WARGA~~~

Where did wargames come from? Who participated in them, and why? How is their development related to changes in real-life warfare? Which aspects of war did they capture, which ones did they leave out, how, and why? What do they tell us about the conduct of war in the times and places where they were played? How useful are they in training and preparation for war? Why are some so much more popular than others, and how do men and women differ in their interest? Starting with the combat of David versus Goliath, passing through the gladiatorial games, tournaments, trials by battle, duels, and board games such as chess, all the way to the latest simulations and computer games, this unique book traces the subject in all its splendid richness. As it does so, it provides new and occasionally surprising insights into human nature.

MARTIN VAN CREVELD is Emeritus Professor at the Hebrew University, Jerusalem, and one of the world's best-known experts on military history and strategy. He is the author of over twenty books, covering all aspects of these and other subjects, which have now been translated into twenty languages including Chinese, French, German, Greek, Italian, Japanese, Korean, Polish, Portuguese, Russian, Serb, and Spanish. Professor van Creveld has consulted to the defense establishments of various countries and taught or lectured at many institutes of higher learning, both military and civilian. He has also written hundreds of articles and conducted interviews with newspapers, television, and radio all over the world.

WARGAMES

From Gladiators to Gigabytes

MARTIN VAN CREVELD

CAMBRIDGE UNIVERSITY PRESS
Cambridge, New York, Melbourne, Madrid, Cape Town,
Singapore, São Paulo, Delhi, Mexico City

Cambridge University Press
The Edinburgh Building, Cambridge CB2 8RU, UK

Published in the United States of America by Cambridge University Press, New York

www.cambridge.org
Information on this title: www.cambridge.org/9781107684423

First published 2013

Printed and bound in the United Kingdom by the MPG Books Group

A catalogue record for this publication is available from the British Library

Library of Congress Cataloguing in Publication data
Van Creveld, Martin, 1946–
Wargames : From Gladiators to Gigabytes / By Martin van Creveld.
pages cm
ISBN 978-1-107-03695-6 – ISBN 978-1-107-68442-3 (pbk.)
1. War games – History.   2. Computer war games – History.   I. Title.
U310.V327   2013
793.9′2–dc23
2012039203

ISBN 978-1-107-03695-6 Hardback
ISBN 978-1-107-68442-3 Paperback

For Uri. My son

Mirror, mirror on the wall:
What is the most exciting game of all?

CONTENTS

ACKNOWLEDGMENTS

This volume owes its existence to my one time mentor, Edward Luttwak. It was his brilliant 1987 book, *Strategy: The Logic of War and Peace*, that first made me think about a topic which has now been preoccupying me for a quarter-century. I remember an afternoon spent at his home in Chevy Chase, Maryland, when we went over the manuscript together. Both before and after that day Edward has not only astonished me with his intellect but has proved a very good friend too. I am proud and honored to be his.

I cannot remember all the people who, over the years, have been forced to listen to me expounding my ideas. One is Stephen Glick, another old friend. Along with Ian Charters, he did a wonderful job writing an article on wargames for a special issue of a periodical for which I was responsible (*Journal of Contemporary History*, 18, 4, October 1983). Another is Seth Carus who himself designed a wargame around the 1973 Israeli–Syrian battle for the Golan Heights; yet another is my friend and former student Robert Tomes. As always, Israel Defense Force Colonels (ret.) Moshe Ben David and Raz Sagi, as well as Lieutenant Colonel (ret.) Eado Hecht, have been generous with their time and interest. Eado also allowed me to use a short paper he has written about the subject. Amihai Borosh has helped me find my way in some rabbinical literature that would otherwise have remained closed to me. Just as he and his partner, Shmuel Alkelai, have long treated Dvora and me as if we were their parents, so she and I have tried to treat them as if they were our sons. Last but not least, I have had the usual splendid arguments with my stepson Jonathan Lewy. Before following in my footsteps and deciding to become a historian, he himself used to be an avid player of wargames.

Parts or all of the manuscript have been read, and corrected, by Colonel (ret.) Moshe Ben David, Dr. Alex Yakobson, and Dr. Julie Thompson: thank you all for your useful comments.

Some financial assistance towards the writing of this book has come from the Axel and Margaret Axson Johnson Foundation in Stockholm, Sweden. In particular, it helped me buy books that, since I like the feel of paper and dislike reading from screens, I might not otherwise have been able to obtain or to afford. I wish to thank the Foundation and its director, Mr. Kurt Almquist, for its generous support over the last decade or so, and express the hope that I may continue to rely on it in the future.

Concerning Dvora, I have already said whatever there is to be said – not once, but many times. Thank you, Dvora, from the bottom of my heart. Not just for what you do – producing wonderful paintings, running a household, looking after grandchildren, generously giving your time and brains to help anyone who asks you to – but for what you are: the best spouse God has ever given a man.

~

Introduction

Where did wargames come from? What purposes did they serve? Who participated in them, why, and what for? What forms did they take? What factors
drove their development, and to what extent did they reflect changes in the art
of war itself? What did they simulate, what didn't they simulate, how, and why?
What do they reveal about the conduct of war at the times, and in the places,
where they were played? How useful are they in training for war and preparing
for it? Why are some so much more popular than others, how do men and
women compare in this respect, and what can the way the sexes relate to
wargames teach us about the relationship between them? Finally, what does
all this tell us about real war, fake or make-believe war, and the human
condition in general? These are the sorts of questions the present volume will
try to answer. Before it can do so, however, it is first of all necessary to say a
word about what wargames are, where they stand in relation to other kinds of
games on the one hand and to "real" war on the other, what has been written on
them, what may be learnt from them, and where all this may lead.

What is a wargame?

Games, including wargames which form the subject of this book, are all around
us. Even the most superficial observation will soon conclude that not only
humans but many kinds of animals engage in games, i.e. play. The great Dutch
historian Johan Huizinga has argued, to my mind with very good reason, that
not economic needs (as Karl Marx thought) but play and games represent the
real source from which all human culture, everything beautiful, true and good,
springs.[1] In his view, a game is an activity characterized above all by the fact that
it creates its own little world. To this end it is carefully and often ceremoniously
separated from "real life," standing to the latter as the terrarium or tableau in a
glass paperweight does to the room in which it is positioned. Within the space
where the game is held, and for as long as it lasts, cause and effect are abolished.

---

[1] J. Huizinga, *Homo Ludens*, Boston, MA: Beacon, 1950 [1938].

1

The nature of the activity does not matter much. Provided it is done for its own sake, for "fun," as people say, almost anything may be turned into a game.

Another way of putting the same idea would be to say that men (in all that concerns wargames women are a separate species, and will be considered toward the end of this volume) and animals (as far as we can judge) engage in play primarily because doing so provides them with some kind of thrill. A thrill, in turn, results when we are engaged on, or have accomplished, something that is not too easy. Even if that something is, "realistically" speaking, of no value whatsoever, such as driving a ball over a net or into a goal; and even if it does not involve any activity but simply confronting danger, real or simulated, in a passive way, like people riding a roller coaster. Again it is apparent that, depending on personality, age, experience, and the culture of which the individual forms a part, almost any activity that is neither too easy nor impossibly hard – in which case it will lead to frustration or despair – can produce a thrill. To the extent that it does, some people will turn it into a game and enjoy it as such.

The variety of games found in nature and among humans is almost infinite and there is no point in trying to list them here. They range from the simplest to the most complex, from the unstructured to the highly structured, and from those that require little more than imagination and creativity to those that demand equipment worth hundreds of millions of dollars. One very good way to classify games is to distinguish between those that involve chance, those that require physical skill and/or force, and those that involve strategy. Some anthropologists have tried to link each type to a certain kind of society, but these attempts are not very convincing and need not preoccupy us here.[2] Concerning games of chance, presumably no explanation is needed. Think of a game of dice, think of roulette. Such games do not require either physical or intellectual resources. Usually they are considered childish, unless, that is, they are played for high stakes, in which case they turn into tests of character. Games of physical skill or force are just what the name implies. However, the more strenuous among them also test such emotional qualities as determination ("grit"), endurance, and the ability to cope with pain. This fact goes far to explain why, from the ancient Olympics on, they have often drawn crowds of spectators and generated tremendous excitement.

This brings us to the third kind, i.e. games of strategy. According to Clausewitz's classical definition, strategy is the art of using battles, which themselves are the province of tactics, in order to achieve the objectives of a campaign.[3] Nowadays it is often used to describe a carefully planned series of steps needed to achieve an objective. Here I shall employ it in a different sense

[2] J.M. Roberts et al., "Games in Culture," American Anthropologist, 61, 4, August 1959, pp. 597–605.
[3] C. von Clausewitz, On War, Princeton University Press, 1976, p. 127.

suggested by Sun Tzu, Thomas Schelling, and Edward Luttwak:[4] namely, the art of seeking to achieve your objectives in the face of an opponent who thinks and acts. That opponent is allowed not just to try to achieve *his* objectives but to actively prevent you from doing the same – by killing you, if appropriate and necessary. Strategy, in other words, does not just mean planning one's own moves, as in a bicycle race or a swimming contest. It is that, of course; but it is also, and above all, a question of trying to detect, predict, interfere with, and obstruct those of the opponent. Briefly, it consists of the *interplay* between the two sides. Whether that interplay takes place on a board, or in a court, or on a computer screen, or between two squads, or between two army groups, is immaterial. So are the kinds of weapons used and the state of military technology in general.

In the present context, the most important of the three elements is strategy. No exercise that does not involve the kind of interplay just mentioned can be considered a wargame. This is true even if it is used, as a great many are, by the military in order to prepare men for war. For example, attacking a stake with a sword, as was the practice of Roman legionaries and gladiators; or riding a galloping horse and using a lance to hit an object suspended on a rotating pole, as medieval knights, the Mongols and the Mamluks all used to do; or having thousands of troops pretend to "storm" a beach. Many such exercises require a very high degree of skill and take years to master. However, in them the stake, or the object, or the beach, cannot hit back. Unlike flesh and blood humans and, nowadays, some kinds of computer programs, they have neither intentions that must be discovered nor capabilities which they can bring to bear. Hence such exercises will be mentioned in this volume only for purposes of comparison. Also excluded is the kind of exercise where an individual or team plays not against an opponent similar to themselves but against some sort of "control" which determines the course of the game but cannot be influenced in return. Such games may have their uses; however, they involve not strategy but a puppet-master and his puppet.

Since the number of possible combinations is limited, the strategy required in one-on-one engagements is relatively straightforward. Conversely, the more numerous the participants and the more heterogeneous they are – in other words, the more differentiated their capabilities and the larger the number of possible ways of combining those capabilities – the harder the problem of developing a strategy and applying it against the opponent becomes. The substitution of complex terrain for a simple arena or court adds to the difficulties. That is even more the case when each participant must make his moves while only having at his disposal limited information about his own forces,

---

[4] Sun Tzu, *The Art of War*, Fairfield, IA: World Library, 2006; T. Schelling, *Arms and Influence*, New Haven, CT: Yale University Press, 1966; E. Luttwak, *Strategy: The Logic of War and Peace*, Cambridge, MA: Belknap, 1987.

those of the opponent, and the environment in which the game takes place. As Napoleon is supposed to have said, under such conditions the conduct of strategy requires intellectual resources not inferior to those which a Newton or an Euler might command.[5] Furthermore, nothing prevents two or more of the above-listed elements from being joined in a single game. To the contrary: often the way this is done is just what distinguishes one kind of game from another.

How are games and war related?

In the words, of Jonathan Swift, war is "that mad game the world loves to play."[6] As expressions such as "the great game" confirm, the two are linked in so many ways that separating them is sometimes impossible. Specifically, in war skill/ force, chance, and the two-sided activity known as strategy mix. Conversely, war is separated from games by two principal factors. First, whereas war only makes sense to the extent that it is the continuation of politics, the very existence of games depends on that *not* being the case. Games, in other words, even those that incorporate political factors, possess a certain kind of autonomy that war does not have and cannot have. Second, games differ from war in that they are subject to certain highly artificial limits: such as those that govern the location in which they may be held, the way in which they may be played, the equipment that may be used, and, above all, the time they may last and/or the conditions under which they must come to an end. Think of the peculiar size and shape of a basketball court with its hoops; or of the twice forty-five minutes a game of soccer lasts; or of the rules that define just what counts as victory in tennis, bridge, or chess.

Fundamentally, the restrictions in question can take two forms. The first consists of pretense, i.e. some way of signaling that the encounter is "unreal." Not by accident does the Latin word for game, *ludus*, have everything to do with "illusion." The second is a set of formal, often written, rules. Generally the more developed and specific the rules are, the less the need for pretense, and the other way around. The rules' function, in other words, is precisely to eliminate the need for pretense; within the framework that they create, anything goes. For example, a medieval knight who had his servants strew the tourneying field with caltrops could expect to be disqualified by the umpires. However, he did not have to worry that he would be punished for hitting too hard.

A wargame might be defined as a game of strategy which, while clearly separated from "real" warfare by one or more of the above means, nevertheless simulates some key aspects of the latter: including, quite often, the death and/or

---

[5] Quoted in Clausewitz, *On War*, p. 112.
[6] Quoted in W. Hardcastle Brown, *Odd Derivations of Words, Phrases, Slang, Synonyms,* General Books, 2010, p. 312.

injury and capture that results from warfare's quintessential element, i.e. fighting. The more aspects a game simulates, and the more accurate the simulation, the closer to real-life warfare it is. This proposition can be turned around. Just as warfare has often served as inspiration for wargames, so wargames can be, and often have been, played not just by amateurs (from the Latin *amatores*, lovers) for their own sake but by the military for training, planning, and preparation too. To the extent that they allow and force players to strategize, indeed, they are not merely the best form of training but the only available one.

However, a game capable of simulating every aspect of war would *become* war. Generally the larger the scale on which warfare is waged, and the more important the role of political factors as opposed to military ones, the greater the difficulties of simulating it. Above all, unrestricted physical violence, the very factor that forms the essence of war and sets it apart, is hard to capture in a realistic way. Most people will probably refuse to play a game that claims too many casualties. Such a game is also very likely to be condemned and banned by the authorities, as many in fact were. Another possibility is that the game, by escalating out of hand, will develop into the real thing. That was just what happened in 1273 when an Anglo-French tournament turned into the so-called "Little Battle of Châlons" after King Edward I of England, who was among the participants, claimed that one of his opponents had committed a foul.[7]

As a result, all wargames seek to limit violence in one way or another. The place where it takes place may be controlled very carefully so as to affect only the direct participants, thus making sure that escalation does not ensue; or it may be represented by purely symbolic means, as in chess and similar games; or it may be committed by, and on, figures that only exist in virtual reality, as in computer games; or the rules may ban the use of the most lethal weapons, as in some forms of tribal games and tournaments, as well as paintball, laser tag, and their like; or an element of pretense may be introduced, as in many kinds of sham fights and reenactments. Incidentally, the way various games manage violence and restrict it provides another excellent method for classifying them.

Why study wargames?

As I learnt at first hand when students at a seminar literally started jumping up and down on tables, wargames have always been enormously exciting. This fact, as well as the growing involvement on the part of government and big business, explains why the literature on them is vast. However, practically all modern workers in the field seem to have committed a fundamental error: their definition of wargames is both much too broad and much too narrow. It is too broad in that the term is applied to any kind of mock adversarial engagement without regard to whether what is simulated is war, or politics, or economics, or whatever. It is too

---

[7] See M. Keene, *Chivalry*, New Haven, CT: Yale University Press, 1984, p. 87.

narrow in that they focus on the kind of games played by opposing individuals or teams in some kind of room, with the aid of maps and/or boards or, beginning in the 1960s, either on the screens of computers or inside them.[8]

Furthermore, the obligatory reference to chess and its alleged failure to present an adequate portrait of war apart, existing studies of wargames focus on the period since the elder Baron von Reisswitz invented modern wargaming exactly two centuries ago. That, of course, reflects on their understanding both of wargames and of war itself. Most leave out the games played by many tribal societies around the world, some of which are all but indistinguishable from "real" war; single combat and combats of champions from the Old Testament and the *Iliad* onwards; the Roman gladiatorial fights, which were probably the most popular, and certainly the most deadly, wargames of all time; as well as trials by combat, tournaments and duels, to mention but a few. Nor is it simply a question of leaving out most of history. Many modern wargames, be they of the kind "fought" by the American military at the National Training Center, or those that paintball and laser tag enthusiasts practice in their spare time, or those which reenact historical battles, are also given the cold shoulder. Even that, however, is but one side of the problem. Just as modern writers on wargames habitually ignore most of history, so anthropologists, ancient historians, and medievalists have stubbornly refused to look beyond their own specialties. As a result, their work has made little or no contribution to the field. Needless to say, truncating the subject in such a way imposes serious restrictions on what can be learnt from it.

It is in order to avoid repeating this error that the present volume has taken the historical approach in an attempt to trace the games' development from its origins to the present day. Here it may be worth mentioning that this approach is in many ways the exact opposite of the one that "game theorists" use. They have set themselves the task of reducing real events to games and games to a series of precise mathematical formulae; I, to the contrary, wanted to reintegrate wargames, a subject that is too often neglected or looked down upon, with human culture as a whole. Their objective was reductionist; mine, inclusivist. As we shall see, their method is in danger of producing results that are too abstract to be of use in the real world; mine, I hope, will prove fruitful and interesting to those who take the trouble to follow my work to the end.

---

[8] Just a few of the more important works that have taken this approach include: T. B. Allen, *War Games*, New York: McGraw-Hill, 1987; J. F. Dunnigan, *Wargames Handbook*, 3rd edn, iUniverse, 2000; P. Perla, *The Art of Wargaming*, Annapolis, MD: Naval Institute Press, 1990; T. C. Schelling, *The Strategy of Conflict*, Cambridge, MA: Harvard University Press, 1960; M. Shubik, *Games for Society, Business, and War*, Amsterdam: Elsevier, 1975; and A. Wilson, *The Bomb and the Computer*, London: Crescent, 1968. To my knowledge, the only volume that attempts to cover earlier periods as well is T. J. Cornell and T. B. Allen, eds., *War and Games*, Woodbridge: Boydell, 2002.

The outline of the volume is as follows. Chapter 1, "On animals and men," opens with a brief look at hunting as well as the "wargames" animals play. Following a discussion of unarmed combat sports and contact sports, it proceeds through the various kinds of sham fights held by many tribal societies toward combats of champions and single combats. Chapter 2, "Games and gladiators," is devoted to what were easily the most deadly wargames in the whole of history. Here the objective is to find the cultural factors that made them possible, what aspects of war they simulated, what aspects they did not simulate, why they were as popular as they were, and why they were finally brought to an end. Chapter 3, "Trials by combat, tournaments, and duels," explores certain types of wargames which for centuries used to form an important part of Western culture but are now defunct. As was the case with Rome, not the least interesting question is *why* they are defunct, and what, if anything, has taken their place.

Moving closer to the present, Chapter 4, "Battles, campaigns, wars, and politics," focuses on various types of wargames that, resting on much older foundations, became very prominent in the nineteenth century when both amateurs and professional soldiers developed them and played them. Since the latter often used the games for training, simulation, and planning, this is also the place to take a look at their possibilities and limitations in these respects. Chapter 5, "From bloody games to bloodless wars," deals with the kind of wargames that, instead of using floors, boards, or tables, are played by real people on real terrain. Chapter 6, "Enter the computer," explains how those machines have transformed the field in which we are interested and how they are causing real reality and virtual reality to merge. Chapter 7, "The females of the species," asks some questions about the way 50 percent of humanity relate, or do not relate, to wargames; here the goal is to use such games as a prism for examining what, to me, looks like some fundamental differences between the sexes. Finally, Chapter 8, "The mirrors and the mirrored," represents our conclusions.

Going beyond the obvious questions – why wargames are/were held and how, how they relate/d to war, and how useful they are/were in helping train for it, simulate it, and prepare for it – what can a study of wargames teach us? To answer, consider an old story by Ephraim Kishon (1924–2005), a Hungarian-born Israeli humorist whose books, translated into German and other languages, sold in the tens of millions. A man is sitting on a park bench. After a while he is joined by an older man who takes out a photograph of a child and shows it to his companion. "My grandson," he says. Once the stranger has expressed his admiration, the grandfather calls one of the children playing on the grass and presents him. "Why did you not call your grandson in the first place?" the younger man asks. "Because," the proud grandfather answers, "recently the child has not been eating very well. The picture looks more like him than he does!"

Though the story is deliberately silly, the point the grandfather is trying to make is anything but. "Reality," after all, is an elusive, ever-shifting, thing. It exists, if at all, only for a moment, and that moment itself may very well be entirely untypical. That is why some representations of it can capture its essence better than reality itself can. Studied both as they were held at certain times and places and across time, wargames provide a singularly useful tool for understanding the nature of war and the way various societies related to it. Like Kishon's photograph, they can present us with war in its purest form, so to speak. At the same time, the way people related to them can tell us something both about changing social attitudes and about human nature in general.

War, to quote one modern scholar summing up what many have said before him, "offers the individual an escape from debilitating tedium and existential boredom, a glorious alternative to the banality of everyday life and work. It appeals to his need for excitement, adventure, stimulation, sensation, spectacle, and his craving for power, grandeur and self esteem."[9] Whether that applies to real-life war may be, and often has been, disputed. But when it comes to wargames there can be no doubt concerning its truth. After all, one of their main functions is precisely to provide the thrill at little or no cost to partic*ipants, spectators, or both; their very existence proves how successful they are in doing just that. If only for this reason, it is important that they be studied and understood.

---

[9] J. M. G. van der Dennen, *The Origin of War*, PhD dissertation submitted to the University of Groningen, 2000, vol. I, 245.

1

On animals and men

Hunting, combat sports, and contact sports

To begin at the beginning, both humans and many species of animals hunt. In so far as hunting is a question of using violence to catch, overcome, and kill a living creature, unquestionably it has certain things in common with warfare. Unless the animals are driven to be killed, physical effort and/or skill play an important role. So does chance in the form of a sudden gust of wind that may carry the hunter's scent, or, in the days of edged weapons, deflect his arrow from its intended target. Hunting also involves strategy, although it differs from the kind commonly used in war. Not many animals will stand and fight the hunter just as he fights them, and almost none will do so unless it is cornered first. Even if it is, normally precautions are taken to ensure that the killing is one-sided. That is why, in English, hunting is also known as the "chase," from the French *chasse*, "pursuit." Semantically it is closely associated with its opposite, to flee; the same is true of its German and Dutch equivalents, *Jagd* and *jacht*.

Other similarities between hunting and war, specifically including the willingness to shed blood and the outdoor life that both require, do not have to be explained in any great detail. Plato at one point claimed that war was simply a different form of hunting,[1] which was not meant exactly as a compliment to soldiers. Xenophon and Machiavelli, both of whom had commanded men in war, saw things in a different light. To them it was a useful form of military training.[2] Pigsticking and other forms of big-game hunting continued to be advertised as such down to the last years of the nineteenth century.[3] Warriors of

---

[1] Plato, *Laws*, London: Heinemann, Loeb Classical Library (LCL), 1926, 823b; also Isocrates, *Plataicus*, LCL, 1945, 163.
[2] Xenophon, *On Hunting*, R. D. Doty, ed., Lampeter: Mellen, 2001, 2.1, 12.1. See, for similar views, Xenophon, *Cyropaedia*, 12.10–1; Plato, *Republic*, LCL, 1919, 549A; Plato, *Laws*, 763b; Plato, *Sophist*, LCL, 1921, 219d–e, 222c; N. Machiavelli, *The Discourses*, bn Publishing, 2005 [1517], p. 511.
[3] See on this J. A. Mangan and C. McKenzie, "'Pig-Sticking is the Greatest Fun': Martial Conditioning on the Hunting Fields of Empire," in J. A. Mangan, ed., *Militarism, Sport, Europe: War without Weapons*, London: Cass, 2003, pp. 97–119.

all periods have often hunted during their leisure hours. For example, the Roman Emperor Hadrian is said to have incurred a scar when hunting, causing him to grow a beard and ending a centuries-old tradition when Romans had shaved. During the Middle Ages, and indeed for centuries after they had ended, hunting was the warrior's sport par excellence; before he was killed at the ripe old age of twenty-six, World War I flying ace Manfred von Richthofen spent his leave hunting.[4] One anthropologist, investigating the Avatip of New Guinea, has suggested that they see warfare as a superior form of hunting in which the prey is human beings.[5]

Certainly among humans, and probably among some animal species such as chimpanzees, hunting is often practiced not simply for nutrition but for fun as well. Cats will even try to catch images floating on a screen; at least one dog I knew used to chase spots of light thrown on the floor by a flashlight. Whether these and other animals behave as they do because of some "hunting instinct," or because the activity generates a thrill, it is, of course, impossible to say. Possibly both motives are involved, and possibly motives differ not only from one animal to another but also from one moment to another; after all, human behavior in these matters is not always consistent either.

Some evolutionary biologists believe that hunting, passed to us by our primate-like ancestors, is the oldest sport of all.[6] In this context it is worth pointing out that, several centuries before the word "sport" came to acquire its present meaning of serious physical exercise, it was used in the sense of "joke," "amusement," or "game." Be that as it may, hunting, whether carried out by animals or by humans, differs from war in that it is an interspecies activity and not an intraspecies one. One sometimes comes across "manhunts," as well as attempts to institute games in which some people are tasked with running away and others with tracking them and hunting them down. However, the former are not games, whereas most of the latter seem to fizzle out almost as soon as they are started. Both involve a chase, not strategy. Hence hunting, though useful for purposes of comparison, will not be further considered in these pages.

As is the case with human games, those played by animals may be divided into different kinds. In many of them there is no sentient opponent capable of putting up resistance, and therefore no strategy as defined in the introduction to the present volume. For example, ravens and otters sometimes engage in sliding games. Squirrels seem to like to manipulate pine cones, dogs to chase objects, shake them, and tug at them. My late poodle, Poonch, even developed a whole

---

[4] See J. Castan, *Der Rote Baron: Die ganze Geschichte des Manfred von Richthofen*, Stuttgart: Klett-Cotta, 2007, *passim*.

[5] S. Harrison, "The Symbolic Construction of Aggression and War in a Sepik River Society," *Man*, 24, 1989, p. 586.

[6] See D. M. Carroll, *An Interdisciplinary Study of Sport as a Symbolic Hunt*, Lewiston, NY: Mellen, 2000, especially pp. 29–69.

series of signals to show me, whenever we arrived at a certain spot during a walk, that he wanted me to throw objects so he could retrieve them. First he would start breathing hard. If that did not work, he would rub my leg; if I still did not get the idea he would emit a special high-pitched bark he used exclusively for that purpose. Monkeys and apes regularly seize branches and swing on them even when there is no obvious need for doing so. In these and a great many other activities the objective seems to be not "usefulness" but plain fun. Some of the games in question are extremely demanding in terms of the skills they require. Still they cannot be classified as wargames and will not be considered here.

Many kinds of animals also engage in fighting between individuals. To repeat, what distinguishes serious fighting from play, or games, is the presence in the latter of certain restrictions that may take the form either of pretense or of rules. To start with the former, distinguishing between the "real" thing and make-believe demands a considerable amount of intelligence. Before play can get under way, one of the parties must send out some kind of signal, such as a bow (dogs) or jerky head and body movements accompanied by a raised tail (cattle).[7] The other must understand what it is all about, and of course signal its consent by using similar means. To bring the game to an end it is necessary to send out another signal; some psychologists speak of different "degrees of intentionality."[8] Hence it comes as no surprise that all observable animal "wargames" seem to occur among vertebrates, and specifically mammals. When Darwin accepted the claim of another biologist that he had seen ants clashing and pretending to bite each other "like so many puppies," he was almost certainly wrong.[9]

In particular, such games are something practically all carnivores and primates engage in as a matter of routine, especially but by no means exclusively when they are young. Generally the longer the period of youth, i.e. the larger the percentage of their entire life that members of a given species have to go through before reaching sexual maturity, the more they engage in play, agonistic play included: an hour a day spent in this way is by no means unusual.[10] One must, however, keep in mind that deliberately formulating a set of rules that will govern some future activity, let alone maneuvering among the rules so as to use them in one's favor while putting one's opponent at a disadvantage, is even more intellectually demanding than putting on an act. This explains why,

[7] See e.g. M. Bekoff, "Play Signals as Punctuation: The Structure of Social Play in Canids," *Behavior*, 132, 5/6, May, 1995, pp. 419–29; V. and R. Reinhardt, "Mock Fighting in Cattle," *Behavior*, 81, 1, 1982, pp. 1–13.
[8] See, on the mechanisms that may be involved, "Is There an Evolutionary Biology of Play?," in M. Bekoff and D. Jamieson, eds., *Interpretation and Explanation in the Study of Animal Behavior*, Boulder, CO: Westview, 1990, pp. 180–96.
[9] C. Darwin, *The Descent of Man*, New York: Random, 1936 [1871], p. 448.
[10] O. Aldis, *Play Fighting*, New York: Academic Press, 1975, pp. 157, 158.

even among our nearest relatives the primates, there seems to be no question of formal rules similar to those that govern the higher forms of human play.

Depending on the species, the "fighting" may take many forms. Normally the first stage consists of maneuvering for position, which can easily be observed in dogs and some species of monkeys, and assuming offensive or defensive postures. This is followed by various kinds of wrestling. Some animals also push and butt and ram and horn one another. Other species engage in scratching and biting which, if done in earnest, can result in very serious injuries indeed. In the animal world as a whole, biting is by far the most common form of inflicting injury. When done in play rather than in earnest, it is replaced by mouthing which either causes no wounds or very minor ones. Close observation shows that two mechanisms are at work. First, the biting animal, when closing its jaws on the opponent, will not apply the full force of which it is capable. Second, the bite, while applied with full force, may be directed against body parts that are relatively invulnerable. The first pattern is common among dogs and bears, the second in jackals. The latter seem to obey the maxim, "thou shalt not bite thy playmate's ear."[11] Incidentally, dogs that play with humans soon learn which parts of the body are protected by clothing and can therefore be bitten with greater force.

Whatever the form they take, play-fights are not always easy to separate from the real thing. Yet three differences seem to be involved. First, play, precisely because it is not in earnest, tends to last longer than fighting does. Second, as long as play lasts, retaliation, instead of being blocked, is permitted. Third, look at what happens after the fight is over; does one of the combatants flee the field, or do they stay together and resume peaceful relations?[12] Since animals cannot explain their motives, we can only try to guess why so many of them engage in sham fighting. As with humans, probably the "conscious" – if one may use that word – motive is to experience a thrill. Like many other forms of play, sham fighting may also serve as a useful method to train for the real thing, in which respect it is similar to many forms of human play. Finally, it may help define social relationships and preserve the peace inside the group.

For example, it is one of the distinguishing features of mock fighting that, among many primate species, it involves much younger and smaller animals "attacking" older, larger, and more dominant ones. The latter react, but in doing so they use a small fraction of the force they are capable of. As long as the game

---

[11] See A. Seitz, "Beobachtungen an handaufgezogenen Goldschakalen," *Zeitschrift fuer Tierpsychologie*, 16, 1959, pp. 747–71.

[12] See on these differences D. M. Watson and D. M. Croft, "Age-Related Differences in Play Fighting of Captive Male Red-Necked Wallabies," *Ethology*, 102, 1996, pp. 336–46; J. H. Kaufmann, "Social Ethology of the Whiptail Wallaby," *Animal Behavior*, 22, 1974, pp. 281–369; S. M. Pellis and V. C. Pellis, "Structure–Function Interface in the Analysis of Play," in M. Bekoff et al., eds., *Animal Play*, Cambridge University Press, 1998, pp. 123–9; and Aldis, *Play Fighting*, pp. 29–31.

lasts, ordinary behavior is suspended and the two animals, each in its own way, pretend they are equals. However, if the younger one goes too far, a sudden sharp, but still largely harmless, response may put it in its place, drawing a line between what is and is not allowed and terminating the game, at least for a time.[13] Whatever the motive, the advantage of sham fighting over the real thing is that the cost, and the risk involved, is very low (though not nonexistent, for presumably that would eliminate the thrill).

Human children who are too young to understand an existing set of rules or to create one of their own also engage in sham fighting. More important for the topic at hand, so do some adults. There are even cases, such as "professional" wrestling matches, when the fighting is made to follow a pre-arranged script. The combatants open their matches with noisy verbal contests, pretending that they are boiling with rage and ready to tear their opponents to pieces. Not seldom they resort to extraordinary methods such as using chairs to hit their opponents or else banging their heads against the steel floor of the arena. In fact, though, professional wrestling is a "sophisticated theatralized representation of the violent urges ... [consisting of] largely pantomimed confrontations," which is why it is discussed, among other places, in *The Drama Review*.[14] Some organizers go further still by providing a story line, comparable in some respects to a scene in a theatrical drama or a film. Allegedly the fight is the result of a long-running feud, or else it represents an attempt to avenge an injury. In many ways the stories are like the scenarios routinely dreamt up by those responsible for organizing many kinds of political-military and military wargames described later in this volume; another analogy is with the thin stories often provided by the makers of pornographic films to surround the main act and make it more interesting.

Professional wrestling sometimes results in serious injuries, especially among long-time fighters who have been through it all many times. Nevertheless, all this makes the "shows" much less of a fight and more of a sham. Almost always the outcome is fixed in advance in such a way as to confirm the spectators' expectations as to what is right and what is wrong. So considered, the fights' closest relative is not war but the morality play. Not just the scenario but even individual moves are planned not merely with an eye to defeating the opponent, but in such a way as to increase their appeal to the crowd; the more important the show and the better known the combatants, the less "real" it is likely to be. All of which explains why the matches are not held in high esteem by those who engage in, or watch, "serious" combat sports.

[13] See, for the way these things work among buffaloes, for example, A. R. Lumia, "The Relationship between Dominance and Play Behavior in the American Buffalo," *Tierpsychologie*, 30, 1972, pp. 416–19.
[14] S. Mazer, "The Doggie Doggie World of Professional Wrestling," *Drama Review*, 128, 4, Winter 1990, pp. 96–122. The quote is from p. 97.

Unarmed – and, as we shall see, armed – humans preparing to fight one another resemble animals in that they start by maneuvering for position. Next, they assume either an offensive stance or a defensive one. The fights themselves take on a variety of forms. Since humans only have small and weak teeth and nails, in fights among them biting and scratching are much less important than with animals. In fact it is almost exclusively when women and children (and Mike Tyson) fight that they play any role at all, and in many cases they are banned altogether. That is not the only difference. Primates, as our closest relatives, do not use their legs for kicking and indeed that practice is limited to horses, donkeys, mules, and elephants. Humans, by contrast, often do so. Another difference is that even the members of species that have digits, notably primates, rarely use them to grasp opponents when they wrestle.[15] Above all, humans are able to use their arms to throw punches, something no animal does.

Fights between unarmed humans that are governed by rules are known as combat sports. Probably there has never been a society that did not have them in one form or another, though they are said to be more widespread among warlike societies than among less warlike ones.[16] Often they were associated with religion, particularly during funeral ceremonies when the gods demanded their pound of flesh. Wrestling is known to have been practiced 5,000 years ago in Sumer where the hero Gilgamesh had to engage the undefeated Endiku as part of his epic journey. Judging by the frequency with which it appears on the monuments, in ancient Egypt it almost amounted to a national sport. It is represented on temple walls, tomb walls, and stelae, as well as by hundreds of sculptures and miniatures, some of them carefully made and of a very high artistic quality. Wrestling seems to have been a particular favorite among military personnel who boasted of their achievements and regularly practiced it in front of the Pharaoh. The palace window from which Rameses III (c. 1186–1155 BC) watched the proceedings still exists.[17] On the other hand, though Pharaohs are known to have engaged in various sports such as running, archery, and driving chariots, they did not, as far as the evidence goes, engage in either wrestling or other combat sports.

Present-day tribal societies all over the world also engage in wrestling and appear to have done so for a long time past. In some cultures, such as that of the Nuba of the Sudan, it played a very important role indeed by helping reinforce the social order without resort to actual fighting.[18] Among the Ona, a people of

[15] Aldis, *Play Fighting*, pp. 37, 196–8.
[16] According to R. G. Pipes, "War, Sports and Aggression – an Empirical Test of Two Rival Theories," *American Anthropologist*, 75, 1, February 1973, p. 71.
[17] See, for Sumer, W. J. Baker, *Sports in the Western World*, Totowa, NJ: Rowman & Littlefield, 1982, p. 8; for Egypt, W. Decker, *Sports and Games in Ancient Egypt*, New Haven, CT: Yale University Press, 1987, pp. 71–87.
[18] S. Nadel, *The Nuba*, Oxford University Press, 1947, pp. 136–7, 232–4.

the island of Tierra del Fuego, it even served as a method for resolving conflict. If a feud had gone on for too long and threatened to run out of hand, the leaders of one family would send an old woman not worth capturing to talk to its rival. A meeting would be arranged and a series of individual matches held, attended by the men of both sides. The matches would continue until all wrestlers on one side had been defeated one by one. Then the other side would proclaim its victory, and everybody went home happily enough.[19] The Siriono people of eastern Bolivia had a somewhat similar custom.[20]

Modern wrestling is commonly divided into no fewer than five different kinds, i.e. Graeco-Roman, freestyle, grappling-submission, beach, and folk (Scandinavian). Many other forms of wrestling probably existed at various times and places but have been abandoned and forgotten. Boxing, whether carried out with or without gloves, is probably as old as wrestling is. Once again, the evidence goes back all the way to ancient Egypt; boxing is also shown on vases produced in the island of Thera (in the Aegean) during the fifteenth century BC. Sometimes the two sports may have been combined, as in the ancient Greek *pankration* (literally, "crushing by every available means"). *Pankration* fighters were allowed not only to kick but to aim their kicks at the groin. Some even got away with bending back their opponents' fingers.[21] Like wrestling, boxing is commonly divided into several kinds of which the most important ones are ancient Greek, ancient Roman, and modern. Yet wrestling and boxing in all their different varieties by no means exhaust the list of combat sports; such a list would also have to include Thai kickboxing, judo, karate, kung fu, sumo, cage fighting – which is currently the most violent combat sport of all – and others too numerous to mention.

In all these forms of combat sports the combatants fight unarmed, either bare-breasted or while wearing only light clothing that provides no protection. In some forms of boxing the participants wear gloves. Depending on the culture, the intention may be to increase the damage. Alternatively it may be to protect the wrist or limit the injury that the party that takes the punch can suffer.[22] Modern boxers also wear devices to protect their teeth, and sometimes their heads. These precautions, as well as the fact that weapons are not allowed, do not entirely eliminate the possibility of serious injury and even death. They do, however, considerably reduce their probability. However it is done, the fact that combat is unarmed renders the relationship between it and war problematic, to say the least. Probably at no time or place was this fact more in evidence

[19] S. K. Lothrop, *The Indians of the Tierra de Fuego*, New York: Holt, 1928, pp. 619–20.
[20] A. R. Holmberg, *Nomads of the Longbow: The Siriono of Eastern Bolivia*, Garden City, NJ: Natural History Press, 1969, p. 156.
[21] M. B. Poliakoff, *Combat Sports in the Ancient World*, New Haven, CT: Yale University Press, 1987, p. 57.
[22] Poliakoff, *ibid.*, pp. 68–79, examines the question of gloves in some detail.

than in ancient Greece, the reason being the exceptionally important role that
sports in general, and combat sports in particular, played in the culture.[23]
The belief that combat sports helped achieve success in war was expressed
most clearly by the comic poet Aristophanes. In more than one of his plays he
claimed that it was training in the *palaestra*, best translated as school for combat
sports, which enabled the Athenians to turn back the Persian invasions in 490
and 480 BC.[24] Aristophanes' objective was to make the Athenians of his own
day take up the sports in question which, he thought, had been sadly neglected.
Some modern writers have followed his lead, describing Greek warfare as
"gymnastic" and contrasting it with the Persian one.[25] How such claims may
be reconciled with the weight of armor, which seriously interfered with the
movements of those who wore it, is not entirely clear.[26] Nevertheless it was
hardly accidental that, at Olympia, the statue of Agon, a term that may be
translated as task, or painful burden, or contest, stood right next to that of Ares,
the god of war; throughout the Greek world, the language of inscriptions used
to praise successful athletes was quite similar to that employed to glorify
victorious soldiers.

Several Olympic champions at *pankration* were excellent soldiers, though
whether and just how the two things were connected is not very clear. On the
other hand, the *Iliad* mentions a man by the name of Epheios who admits that
he is not very good at war. He excuses himself by saying that nobody can excel
at everything, and promises to crush anybody who dares to confront him in a
boxing match;[27] incidentally this was the very man who later built the Trojan
horse, thus playing a crucial role in the Greek victory. In a fragment of a lost
play, the late fifth-century BC tragic poet Euripides has one of his characters
claim that no wrestler or any other athlete had ever helped save his city from an
invader and that, in the presence of "steel," their various bends, leaps, grips, and
blows are so much foolishness.[28] Plato in *The Laws* also opined that the tactics
used in wrestling and boxing were worthless in war. In the ideal state, he wrote,
they should be replaced by more realistic, and necessarily more dangerous,
exercises. This included gymnastics in full armor, all sorts of mock warfare, and

[23] See, on the role of sport, M. Golden, *Sport and Society in Ancient Greece*, Cambridge
University Press, 1998, pp. 1–45.
[24] *Clouds*, 984–5, 1052–4; *Frogs*, 1069–73, in *The Complete Plays of Aristophanes*, New York:
Bantam, 1984.
[25] T. Wintringham and J.N. Blashford-Snell, *Weapons and Tactics*, Harmondsworth:
Penguin, 1973 [1943], p. 43.
[26] V.D. Hanson, *The Western Way of War: Infantry Battle in Classical Greece*, New York:
Random House, 1989, pp. 55–88, has a list of complaints about the weight of armor.
[27] Homer, *Iliad*, LCL, 1924, 23.670–1.
[28] Euripides, *Autolycus*, quoted by Galen, in J. Juethner and F. Brein, *Die athletischen
Leibesuebungen der Griechen*, Vienna: Austrian Academy of Sciences, 1965, 1, 95.

"fighting with balls" (*sphaeromachia*) and darts as nearly real as possible – though he did admit that the points of the darts would have to be blunted.[29]

By that time, the individual fights between outstanding warriors that take up so much of the *Iliad* had long been replaced by hoplite warfare in which the exploits of individuals, however brave and however skilled, counted for much less. No wonder classical Greek writers and commanders were divided on the issue. Xenophon claimed that Boiskos, a famous boxer who early in the fourth century BC had won many matches, was unreliable as a soldier, and had once run away from a battle with the excuse that he was tired.[30] During his youth the great fourth-century BC Theban commander Epaminondas engaged in running and wrestling (exceptionally, he felt that in war speed was more useful than strength). Yet his main concern was weapons practice; he once told his troops that, though wrestling shows might impress the enemy, the proper place to prepare for war was not the *palaestra* but the camp. A century and a half or so later, the Achaean commander Philopoemen, who like Epaminondas had wrestled in his youth, went so far as to claim that athletes did not make good soldiers and barred them from competition. Alexander the Great too had little respect for the combat sports of his day, though he did admire fighting with staves.[31]

The view that most combat sports as practiced in ancient Greece were irrelevant to, or at any rate insufficient for, military training seems to have been shared by the most warlike Greek city-state of all. It was hardly accidental that, in the Spartan version of *pankration*, biting and gouging were also permitted. Though there is no indication that they were allowed to practice these "skills" at Olympia, the list of Spartans who won the *pankration* at the games is very impressive. Yet the parallel can be carried only so far. Tyrtaeus, the seventh-century Spartan bard who provided his (adopted) city-state with many of its most powerful martial songs, specifically wrote that skill in wrestling and similar sports did not make a man fit for war. The latter demanded the ability to witness, commit and withstand, "bloody slaughter";[32] as when arms and legs are sliced off, bodies ripped open, and heads sent rolling on the ground.

In ancient Greece sports in general, and combat sports in particular, were an expression of aristocratic culture. As the famous Olympic oath indicates, only free men could participate. True, there was no legal prohibition to prevent members of the lower classes from training and competing; however, to do so it was first necessary to have sufficient leisure, or *scholē*. Furthermore, regularly attending the *palaestra* was not inexpensive. This aristocratic character may be one reason why so many victors whose names are known to us were members of

---

[29] Plato, *Laws*, 796, and 830c–831a.   [30] Xenophon, *Anabasis*, LCL, 1922, 5.8.23.
[31] Plutarch, *Moralia*, LCL, 1959, 192c, 788a; Plutarch, *Philopoemen*, 3.2–4; Plutarch, *Alexander*, 4, both in *Lives*, LCL, 1914.
[32] Tyrtaeus, Fragment 12w.

the upper classes. It also helps explain why, centuries later, the question was caught up in the debate as to which culture, the Greek or the Roman, was preferable. Second-century AD Greek writers often used sports in general, and combat sports in particular, as evidence of Greek superiority. One of them, the philosopher Philostratus, summed up the idea by saying that the great athletes of the past "made war training for sport, and sport training for war." Turning Spartan logic on its head, Plutarch even claimed that the Thebans at the great Battle of Leuctra in 371 BC defeated the Spartans because they had done more training at the *palaestra*; he also wrote that sport, wrestling specifically included, was an imitation and exercise of war. The novelist and satirist Lucian, who was a close contemporary of both, devoted an entire essay to the question. Cast as a dialogue between the Athenian lawgiver Solon and a Scythian visitor, it concludes that athletic training helps citizen-soldiers defend their city's freedom and defeat the enemy if necessary.[33]

By that time the Greek world had long been conquered by the Romans, whose approach to the problem was entirely different. To be sure, as early as the second century BC many "progressive" Romans recognized the excellence of Greek achievements in art, literature, and science as far exceeding anything they themselves produced. The fact that they asked for, and obtained, permission for their citizens to participate in the prestigious Olympic Games also speaks volumes, since it was by such means that they set themselves apart from the remaining "barbarians." Yet side by side with this view there was also one that accused the Greeks of lacking *gravitas*, seriousness. As early as the middle of the second century BC Polybius, a Greek statesman-soldier who spent much of his life in Rome and knew it well, noted how seriously the Romans took military training.[34] Though he does not say so explicitly, clearly he saw them as an example his own countrymen should follow, if they only could.

About a century later we find the statesman and orator Cicero describing the exercises which Greek youths undertook as useless for the purpose of military training. He even coined the term Graeculi, meaning, roughly, "despicable little Greeks"[35] – a fact all the more remarkable because Cicero, along with his other accomplishments, was the most important Roman exponent of Greek philosophy of his day. Several Roman poets claimed that the *palaestra* only produced degenerates incapable of carrying weapons. Both the encyclopedist Pliny and the historian Tacitus warned against the effect it might have on Roman bodies. Plutarch himself sums up the Romans' attitudes by saying that, in their view, the *palaestra* was the real reason why Greece had lost its independence. Instead

---

[33] Philostratus, *Gymnasticus*, LCL, 1931, 9.11.43; Plutarch, *Moralia*, 639a–40a; Lucian, *Anacharis*, in *Works*, LCL, 1968.
[34] Polybius, *The Histories*, LCL, 1972, 6.52–4.
[35] Cicero, *Philippics*, LCL, 1931, Fifth Philippic, 14.

of teaching youths to survive on simple military fare, it made them feed on fine-tuned diets. Leaving no time for weapons practice, it encouraged laziness, profligacy, and pederasty; and ended up by producing wrestlers rather than soldiers.[36]

Both these views, the one which held that combat sports contribute to military preparedness and the one which claimed no such link existed, continued to be heard down to the first half of the twentieth century. Indeed it was probably during the interwar years, when people everywhere were fearfully contemplating the next major conflict, that they reached their peak. Governments, especially but by no means only totalitarian ones, did whatever they could to encourage their populations to engage in sports. The Nazis were particularly interested in boxing and made it compulsory for members of the Hitler Jugend. Along with a breakfast diet consisting of porridge, they saw it as one of the secrets behind Britain's military-political success.[37] Things only started changing after 1945 when the proliferation of nuclear weapons began making war, or at any rate war as waged by major developed countries against each other, obsolete. As conscription was gradually abolished, the number of those involved with war and the military went down. Few today believe that engaging in wrestling, boxing, or even much more violent combat sports such as Mixed Martial Arts (MMA) will help prepare either them as individuals or their nations for eventual armed conflict.

It is of course true that many modern combat sports are extremely demanding in terms of physical force, skill, and endurance. Indeed many athletes are much fitter and better trained than the vast majority of soldiers. However, all those various kinds of sport are based on artificial rules as to what is and is not permitted. Furthermore, and with the exception of fencing, a highly ritualized form of combat to which we shall return, even the most violent ones do not permit the players to use weapons. In their absence, most of those skills are too specialized to be of much military relevance.

In combat sports as in war, and indeed in life in general, a connoisseur is in a much better position to appreciate the refinements of strategy than a layman is. What the latter sees as random and repetitive the former may understand as carefully planned and brilliantly executed movements involving high skill. Skill

---

[36] Pliny, *Natural History*, LCL, 1952, 35.13; Tacitus, *Annales*, LCL, 1937, 14.20; Plutarch, *Moralia*, 274d.

[37] A. Krieger, "Sieg Heil to the Most Glorious Era of German Sport: Continuity and Change in the Modern German Sports Movement," *International Journal of the History of Sport*, 4, 1, 1987, pp. 5–20; J. Tollener, "Formation pour la vie et formation pour l'armée: La Fédération Nationale des Sociétés Catholiques de Gymnastique et d'Armes de Belgique, 1892–1914," *Stadion*, 17, 1, 1991, pp. 101–20; and L. W. Burgener, "Sport et politique dans un état neutre: l'instruction préliminaire en Suisse, 1918–1947," *Information Historique*, 48, 1, 1986, pp. 23–9; M. Spivak, "Un concept mythologique de la Troisième République: le renforcement du capital humain de la France," *ibid.*, 4, 2, 1987, pp. 155–76.

is also what enables the trained combatant to defeat the novice. Nevertheless, it is hard to deny that strategy in the form it is practiced in one-on-one combat sports is rudimentary. It is true that coaches, who in this respect act as commanders, do take care to study the opponent's strengths and weaknesses by watching them in action. However, the one-on-one nature of the fights and the limited possibilities of the human body prevent their strategies from developing beyond mastering a few simple tricks and implementing them against the right opponent at the right moment; the small repertoire of punches used in boxing – just four in all, each capable of being delivered either by the right or the left hand – provides sufficient proof of this. A famous case in point is that of the 1930s German boxing champion Max Schmeling. Watching Joe Louis fight, he noticed that his future opponent sometimes briefly dropped his left arm after throwing a left jab. Doing so left him vulnerable for a split second to a well-placed right cross, which was Schmeling's best punch.[38] Surely this was good observation based on a sound understanding of the sport and implemented by lightning-fast reaction. But it was little more.

Modern contact sports do not allow as much violence as combat sports do, and fortunately so; or else surely many games would degenerate into one or more heaps of struggling, kicking, punching men with little thought for either the ball or scoring. Anybody who has ever witnessed a game of soccer deteriorating into a fistfight will know how flimsy the border between the two is and how real the danger of escalation. Thanks to the fact that they demand close cooperation between team members, though, such sports presuppose the existence of detailed, often quite complicated, rules. Both the rules and the need for cooperation mean that, considered from the point of view of strategy, they are much more sophisticated than individual combats can ever be.

As with wrestling, the earliest known contact sports date back to ancient Egypt where representations sometimes show groups of fishermen engaged in them. Standing in boats and using staves, they tried to push their opponents into the water; the fact that, in one of those reliefs, the fight takes place aboard a processional bark of the war-god Month must be significant, though unfortunately we do not know just what its significance is.[39] Many other pre-modern civilizations were also familiar with contact sports. Their excellence at combat sports apart, the Spartans also developed "strategic" contact sports specifically designed to make not individuals but opposing teams fight one another. In one of those games two teams competed in snatching a piece of cheese placed upon the altar of the goddess Aphrodite. One is reminded of the custom, also much in evidence at other times and places, of having women hand out the prizes to the victor.

---

[38] The story is taken from D. C. Large, *Nazi Games: The Olympics of 1937*, New York: Norton, 2007, p. 337.
[39] Decker, *Sports and Games in Ancient Egypt*, p. 101.

The other game involved a ball and may have been what Plato had in mind, though we do not know the rules of play. Compared with modern games of football or lacrosse, the difference was that kicking, punching, biting, and gouging were also allowed. Casualties, rather than being seen as accidental and regrettable by-products as in modern contact sports, were expected, even encouraged. So ferocious was the *agogē*, or training course, Spartan youths underwent that Aristotle considered it more suitable for beasts than for men.[40] It may also have played a role in the city's decline after about 370 BC, when fewer and fewer entered it and completed it, but that is speculation. Aristotle did, however, approve of athletics in general as suitable training for war. Since we do not understand the details, we can only assume that, then as today, serious coaches and their teams did what they could to keep their own methods secret and also prepared an elaborate "game plan" before each play. Some coaches want to play an offensive game, others a defensive one, and so forth. Often each player, while obliged to stay within the rules, is assigned a role and told to do this and avoid that. Often strategies are changed in mid-game; for example, in order to keep an advantage one has to try and snatch it away from an opponent who seems to be approaching victory.

Strategies of the kind familiar from American football, in many ways the most complex contact sport of all, are quite numerous and sufficiently stand-ardized to acquire names. Terms such as Shotgun formation, Wishbone for-mation, Option Offense, Smashmouth Offense, and of course the famous Hail Mary maneuver which General Norman Schwarzkopf used to explain what he did to Saddam Hussein's army back in 1991, will ring a bell with many readers. Some of these maneuvers are deliberately designed to deceive the opponent. All require teamwork, with the result that players in training spend a lot of time learning how to cooperate with each other. Nevertheless, in truth they are so simple that they are perhaps better described as drills. One reason for this is because, though players certainly vary in strength and speed and also develop some individual skills such as those associated with quarterbacks, linebackers, cornerbacks, and the like, ultimately one human body is not too different from another. In the absence of offensive equipment, which might provide each player with very different capabilities, specialization and division of labor can only be carried so far. Thus there are definite limits on how sophisticated strategy may grow.

Furthermore, the fields on which both football and all other contact sports are played are set aside especially for the purpose. On one hand, they come with all kinds of artificial marks, lines, circles, and the like, whose function is to tell players what may and may not be done on each of their parts. On the other, they tend to be level, symmetrical – every effort is made to ensure that no side obtains an advantage in respect to which side of the field it plays on – and

---

[40] Aristotle, *Politics*, 8.4.1338b.

relatively small. They are also incomparably simpler than the terrain on which real-life warfare is waged. There are no rivers, lakes, mountains, vegetation, or man-made structures of any kind that obstruct movement and/or provide shelter. Not only does this fact simplify strategy, but normally the players on each side can easily and instantly observe what their opponents are doing. The only exception is when players momentarily form some kind of wall to conceal what is happening to the ball. Consequently modest room is left for those vital instruments of war, deception, surprise, and, above all, intelligence (except intelligence of the kind that is gathered before the game starts) and reconnaissance.

Though hand-to-hand combat has become rare, much modern warfare continues to involve physical strain such as those who have not engaged in it can scarcely imagine. Thirst, hunger, heat, cold, discomfort, exhaustion, sleep deprivation, fear, and often pain and suffering as well all remain exactly what they have been since time immemorial. Any commander worth his salt will make sure his troops will get habituated to them, as far as possible, before he leads them on campaign. However, to speak with Epaminondas, the place to achieve this is the field and not the gym or the playing court. The members of football teams do not enter the field hungry; should they suffer a serious injury, they expect to be evacuated and taken care of immediately.

On the whole, changes introduced since ancient times have tended to make combat sports and contact sports less violent than they used to be. For example, the English scholar and diplomat Sir Thomas Elyot (1490–1546) wrote that soccer, a game whose origins seem to go back to the Middle Ages, was "nothing but beastly fury and extreme violence."[41] Though some attempts were made to mitigate it even then, apparently they did not get very far. Even three centuries later players were still permitted not merely to trip and hold opponents but to throttle them and kick them in the shin (hacking, as it was called). Contemporaries sometimes spoke of "mob football."

Things only changed in 1863 when the fledgling Football Association that had just been formed in London outlawed these practices. Even so, it was an uphill struggle. Some teams preferred the old rules and refused to join the Association; one official even insisted that "if you do away with it [hacking] you will do away with all the courage and pluck of the game, and I will be bound to bring over a lot of Frenchmen who could beat you with a week's practice."[42] American football, also known as collegiate football because it was the colleges that first set up a league with regular matches, was more violent still. Players were regularly carried away on stretchers. Crippling injuries were frequent; in 1905 alone nineteen fatalities were incurred. Thereupon US President

---

[41] Quoted in D. Birley, *Sport and the Making of Britain*, Manchester University Press, 1993, p. 62.
[42] *Ibid.*, p. 259.

Theodore Roosevelt, himself no mean sportsman, intervened and ordered the colleges to clean up their play, or else he would have it prohibited.[43] In response, mass formations and gang tackling were banned and some other changes introduced as well. Thus the gap between contact sports and war has grown, not diminished.

All in all sports, including unarmed combat sports and "strategic" team sports that allow the use of some physical contact such as football, can help maintain a general degree of physical fitness. At their best, they also represent useful aids in developing character, encouraging a competitive spirit, and building group cohesion among participants and spectators alike. Some consider them a sublimated form of warfare and a substitute for it, one that can easily be diverted for military purposes if so desired; to that extent, if it is true that the Duke of Wellington never said that the Battle of Waterloo was won on the playing fields of Eton, he should have done so. This explains why sports are often practiced in military academies all over the world and also why many of those academies maintain their own teams. Nevertheless, whether because they do not allow the use of weapons (all the different kinds of sports discussed so far), or because the rules prohibit players from deliberately injuring their opponents, they are too different from war to play a very great role in preparing for it.

Whereas sportsmen have been known to volunteer for the military, it would take an odd recruiter to judge prospective cannon fodder simply by looking at their prowess at football or, for that matter, cage fighting. The larger the scale on which warfare was waged, the more organized it became, the more powerful and more sophisticated the weapons in use, and the longer the logistic "tail" as opposed to the fighting "teeth," the weaker the links became between it and every kind of sport, combat sports and "strategic" contact sports included. Which is why no attempt will be made here to trace the development of such sports, and such links, in any detail; between them, Lucian and Plutarch appear to have said everything there is to say on the subject.

Still, the fact that the analogy between combat sports and "strategic" contact sports on one hand and war on the other can only be carried so far does not mean that the former two are without broader social significance. A mere look at the "stars" they breed, the vast crowds they draw, and the sums of money that are spent on them and earned in them will disprove any such claim. If anything, that was even truer in Lucian's day than it is at present; throughout the millennium or so that the ancient Olympic Games were held, few men could compete with the victorious athletes for glory and fame. Officially the winner's prize consisted of a simple crown of laurel. However, behind the scenes

---

[43] See C. Uygur, "How Teddy Roosevelt Ended Unfettered Football and Saved the Game," *Huffington Post*, April 21, 2009, available at: www.huffingtonpost.com/cenk-uygur/how-teddy-roosevelt-ended_b_189310.html.

successful athletes, those specializing in combat sports included, could earn fabulous sums of money for themselves and for those who had financed and supported them. What is more, side by side with combat sports and contact sports there also existed other kinds of games whose similarity to war was much more pronounced.

Great fights, nothing fights

Let it be said at once: whatever Rousseau and his latter-day followers may have written, life among hunter-gatherers, slash and burn horticulturists, and fishing cultures is not all peaceful fun and games. Not only do the great majority of the peoples in question engage in warfare, here understood in the sense of collective violence directed against the members of another group or tribe, but that warfare is often exceedingly murderous.[44] The most common causes of war are disputes over possessions and women – a commodity which, owing to the widespread combination of polygamy and female infanticide, is often in short supply.[45] Another is insults; these, unless they are avenged, will lead to more insults, and ultimately to the loss of property and life as well. On pain of coming to be treated as "nothing men,"[46] members of the tribe are forced into frequent feuding that can last for years, even decades. Men are killed as a matter of course, women – such as pleased the warriors, as one scholar puts it[47] – and children captured and incorporated into the victor's families. In almost all regions where tribal societies engage in armed conflict, entire villages are known to have been wiped out by such means. Over time, and considering population size, tribal warfare can be quite as deadly as that waged by more advanced societies.[48]

"Operationally" speaking, the most common forms of war were the treach-erous banquet on one hand and the predawn raid on the other. Concerning the former, not much needs to be said. The proceedings started when some pretext, such as the need to forget old grievances and make peace, was used to invite the enemy warriors to a feast. Often assisted by "friendly" women who acted as bait, they were made to drink more than was good for them and, if they carried weapons, disarmed. Next, the doors were shut, the guests were locked inside

---

[44] Only about 10 percent of hunting societies had no war: see K. F. Otterbein, "A History of Research on Warfare in Anthropology," *American Anthropologist*, 101, 4, 2001, p. 797.

[45] See on this A. Gat, *War in Human Civilization*, Oxford University Press, 2006, pp. 67–113.

[46] The expression comes from Melanesia: D. J. J. Brown, "The Structuring of Polopa Feasting and Warfare," *Man*, 14, 4, December 1979, p. 722.

[47] F. Boas, *Kwakiutl Ethnography*, H. Codere, ed., University of Chicago Press, 1966, p. 108.

[48] See, for a useful list of figures, A. Gat, "The Pattern of Fighting in Simple, Small-Scale, Prestate Societies," *Journal of Anthropological Research*, 55, 4, 1999, pp. 574–5.

four walls, and, in their helpless state, cut to pieces. Should any of them escape, they might be ambushed while trying to make their way home. The practice, of course, is far from new. Herodotus describes an episode when Alexander (not the Great, but one of his ancestors, c. 520–454 BC), son of Amyntas and heir to the Macedonian throne, tricked some Persian envoys and had them massacred.[49] If the Greek historian is to be believed, on that occasion it was the Persians who, by molesting their hosts' women, brought their fate upon themselves. Be that as it may, the treacherous banquet, indicative of extreme hostility though it was, had more in common with murder than with war, let alone strategy as defined in this volume. Trusting in the enemy's promises, one side was put into a position where it could not possibly fight back. The only interaction, if that is the correct term, consisted of one side assaulting and butchering the other. Gangsters in New York, Chicago, and other cities around the world also occasionally employ the tactic.

The other common form of tribal warfare was the predawn raid, often directed at people who were not close neighbors but lived several days' march away. Though the scale on which the raids were conducted was necessarily small, typically they represented fairly sophisticated operations. Absent a permanent military organization, first it was necessary to elect a commander and invest him with authority. Preparations, both magical-religious and practical, had to be made. Next, routes had to be selected and a division of labor instituted. Some warriors might act as scouts, others as rearguards, and one, a shaman, as a medic. Since hardly any of the peoples discussed in this chapter had beasts of burden, a couple of women might be taken along to act as food-gatherers, porters, and cooks. To find out the enemy's whereabouts, number, and degree of preparation, reconnaissance was used. As the party approached its objective, its movements were increasingly limited to night-time.

The final jumping-off point having been reached, it was often considered necessary to resort to some ruse so as to outwit the enemy and mislead him concerning the direction from which the attack was about to come. For example, some warriors might raise a clamor while the others made their approach by stealth. Another way to divert the victims' attention was to set some neighboring vegetation on fire. Some warriors might be tasked with stirring up the enemy warriors, others with shooting or axing them as they emerged from their quarters. All this demanded careful advance planning. Both during the approach march and during the retreat the raiders might find themselves involved in ambushes and counter-ambushes. In cases when these resulted in a pitched battle, the outcome could be quite deadly to one side or both.

What all these various forms of organized violence – the treacherous banquet, the predawn raid, and of course the ambush and the counter-ambush – have in

---

[49] Herodotus, *The Persian Wars*, LCL, 1921, 5.18–20.

common was their reliance on *surprise*. The role played by surprise in war cannot be overestimated. By greatly reducing the ability of the enemy to respond, it sometimes enables a victory to be won with relatively little fighting; so well established is the principle that it hardly requires elaboration. By contrast, the outstanding characteristic of the form of "war" we are discussing here, and also of a great many types of wargames, is precisely that encounters were pre-arranged in respect to both time and place.

Time and place having been determined, surprise, notwithstanding that it is perhaps the most important "principle of war" of all, was deliberately sacrificed. Along with surprise went reconnaissance and many, if not most, forms of deception. So did the means normally used to guard against surprise, i.e. security in the form of physical obstacles, lookouts, sentries, and the like. Another factor that very largely lost its role was taking the initiative, meaning the ability to make the enemy dance to one's own pipe instead of the other way around; this might be carried to the point where the combatants took turns trying to hit the opponent. Strategies such as choosing the terrain one wants to fight on and taking advantage of its features also went by the board.

Clearly none of this was done because of ignorance, an idea that is at once offensive and rendered ridiculous by the simultaneous existence of other forms of war. Nor was it due to the force of circumstances, as quite often happens in warfare between more sophisticated armies too;[50] as late as the third decade of the nineteenth century Clausewitz could write that battles took place by a sort of tacit consent between the opposing sides. Instead it was done purposefully on the basis of an explicit agreement openly made between the leaders of the two sides. Given the decentralized nature of the tribes' decision-making apparatus, indeed, it is hard to see how else it could be done.[51] Another reason for this was the low density of the population and the large distances that often separated one tribe from another. Had the encounters not been fixed in advance, quite possibly they could not have taken place at all.

Geographically speaking the incidence of such arrangements is very wide-spread.[52] Peoples living as far apart as the Kalinga of Luzon, the Algonquian of the northeastern United States, and, on the opposite side of North America, several groups of Californian Indians were all familiar with them. So were the Tinglit of the northwestern United States, the Eskimo of Alaska, the Maya of Chiapas in central Mexico, the Yanomamo of the Amazonian rain forest, the Chumash of California (whose battles one modern authority describes as

---

[50] For example, Greek phalanxes: P. Krentz, "Fighting by the Rules: The Invention of the Hoplite Agon," *Hesperia*, 71, 2002, pp. 27–8.

[51] See, for a short account of the apparatus in question, M. van Creveld, *The Rise and Decline of the State*, Cambridge University Press, 1999, pp. 2–7.

[52] See, for a brief survey, B. F. Knauff, "Not for Fun," in Cornell and Allen, *War and Games*, pp. 137–57.

"comic opera encounter[s]"),[53] the Maori of New Zealand, and at least some of the Australian aborigine tribes. It was practiced in Melanesia where it formed part of a peculiar complex involving alternate fighting and feasting.[54] As if to make sure no continent was left out, the Higi of Nigeria-Cameroon, the Nguni of southeastern Africa, and, according to at least one source, the Montenegrins, on the shores of the Adriatic, also practiced the custom. One place where it was particularly common, and where it attracted anthropologists like flies, was Papua New Guinea with its population of numerous, often bitterly hostile, tribes.

Separated by thousands of miles of land and ocean, these and other societies must have developed the custom independently. Hence, though the principle is basically the same everywhere, it is scant wonder that there was considerable variation from one place to another. The encounters' one-time existence, side by side with the other above-listed forms of war, is admitted even by a well-known anthropologist who made his career by showing that tribal war was ferocious and "the noble savage" a myth.[55] Another scholar, while claiming that he had never come across them, forgot that in an earlier publication he himself listed some peoples that had them.[56]

The most detailed description of ritualized combat we have comes from Mervyn Meggitt, an Australian anthropologist. As he notes in the preface to his book, he worked in Papua New Guinea during the 1950s and 1960s. His specific field was the Mae Enga, a people of the Western Highlands that made its living by means of horticulture, raising livestock and engaging in trade with other tribes. Meggitt's objective was to reconstruct Mae life as it has been until about 1950 when the heavy hand of the Australian administration really began making itself felt. One outcome was the abolition of the kind of war we are concerned with here along with all the others.[57] It did, however, survive for another decade or so among some other New Guinean tribes until a combination of more lethal weapons and strict supervision from above brought it to an end.

The total number of Mae people was estimated at about 100,000–150,000. They lived in a very large number of kin-based tribes and clans, forming an interlocking, immensely complicated network where every individual belonged

[53] C. Grant, *The Rock Paintings of the Chumash*, Berkeley: University of California Press, 1965, p. 43.
[54] A. Salmond, *Between Worlds: Early Exchanges between Maori and Europeans, 1773–1815*, Honolulu: University of Hawaii Press, 1997, pp. 462–63; Brown, "The Structuring of Polopa Feasting and Warfare," pp. 712–33.
[55] L. N. Keeley, *War before Civilization: The Myth of the Peaceful Savage*, New York: Oxford University Press, 1996, especially pp. 59–65.
[56] Otterbein, "A History of Research on Warfare in Anthropology," p. 796; K. F. Otterbein, *Feuding and Warfare*, Longhorne, PA: Gordon & Breach, 1994, pp. 75–96.
[57] M. Meggitt, *Blood is their Argument*, Paolo Alto, CA: Mayfield, 1977, pp. 17–21.

to several groups at once. Every adult man was free to participate in war; on the other hand, since government was weak, there could be little question of anybody being compelled to do so. Furthermore, since kin-ties with other people were both numerous and very complex, the men often had a fair amount of freedom in choosing which camp to join. As was also true of other tribes around the world, "great fights," as the Mae called them, did not stand alone, but represented one out of several forms of war. But whereas the remaining types, mostly consisting of raids and ambushes, were directed by one or more clans of one tribe against the clans of another, "great fights" were intra-tribal affairs and involved a larger number of related clans clashing with one another.

The number of warriors on each side might be 250–500, though on one occasion as many as 1,000 may have taken part. This was far more than in any other form of armed conflict. It was certainly more than would ever join a raiding party whose size, owing to the need for speed and secrecy as well as logistics, was kept much smaller. Compared to other kinds of war such fights were relatively rare, taking place every few years on the average. One old man told Meggitt that he could only recall four of them in his lifetime and that his father had told him he could only remember four more.

Like other forms of war, great fights were occasioned mainly by theft, especially of livestock, and insult. However, these were often no more than excuses. Instead, Meggitt says, such fights were "deliberately planned affairs . . . whose main function appeared to be display"; in other words, they served as "tests of strength and as opportunities for individual warriors and groups to enhance their prestige." Sometimes it was simply a question of men "spoiling for a fight." As if to confirm the fact that the entire affair did not serve strictly utilitarian purposes, the dress and equipment worn were more elaborate than those used during raids, when mobility and stealth were at a premium. Both warriors and their so-called "fight leaders" added plumes, shells, and other ornaments to their normal attire of wig, apron, and rump leaves.[58]

The men of the first clan would assemble on a convenient hillside. Mixing boasts and insults, they would call upon their opponents to accept a challenge. The opponents would reply in kind, and a suitable time and place would be agreed on. Early on the appointed day warriors from both sides, decorated and armed with bows, arrows, spears, and shields, presented themselves at the lists. The chosen site was a gently sloping grassy down. It lay on the belligerents' common border and had to be sufficiently large to offer plenty of room for maneuvering. Directed by their fight leaders, the men formed extended lines along opposite sides of the arena, arranged more or less by clans with the two clans that initiated the confrontation located opposite one another. There was, however, no strict order; nothing could prevent individual men from changing their place if they found themselves face to face with close relatives

---

[58] *Ibid.*, p. 53.

on the other side. Friends and kinsmen were also free to participate if they wanted to. Young bachelors in particular were likely to join in, either to help their relatives, or to gain combat experience, or just for the hell of it. The tangled network of kin connections meant that volunteers from one clan might well find themselves operating on opposite sides, in which case they took care not to harm each other.

The proceedings opened with a period of massed chanting, the shouting of insults, and stylized displays of aggression, such as the brandishing of weapons, feints, and the like. Next, fight leaders on each side challenged men of comparable reputation from the other to duels. Each pair might begin by firing arrows, which of course implies that a considerable space had to be left for them to maneuver in. Later, using shields and spears, they fought at close quarters in the middle of the field. These encounters were rarely fatal, partly because the antagonists were evenly matched, partly because they were more concerned to wound than to kill. The duel ended when one man was injured or weapons had been expended. At that point the champions would congratulate each other, embrace, and exchange decorations, which might include plumes, shells, and the lethal stone axes that they carried but were not supposed to use in combats of this kind. Next, each one rejoined the warriors of his own side.

During these "balletic" episodes, to use Meggitt's term, the remaining warriors on both sides simply acted as interested and knowledgeable spectators. They shouted advice and encouragement while also occasionally helping wounded men off the field and looking after them. On no account were they supposed to fire their bows on an enemy duelist. If a man were to do so, angry Big Men or fight leaders of his own group might well attack him, the reason being that his action, especially if he killed the opposing champion, counted as a foul. It could easily convert the tourney into serious warfare.

Once one-on-one dueling had ended, the two sides opened fire with their bows. The field would be filled with men moving rapidly about, advancing, shooting, dodging arrows, advancing, and falling back. Though the skirmishing went on at a great pace, it was not unusual for warriors to withdraw from time to time to catch their breath and replenish their arrows. Doing so, they also formed a changing reserve force that the fight leaders or Big Men could use to strengthen weak points in the front line. The fight leaders themselves alternated between observing and advising from behind and rushing into the fray to rally faltering groups. On the whole, hand-to-hand combat was carefully avoided and most casualties resulted from arrows fired at a distance.

While formations were very loose – in New Guinea as elsewhere, bows and arrows, unless they are fired from behind some kind of shelter, are hardly conducive to anything else – the warriors on each side did have a definite objective: namely, to preserve their own extended skirmishing line while trying to turn the others' flank. If successful, the maneuver would enable them to take the opponent under a heavy death-dealing crossfire. Both groupings had the same goal in mind. However, neither was supposed to move off the field into the trees and gardens or among the houses to achieve it, and in any case people were watching. Thus the normal outcome was a stalemate.

Given the numbers involved and the style of battle, for one side to suffer such disproportionate losses that it unilaterally broke off the engagement and withdrew was very unusual. If the weather held, the fighting went on until dusk; however, normally it was halted by the late afternoon rain. In the highlands the downpours are miserably cold and uncomfortable, so that allowing the fighting to continue might cause great damage to the highly prized plumes. Besides, the poor light made it hard for the bowmen to see their targets so that they might hit relatives on the other side by mistake.

When the fight leaders and Big Men decided that enough was enough they told their men to fall back in an orderly manner into their own territory, if necessary reining in young blades who had not yet had their fill of fighting. Weather permitting, some fight leaders might formally bring the proceedings to an end by once again engaging in duels. The final act consisted of speeches by the Big Men on each side. They would sum up the day's events, list the dead (if any), and, since the speeches were aimed at their opponents as well as their own followers, set the scene for future relations between the two groups. That accomplished, everybody would go home.

Understood as one among several forms of war, great fights formed a sharp contrast with the vicious warfare fought by clans against each other. The latter was an expression of realpolitik in which almost any action was acceptable. Whereas in "real" warfare anybody was free to engage anybody else, great fights were supposed to pit equals against one another. Whereas war was waged by means of mobility and stealth, great fights were largely stationary affairs, both spectacular and noisy. Whereas war could take place anywhere, great fights were confined to an agreed-on location so that property such as houses, gardens, and valuable trees was immune. Wounded warriors were also immune – the rules prohibited any interference with attempts to help them – together with what we would call noncombatants, meaning women and children. Members of those two groups were allowed either to go about their day-to-day business or to observe the proceedings. Boys in particular were encouraged to watch what their elders were doing. However, they were not supposed to participate by gathering spent arrows and the like.

Still, perhaps the most striking aspect of the whole business was the fact that, if one of the contending groups was so badly mauled that it had to withdraw (as sometimes happened), the victors' only profit consisted of enhanced prestige, and perhaps deterrent power. A great fight, Meggitt concludes, corresponded to participants' memories of it. Differing sharply from other forms of war, it was mainly a day of good sport, spiced with moderate danger. Its main function was to present men – young men in particular – with an opportunity both to increase their skill in case it was needed in "real" warfare and to put it on display for the benefit of friends and enemies alike.

In the words of another expert on warfare in Papua New Guinea, the opponents were there to be fought, not annihilated.[59] The number of injured was much larger than the number of dead. The fights were expected, recurrent, and coordinated between the two opposing groups. They bore a noticeable ceremonial character. Among the Kiwai, another New Guinean tribe, this was carried to the point where the fights took place at night; to assist the proceedings, the scene might be illuminated by bonfires on the ground or else with the aid of torches held by the women. The scene, consisting of two opposing groups of men throwing objects (including firebrands) at each other, while simultaneously leaping about their own shadows, is hard even to imagine.[60]

To modern strategists raised on Clausewitz's dictum that war is the continuation of policy by other means, all this will sound strange indeed. It is, however, confirmed by other travelers and anthropologists who lived among, or did work with, other peoples around the world. Take the Yanomamo, a people of the upper Amazonian rain forest whose war-making system, thanks to Napoleon Chagnon in his 1968 volume, *The Fierce People*,[61] has attracted much attention. Widely seen as one of the socially and technologically least advanced tribal societies left on Earth, the Yanomamo make their living by gathering, hunting, fishing, and cultivating small transient gardens. As in New Guinea, kin relationships are extremely complex and spread their net far and wide. However, political authority exists, if at all, only within individual villages.

As with other tribes, normally conflicts grew out of disputes over property, women, or insults. The relative importance of these three causes is hotly disputed among anthropologists. Depending on how many friends and relatives each man could gather in his support, the antagonists could be either individuals or groups. Either way they would face each other and exchange blows. The mildest form of conflict, fought with bare hands, consisted of chest-pounding, which the antagonists inflicted in rotation on each other. Next came side-slapping, also performed with bare hands on unresisting opponents. These two forms of combat, if that is the right word, put greater emphasis on the ability to withstand blows than to deliver and avoid them. To that extent they were similar to the European pistol duel as it developed from about 1850 on.

Matters might very well end at this point, proving that escalation was by no means inevitable. When it did occur, or when the grievances at stake were of a

[59] R. M. Berndt, "Warfare in the New Guinea Highlands," *American Anthropologist*, 64, 4, August 1983, p. 183.
[60] According to G. Landtman, *The Kiwai Papuans of British New Guinea*, London: Macmillan, 1927, p. 148.
[61] N. A. Chagnon, *Yanomano: The Fierce People*, New York: Holt, 1977, pp. 113–37. It is only fair to say that, like all famous works, that of Chagnon has been widely criticized.

more important kind, the outcome was club fights. These were much more
serious affairs and often led to injuries, though fatalities rarely ensued. Many
Yanomamo men proudly displayed the resulting physical deformations, especially dents in the head. Much like modern decorations, they acted as proofs of
courage and told everybody that their owner was able and willing to avenge any
insult to which he might be subjected.

The bloodiest fights of all were waged with wooden spears and bows and
arrows which, until the arrival of white traders who brought with them steel
axes and machetes, formed the Yanomamo's most deadly weapons for both
hunting and war. Yet even so things were rarely taken to extremes. Injuries were
frequent, but not deaths. So highly ritualized – in other words game-like – were
all these forms of combat that some commentators did not regard them as war
at all. Instead they spoke of "a complex cultural construct consisting of a
classification of socio-political distances, a theory of physical and supernatural
aggression, and a system of symbolic exchanges via funerary and war rituals."[62]
Others used them to argue that the Yanomamo are not really "fierce": a view
that is not without implications either for our understanding of early mankind
in general or for ongoing political discussions concerning the best way to treat
tribal peoples in today's Brazil and Venezuela.[63] However that may be, the
contests were certainly far less lethal than the predawn raids and the treacherous banquets on which Yanomamo warriors, when truly angry at members of
some another tribe to whom they were not closely related, also engaged. Indeed,
the great majority of men who met a violent end seem to have died as a result of
raiding in particular.

Some sixty miles south of New Guinea lies the northern tip of Arnhem Land,
Australia, home of the Murngrin tribe.[64] According to W. Lloyd Warner,
another Australian anthropologist, the Murngrin had no fewer than six forms
of war, all of which were sufficiently distinct to be called by their own names.
Some, such as the *maringo* (death adder), a night raid on a neighboring village,
and the *gaingar* (ghost spear), a pitched battle, were as lethal as the available
weapons and techniques permitted. Yet there was also *makarata*, best described
as a ceremonial peace-making fight.

A *makarata* ensued when, a considerable time having passed since a killing,
the men of the injured clan sent a message to their opponents that they were
ready. The ceremony itself involved the two sides taking up positions at a little
more than spear-throwing distance. First, those indirectly involved in the

[62] B. Albert, "On Yanomami Warfare: Rejoinder," *Current Anthropology*, 31, 5, December
1990, p. 561.
[63] L. E. Sponsel, "Yanomami: An Area of Conflict and Aggression in the Amazon," *Aggressive
Behavior*, 24, 1998, pp. 107–9; B. Albert, "Indian Lands, Environmental Policy, and
Geopolitics of Amazonian Development in Brazil: The Yanomami Case," *Urihi*, 8, 1989,
pp. 3–36.
[64] W. Lloyd Warner, *A Black Civilization*, New York: Harper, 1937, pp. 174–6.

injury, known as the pushers, and accompanied by relatives from the other side, had to run between the lines. They thereby exposed themselves to spears thrown by men of the injured side from which, however, the stone heads had been removed. Next those actually responsible for the injury had to do the same, except that this time the spears were sharp. The ceremony went on until the elders on the injured side declared that enough was enough. Then a man on the injured side jabbed a spear through the thigh of one of the killers, signifying the end of the dispute. Finally the two sides danced together as a gesture of solidarity.

The following refers to a similar encounter among the Tiwi, another tribe of northern Australia:[65]

> Thus Tiwi battles had to be the confused, disorderly, inconclusive things they always were. They usually lasted all day, during which about two-thirds of the elapsed time was consumed in violent talk and mutual abuse ... The remaining third of the time was divided between duels involving a pair of men who threw spears at each other until one was wounded, and brief flurries of more general weapon-throwing involving perhaps a dozen men at a time, which ended whenever somebody, even a spectator, was hit.

What set some of the Australian tribes apart was their use of a unique device, the boomerang. Elsewhere, long-range weapons consisted of throwing spears as well as bows and arrows. Yet whatever the weapons of choice, some measures were taken to make them less lethal than those used for "real" war as well as hunting. For example, the effective range of the bows used by the Huli, another New Guinean tribe, was about fifty yards. In "battle," though, the two parties would exchange arrows at 50–100 yards, making it hard to hit one's target and allowing one's opponent plenty of time to dodge the arrows coming at him.[66] In other cases the arrows were not provided with feathers, thus making them less accurate. In others still, special large shields were used, offering better protection than those commonly carried during raids; what made this possible, of course, was the fact that they did not have to be carried very far, as on raids. Finally, the Higi of the southwestern United States simply discarded the weapons normally used for hunting and war, using staffs instead.[67]

In the Marquesas Islands, as in French Polynesia as a whole, weapons were made of heavy hardwood studded with razor-sharp shark teeth. Internecine warfare tended to be ferocious and was marked by great cruelty, as warriors literally sawed each other to pieces, and by some accounts engaged in ritual

---

[65] C. W. Hart and A. R. Piling, *The Tiwi of Northern Australia*, New York: Holt, 1960, p. 807.

[66] R. Glasse, *Huli of Papua: A Cognatic Descent System*, The Hague: Mouton, 1968, p. 2.

[67] K. F. Otterbein, "Higi Armed Combat," *Southwestern Journal of Anthropology*, 24, 2, Summer 1968, pp. 202–3.

cannibalism. Yet there were also occasions when the warriors put their weapons aside. Instead they formed skirmishing lines and pelted each other with chestnuts, young coconuts, young breadfruit, and even small stones. This method resulted in a very great reduction in the number of casualties, but it did not altogether eliminate them. Here and there a hit, fortunate or unfortunate as the case might be, led to a man being killed.[68] In all the encounters discussed so far, not only were casualties very low in comparison with the length of time spent "fighting," but the proceedings might end after a single warrior on either side died or was seriously wounded. To that extent it is even possible to speak of "victory points," similar to those used in many other kinds of wargames.

William Buckley was an English convict who was deported to Australia in 1803. He escaped and spent the next thirty-two years living with the Aboriginal tribes. In his memoirs, dictated after he had returned to "civilization" (he himself was illiterate), he says that he witnessed about a dozen encounters of this kind. Though conducted with the aid of spears and boomerangs and lasting for hours, they were leisurely affairs that allowed for interruptions and regularly resulted in just one to three people dead.[69] The aborigines were hardly unique in this respect; one seventeenth-century eyewitness of Algonquian Indian warfare claimed that, taking turns to fire their arrows, they might "fight for seven years without killing seven men."[70] According to the testimony of an old Blackfoot in 1787–8, a day-long engagement might leave several warriors injured but none killed. By dusk nobody had taken even a single scalp; since doing so was one of the main objectives of Blackfoot warfare, that fact was a miracle indeed.[71] Much the same applied to the Eskimo of the Bering Strait, whose customs in this respect resembled those of the other tribes considered here.[72]

Clearly one thing the encounters did not aim to do was inflict large-scale slaughter. That much was admitted even by some pre-1914 German missionaries and administrators in Papua New Guinea, whose normal objective in writing was to show how uncivilized, how utterly barbarian, their charges were – and, by implication how strong their need to be ruled by Europeans in

---

[68] E. S. C. Handy, "Native Culture in the Marquesas," B. P. Bishop Museum Bulletin, 9, 1923, pp. 262–3.

[69] See the description in J. Morgan, The Life and Adventures of William Buckley, Canberra: Australian National University Press, 1980 [1852], pp. 40, 41, 42, 49–50, 60, 68–9, 76–7, 81, 82. Most anthropologists now agree to take Buckley more or less seriously.

[70] R. M. Utley and W. E. Washburn, Indian War, Boston, MA: Houghton Mifflin, 1977, pp. 42–3.

[71] See F. R. Secoy, Changing Military Patterns of the Great Plains Indians, New York: Augustin, 1953, pp. 34–5.

[72] E. W. Nelson, The Eskimo about Bering Strait, Washington DC: Smithsonian, 1983 [1899], p. 327; E. Burch, "Eskimo Warfare in Northwest Alaska," Anthropological Papers of the University of Alaska, 16, 1974, pp. 2, 4.

general and by Germans in particular.[73] Nor do they fit easily into neo-Malthusian "ecological" theories that seek the origins of war in the need to keep a balance between population and resources, especially land. Indeed it has been suggested that land ownership, to the extent that it played any role, did not act as one of war's causes but only underwent accidental change as a result of it.[74]

Some anthropologists see the encounters as a Machiavellian device in the hands of tribal elders, enabling young men to discharge their aggression at relatively low cost. Meanwhile the elders, working behind the scenes, kept their own influence intact. To students during the 1970s and 1980s they were part of an elaborate "male supremacist" complex. The goal was to keep women firmly in their place and willing to accept male decisions concerning such vital matters as marriage, property, custody over children, etc. It was done by providing a graphic, if comparatively harmless, display of what men could do should the appropriate circumstances arise, much in the same way as other forms of sport, wrestling and dueling specifically included, did.[75] This would explain why women's presence at the matches was tolerated, indeed encouraged; as we shall see, it was not the only time women enjoyed watching men pretending to kill each other or actually doing so. Others still saw mock warfare as a method for reinforcing group solidarity.[76] If so, then it had something in common with the kind of modern educational institute, military or civilian, that maintains a football team.

Whatever the truth, the danger always existed that the skirmishing would get out of hand. Deliberately or not, it might turn into the real thing. Returning to the Mae, this was most likely to happen if one side pushed through its design of outflanking the other, made its way among the houses and gardens, and reemerged in the open; or else if the warriors who made the attempt were caught in the act. In the second case they were regarded as outlaws. Circumstances permitting, they might be killed and have their bodies left in the field as a warning to the rest. The same might happen if bystanders were killed either by accident or by design. Most serious of all, so-called "rubbish men," meaning those whose social status was low, sometimes presumed to take on an opposing fight leader. In that case, so great was the danger of escalation

---

[73] See the diary of a certain Bayer, missionary, quoted in H. Fischer, ed., *Wampar: Berichte ueber die alte Kultur eines Stammes in Papua New Guinea*, Bremen: Uebersee Museum, 1978, p. 181.

[74] See e.g. P. Brown, "New Guinea: Ecology, Society and Culture," *Annual Review of Anthropology*, 7, 1978, pp. 263–91; A. P. Vayda, "Why Marings Fought," *Journal of Anthropological Research*, 45, 2, Summer 1989, pp. 159–77.

[75] W. T. Divale and M. Harris, "Warfare and the Male Supremacist Complex," *American Anthropologist*, 78, 3, September 1976, pp. 525–7.

[76] Harrison, "The Symbolic Construction of Aggression and War," pp. 583–99.

that such a person, should he have killed the enemy, might be put to death by his own comrades.

Other peoples had their own ideas as to what was, and was not, acceptable. For example, sanctuaries might or might not be provided. Noncombatants might be allowed to assist their warriors by warning them, feeding them, and providing them with arrows, or they might not. The victorious party might be permitted to pursue – which might very well lead to a much larger number of casualties and permanently embitter relations between the two sides – or it might not. Some communities had rules that only allowed arrows to be fired at the opposing men's legs.[77] Though escalation was by no means inevitable, often Big Men and fight leaders must have had their hands full trying to prevent greater damage from being done. On other occasions, of course, they were looking at ways to cheat the opponent and get the better of him. A deliberate violation of the rules was always likely to lead to very serious consequences; the more so because, in contrast to many other types of wargames, there were no neutral referees to control the fighters or mediate between them.

The skirmishing, limited to daylight time and interrupted as each evening fell, might go on for weeks or even months on end, resulting in little if any bloodshed. Then one day a few warriors might lose their lives, incidentally proving that, until that point, it was restraint and not incapacity that had governed the proceedings. The outcome could be some of the most brutal warfare imaginable. Houses and gardens might be plundered and set on fire. Dozens if not hundreds might be killed without distinction of age or sex, and villages depopulated as their surviving inhabitants sought refuge among their friends and relatives in other tribes. Repairing the damage, if it was done at all, might take years.[78] Yet using these facts to deny the existence of the kind of encounters we have described is equivalent to saying that, since the 1969 "100 hours war" between Honduras and El Salvador broke out after a football match had brought tensions between the two countries to a head, there is no such thing as football.

Closely linked with political, economic, and family grievances as they were, the encounters in question did not stand entirely on their own. To that extent they were clearly part of the "ordinary" life of the tribes in question. Yet they were also separated from that life by the arrangements that preceded them and enabled them to take place; as long as they lasted, "ordinary" life, both that of the participants and that of the spectators, was suspended. Compared with the other forms of war practiced by the same societies, clearly the combats were governed by highly artificial rules in respect to the kind of weapons used, how they might be used, and against whom. Not only were they held at a location especially selected for the purpose, but they were organized in such a way as to

---

[77] Landtman, *The Kiwai Papuans*, p. 148.
[78] See Vayda, "Why Marings Fought," pp. 166–70.

match like with like, contain any damage that might result, and allow the participants to have some fun. Some of the objectives of "real" warfare, such as capturing women, were left out; whereas in predawn raids women and children often accounted for half or more of the casualties, in great fights such casualties were quite rare.[79] Instead, great emphasis was put on sheer display, to the point where "war" almost turned into a ceremonial dance. The day having ended, the parties parted, or at any rate were supposed to part, as friends rather than as enemies.

In all these ways the fights were a perfect fit for games as defined by Huizinga and others. In so far as they mimicked battle and involved coping with opponents well able to respond in kind and even specially chosen for that purpose, they are rightly called wargames. As if to clinch the argument, some of the tribes that practiced the custom seem to have been well aware of the paradox it involved, or else one is hard pressed to understand why the Maring, another New Guinean tribe, when referring to what their Mae neighbors called "great fights," called them "nothing fights" or "nonsense fights."[80] Apparently each of these two peoples, while engaged in very similar encounters, saw them from a completely different angle. Both, of course, had perfectly valid reasons for using the terminology they did. Yet together they expressed what may very well be the most outstanding single feature of games, the wargames played by men and animals alike included: namely, their extraordinary ability to combine light-heartedness with absolute – one is tempted to say deadly – seriousness. This may be carried to the point where not even the players can be sure which is which, as in the Trobriand Islands where war itself is regarded as one of the games men (as opposed to women) play.[81] So it has been in the past, and so – though the way games are played has changed very much – it remains to the present day.

Combat of champions and single combat

Hunting aside, what the various kinds of combat sports, team sports, and sham fighting discussed so far had in common is that, in them, bloody slaughter was neither the main objective nor the principal instrument employed. On the contrary, it was in order to contain slaughter that challenges were issued, arrangements concerning time and place agreed on, certain weapons and/or tactics prohibited, sanctuaries provided, bystanders granted immunity, and the proceedings brought to an end by mutual agreement. Thus slaughter, to the

---

[79] R. C. Kelly, *Warless Societies and the Origins of War*, Ann Arbor: University of Michigan Press, 2003, p. 100.
[80] Meggitt, *Blood is their Argument*, p. 17; Vayda, "Why Marings Fought," p. 166.
[81] P. A. B. Weiner, *Women of Value, Men of Renown: New Perspectives on Trobriand Exchange*, Austin: University of Texas Press, 1976, p. 91.

extent that it took place at all, was largely incidental. In case too many men were killed, either the games would be brought to an end or, by leading to escalation, turned into something much more serious. However, there also exists a very different class of wargames, such as, seen from the point of view of the participants, could be quite as deadly as war itself and sometimes even more so. I am referring to combat of champions, single combat, and gladiatorial shows. Of these, the first two are treated in the present section, the third in the next chapter.

While there have been attempts to distinguish between combat of champions and single combats, they seem to lead nowhere; here the two terms will be used interchangeably. Some modern historians have confused them with feuding.[82] In fact, however, they are the exact opposites. Feuding consists of intermittent, if normally small-scale (owing to the limited number of participants and their consequent inability to acquire and use heavy weapons), warfare between rival families or clans. Though it sometimes took the form of regular duels, very often it was, and in some places still is, conducted by the most underhand means available, including the ambush, the *ruse de guerre*, and even the treacherous banquet. In one recent case in Afghanistan, the place of the banquet was taken by a fake television crew. Carrying a bomb concealed inside their video camera, its three members applied for an interview with Sheikh Ahmad Massoud, a rival of Al Qaeda and Osama bin Laden. Granted access to him, they blew him up, along with two of their own number who also went to heaven.[83]

By contrast, to hold a combat of champions or single combat it was first of all necessary to suspend what hostilities were going on at the time. Often this was done by means of an explicit covenant crafted by spokesmen on both sides. Even when this did not happen, some kind of tacit agreement was needed if the enemies were temporarily to put down their arms, separate, create some kind of ring or arena, and permit the encounter to take place. As the contestants challenged and faced one another in the open, most of the strategies commonly used in feuding were rendered irrelevant. Another reason for this was the presence of spectators on both sides who, in case of a foul, could be counted upon to intervene and end the fight. Very often the declared objective of the exercise was to end the war without further bloodshed (an objective, as we shall see, that was rarely if ever achieved). In other cases it was simply a question of taking time off to admire an exceptional performance by exceptional fighters. In any case there can be no mistaking the game-like character of the encounters. They were isolated, clearly separated from "ordinary" warfare, and often enough allowed to run their course as if the latter did not exist.

---

[82] E.g. V. G. Kiernan, *The Duel in European History*, Oxford University Press, 1988, pp. 20–34.
[83] See on this story, Ahmad, Sheikh Massoud, at: http://en.wikipedia.org/wiki/Ahmad_Shah_Massoud.

Leaving aside the combats between fight leaders that sometimes opened the encounters described in the previous section, the earliest known account of an encounter of this kind is found in an Egyptian literary work dating to the twentieth century BC. It refers to events that supposedly took place not long before. The story is narrated in the first person by Sinuhe, formerly an Egyptian official of some rank. Sent into exile by the reigning Pharaoh, he lived in the Land of Canaan where he married the daughter of a local chief and ultimately rose to become a chief in his own right. Challenged to single combat by a local "mighty man," he consulted his father-in-law before taking up the challenge. His preparations for the fight are described in some detail. Time and place having been duly agreed on, the two met. A large crowd, made up partly of local people and partly of Sinuhe's own followers, was in attendance. Unusually in fights of this kind, the encounter was fought entirely with bows, i.e. without any hand-to-hand fighting. The contestants, presumably confronting one another in the open, exchanged shots until one of Sinuhe's arrows pierced his opponent's neck. Thereupon he used the man's own battleaxe to deliver the *coup de grâce* "while every Asiatic roared." The story ends when the Pharaoh, having heard of Sinuhe's exploit, pardons him, allowing him to spend the evening of his life in his native land.[84]

Another early battle of champions is described in a Babylonian epic, the *Enuma Elish*.[85] It was probably written somewhere between 1800 and 1600 BC, though some scholars believe that the correct date is closer to 1100 BC. This time the opposing forces consisted of divine beings, not men. On one side were the god Marduk, a four-eared, four-eyed creature (which probably means that he had two heads) and his allies. They were confronted by the sea-goddess Tiamat and *her* allies. Certainly Marduk, and possibly Tiamat as well, came under pressure from members of his or her own coalition. The two of them having agreed to meet and fight it out, things developed as follows:

> Tiamat and the expert of the gods, Marduk, engaged,
> Were tangled in single combat, joined in battle.
> The lord spread his net encompassing her,
> The tempest, following after, he loosed in her face,
> He drove in the tempest lest she close her lips,
> The fierce winds filled her belly,
> Her insides congested and she opened wide her mouth,
> he let fly an arrow, it split her belly,
> cut through her inward parts and gashed the heart,
> he held her fast, extinguished her life.

[84] A translation of the part of the text referring to these events is printed in Y. Yadin, *The Art of Warfare in Biblical Lands*, New York: McGraw-Hill, 1963, pp. 72–3.

[85] For what follows, including the translation, see T. Jacobsen, "The Battle between Marduk and Tiamat," *Journal of the American Oriental Society*, 88, 1, January–March 1968, pp. 104–5.

Other translations have Marduk cutting open and laying out the defeated Tiamat "as if she were a fish." The story has been interpreted in various ways. Depending on the scholar, Marduk's victory over Tiamat may have represented the triumph of order over chaos, of the land over the all-encompassing sea, of the new over the old, of civilization over nature, or of the wicked male principal over the female one who, from then until the present, was condemned to eternal submission. Later, during the age of the Assyrian Empire, Marduk was identified with the god Asur. Some scholars believe that the combat was reenacted each year, with the king playing the role of Marduk/Asur;[86] just who his opponent was, and what happened to him, we have no idea. Others have tried to link the story to the Egyptian god Osiris and to the Old Testament.[87] To us, it does not matter. The decisive point is that two coalitions of divine beings were facing each other. Rather than engage in a pitched battle, two champions were chosen. They challenged one another and fought one another to the death.

To return from the world of gods to that of men, we have the famous story of David versus Goliath (strictly speaking Goliath versus David, because it was Goliath who first issued the challenge).[88] The date, as far as it may be determined, was around 1065 BC. The Philistines and the Israelites, long-time enemies in a land to which both of them were destined to give their names, were drawn up in two opposing battle arrays in the Valley of Ellah, about twenty miles west of Jerusalem. Since the heavily armed Philistines were less able than their enemies to fight on hilly terrain, and vice versa, apparently neither side was keen to be the first to attack. The outcome was a stalemate that lasted for some time. Day after day, a Philistine giant by the name of Goliath marched into no-man's-land and challenged the Israelites to a combat of champions. However, "when Saul" – the Israelite king – "and all Israel heard his words, they were dismayed, and greatly afraid." None dared take up the challenge. Enter David, a shepherd lad from Bethlehem whom his father had sent to the Israelite camp to provision his older brothers who were stationed there. Having heard Goliath bellow, he went to Saul and, claiming that the Lord would be on his side and not on that of the Philistines, succeeded in persuading the king to allow the encounter to take place.

As we shall see, normally in games/combats of this kind every effort was made to ensure that the fighters would meet one another on equal terms. Not

[86] W. G. Lambert, "The Great Battle of the Mesopotamian Religious Year: The Conflict in the Akitu House," *Iraq*, 25, 2, Fall 1963, pp. 189–90.
[87] See e.g. P. H. Seeley, "The Firmament and the Water Above," *Westminster Theological Journal*, 53, Fall 1993, pp. 241–61. The paper is available at: http://www.thedivinecouncil.com/seelypt1.pdf.
[88] 1 Samuel 17.

so, however, on this occasion. On the Philistine side there was Goliath, six cubits and a span tall.

> And he had a helmet of brass upon his head and he was armed with a coat of mail; and the weight of the coat was five thousand shekels of brass. And he had greaves of brass upon his legs, and a target of brass between his shoulders. And the staff of his spear was like a weaver's beam; and his spear's head weighed six hundred shekels of iron; and one bearing a shield went before him.

His opponent was young and lightly armed – he had tried on Saul's arms, but not being used to them he decided to do without them. All he had was a staff, a sling, and five pebbles. So great was the disparity between the two that the expression "David versus Goliath" has become proverbial.

In fact, appearances were deceptive. Admittedly David was greatly inferior in strength and the power of the weapons he carried. Nor did he wear any defensive armor. However, in terms of mobility and range he was clearly superior. While the Bible provides few details, obviously there was sufficient space between the opposing armies to allow David to develop a strategy that exploited these advantages to the full. Having "run" until he was within range of his opponent, he halted, put a pebble in his sling, whirled it around, aimed and fired. Had he missed, then of course he could still have run away, taken up some other position, and repeated the attempt. There simply was no way Goliath could have chased him and caught up with him. In the event he hit his enemy on the forehead, causing him to fall, unconscious. Next, using the giant's own sword, he cut off his head. In all the records of single combat a more asymmetrical fight is hard to find. The preliminary exchange of taunts and curses apart, so limited was the interplay between the two that it hardly deserves to be called a fight at all.

When issuing his challenge, Goliath suggested that the fight, however it turned out, would bring the war to an end. Should he himself be defeated, then the Philistines would agree to become the Israelites' "servants"; if things turned out differently, then the relationship would be inverted. The text does not tell us whether Saul, when he agreed to allow David to try his luck, accepted those conditions. As it turned out, the Philistines, having watched their mighty champion fall and die, fled the field. The Israelites went in pursuit and wounded many (the text does not say explicitly that they were killed). They ended by plundering the enemy's camp. The clear implication is that if hostilities were resumed and further bloodshed took place, it was the Philistines' fault.

The next book of the Old Testament, 2 Samuel, also contains a description of a combat of champions. This time it was not individuals but two groups which met and fought. Following Saul's defeat and death at the Philistines' hands, civil war broke out between the forces of his son and putative heir, Ishbosheth, and those of his son-in-law, the pretender David. The former were commanded by Abner, the latter by Joab, who also happened to be David's nephew. The armies met on two sides of a pool at Gibeon, a few miles north of Jerusalem.[89] The two men knew one another well. Abner, who was older and more experienced, suggested "let the young men now arise, and play before us." Joab immediately agreed. The extremely terse language – much more so in the original Hebrew than any English translation can reproduce – may suggest that they were not volunteers but acted under orders. "Then there arose," the text proceeds, "and went over by number twelve ... which pertained to Ish-bosheth ... and twelve of the servants of David. And they caught every one his fellow by the head, and thrust his sword in his fellow's side; so they fell down together." Whereupon the war was resumed, many were killed, and Abner's forces were badly beaten.

Starting as long ago as the fourth century AD, rabbis and scholars have often commented on this text.[90] Some things seem clear enough. First, there were no speeches and apparently no attempt to negotiate an agreement concerning what would happen in case one side won and the other lost. Judging by the use of the term "play," the only goal Abner had in mind seems to have been pure entertainment. Perhaps the word, which like the English "sport" is closely linked with "fun" and "laughter," was deliberately chosen to bring out this aspect of the matter. Some rabbis, indeed, have condemned Abner, claiming that his death, which took place soon afterwards, was a divine punishment for making light with men's blood. Second, evidently what took place was a series of one-on-one fights, not a struggle between two organized teams; each fight involved both wrestling and weapons play. Just such a fight, dating to approximately the same period and involving two men holding one another by the beard and stabbing one another, is shown on some reliefs from Tel Halaf in northern Syria.[91]

Third, as is normal in combats of this kind, there were no rules to limit the amount of violence the combatants might use and no attempt to prevent a deadly outcome. To the contrary, the death of at least one combatant was expected. Though the text does not explicitly say so, clearly what made this possible was the fact that they fought in a location specially set aside for the purpose. Some modern archeologists even believe that they may have discovered it. Finally, since the forces on both sides were perfectly symmetrical, the fight was much more typical of the genre of single combat and combat of champions than the one between David and Goliath.

We are told in 2 Samuel that several of David's "heroes" also killed their opponents in single combat, but too few details are provided for these episodes

---

[89] 2 Samuel 2.
[90] Thanks to my friend Amihai Borosh, who is both a rabbi and a scholar, for bringing the relevant texts to my attention.
[91] M. von Oppenheim et al., Der Tell Halaf: Eine neue Kultur im ältesten Mesopotamien, Leipzig: Brockhaus, 1931, plate 35b.

to be worth commenting on.[92] Whether they involve gods or men, one thing all these encounters have in common is their mythological or semi-mythological character. This even applies to the one built around the Egyptian hero Sinuhe. Determined attempts have been made to show that the one between David and Goliath could not have taken place in the form the Bible describes it. First, it turns out that Goliath's equipment, strongly reminiscent of that described by Homer though it is, fails to match what various contemporary sources reveal about that used by the Philistines during the period in question. Second, it is claimed that the account of the fight was written many centuries later. By this view, the consciously held objective was to demonstrate the superiority of Jewish over Hellenistic culture.[93] Similar questions have been raised concerning three other combats to which we must now turn. They are described in the *Iliad*, an eighth-century BC epic whose relationship to "what really happened" is by no means clear.

Modern scholars place the Trojan War, if it ever took place, about two centuries before the reign of King David. The first combat took place after the Trojan hero Hector called his brother Paris, whose abduction of the beautiful Helen from her husband Menelaus had caused the war, a coward. Thus challenged, Paris admitted that he was a better man in bed than on the battle-field. However, he also said that he was prepared to meet Menelaus in a duel for Helen's hand and treasure, thus ending the conflict his deed had initiated. Hector, whose heart was full of forebodings concerning the eventual fate of his city, leapt at the proposal of saving it. Stepping between the lines, he stopped the fighting and repeated Paris' consent for the enemy forces to hear. Menelaus having agreed – after ten years of hostilities everybody had grown sick and tired – some sheep were slaughtered, and both armies swore a solemn oath that whoever won the fight would be allowed to keep Helen, together with all her treasure. A piece of ground was staked out; on both sides, the warriors sat down in orderly rows to watch the proceedings.

As in many a modern pistol duel, lots were drawn to see which of the combatants would be the first to cast his spear. Paris won, but his spear failed to penetrate Menelaus' shield. Next Menelaus, a much better warrior than his rival, cast *his* spear. It penetrated and tore Paris' shirt, though the text does not explicitly say that he was wounded. Reaching for his sword, Menelaus sought to kill his opponent, but it broke. He thereupon seized Paris by his helmet's strap, and would have overcome him if the strap too had not broken. Paris' life was only saved by the intervention of his patroness, the love-goddess Aphrodite. Having enveloped him in a cloud, she spirited him away from the battlefield back to his house in Troy where she ordered Helen to sleep with him.

---

[92] 2 Samuel 17.1.
[93] A. Yadin. "Goliath's Armor and Israelite Collective Memory," *Vetus Testamentum*, 54, July 2004, pp. 373–95.

Meanwhile a mystified Menelaus searched for Paris all over the battlefield. Since he could not be found, King Agamemnon proclaimed that Menelaus had won the fight and called on the Trojans to keep their oath and return Helen. This might indeed have happened. However, Athene, who hated Troy and wanted to bring about its destruction, persuaded a Trojan hero, Pandaros, to fire an arrow at Menelaus, which wounded him. The oath having been treacherously broken, hostilities were resumed.[94]

The second fight was instigated by Paris' brother Helenos. Acting on the advice of Athena and Apollo, he persuaded Hector, who was also his brother, to call a halt to the fighting. Obeying Hector's call, the Trojans sat down on the ground, whereupon the Greeks, on the order of Agamemnon, did the same. Addressing both armies, Hector suggested a combat between himself, as the most powerful Trojan warrior by far, and a Greek champion. This time, though, the text does not say anything about any conditions that may have been attached to the outcome of the anticipated fight.

At first Menelaus wanted to answer the challenge. However, he was prevented from doing so by his brother, King Agamemnon, who argued, with good reason, that Hector was much the greater warrior and that the outcome of such a fight would be a foregone conclusion. After some hesitation no fewer than nine Greek heroes volunteered to take his place. A lottery was held, and it fell on the giant Ajax. Following some mutual taunting, he and Hector went after one another with spear and heavy rock. It looked as if Ajax might win, but as the day ended and darkness approached the heralds on both sides called a halt to the fight. At this point one "wise" Trojan leader, Antenor, suggested that Paris return Helen with all her treasure so as to put an end to the war. Paris on his part was prepared to return the treasure but not Helen. His father Priam, King of Troy, agreed to have that proposal submitted to the Greeks. When the latter had heard it, they understandably decided that the war should go on.[95]

The *Iliad* also describes a third encounter of the same kind. This time the objective was not to end a war but to observe religion and provide entertainment; the combatants, though they were rivals, were not enemies and did not represent anybody except themselves. After Patroclos had been killed and buried, his friend Achilles held funeral games in his honor. The highlight was formed by single combat between two great heroes, Diomedes and the abovementioned Ajax. Three times the antagonists clashed, only to separate again. Ajax struck hard but did not penetrate Diomedes' armor. Diomedes on his part was directing his "glittering spear" at Ajax' throat when the Greeks, "worried about Ajax," called an end to the fight, leaving Diomedes to carry the prize. Like some of the rest, the story is not as clear as it should have been. Before the fight began, Achilles announced that the first combatant to "dip his spear in his opponent's blood" would be pronounced the victor. Yet he also promised that

---

[94] Homer, *Iliad* 3.15–4.126.   [95] *Ibid.*, 7.37–404.

after everything was over he would invite both fighters to feast in his tent. Clearly, then, though injury was expected, there was no intention of having the two men fight to the death.[96]

The poet has arranged the fights in a definite order. Menelaus did defeat Paris, but he was no match for Hector who was much stronger than him. Hector was injured by the gigantic Ajax and, had nightfall not interrupted the fight, might very well have been left dead in the field. Ajax in turn was overcome by the great warrior Diomedes, who as it happened was the favorite of the war-goddess Athena and took on the war-god Ares himself. Thus it is the greatest heroes who are made to fight one another last.

Tactically speaking, these three encounters were all but indistinguishable from countless other fights described in the *Iliad*.[97] First two heroes, often known to each other by name (and sometimes related, which causes them to part peacefully) met on the battlefield. Sometimes they exchanged speeches, sometimes not. The fight opened with the casting of spears – naturally there could be no question of throwing lots to see who would do so first. The spear having failed to kill the opponent, they followed up with swords and heavy rocks. Two principal differences distinguished the Homeric duels from "real" combat. First, they were pre-arranged. In the one between Paris and Menelaus explicit conditions were agreed on concerning what would happen in case it turned out this way or that. Though the poet does not say so, presumably that was also true in the one between Hector and Ajax. Second, and even more important, and as Hector reminded his opponent in his pre-battle speech,[98] the use of cunning and dirty tricks was prohibited. Responsibility for making sure that the proceedings would be fair rested with the spectators on both sides, acting as witnesses. All three duels bore a solemn, even festive, character. In this they differed sharply from the confused, often anything but fair and even-handed, reality of war so well described elsewhere in the *Iliad*.[99]

Taking all the above-mentioned seven encounters, between them they encompass almost every type of duel known to man. Mostly the combatants were volunteers, but if I interpret 2 Samuel correctly they might also be ordered to participate. Now individuals met, now groups. Sometimes explicit conditions concerning what would happen if one side won and the other lost were set, sometimes not. Usually care was taken to provide a certain symmetry on both sides, or else presumably one or the other would have refused to fight, but this was not always the case. Normally the combatants fought with short-range weapons, presumably because they were considered fit for heroes because they did not endanger the spectators; but we have also noted cases when bow and

---

[96] *Ibid.*, 23.800–23.
[97] See, on the fighting techniques of Homeric armies, V. M. Udwin, *Between Two Armies: The Place of the Duel in Epic Culture*, Leiden: Brill, 1999, pp. 71–5.
[98] Homer, *Iliad*, 7.242–3.   [99] See Udwin, *Between Two Armies*, pp. 89–90, 107–8.

arrows and even the sling were used. Many duels were fought to the death, others stopped before they got that far. All are clearly wargames as we have defined the term. The difficulty is that none of the sources even comes close to historical objectivity as we understand it today. Not only do historians question Goliath's equipment, but it is not at all certain that the Greeks ever fought in the way described in the *Iliad*. The fact that later vase paintings often show the combats, complete with the protagonists' names, does nothing to resolve the issue. The question is whether the protagonists ever existed and whether the fights did take place.

Subsequent Greek authors, notably the seventh-century BC poet Hesiod, the fifth-century BC playwright Euripides, and the first- and second-century AD geographers Strabo and Pausanias also tell us of single combats between champions.[100] However, in every case the events they describe took place centuries before their own time, either shortly before the Trojan War or not long after it. As a result, though Strabo and Pausanias both claim to have seen monuments erected to the heroes in question (and though there is no reason to question their veracity in this respect), neither their accounts nor those of the others can be authenticated any more than the *Iliad* can. The same is true of Herodotus' story concerning a fight that took place at the Isthmus between a Heraclid (Dorian) champion and a Tegean one. This, incidentally, is one of the few cases when the conditions surrounding the fight, assuming it did in fact take place, were actually observed; the outcome was said to have been fifty years of peace.[101] As with Homer, all one can surmise is that there is nothing intrinsically impossible about these accounts: even if the specific champions whose names have come down to us never existed; even if the specific combats mentioned never took place; and even if some of the stories are clearly intended to provide an explanation for certain strange facts and proceedings whose origins were obscure.

Ancient historians dealing with the seventh and sixth centuries BC mention several cases of combat by champions, the last of which supposedly took place in 512 BC. Supposedly on this occasion the people of the two kings concerned, Perinthis and Paeonia (both on the Hellespont), matched not only man against man but horse against horse and dog against dog.[102] Roman history also provides several examples of combat of champions and single combat, but none appears to be historical. The poet Virgil in the *Aeneid* has the Trojan hero Aeneas challenge his enemy Turnus. At stake was the hand of Lavinia, daughter

---

[100] Hesiod, *Fragments*, LCL, 2007, nos. 90 and 93; Euripides, *Phoenician Women*, LCL, 2007, 1255, 1274–6, 1361, 1468ff; Strabo, *Geography*, LCL, 1932, 393 and 633; Pausanias, *Description of Greece*, LCL, 1933, 9.25 and 8.53.

[101] Herodotus, *The Persian Wars*, 9.26. This story is also mentioned by a much later ancient historian, Diodorus Siculus, *Library of History*, LCL, 1933, 4.58.2–5.

[102] Herodotus, *The Persian Wars*, 5.1–2.

of King Latinus, and with her rule over Latium. Conditions were agreed on and everything made ready for the fight; however, Turnus' allies violated the truce. The war, which had been going on for some time, was resumed and Turnus was killed. The historian Livy tells of an episode that supposedly took place around 650 BC when three Roman volunteers, the Horatii, agreed to meet with, and defeated, their three opponents, the Curiatii of Alba Longa, settling the war between the two cities in Rome's favor.[103] Both authors lived many centuries after the events they describe. Neither invented their stories out of thin air, and both are known to have utilized, and elaborated on, much older sources. Yet no more than Paris, Menelaus, and the rest can the existence and deeds of Aeneas, Turnus, and the Horatii be verified.

One of the consuls for 202, BC, Marcus Servillius Pulex Geminus, claimed to have challenged and fought individual enemies no fewer than twenty-three times.[104] Another uniquely Roman institution was the famous *spolia opima*. Physically it consisted of the equipment of an enemy commander whom a Roman commander had slain in single combat. More important, though, was the right to carry it in triumph and dedicate it to the gods, a right only the Senate could grant. According to Plutarch, the first to win the *spolia* was none other than Romulus. The text, which Plutarch derived from much older sources, is as explicit as anyone could wish for: "when they [Romulus and the Caeninensian king, Acron] were face to face and had surveyed each other, they challenged mutually to single combat before battle, while their armies remained quiet under arms." As also happened in the encounter between David and Goliath, Romulus' victory was followed by a battle in which the Romans routed their enemies.[105]

Early in the fifth century BC a military tribune, Aulus Cornelius Cossus, is said to have repeated Romulus' feat by fighting and killing an Etruscan king, Lars Tolumnius.[106] Like its predecessors, though, this case is probably mythological. Switching to "real" history, during all the thousand and more years of the Roman Republic and Empire only one man actually received the award. His name was Marcus Claudius Marcellus and he was consul in 222 BC. The enemy was a "king" of the Gauls whose name is not given.[107] Another man, Marcus Licinius Crassus, grandson of the former "triumvir," should have received the *spolia* in 27 BC, but was denied the award by the Emperor Augustus, apparently for political reasons.[108] All four encounters took place in the no-man's-land between the assembled armies, as indeed they would have to since each commander had to part with his bodyguard and ride ahead. To that extent they answer our definition

---

[103] Livy, *History of Rome*, LCL, 1919, 1.24–6. [104] *Ibid.*, 45.39.16.
[105] Plutarch, *Romulus*, in *Lives*, 16.3–4. [106] Livy, *History of Rome*, 4.19–20.
[107] Plutarch, *Marcellus*, 8.
[108] See for this episode H. I. Flower, "The Tradition of the *Spolia Opima*: M. Claudius Marcellus and Augustus," *Classical Antiquity*, 19, 1, 2000, pp. 34–64.

of wargames. However, only the first one was preceded by a formal challenge. The others were more a question of one general, having observed his rival exposed, taking the opportunity to charge and fight him.

Arriving in Byzantium, we seem to be on safer ground. According to Procopius, a sixth-century chronicler who wrote under Justinian, the battles of Faenza (AD 542) and Busta Gallorum (AD 552) were preceded by single mounted combats between carefully chosen champions of both sides. Both encounters were pre-arranged following a formal challenge. Both were held in full view of the assembled armies and Procopius provides us with blow-by-blow accounts of them. On the first occasion both protagonists were killed and it was the Ostrogoths under King Totila who won the battle that followed. On the second, it was the "Romans," as the Byzantines always called themselves, who prevailed both in the single combat and in the battle.[109] In so far as there was no attempt to negotiate a settlement, apparently the encounters' purpose was not much more than entertainment. Perhaps each side also hoped that the victory of its champion would not be without some moral side-effect on its opponent.

There has never been any question but that the two battles were historical. Both were part of Justinian's attempt to reconquer Italy and took place within Procopius' own lifetime. On both sides, the generals in charge were well known. Both involved thousands of troops, many of whom were still alive at the time Procopius wrote. Unlike some of his predecessors, clearly he could not just invent details, including the combatants' names, out of thin air. Adding to his credibility is the fact that, on both occasions, the Byzantines were fighting not some other ancient city, kingdom or empire but a barbarian tribe. Both before and after Procopius' time, societies that lacked the fundamental division between the private and the public, i.e. such as were constructed either on tribal principles or on feudal ones, were especially likely to engage in the kind of wargame known as combat of champions and single combat.[110]

Here is another description of such an encounter, taken from the work of Liutprand of Cremona (c. 922–72). The reference is to Pavia in 773, scene of an impending battle between some Bavarian and Italian chiefs and their respective armies:

> Already twenty-one days had passed while . . . neither side could harm the other, and every day one Bavarian, reproaching the lines of the Italians, shouted that they were weaklings and poor riders. To the increase of this insult he jumped amidst them and knocked the spear from one man's hand and thus returned elated to his side's fortification. Therefore [one] Hubald . . . desiring to avenge so great an insult against his people, having taken up his shield, soon went out to meet the aforementioned Bavarian . . . Certain of victory, that fellow advanced elated against him, and he began at

[109] Procopius, *History of the Wars*, LCL, 1914, 7.4.21–9; 8.31.11–16.
[110] See on such societies van Creveld, *The Rise and Decline of the State*, pp. 1–58.

times to spur on his agile horse with vigorous charges, and at other times to pull him back with tightened reins. The aforementioned Hubald began to advance straight on. When they reached the point that they struck each other with blows, in his usual way the Bavarian began to gallop in swirls with the horse taking various complicated turns, so that with these maneuvers he could trick Hubald. Instead, when according to these tactics, he turned his back so that, suddenly turning around, he could strike Hubald from behind, the horse upon which Hubald rode was vigorously urged on with spurs, and the Bavarian was pierced between his shoulders through to his heart before he could turn around ... Once this had been done, no small fear gripped the Bavarians, and no small boldness the Italians.

After which the Bavarians were content to receive some silver and return to their own country.

Other medieval sources fairly bristle with such encounters. Gregory of Tours in his sixth-century *History of the Franks*, Paul the Deacon in his eighth-century *History of the Lombards*, Richerus of Rheims in his tenth-century *Histoire de France*, all refer to them. So do the historian known to us as Saxo Grammaticus in his *Deeds of the Danes*, William of Malmesbury in his *Historia Novella*, and Henry of Huntington's *History of the English People*, all of which were written in the twelfth century. From the thirteenth century come the anonymous *L'Histore de Guillaume le Maréchal* and Joinville's *Life of Saint Louis*; from the latter part of the fourteenth, Froissart's *Chronicles*. All of these tell of countless combats of the kind we are interested in.[111] All these were respectable works written by acknowledged scholars. But for them, our knowledge of the early Middle Ages in particular would be nearly nonexistent. Each according to his lights sought to record the most important events that took place during the period he covered. Though each had his biases, none set out to invent history as epic poets so often do. They could have elaborated and embroidered and undoubtedly did so at times; but they could not create an entire class of combats out of nothing without, at the very least, causing their readers' eyebrows to rise.

Though obviously no two encounters were exactly alike, most of them seem to have been governed by a fairly orderly procedure. First two armies would confront each other in the field, parade-like, as was the normal practice until Napoleonic times.[112] Another good time for delivering a challenge might be a siege, given that many investments were lengthy and marked by periods during which nothing much happened. A champion, either acting on his own initiative

---

[111] Saxo Grammaticus, *The History of the Danes*, H. E. Davidson, ed., Cambridge: Brewer, 1979, p. 131; Paolo Diacono, *Storia dei Longobardi*, Milan: Rizzoli, 1967, 5.31; Richer, *Histoire de France*, R. Latouche, ed., Paris: Les Belles Lettres, 1937, p. 93; Joinville, *History of the Crusades*, C. Smith, trans., London: Penguin, 2009; Henry of Huntington, *History of the English People*, D. Greenway, trans., New York: Oxford University Press, 1997; Froissart, *Chronicles*, G. Brereton, ed., Harmondsworth: Penguin, 1978.

[112] See on this van M. van Creveld, *The Culture of War*, New York: Presidio, 2008, pp. 9–10.

or after having received his superior's permission, would step forward and give a speech. Having boasted about the importance of his lineage and his personal prowess in war, he would hurl insults and demand that an enemy warrior come out and meet him in mortal combat. Long-range arms such as bows and arrows do not seem to have been allowed; that apart, the same weapons were used, and the same lack of restrictions applied, as in "real" warfare. While there may have been exceptions, the normal outcome was the death of one of the parties. Finally the victor would praise God and approach his superior to receive his reward. All this applied as much in medieval Europe as it had during the Trojan War. For example, both the battles of Hastings (1066) and of Halidon Hill (1333) opened with a combat of champions; on both occasions the challenger was killed.

There were also some occasions when things worked the other way around. Instead of a game serving as a prelude to "real" war, "real" war was interrupted to allow a game to take place. The *Iliad* apart, just such an occasion is described by Froissart, the late fourteenth-century French chronicler whose ties to both the French and English courts enabled him to produce what is perhaps our best source for the middle decades of the Hundred Years War.[113] The setting was the English siege of Limoges, the year 1370. At one moment, three French and three English knights met each other by accident. Those three against three [their names are carefully recorded] gave a masterly display of skillful fighting. The others let them fight it out . . . Presently the [English commander, the Black] Prince came that way and . . . watched them with keen interest, until at length the three Frenchmen stopped fighting with one accord and said, giving up their swords: 'Sirs, we are yours, you have beaten us. Treat us according to the law of arms'." "We would never dream of doing anything else," was the answer. Quarter was granted as a matter of course; later, this fact did not prevent the city from being "pillaged and sacked without mercy, then burnt and utterly destroyed."

Many medieval and even early modern rulers are also known to have challenged their enemies to single combat. William the Conqueror challenged Harold but was refused. Richard the Lionheart challenged Philip Augustus of France: proposals were exchanged, but nothing came of it since each side tried to bend the rules in their favor and no agreement was reached. Their successors Edward III and Philip of Valois repeatedly challenged one another to single combat for the crown of France. In 1402 Louis of Orleans, the brother of Charles VI of France, defied Henry IV of England to meet him, declaring that he wanted to revive chivalric glory by such means; Henry, of course, refused. Philip the Good of Burgundy appears to have had a passion for such contests and challenged many other lords in turn. In 1525 Emperor Charles V challenged King Francis I of France. Even as late as the 1640s, during the early years of the English Civil War, many aristocrats on both sides challenged one another

---

[113] Froissart, *Chronicles*, p. 179.

as if nothing had changed and the Middle Ages still lasted.[114] Repeatedly we are told that the recipients wanted to accept. Some started preparing, purchasing special equipment, going on a diet, exercising and training, only to be dissuaded by their advisers; that way, "practical" policy could prevail while honor was assuaged. In all these cases the declared objective was to spare Christian blood and obtain a settlement, but rarely did the negotiations reach the stage where specific conditions were set.

Like most others throughout history, medieval battles tended to be the province of screaming chaos as the men on both sides maneuvered, clashed, got mixed up, called on others for help, and so on. Combats of champions and single combats were no less bloody, but they were fought out in the spaces deliberately left open by both sides and were keenly observed by them. As with the kind of mock combats discussed in the previous section, surprise was set aside. All this may explain why, especially during the early Middle Ages, they often provide us with much the most detailed descriptions of tactical methods in the literature of the period.[115] Nor was northwestern Europe the only region where they took place. Fredegar, presumably a Frankish monk who lived and wrote his chronicle during the first half of the seventh century, comes up with the following story. It originated, he says, with a Byzantine embassy that visited King Dagobert of Austrasia in 629.[116]

> Following his usual practice, the Persian emperor sent an army against [the Byzantine emperor, reigned 611–40] Heraclius . . .But Heraclius came out to meet them with an army. He sent a mission to Chosroes [Kosrau II, reigned 590–627], the Persian emperor, to require him to do single combat with him . . . The Persian emperor agreed to this and promised to do single combat. Heraclius armed himself, left behind him his army drawn up in fighting array, and advanced to the fray like a second David . . . But the Persian emperor Chosroes honored their pact by sending one of his patricians, whose great valor he knew, to fight in his place . . . The patrician turned his head to see who was following him, whereupon in a flash Heraclius spurred his horse forward, drew his short sword and cut off his opponent's head. So the Emperor Chosroes was defeated with his Persians, and all in confusion he turned in flight.

At about this time, on 17 March 624, there took place the battle of Badr. On this occasion Mohamed and his small army were trying to capture a caravan that was traveling from Syria, whereas the people of Mecca were determined to

[114] See J. S. A. Adamson, "The Baronial Context of the English Civil War," *Transactions of the Royal Historical Society*, 40, 1990, pp. 93–102.

[115] See H. E. Davidson, *The Sword in Anglo-Saxon England*, Woodbridge: Boydell, 1994, p. 193.

[116] J. M. Wallace-Hadrill, ed., *The Fourth Book of the Chronicle of Fredegar*, Westport, CT: Greenwood, 1981 [1896], pp. 51–3. See, for the entire episode, S. T. Wander, "The Cyprus Plates and the Chronicles of Fredegar," *Dumbarton Oaks Papers*, 29, 1973, pp. 345–6.

defend it. Once the two armies had met, the Meccans sent out three champions. Thereupon the Moslems in turn sent out three "assistants" (*ansar*) to confront them. Needless to say, the Moslems won. They also emerged victorious from the battle that followed, which at the time and later was taken as proof of Allah's favor.[117] Both later Islamic and Japanese sources also contain frequent references to the practice.[118] To repeat, it was especially widespread among societies, whether tribal or feudal, that did not recognize a strict separation between the public and the private. In such societies every "public" war was *ipso facto* a private quarrel between rulers. No wonder they wanted to settle, or at any rate claimed their desire to settle, those quarrels by such means, either themselves challenging their opponents or sending champions to do so in their stead.

Considering themselves "realists," many modern historians have been unkind to the kind of challenge, combat of champions and single combat just described. Some of them argue that if the challenges were issued but left unanswered, then surely this proves the "decline" of chivalry from some lofty standard set in some past period when people were more "innocent" and less "realistic." If they were answered and resulted in actual fighting, then equally surely they were the product of "childish exhibitionism," "a total lack of military discipline" and "stupidity."[119] Other historians take the easy way out by dismissing the entire subject as a figment of the imagination. They deny that the challenges and combats ever did take place or could have taken place.

In fact, there is little about the combats that is intrinsically impossible. The fight between Marduk and Tiamat, of course, is in a class of its own. Perhaps it was meant to be taken allegorically, as were similar tales told by other societies around the world. Yet the fact that it was reenacted on an annual basis casts a different light upon the matter; while we do not know the details, the reenactment itself represented a wargame of sorts. Elsewhere, though the protagonists may be mythological, and though a little divine help is occasionally mentioned and much appreciated, there can be hardly any question of miracles or supernatural deeds. If Goliath, Hector, Romulus, and the rest did not exist and did not engage in single combat, men like them *could* have existed. *Pace* so many historians, too, the fact that the oft-stated objective of saving blood was rarely achieved and that very few wars were brought to an end by such means does not necessarily prove that the whole thing was a "childish" exercise in futility. As

[117] See, on the battle of Bader, M. Lings, *Muhammad: His Life Based on the Earliest Sources,* London: Islamic Texts Society, 1983, pp. 138–9; also M. M. Pickthall, *The Meaning of the Glorious Koran,* New York: Mentor, 1953, pp. 7–9, 17.
[118] Boha ad Din, *The Life of Saladin,* C. L. Conder, trans., London: Palestine Pilgrims' Texts Society, 1897, vol. XII, pp. 161–2; S. Trumbull, *Samurai Warfare,* London: Arms and Armor, 1996, p. 22.
[119] R. L. Kilgour, *The Decline of Chivalry as Shown in the French Literature of the Late Middle Ages,* Gloucester, MA: Smith, 1966 [1937], pp. 10–11, 375–6; J. J. Glueck, "Reviling and Monomachy as Battle-Preludes in Ancient Warfare," *Acta Classica,* 7, 1964, pp. 26, 31.

Napoleon once said, in war the moral is to the physical as three to one. Psychologically speaking an unanswered challenge, if properly stage-managed and publicized, could have its uses. This was even more the case if and when it was answered, resulted in combat, and ended in the champion on one side winning and the other being killed.

However, it is also possible that the real significance of the fights, which is brought out so clearly and so often both by the terminology used and by the spectators' reactions, should be sought in another field altogether. I am refer- ring not to any "useful" military purpose they may have served but the enter- tainment they provided, the excitement they generated, and the cathartic powers they possessed. That certainly applied to the next type of wargames we must consider, i.e. the Roman gladiatorial shows.

2

Games and gladiators

Origins and development

The Roman *ludi*, best translated as festivals or games, have a long history. Held on fixed days of the calendar to honor some god, they went back at least as far as the monarchy which itself came to an end in 510 BC. Originally they featured a procession (*pompa*, in Latin). This was followed by chariot races, stage plays, and similar popular entertainments.[1] From 275 BC on, hunts, animal fights, and the throwing of condemned criminals to the beasts were added. Over time, the number of festivals and their duration grew; by the time of Augustus they took up no fewer than sixty-one days each year. Since we know that Emperor Marcus Aurelius (AD 161–80) decided to cut them to 135, his successors must have added even more.

Apparently it was only towards the middle of third century BC that the *ludi* began to be supplemented by the introduction of life-to-death fights between pairs of specially selected gladiators (from *gladius*, the short sword that, along with the *pilum* or javelin, formed the legionaries' principal offensive weapon). The clearest account of the fights' origins is found in Nicolas Damascus. A Syrian/Greek historian, philosopher, and naturalist who lived at about the time of Christ, he had been tutor to the children of Anthony and Cleopatra. He was also a friend of Herod the Great and spent the last years of his life in Rome. While most of his books have been lost, fragments of them are quoted in the works of other ancient historians. In one of them, called *Athletics*, he wrote:[2]

> The Romans organized performances by gladiators, a habit they had acquired from the Etruscans, not only at festivals and in the theaters but also at feasts. That is to say, certain people would frequently invite their friends for a meal and other pleasant pastimes, but in addition there might be two or three pairs of gladiators. When everyone had had plenty to eat and drink they called for the gladiators. The moment anyone's throat was

---

[1] See, for a general account, A. Futrell, *A Sourcebook on the Roman Games*, Oxford: Blackwell, 2006, pp. 1–4.

[2] Quoted in Athenaeus, *The Learned Banqueters*, LCL, 2007, 4.153f–154a.

cut, they clapped their hands with pleasure. And it sometimes even turned out that someone had specified in his will that the most beautiful women he had purchased were to fight each other, or someone else might have set down that two boys, his favorites, were to do so.

An early seventh-century writer, Saint Isidore of Seville, believed that the Latin *lanista*, or manager of gladiators, derived from the Etruscan word for executioner. The title of Charun, an official whose task was to look after the remains of those who had been killed in the arena, also betrayed an Etruscan origin. Yet no known painting in any of the numerous Etruscan graves that have been excavated shows gladiatorial games.

These facts have caused recent historians to doubt that the Etruscans did in fact invent the fights. Other evidence, in the form of buildings or installations that may have been used for the purpose, is also scant or nonexistent.[3] These historians point to Campanula, south of Rome, as the region where the shows may have originated. They base their argument on Livy who, writing a little later than Nicolas, says that "the Campanions, on account of their arrogance and their hatred of the Samnites, armed their gladiators, who performed during banquets, in the fashion of [the captured men] and addressed them as 'Samnites.'"[4] Livy's account is supported by that of his contemporary Strabo. "As for the Campanians," the traveler and geographer writes, "it was their lot, because of the fertility of their country, to enjoy in equal degree both evil things and good. For they were so extravagant that they would invite gladiators, in pairs, to dinner, regulating the number by the importance of the dinners."[5]

Fourth-century BC grave paintings from the town of Paestum, southeast of Naples, as well as the fact that the earliest known Roman gladiatorial schools were located in Campania, reinforce these claims.[6] So does the fact that during the Republic gladiators equipped as "Samnites" are mentioned more often, and were presumably more numerous, than any other type.[7] Perhaps, though, the question is unanswerable. That is because funeral games in which men fought one another, sometimes to the death, appear to have been fairly widespread in the Greek world, from which they may have reached Rome with or without intermediaries. The Homeric combat between Diomedes and Ajax has already been mentioned, but it is hardly the only one. Herodotus says that, around the time of the Persian invasion of 480 BC, the people of Thrace used to honor their richest dead by holding funeral games wherein the single combat

---

[3] See K. E. Welch, *The Roman Amphitheater: From its Origins to the Coliseum*, Cambridge University Press, 2007, p. 15.

[4] Livy, *History of Rome*, 9.40.17.   [5] Strabo, *Geography*, 5.4.13.

[6] Futrell, *A Sourcebook on the Roman Games*, pp. 3–5.

[7] According to M. Junkelmann, "Familia Gladiatoria: The Heroes of the Amphitheater," in E. Koehne and C. Ewigleben, eds., *Gladiators and Caesars*, Berkeley: University of California Press, 2000, p. 37.

(*monomachia*) carried the highest prize. According to the third-century BC writer Diylos, who was the son of one of Alexander the Great's generals, the Macedonian chief Cassander had four of his soldiers fight each other at the funeral of a king and queen of Boeotia. Plutarch goes so far as to claim that, long before his time, the preeminent symbol of Greek civilization, the Olympic Games, used to include armed combat. However, he also admits that, when he saw the report, he was somewhat the worse for wine and that he was unable to remember where he found it.[8]

Whatever the truth, different interpretations concerning the early fights' precise function are still possible. Strabo apart, we have the testimony of Silius Italicus, a Roman poet who flourished toward the end of the first century AD. "It was [the Campanians'] ancient custom to enliven their banquets with bloodshed, and to combine with their feasting the horrid sight of armed men fighting; often the combatants fell dead above the very cups of the revelers, and their tables were stained with streams of blood."[9] The goal, in other words, was pure entertainment of the crudest sort, as befitted the spoiled inhabitants of a famously rich country such as Campania. The Romans, we are told, behaved differently; both Livy and his contemporary, the historian Valerius Maximus, date the earliest Roman gladiatorial fights to 264 BC, i.e. the year when the First Punic War got underway. Both tell us that one Decimus Iunius Brutus Scaeva, along with his brother, had three pairs of gladiators fight to the death in Rome's "cattle market" (Forum Boarium) as a tribute to their deceased father.[10] Presumably they refer to the former consul (292 BC) Brutus Pera, though modern historians have also considered other possibilities. In this way they emphasize the religious roots of the fights which neither Nicolas nor Strabo mention.

The term used by Livy to describe the games is *munus*, a sacred obligation to the dead. By calling the fighters *bustuarii*, from *bustum*, a funeral pyre or grave, the orator and statesman Cicero also suggests a religious connotation. For as long as the shows existed, the official directly responsible for organizing them never lost his title of *procurator munerum*. To the late second-century AD historian Cassius Dio, the fact that Augustus' longtime companion and partner in government, Marcus Vipsanius Agrippa, always took care to hold them at the time they were due was proof of his piety.[11]

After 246, the next time a gladiatorial fight is mentioned is in 216 BC, the year in which the Romans suffered their disastrous defeat at the hands of Hannibal

[8] Herodotus, *The Persian Wars*, 5.8; Diylos quoted in Athenaeus, *The Learned Banqueters*, 155a; Plutarch, *Moralia*, 675c–d.

[9] Silius Italicus, *Punica*, LCL, 1934, 11.51–4.

[10] Livy, *History of Rome*, 16; Valerius Maximus, *Memorable Doings and Sayings*, LCL, 2000, 2.4.7.

[11] Cassius Dio, *History of Rome*, LCL, 1924, 58.29.

at Cannae.[12] Again it was the sons of a deceased ex-consul, Aemilius Lepidus, who organized the show. From this point on, both the number of occasions when fights were staged and the number of the gladiators who participated in each one seems to have grown steadily. In 200 BC, twenty-five pairs of gladiators fought at the funeral games held for Marcus Valerius Laevinus (consul, 210). In 183 the number rose to sixty, whereas in 174 a number of fights were staged, the largest of which involved no fewer than seventy-four.[13] Among the organizers (editores) of these and subsequent shows were some of Rome's most important field commanders; indeed it is probably for this reason, rather than because of anything special that happened in them, that Livy, as our principal source, mentions them. Both Titus Flamininus, the general who prevailed over Philip V of Macedonia in 197 BC, and Aemilius Paulus, who defeated Philip's son Perseus and finally destroyed the kingdom in question twenty-nine years later, gave shows.

Over two and a half centuries separate the outbreak of the first Punic War, when the earliest known shows were held, from the death of Augustus in AD 14. Since in his political testament Augustus was the first to suggest that territorial expansion should come to an end, the period in question saw Roman imperialism at its height. With rivers of booty and countless prisoners coming, many aristocratic families became incredibly wealthy. Among other things, this fact was reflected in the size of the shows that they held. In 65 BC Julius Caesar, though already almost forty years old (he was born in 102 BC), was still an aspiring politician occupying a comparatively junior position. To advance himself he was planning a show involving no fewer than 320 pairs of gladiators. His excuse was the need to honor his father who, however, had died many years before. This time the Senate, aware that the city of Rome did not have a proper police force, intervened. It feared the result might be public disorder – perhaps, indeed, an attempt at a coup d'état – and limited the number of fighters.[14]

Nineteen years later, having conquered both Gaul and Egypt, defeated all his opponents in the various civil wars, and while serving as a dictator, Caesar's power had reached the point where he was no longer obliged to pay heed to such restrictions. Suetonius, the early second-century AD historian, says that he organized two armies of gladiators. Each consisted of five hundred infantrymen, twenty elephants, and three hundred cavalrymen; they fought in a facility erected especially for the purpose in the Campus Martius, the field where the consuls used to assemble their troops before going to war. Still not content, he had an artificial lake dug. On it warships with two, three, and even four rows of

[12] Livy, History of Rome, 23.30.
[13] All this is recorded by Livy, ibid., 31.50, 39.46, and 41.28.
[14] See for this episode, Suetonius, Julius Caesar, in The Lives of the Caesars, LCL, 1914, 10; Cassius Dio, History of Rome, 37.8; and Plutarch, Caesar, in Lives, 5.9.

oars as well as "a large number of fighters" clashed. Caesar, incidentally, was also the first to hold a show in honor of a woman, his daughter Julia.

Originally the shows had been held by private individuals on their own initiative. To the extent that they were opened to the wider public, tickets had been sold in order to generate a profit. Things changed in 122 BC when Gaius Gracchus, who was serving as a people's tribune, broke with the tradition and arranged for free seats to be distributed instead. Though his fellow tribunes did not take kindly to the idea and saw to it that he should not be reelected, it stuck and was to have a great future in front of it.[15] Another important turning point came seventeen years later. For the first time it was the consuls who organized the shows, with the result that the distinction between the *ludi*, the ancient state-organized festivals, and the more recent *munera* (plural of *munus*), the privately sponsored gladiatorial fights, became fuzzy. The last decisive step in this direction was taken in 42 BC. That was when the serving aediles, apparently to fend off an exceptionally threatening series of omens that seemed to promise ill to the Republic,[16] officially merged the two kinds of festivities with one another. Henceforward gladiatorial combats were regularly held on the same occasions, and in the same locations, as the hunts, the animal fights, and the execution of condemned criminals. All these were amalgamated to form part of a single bloody complex.

In his *Res Gestae*, the political testament that he wrote before his death and which, inscribed on bronze or stone, was distributed throughout the Empire, Augustus boasted that he had three times held gladiatorial games in his own name and five times in those of his various sons and grandsons. No fewer than 10,000 men were assembled and fought;[17] for the pedants, this means that, on the average, 1,250 participated in each show. Even so there were certain limits. Of all the various events that comprised the *ludi*, gladiatorial fights were the most expensive by far. Before they were ready to fight the gladiators had to be maintained for months, fed, trained, provided with medical treatment, and guarded. This fact may explain why Augustus himself limited them to fixed dates – December 2 to 8, December 17 to 23, and March 19 to 23 – and why his successor Tiberius tried to reduce the number of fighters who were allowed to take part. Later Caligula lifted Tiberius' restrictions. He may also have been the first emperor who himself performed in the arena as a gladiator of sorts.

Claudius distinguished himself by his love of the fights – he even had his dinner while watching men tear each other to pieces. He also organized mass fights between condemned prisoners instead of simply throwing them to the beasts. On one occasion he set up a huge battle, the largest on record, in which

---

[15] Plutarch, *Gaius Gracchus*, in *Lives*, 12.
[16] This is the interpretation advanced by A. Futrell, *Blood in the Arena: The Spectacle of Roman Power*, Austin: University of Texas Press, 1997, pp. 1–2.
[17] Augustus, *Res Gestae divi Augusti*, in *Compendium of Roman History*, LCL, 1924, 22.

no fewer than 19,000 men participated either as oarsmen, fighters, or guards. Nero once sent 400 senators and 600 knights into the arena in order to humiliate them, with what results is not clear. Nero also built a vast wooden amphitheater which, however, was burnt to the ground in the huge conflagration of AD 64 that he himself was later suspected of having started. Perhaps the most lasting contribution of all was that of Vespasian (69–79). He employed the Jewish prisoners taken in the war of 66–69 to build the Colosseum, thus finally putting an end to the various temporary installations in which the shows had been held until his time and seeing to it that his name would be eternalized.

As far as the sources allow us to see, the gladiatorial fights reached their apogee during the century and a half or so that separated Julius Caesar from Trajan. The latter, when celebrating the subjugation of Dacia, is said to have sent 10,000 gladiators into the arena within four months, as many as Augustus did during his entire reign.[18] The total number of those who fought during his reign was much larger still. Not just pairs of individuals but entire armies were made to fight each other. Apparently the largest shows of all were those involving naval battles, given that, for each man who fought aboard ship, there had to be several others who pulled on the oars.

To what extent did the shows resemble real-life wars, and how were the two linked? While some of the above-mentioned "armies" and "navies" were quite large, unfortunately we have not the slightest idea how they were organized. Were the participants made to practice together until they formed some kind of cohesive unit or units? Probably not, because people still remembered the Spartacus Revolt of 73–71 BC. Even after Augustus for the first time provided the city with proper police forces in the form of the *Praetoriani* and the *Vigiles*, such units, made up of highly trained but desperate men with nothing to lose (many, like Spartacus himself, foreigners) would pose a real threat to public order. Accordingly, when famine threatened Rome in AD 6, he took the precaution of sending the gladiators to places some hundred miles away.[19]

Or should we assume that they were just hordes of men hastily assembled by the *procuratores* (those who bought or rented the fighters on behalf of the *editores*) and the *lanistae* and thrown together for the occasion? Since gladiators could sometimes be rented by the day and even by the hour, undoubtedly there were instances when that was the case. Yet it is also clear that shows involving numerous fighters could not be improvised at a moment's notice. Sailors and oarsmen in particular required considerable training before they could act in unison or maneuver their vessels. The restricted available space made doing so all the more difficult.[20] We are told that, in the largest naval "battle" of all, "sufficient space was left to allow the oarsmen to display their strength, the

---

[18] *Ibid.*   [19] Cassius Dio, *History of Rome*, 55.26.
[20] See, on the role of training, H. R. Hale, *Lords of the Sea: The Epic Story of the Athenian Navy and the Birth of Democracy*, New York: Viking, 2009, pp. 20 and 112.

steersman their skill, the ships' speed, and all the normal stratagems of [naval] war."[21] To achieve such results joint training was indispensable; one could not just put together two undisciplined mobs and hope for the best.

Nor was the problem confined to naval fights alone. But for proper coordination, different arms such as infantry, cavalry, chariots, and elephants were unable to fight effectively. From the point of view of both organizers and spectators, they might well present a greater danger to each other than to the enemy, thus spoiling what could have been a nice show. Fighting Antiochus III of Syria at Magnesia in 190 BC, the Romans themselves had seen this happen. But how could the necessary coordination be achieved? Or did each of the "arms" fight others of the same kind exclusively, thus dividing the show into different acts? Did each side in the amphitheater have a commander-in-chief and unit commanders? If so, how were those commanders selected and what powers did they wield? Were there rehearsals? In fact we know that, for some kinds of shows, rehearsals were held. As is also sometimes the case with modern concerts and theatrical shows, spectators were even invited to watch them. However, our sources' main concern is to describe the size and extravagance of the shows, any unusual incidents that took place in them, and, during Imperial times, how various emperors saw them and treated them. Rarely do they discuss organization and tactics: hence no answers to these questions are provided.

We do, however, receive some hints. Contrary to the view of some modern historians who claim that gladiators always fought in pairs, Cassius Dio tells us that Caligula had large numbers of gladiators "drawn up in a kind of military formation."[22] Second, the same historian, describing some of the shows organized by Titus (AD 70–8), says that gladiators sometimes fought in groups. Titus' brother and successor Domitian organized battles with groups of infantry and cavalry.[23] Third, it is known that, to add interest, some of the larger events were intended as replicas of well-known historical battles. One, organized by Claudius whose mind contained an antiquarian streak, simulated the battle of Salamis in 480 BC; another, the one between the navies of Corcyra and Corinth that marked the opening of the Peloponnesian War forty-nine years later. A third did the same for the famous battle between Athenians and Syracusans in 415 BC; however, the limits of the discipline imposed on the combatants are shown by the fact that, this time around, the Athenians won. Claudius also celebrated his conquest of Britain – which he did not command in person – by leading his troops in a simulated attack on a British town. As is also true in modern reenactments of historical battles, on these and similar occasions it was necessary to ensure that the fight, instead of degenerating into a free-for-all, would in fact follow the script. Doing so implies the existence of a command system of some kind.

---

[21] Tacitus, *Annales*, 12.56.   [22] Cassius Dio, *History of Rome*. 59.10.
[23] *Ibid.*, 66.25; Suetonius, *Domitian*, in *Lives of the Caesars*, 4.

However large the shows, however numerous those who participated in them, and whatever command arrangements may have existed, clearly there were some aspects of real-life war they could not and did not duplicate. As with all the other kinds of games discussed so far, and with many that will be discussed later too, there was no question of bringing logistics into the picture. Gladiators entered the arena well fed after having a final ceremonial meal the evening before; once in it they fought until they killed their opponents, were killed themselves, or were granted quarter. Most fights between individual gladiators were over in a matter of minutes. Even the largest naval combats cannot have lasted for more than a few hours. Considering that, to quote Cardinal Richelieu, "many more armies [have been] ruined by want and disorder than by the efforts of their enemies,"[24] the absence of logistics was very significant indeed. Furthermore, the place and time of the fights was decided not by the participants but by *force majeure*. Hence there was no room for what today is known as strategy and operational art. Instead, the two sides were made to take up their appointed places and a signal was given so that the fight could get under way. As in combat sports, what strategy was involved was limited to fighting technique.

For the same reason, many forms of what Clausewitz calls friction – the endless number of unforeseen incidents that make the conduct of war so complicated and so difficult – were excluded.[25] Indeed the whole purpose of holding the shows at certain well-defined places and times was precisely to exclude it so as to focus on combat alone. To the extent that any trace of it remained at all, it must have been experienced as an annoyance. Last but not least, even the largest shows merely simulated battles, not campaigns or war as a whole. Since all battles were fought at very close range, in fact face-to-face, little role was left for intelligence. It was standard practice for the fights to be preceded by processions in which the fighters, marching to musical accompaniment, presented themselves to the spectators. As a result, both sides must have known almost everything about the other right from the outset; there was no question of sending out scouts (*exploratores*) or using other accepted methods for obtaining information.[26] The role that surprise and ruses of every kind could play was also limited.

Again it is tempting to speculate on the kinds of equipment that were issued to the participants in these large, collective fights. As is sufficiently well known, during classical times the Greeks' main weapon at sea was the ram. The Romans, however, increasingly came to fight sea battles as if they had taken

[24] L. André, ed., *Le testament politique du Cardinal de Richelieu*, Amsterdam: Hay, 1749, p. 480.
[25] Clausewitz, *On War*, pp. 119–21.
[26] See, on Roman methods of gathering intelligence, N. J. E. Austin and N. B. Rankov, *Exploratio*, London: Routledge, 1995.

place on land, grappling and boarding their enemies' ships. During their last major naval battle, i.e. the one at Actium in 29 BC, light stone-throwing catapults, arrow-firing bows, firepots, javelins, and of course swords and daggers were employed. Could those have been used in the arena too? The answer seems to be, to some extent. Certainly equipping gladiators, a rowdy lot at the best of times, with long-range weapons would have been much too dangerous. On the other hand, as Tacitus explains, the lake that Claudius used for his *naumachia*, or naval battle, was ringed with rafts. The Praetorian cohorts that manned the rafts did have war engines, though whether they participated in the action or simply stood in reserve lest any of the gladiators should try to escape is not clear.[27] All in all, it seems obvious that even the largest collective fights could not match up with "reality." Bloody as they undoubtedly were, there could be no question of simulating either the complexities of real warfare or the kind of coordination needed for waging it.

In any case, large as the Colosseum was, and extensive as the artificial lakes on which the naval fights took place were, they could offer no substitute for nature. Clearly there were limits to what could be done even in the largest shows. For example, as far as we know not once did the standard warship of the time, i.e. the quinquereme (with five banks of oars) make an appearance. Instead the fighting was done by fleets consisting of considerably smaller vessels, probably with no more than two or three rows. On land, too, what took place in the arena were in reality not battles but skirmishes. We know that most gladiators were simply organized in pairs, which means that there was room only for fighting technique but hardly for tactics of any kind. The nature of the arena and the flat "terrain" it provided worked in the same direction; nowhere was any shelter to be found, and gladiators who instead of fighting their opponents spent too much time running away from them were prevented from doing so by specially appointed guards armed with cattle prods and red-hot iron plates. On the other hand, watching hundreds of separate pairs fighting in sequence must have taxed the patience even of the most enthusiastic Romans. That is another reason for thinking that many gladiators were organized in groups.

Perhaps surprisingly, the equipment in use was not closely modeled on that of contemporary soldiers. Apparently no gladiator ever entered the arena dressed as a Roman soldier would be; possibly this had something to do with the need to keep the two types separate in the public mind.[28] In time, the gap between games and reality grew.[29] The earliest, and for a long time the most

---

[27] Tacitus, *Annales*, 12.56.
[28] T. G. Cornell, "On War and Games in the Ancient World," in Cornell and Allen, *War and Games*, p. 51.
[29] See on this subject G. Ville, "La guerre et le *munus*," in J. P. Brisson, ed., *Problèmes de la guerre à Rome*, Paris: Mouton, 1969, pp. 185–95.

common, type of gladiator was the Samnite. According to Livy,[30] his origins went back to the time when the first shows were held in Campania during the fourth century BC. Samnites carried a rectangular, curved, and elongated shield similar to that of legionaries. Like legionaries they only wore greaves that reached up to the shins; unlike them, they did not have body armor. Offensive arms were broadly similar to the ones legionaries carried, consisting of a sword – as time went on, its length tended to increase – and/or a javelin or spear. Though we do have images of them, the last two are often a little hard to tell apart. After all, a spear is not much more than a longer, heavier javelin, and vice versa. The two were often confused with one another, and not just in antiquity either. Suppose that what we see on one first-century AD grave monument are indeed *pila*, which in skilled hands were very effective weapons with a range of perhaps 80–100 feet.[31] In that case serious safety problems would have ensued: either a javelin might have inadvertently struck the spectators, or some gladiator, despairing of life, might have deliberately set out to take one or two of them with him to the nether world.

Another well-known type was the *Thrax* or Thracian – presumably Spartacus, who originated in that country, was one of them. Then there were the *secutores*, the *murmillones*, the *retiarii*, the *hoplomachi*, the *provocatores*, the *equites*, the *crupellarii*, the *praegenarii*, the *laquerarii*, and the *sagittarii*. The list ends with the *essedarii*.[32] As countless monuments show, Roman military equipment was never completely uniform – no more so than that of modern armed forces, one could add. Not only did that of the legionaries vary considerably, but as time passed the army took on a growing number of auxiliary units. The troops who made up those units originated from different nations and carried a wide array of different weapons. Furthermore, these things did not remain constant. Over time some arms were added, others put aside.

Even taking all this into consideration, though, one cannot help but be struck by the strange nature of some of the above-mentioned types. For example, *Thraeces* were armed with a small curved sword (*sica*) and carried a small shield that might be either round or square. Apparently to compensate for this lack of protection, they wore long leg pieces that covered both thighs and shins. *Secutores*, "pursuit men," carried a sword and a long shield, and wore greaves that only covered the shins. Both were evidently light troops. The *murmillones*, or "fish men," were akin to the *secutores* but were distinguished by having the top of their helmets decorated with a fish. This in turn was because they were most frequently matched with the *retiarii*. The latter were a highly specialized kind of fighter who wore no armor – not even a helmet – apart from a plate that covered

[30] Livy, *History of Rome*, 9.40.
[31] See the illustration in F. Meijer, *The Gladiators: History's Most Deadly Sport*, New York: St. Martin's, 2007, p. 27.
[32] Junkelmann, "Familia Gladiatoria," pp. 45–64.

their left shoulder and upper arm and wielded, as their offensive weapons, a net and a trident. *Hoplomachi*, literally "arms-bearing fighters" were similar to *Thraeces* but wore a distinctive "Boeotic" helmet with a visor that only left narrow slits for the eyes. They also carried a spear (*hasta*) as well as a sword.

Provocatores, or "challengers," carried long rectangular shields, wore breast-plates and leg-plates (on the left leg only) and used short swords for stabbing. Apparently they were employed mainly for fighting each other; some modern authorities consider that the men were beginners who, having been tested in this way, would later be assigned to one of the remaining categories on the basis of their performance. The *equites* were what their name implies, i.e. horsemen. Provided with curious helmets with wings that made them look like latter-day Vikings, they too fought each other. References to *sagittarii* or "bowmen" are rare. In case they did participate, their use must have required considerable security precautions. Finally, the term *essedarius* is derived from *essedum*, a two-wheeled war chariot. The conquering Romans encountered it first in Gaul and subsequently in Britain where, famously, it was used by Queen Boadicea. Charioteers too may have fought mainly each other. Yet considered as a real-life weapon system chariots were hopelessly antiquated: they were much more at home in the first half of the first millennium BC than in the second. Just how they were used in the limited space of the arena is a little hard to imagine. At least one author has argued that the name is misleading and that the *essedarii* must have been some other kind of fighters about whom, however, we know nothing.[33]

Obviously some types of gladiators originated with peoples whom the Romans had defeated and who, taken prisoner, were made to fight in the arena. However, there were also some even stranger, if apparently less common, kinds. One was the *dimachaerus* ("man with two swords"); another, the *veles* ("fast one"), who may have used a spear; another still, the *laquearius*. He came into the arena armed with a lasso and was often matched with a *retiarius*. Of the *retiarii* we know, and of the *laquearii* we may suspect, that they stood at the very bottom of the social ladder. Probably this was because their light equipment forced them to be on the run much of the time, looking for an opportunity to stop, turn around, and kill their imprudent adversaries. Perhaps strangest of all were the *crupelarii*, a Gallo-Roman type who carried such heavy armor that, once they had lost their footing, they could not get up, and the *praegenarii*, who seem to have been unarmed. Both are rarely mentioned and both may have been intended more for comic relief rather than serious fighting.

Most gladiators, having been assigned to one class or another, remained in it. Men able to master more than one fighting technique were rare. Judging by some pictures and statuettes, the various types were not always kept strictly separate. Hybrid types, designed to increase interest or simply made necessary

---

[33] M. Junkelmann, *Gladiatoren: Das Spiel mit dem Tod*, Mainz: Zabern, 2008, p. 99.

by a momentary shortage of this or that kind of fighter and/or this or that kind of equipment, also made their appearance. As far as may be seen, the various types were remarkably uniform throughout the Empire: in all probability, provincial towns looked to Rome for inspiration.

A graffito found at Pompeii, representing the score of a four-day show held in that city during the early Imperial period, explains how some of the types were paired with each other. First a *Thrax* fought a *murmillo*. Then it was the turn of a *hoplomachus* to do the same. Then a *dimachaerus* engaged a *hoplomachus*. Then again two *Thraeces* sequentially fought two *murmillones* (*murmillones* seem to have been very popular at Pompeii). Then a *hoplomachus* fought a *Thrax*. Then another *Thrax* fought a *murmillo*. Then two *essedarii* fought one another. The proceedings ended with two more fights between *Thraeces* and *murmillones*.[34] None of the above-listed types seem to have had much in common with the heavy infantry that formed the backbone of the legions from Republican times until at least the early years of the fourth century AD. By that time even the one that came closest, i.e. the Samnite, had long disappeared. Nor were gladiators supposed to carry the kind of digging and building equipment that, during the first century BC, caused legionaries to be nicknamed "Marius' Mules": modern trials have confirmed how heavy and cumbersome it was.[35]

Even if we assume that the larger gladiatorial shows did not consist simply of a free-for-all, and even if some of them involved some kind of command arrangement, clearly there was little the fights had to offer commanders. The goal was to provide amusement by demonstrating prowess, not to achieve military objectives at the least possible cost to oneself. As a result many experienced military men probably regarded most gladiators' weapons, along with the fighting techniques that went with them, as sheer foolishness. One who certainly took this point of view was Pompey: Cicero in one of his letters says that he saw the shows as a waste of time and money. Caesar himself displeased the crowd by using the time he spent at them to do his paperwork. Tiberius, who as a soldier was almost equally experienced but whom the sources present as a miser and a morose character, hardly bothered to hide his aversion to the shows. Vespasian too did not much enjoy them.[36] Toward the end of the first century AD Vespasian's son Domitian annoyed the crowed by failing to watch the proceedings and conversing with what looked like a deformed dwarf instead. Marcus Aurelius, and after him Julianus the Apostate, were equally contemptuous.[37]

---

[34] *Corpus Inscriptionum Latinarum* (CIL), Berlin: de Gruyter, 1995, 4.2508.
[35] See M. Junkelmann, *Die Legionen des Augustus: Der roemische Soldat im archaeologischen Experiment*, Mainz: Zabern, 2003, especially p. 106.
[36] Suetonius, *Tiberius*, in *Lives of the Emperors*, 34.
[37] *Ibid.*, 45; Cassius Dio, *History of Rome*, 66.15; Suetonius, *Domitian*, in *Lives of the Caesars*, 4. Marcus Aurelius, *Meditationes*, LCL, 1915, 1.6, 6.46, and 10.8; Zosimus, *The History of Count Zosismus*, London: General Books, 2010 [1814], 11.3.11.4–5.

Descending from the level of the commander to that of the ordinary soldier, things were different. For all that many of the weapons that gladiators wielded were strange and outlandish, the training they received was of a very high order and the discipline to which they were subjected extremely strict. Strength, technique, agility, and endurance all counted; many gladiators had enough in common with soldiers for some of their skills to be transferrable to the latter. As far as we know, the first time instructors (*doctores*) from the schools were asked to lend a hand in training troops was in 105 BC; probably it is no accident that this was very close to the time when the old Republican system of part-time citizen soldiers was finally abolished and a professional army established. The reform is attributed to one Publius Rutilius Rufus (158–c. 78 BC). A great-uncle of Julius Caesar, he had gained considerable military experience while campaigning in Numidia. Serving as consul, it was he, along with his colleague Gnaeus Malius Maximus, who completed the process that turned privately organized combats into public, even official, occasions. Two centuries later Frontinus, or rather the anonymous author who wrote the fourth book of the *Strategemata* in his name, tells us that Marius, who by any standard was one of the greatest Roman commanders, was so impressed by the troops Rutilius had trained that he preferred them to his own.[38] Clearly soldiers had to be physically fit, and clearly they had to know how to use their weapons to best effect. In these fields gladiators, as professional fighters who spent much of their lives in training, were at an advantage.

Vegetius, a late fourth-century author who penned what was destined to become the best-known treatise on Roman military organization of all time, provides a fairly extensive description of the *armatura*, or weapon-training course.[39] First, each gladiator or soldier was assigned a stake, or *palus*, which, firmly planted in the ground, projected six feet above it. Wielding a wickerwork shield and a wooden sword, both of them twice as heavy as those used in combat, trainees "fought" the stake under the watchful eye of the instructors. Now they advanced, now they retreated. Now pretending to attack this body part or that, now defending themselves, they would learn how to inflict injuries without exposing their own bodies. Above all, it was considered vital that they should get used to stabbing rather than slashing, since doing so both inflicted more serious injuries and, since the swordsman did not have to raise his arm away from his body and expose himself, was much safer. The importance of training at the stake is brought out by the fact that the group of best combatants were called *primi pali*, the next one *secundi pali*, and so on. In the words of Valerius Maximus,[40] training joined courage with craft, and craft with courage.

---

[38] Frontinus, *Stratagems*, LCL, 1925, 4.2.2.
[39] Vegetius, *Epitome of Military Science*, Liverpool University Press, 1997, *passim*.
[40] Valerius Maximus, *Memorable Doings and Sayings*, 2.3.2.

Craft was made bolder and more vehement by courage, and courage was rendered more circumspect by craft.

For displaying courage, both soldiers and gladiators could be decorated with the *torques* (necklace) and the *hasta* (honorary lance). In spite of their very different social status – the army would not take slaves – they were interchangeable to some extent. A public person who owned too many gladiators could become dangerous. Realizing this fact, in 63 BC the Senate became sufficiently alarmed to take some precautions against Catilina using them for the purpose of the conspiracy on which he had embarked. At the outbreak of the civil war between the *duumvirs* in 49 BC Caesar was suspected of planning to enlist gladiators from Capua. However, he was preempted by Pompey who, though he did not himself use them, broke up the schools in which they were concentrated and dispersed them. If Decimus Brutus, one of the conspirators against Caesar, was able to play an important role after the latter's murder then this was primarily because he was in charge of the gladiator teams that were housed in Rome. Caesar's would-be successor Antony enlisted some gladiators. They fought against Augustus and remained loyal to the bitter end.[41] As our sources disapprovingly note, both Caligula and Nero sometimes recruited gladiators as bodyguards.[42] So, three hundred years later, did Pope Damasius (366–84). At least one woman, the wife of an Asiarch, did the same; unfortunately the inscription to which we owe this information, which was found on Cos, cannot be dated.[43]

Though both Otho and Vitellius recruited gladiators into their armies when fighting over the Imperial throne in AD 69, they do not seem to have served them very well. Vitellius' gladiators later betrayed him and went over to his rival Vespasian, but their performance still remained below par. Faced with the *n*th German invasion, Marcus Aurelius at one point enlisted gladiators (and bandits) into his army. The outcome was to raise prices, much to the chagrin of the population of Rome which was loath to lose its beloved circuses and suspected that the emperor wanted to turn all of them into philosophers! Aurelius' successor-once-removed, Didius Julianus, followed his example. Conversely, in 193 after Septimius Severus replaced the personnel of the Praetorian Guard with his legionaries, some of the former took up the gladiator's profession. Around AD 360 Ammianus Marcelinus, an officer of no mean experience, mentions soldiers who fought in the manner of *murmillones*. Possibly they did so by crouching behind their shields and waiting for the enemy to make a wrong move.

However, important differences between soldiers and gladiators also existed. Whether or not *pila* were permitted in the arena, few gladiators appear to have trained with the bow or with the sling, let alone used those long-range weapons

---

[41] Cassius Dio, *History of Rome*, 51.7.   [42] Tacitus, *Annales*, 13.25.
[43] *Inscriptiones Graecae*, I. Delamarre, ed., Berlin: Reimer, 1908, pt. 12, sect. 8, no. 547.

in a fight against their own kind. In fact the rare references to *sagittarii* that we do have are not at all clear as to what these men actually did. Lack of real-life experience in fighting real-life soldiers may have been one reason why the gladiators recruited by Otho and Vitellius gave such a disappointing perform-ance.[44] Given that they were not free men and were only expected to fight, not to campaign, it is hard to imagine gladiators participating in road marches that, again according to Vegetius, were standard in the legions. Instead, living in the schools, they were carefully locked up at night. For the same reason, and also because their lives were forfeit, it is hard to think of them as taking the swimming lessons Vegetius also mentions. On the other hand, there could be no question of training soldiers with some of the more exotic weapons gladi-ators were made to wield.

To sum up, there were very strict limits to what the shows, bloody though they were, could do to represent real-life war. The artificial conditions under which they took place prevented anything of the sort, as indeed they were designed to do. Tactically the similarities were somewhat greater, but still rather limited. This was particularly true when it came to the choice of weapons which in turn went far in dictating fighting techniques. Many of the weapons used by the gladiators would have been useless in war. A few were so outlandish that they were probably intended to provide little but comic relief. Yet strategy and tactics are not the most important factors of all; rather, they are merely by-products of the spirit that often causes people to fight each other in the first place. Just how did the shows reflect that spirit, which more than anything else lies at the very heart of both war and games?

Games, crowds, and emperors

First things first: regardless of who invented the gladiatorial shows, and regard-less also of their original purpose, there can be no doubt concerning their popularity. The Romans did not have mass media and could not broadcast the fights on TV. Nevertheless, that popularity has probably never been equaled before or since. One person who came to feel the effect of this was the play-wright Terence. In 160 BC the premiere of his comedy *Hecyna* had to be interrupted because the crowd, deserting the theater en masse, ran to the nearby Forum Romanum where gladiatorial fights were being held.

The Forum in question was the largest open space in the entire city. A century and a half later, the architect and town-planner Vitruvius went so far as to claim that the reason why Roman squares, unlike Greek ones, were given an oblong shape and did not carry as much decoration was because "it is a custom, handed down from our ancestors, that gladiatorial shows should be given in the forum." Accordingly he recommended that the squares be provided with certain kinds

---

[44] See M. Grant, *Gladiators*, London: Weidenfeld and Nicolson, 1967, p. 89.

of colonnades rather than others.[45] Each time a show was planned it was advertised by every available means. A special class of scribes was employed to spell out the details of the forthcoming contests on tablets that were strategically placed along the roads leading to cities. One surviving tablet of this kind reads as follows:[46]

> Twenty pairs of gladiators, owned by D. Lucretius Sater Valens, lifelong priest to Nero Caesar Augustus, and ten pairs of gladiators, owned by his son D. Lucretius Valens, will engage in combat in Pompeii on the 8th, 9th, 11th, and 12th of April. There will also be wild animal hunts, as permitted by law. The seats will be shaded with awnings.

At the time Pompeii was destroyed in AD 79 many of its buildings carried similar advertisements, some of them referring to events that had taken place years previously. The measures taken in other cities were no different. Programs (*libelli munerarii*) on sale at the entrance to the amphitheater con-tained the names of the gladiators scheduled to participate.[47] A standardized system was used to note the past achievements of individual combatants; V meant *victor*, M *missus* (i.e. that the man, though defeated, had fought sufficiently well to leave the arena alive). Each sign was accompanied by a number. However, to increase tension they did not say who was to fight whom.

As with modern "professional" wrestlers, the wish to generate excitement accounts for the strange outfits many gladiators wore and the weapons they used. The outcome was a considerable variety of different fighting techniques. Some emphasized strength, others agility. Mastering such exotic instruments as the net and the lasso must have been no mean feat. The number of possible combinations was in the dozens. Probably about eight out of every ten pairs of fighters involved a different type on each side. Yet things were not simple; care had to be taken to match the combatants in such a way as to give each individual or group a fair chance, or else the fights would have come to an end almost before they began and the crowd would have lost interest.

Similar considerations may explain why, in marked contrast to what went on in "real" war, most gladiators, though they normally wore helmets and had their limbs protected in some way, fought bare-breasted. This even applied to the *hoplomachi*, notwithstanding that the original meaning of *hoplon* is "suit of armor." The intention must have been to shelter vulnerable body parts, such as heads, arms, and legs, where even a slight injury might seriously handicap a fighter and either put an end to the show or make it uninteresting. It has further been argued that exposed torsos both made for better athletic performance and enabled spectators to get a much better view of the wounds being inflicted and

---

[45] Vitruvius, *On Architecture*, LCL, 1931, 5.1.1–2.
[46] CIL, l.4, no. 3884. The translation is by F. Meijer.
[47] *Scriptores Historiae Augustae*, LCL, 1921, *Claudius Gothicus*, 5.5.

the blood flowing out of them. Last but not least, bare chests increased the sex appeal of the shows, already reeking of testosterone, further still. Where the Romans drew the line was in that they made even the most lightly armed gladiators wear leather belts with loincloths suspended from them. Gaily decorated, the cloths did as much to draw attention to the genitals as to cover them. However, gladiators did not enter the arena naked as Greek athletes were expected to do.

Awaited with impatience, the combats and the *ludi* of which they formed part imposed their rhythm on everyday life. On the appointed day both men and women flocked to the amphitheater. The fights took up much less time than the other parts of the program, such as executions, animal hunts, and various forms of entertainment and athletic competition. Nevertheless they easily over-shadowed all the rest and were accordingly reserved for the end of the day. The gladiators were the subject of everyday conversation and of countless graffiti. An entire industry specialized in producing images of them. There was money to be made even by having them painted and the pictures exhibited in public; indeed Pliny the Elder claims that, "for many generations" this art commanded the greatest interest of all.[48] People dreamt of being gladiators, and specialists were called upon to explain the meaning of the dreams. Even children played at being gladiators.[49] Some technical terms originating in the arena left it and entered everyday language, particularly that of rhetoricians and lawyers.

As in modern sports events, people placed bets on the outcome of the fights. Here and there the gladiators' enthused supporters fought regular battles against each other, even resorting to weapons.[50] So many spectators came to watch one of Caesar's shows that some, including two senators, were crushed to death by the crowd.[51] As the first-century AD philosopher Seneca tells us, people abandoned their normal occupations and flocked to the amphitheater. The outcome, an unnatural quiet interrupted only by an occasional roar, provided him with an opportune time for some of his meditations.

From the city of Rome the combats spread all over the Empire, albeit that the scale on which they were held was normally much smaller than in the capital. The most affected, or perhaps one should say infected, were the western provinces, i.e. Gaul and Spain. Yet Africa and the east did not remain immune: long before Rome took over the Middle East, Antiochus IV Epiphanes (reigned 175–164 BC) introduced the shows into Syria. Probably this was because he had spent part of his youth as a hostage in Rome, and significantly his objective was to "rouse in young men a joy in arms." After all, his father had been badly defeated by the Romans and he himself might very well have to face them again. Another explanation is that he wanted to upstage the above-mentioned

---

[48] Pliny, *Natural History*, 35.2.   [49] Epictetus, *Discourses*, LCL, 1925, 3.15.6.
[50] Tacitus, *Annales*, 14.17.   [51] Suetonius, *Julius Caesar*, in *Lives of the Emperors*, 39.

Aemilius Paulus.[52] If the sources may be believed, at first his subjects were terrified, but later they turned to the shows as enthusiastically as anyone else. Inscriptions from the island of Delos show that gladiatorial games were being held there during approximately the same period; countless later ones, found all over Greece and the Middle East, prove how popular they became.[53]

Josephus Flavius, the late first-century AD Jewish historian, says that Herod's grandson, the puppet monarch Agrippa, once had 700 pairs of gladiators fight at Berytus, the modern Beirut.[54] According to Philostratus, a second-century AD writer, a hundred years before his time the Athenians used to "run in crowds to the theater." Their enthusiasm, he adds, was even greater than that of the Corinthians in his own day.[55] Archaeological finds tell an even clearer tale. Besides over two hundred amphitheaters, not all of which have been excavated,[56] they include extensive mosaics showing the fights as well as statuettes of gladiators and objects decorated with images of them. Thousands of such objects, including lamps, vases of every size and description, drinking cups and weapons have been found in practically every province of the Empire. Clearly the shows acted as instruments of Romanization just as roads, aqueducts, baths, statues of the emperor and coins bearing his portrait also did.

To speak with a well-known modern political scientist, they were an important element in Rome's "soft power" – part and parcel of everything it stood for.[57] Conversely, one reason why cities all over the Empire vied with each other in staging the combats was to prove that they, too, were an integral part of it. This was especially true during the first century AD when an Imperial visit to this city or that might be promptly followed by the erection of an amphitheater there, but as late as 217 major improvements were made to the theater at Corinth in anticipation of a visit by Caracalla who, however, was killed before he got there.[58] The process of cultural assimilation may not have been entirely one-sided. Some historians believe that what took place was a gradual fusion of Roman and Greek values which led to changes in both.[59] Several legionary bases

[52] Livy, *History of Rome*, 41.20; Polybius, *The Histories*, LCL, 1923, 30.25.1.
[53] See, for this subject, G. Ville's magisterial *La gladiature en Occident des origines à la mort de Domitien*, Rome: École française, 1981.
[54] Josephus, *Jewish Antiquities*, LCL, 1930, 15.8.1.
[55] Philostratus, *Life of Apollonius*, LCL, 1912, 4.22.
[56] A list of all known amphitheaters in the West is found in Futrell, *Blood in the Arena*, pp. 217–21.
[57] J. S. Nye, *Soft Power: The Means to Success in World Politics*, New York: Public Affairs, 2005.
[58] B. Levick, *The Ancient Historian and his Materials*, Farnborough: Gregg, 1975, pp. 155–65; H. S. Robinson, "Chiron at Corinth," *American Journal of Archaeology*, 73, 1969, pp. 193–7.
[59] M. J. Carter, "Gladiators and Monomachia: Greek Attitudes to Roman 'Cultural Performance,'" *International Journal of the History of Sport*, 26, 2, February 2009, pp. 298–322.

in countries far from Italy had amphitheaters, and some army units may even have owned their own troupes of gladiators; Julius Capitolinus, the biographer of Emperor Antoninus Pius, is quoted as saying that soldiers were obliged to watch gladiatorial combat to learn how to fight and die fearlessly.[60]

The shows' immense popularity explains both the growing scale on which they were held and the readiness of people to pay for them. Things reached the point where, during the late Republic, men sometimes left money in their wills for games to be held in their names much in the way that medieval people often set aside money so that monks might continue to say masses for their souls. Over time the identity of the *editores* underwent a gradual change. Originally anyone was permitted to hold the games, whether for pure entertainment or as an act of piety towards some deceased family member is immaterial. Later they turned into an instrument in the hands of the rich, the powerful, and the ambitious who used them in order to gain popular support, win elections, and build their careers. Cicero on one occasion warned a young friend that character and diligence were more useful in creating admiration than giving shows. However, the man in question, Gaius Scribonius Curio, did not heed the advice; instead he went on to ruin himself by spending money on them, and had to be rescued by Caesar who appreciated his rhetorical skills.[61] By that time holding the shows had become part of the duty of certain magistrates, which placed the entire bloody business on an official basis. Later the same task was taken over by the emperors. Most of them played ball, but not all: probably one reason why, at the end of his life and after his death, Tiberius was so hated was because he had sought to limit the number and cost of the shows.

Whether for personal or political reasons, most emperors did not follow Tiberius' example. Augustus took good care to demonstrate that he, unlike his great-uncle Julius Caesar, was keenly interested in the shows. He and his successors turned them into one of the normal benefits granted to the citizens of Rome, akin to the distribution of free grain; it was the satirist Juvenal who coined the phrase "bread and circuses" as the means par excellence of keeping the population in its place.[62] The cost, needless to say, rose into the stratosphere. As time passed, the tendency to turn the shows into an Imperial monopoly became more pronounced. During the civil wars of AD 68–9 all four emperors tried to legitimize their rule by holding games. In Rome itself they could only be held by the emperor or in his name, with his explicit permission. Domitian went a step further, prohibiting private persons from owning gladiators; perhaps this reflected his fear of conspiracies (he ended by being killed in one). Elsewhere the shows were often organized by the local colleges of Imperial priests of whom the above-mentioned Lucretius Sater was

---

[60] *Scriptores Historiae Augustae, Antoninus Pius,* 21.8.7.
[61] Cicero, *Epistolae ad Familiares,* New York: Oxford University Press, 1982, 2.3.
[62] Juvenal, *Satires,* LCL, 1924,10.81.

one. As with other public ceremonies, there can have been few in which the emperor was not honored in one way or another.

Conversely, when Marcus Aurelius wanted to punish the city of Antioch for its support for a rebellion in AD 176 he forbade it from holding gladiatorial shows as well as public assemblies of any kind. The ban was only lifted after several years. The role the shows played in political and social life is brought out by the fact that Suetonius in his biographies of the emperors regularly includes a chapter on the way each of them dealt with the issue. Unless there was some special reason to think otherwise, he praises the generous and condemns the miserly. The *Historia Augusta*, which is our main source for the emperors of the third century AD, does the same. To cap it all, not only Caligula but some of his successors – Titus, Hadrian, Lucius Verus (dual emperor along with Marcus Aurelius) and Didius Julianus (who reigned for several months in 193) all fought, or pretended to fight, as gladiators. The most notorious emperor in this respect was Marcus Aurelius' son and successor Commodus (reigned from 180 until 192). Dressed as a *secutor*, carrying a shield on his right and a wooden sword in his left (as in modern tennis, a left-handed gladiator enjoyed a certain advantage), he regularly entered the arena and fought opponents likewise armed with wands.

Cassius Dio, who claims to have been present during a number of Commodus' fights and to whom we owe this account, says that they were simply "a little game."[63] With good reason, since obviously very great precautions had to be taken to make sure that neither he nor any of the other emperors should be hurt. Not only is there no record of this happening, but it is hard to imagine how an emperor could have allowed himself to lose and his opponent to win: that, incidentally, is a problem with which many other kinds of wargames besides the Roman gladiatorial ones also had to cope. Both ancient and modern historians have wondered what may have motivated these men. Some, notably Caligula and Commodus, were probably more than a little mad. That is how many sources, especially literary ones written by high-class historians such as Cassius Dio himself, present them. If so, then the engagements in which they took part were simply a continuation of other strange acts they committed inside and outside the arena. Caligula for one was determined to prove that he was shameless and up for anything.[64] Perhaps it is not surprising that the man who used to take away other men's wives, sleep with them, and then describe their performance in public entered the arena with a real sword and ran through opponents armed only with a wooden one. Commodus went further still: we are told that, had they not feared for their lives, his "exploits" would have made the spectators

[63] Cassius Dio, *History of Rome*, 73.19.5.
[64] Suetonius, *Caligula*, in *Lives of the Emperors*, 29.1; A. A. Barrett, *Caligula: The Corruption of Power*, London: Batsford, 1989, p. 43.

laugh out aloud.[65] On one occasion he ordered all people who, owing to accident or illness, had lost their left foot to enter the arena, gave them sponges to fight with, and went on to kill them with a heavy club.

It is, however, possible that, in some of these cases, there was method behind the madness. This was because the shows, like so many others at all times and places, did not only seek to duplicate some aspects of war but represented grand theater as well.[66] To do so, even the seating arrangements at the amphitheater were made to reflect the Roman world in miniature. During Republican times, people had been allowed to select their own seats and mix freely; not so under the Empire when various emperors issued decrees to separate them by class. The higher the class to which a person belonged the better the seat he was entitled to occupy. He also gained other privileges such as the right to use cushions or wear a sunhat.[67] The emperor, of course, occupied the best seat of all. It not only offered an excellent view of the arena but was located in such a way that everybody could see the occupant. Thus the shows gave emperors a unique opportunity to demonstrate both their unity with the people and their power over them. That power was accentuated by the fact that, in deciding whether defeated gladiators should be allowed to live, they might or might not adhere to the spectators' demands. Furthermore, precisely because the fights in which emperors participated were sham, they provided another proof of their ability to kill anyone they pleased at any time they pleased in any way they pleased. So did the displays of summary "justice" when people were simply ordered into the arena without further ado.

To show that he had indeed become a Spaniard, Emperor Charles V once entered a ring and killed a bull in a *corrida*. Much later, a drawing of the episode was made by Francisco Goya. Some Roman emperors may have participated in gladiatorial shows because, in a way, they stood for everything Roman. Here is what Cicero, as good an observer of social and political life as one might wish for, had to say about them: "this countless throng of men, this unanimous expression of the whole Roman people."[68] With the exception of the various forms of single combat, most wargames at most times and places did their best to limit the number of casualties. In fact, the limited number of casualties was what mainly differentiated them from "real" war and allowed them to be held in the first place. Not so in Rome, where the gladiatorial games, and of course the executions and the animal hunts as well, owed their appeal precisely to the unapologetic way in which copious amounts of blood were shed. To make sure

---

[65] Cassius Dio, *History of Rome*, 73.21.

[66] See, for the political uses of the games, O. Hekster, *Commodus: An Emperor at the Crossroads*, Amsterdam: Brill, 2002, pp. 128–9, 138–50.

[67] J. C. Edmondson, "Dynamic Arenas: Gladiatorial Presentations in the City of Rome and the Construction of Roman Society during the Early Empire," in W. J. Slater, ed., *Roman Theater and Society*, Ann Arbor: University of Michigan Press, 1996, p. 111.

[68] Cicero, *Pro Sestio*, LCL, 1958, 125.

it *would* be shed, each fight was preceded by a special ceremony in which the quality of the weapons was carefully and publicly examined.

Two factors made the bloodshed possible. First, unlike the tribal contests we have described and also unlike early medieval tournaments, gladiatorial combat took place inside temporary or permanent structures specially designed for the purpose. Every precaution was taken to protect the spectators and prevent escalation; this was just what enabled the fights to proceed without any restrictions whatsoever. Second and even more importantly, the vast majority of gladiators were men who had been compelled to fight against their will, if necessary by the most brutal available means. Livy's description of one of the rare exceptions to this rule, which supposedly took place fairly early in the history of the games, merely serves to bring out this aspect of the matter even more:[69]

> [After the end of the Second Punic War] Scipio [Africanus] returned to [New] Carthage [in Spain] to pay his vows to the gods and to conduct the gladiatorial show which he had prepared in honor of his deceased father and uncle. The exhibition of gladiators was not made up from the class of men which *lanistae* are in the habit of pitting against each other, that is slaves sold on the platform and free men who are ready to sell their lives. In every case the service of the men who fought was voluntary and without compensation. For some were sent by their chieftains to display an example of the courage inbred in their tribe; some declared on their own motion that they would fight to please the general; in other cases rivalry and the desire to compete led them to challenge or, if challenged, not to refuse.

Apparently Livy, as he went over his sources, was initially incredulous and could hardly make himself believe that, once upon a time, such things had indeed been possible.

This unique episode apart, and disregarding the sprinkling of volunteers of whom Livy also speaks and on whom more later, those who fought in the arena fell into four classes. First and for a long time most numerous were prisoners of war. The Romans – and, to be fair, not only the Romans – convinced themselves that anybody who refused to accept their rule and put up armed resistance instead was a criminal and deserved to be punished if the opportunity offered. One only has to look at the Germans, their hands tied behind their backs and about to be beheaded, who figure on Marcus Aurelius' victory column to see what this could and often did mean. In cases when prisoners *were* taken, their captors often did not know what to do with them. That was why, for centuries on end, slave dealers armed with chains and similar instruments of coercion used to follow every army into the field. They bought the prisoners and later sold those who seemed fit for the purpose to the *lanistae*. But for them, the huge

---

[69] Livy, *History of Rome*, 28.1.10.

shows of the period from 100 BC to AD 200 would almost certainly have been impossible.

Second came men convicted of one of four cardinal crimes, i.e. murder, treason, robbery, or arson. The third category was formed by slaves whom their owners had condemned by way of a punishment. Presumably all these had to undergo some kind of preliminary physical examination, training, and preparation. Not so those who comprised the fourth group. They were sent into the arena at a moment's notice on the whim of some ruler (known cases are limited to emperors, but one cannot rule out the possibility that lesser potentates in provincial cities imitated them) without any regard as to whether they were or were not fit for it. Caligula, Claudius, and Commodus were particularly notorious in this respect. During their reigns anybody who offended them inside or outside the theater, or simply attracted their unfavorable attention for some other reason, might find himself (rarely if ever, herself) sharing the gladiators' fate.[70]

However it was done, clearly those who fought in the arena were the lowest of the low, socially speaking. Having been captured, convicted, sold by their owners, or simply singled out by some ruler, they had literally lost the right to live. Their blood, unlike that of other people, was a free commodity, so to speak. To emphasize this fact even more they were made to swear a solemn oath (*sacramentum*), promising to endure even the worst kinds of humiliation and to suffer death by fire, in chains, or by the sword. Of this oath Seneca says that it was the most honorable of all.[71] A festive meal held on the eve of the fight, used by some to engage in all kind of excess and by others in quiet preparation for the morrow, put the last seal on their situation. Briefly, gladiators were men who had taken their leave of this world. As they presented themselves to the crowd and made ready to fight, legally if not physically they were already dead.

Drenched with blood as they regularly were, doubtless the Colosseum and other amphitheaters throughout the Empire were hell for many, possibly most, of those who fought in them. Still they did not bear over their gates the inscription, "Give up all hope, you who enter here." To be sure, some emperor might take a special dislike to this or that gladiator and inflict arbitrary punishment on him regardless of his performance. Provided prowess was allowed to speak for itself, though, if anything their motto might have been "Bravery in battle makes free," even if one was a prisoner of war; and even if one was a condemned criminal of the worst kind. Compared with the alternatives – suffering execution in one of many exotic ways or being thrown to the beasts – being selected as a gladiator almost amounted to a reprieve.

---

[70] Suetonius, *Caligula*, in *Lives of the Emperors*, 14; for Commodus' deeds and misdeeds in the arena see Hekster, *Commodus*, pp. 137–62.

[71] Seneca, *Epistles*, LCL, 1925, 37.1–2.

Having reached the lowest possible point in life a gladiator could redeem himself by offering proof of courage and fighting ability. Cicero, who as we shall see was by no means uncritical of the games, has the following to say about this aspect of the matter:[72]

> Down-and-outs or barbarians the [gladiators] may be, but just like well-brought up men, they'd rather take a hit than dodge away in cowardly fashion. Look at how often their main concern seems to be to court the approval of either their master or the people. Even when covered in wounds, they will send someone to their master to ask what he wants of them. If he feels they have done enough, they are prepared to die. What gladiator of even the most mediocre caliber has ever groaned or so much as winced? Which of them has ever disgraced himself by failing to move, let alone by giving in? Which of them has ever pulled his head in after submitting and hearing the coup de grâce announced?

Dionysius Halicarnassus, the Greek historian who did his work a generation or so after Cicero, likewise expressed his admiration for the gladiators' valor. It stood, he says, in strange contrast to the terrible things they saw and often underwent. The philosopher and lawyer Pliny the Younger praised a friend for holding a *munus* in honor of his deceased wife; unlike many other kinds of shows, he added, gladiatorial shows did not enfeeble the mind. Indeed they were capable of inspiring even those despicable forms of lowlife, criminals and slaves, to perform courageous deeds.[73] As one modern historian wrote, "by engaging in courageous duels ... gladiators were meant to illustrate the virtues that had made Rome great."[74] In this respect they were not unlike the soldiers who were remembered for having bravely served their country in war.

Seneca, Nero's tutor, who ended up being forced by his former student to commit suicide, went so far as to claim that "the gladiator judges it ignominious to be set against an inferior, as he knows it is without glory to defeat one who can be defeated without danger." He also said that wise men should model themselves on gladiators, accepting the fact that the possibility of death was always there and behaving accordingly.[75] As if to bring out the fact that, at bottom and when everything else had been stripped away, the fights were understood as tests of courage above all, at the beginning of each one the gladiators were made to utter the famous cry, "Hail Caesar, those who are about to die salute you" (*Ave Imperator, morituri te salutant*).[76] However perverted things may have been in practice, the ideal that inspired the words shines through clearly enough. It is only

---

[72] Cicero, *Tusculan Disputations*, LCL, 1927, 2.17.41.   [73] Pliny, *Letters*, LCL, 1969, 6.34.
[74] Meijer, *Gladiators*, p. 19.
[75] Seneca, *On Providence*, in *Moral Essays*, LCL, 1929, 3.4; *On Tranquility, ibid.*, 11.1–6; *De Constantia sapientis, ibid.*, 16.2.
[76] Suetonius, *Claudius*, in *Lives of the Emperors*, 14. The question as to whether this cry was uttered every time or just on the one occasion it is mentioned in the sources has been the

those who, by looking death in the face, have been placed where neither punish-ment nor reward can reach them who are truly free; and whose greeting, there-fore, is worth having in the first place.

It was after many gladiators had engaged in combat and killed each other that Claudius, impressed by their exceptional courage, let the rest go.[77] Conversely, spectators were not slow to boo gladiators who failed to perform as expected or to condemn those who, having surrendered, took up their arms and perfid-iously resumed the fight.[78] Seneca's rough contemporary, the poet Juvenal, describes an occasion when an otherwise unknown aristocrat by the name of Gracchus volunteered to go down into the arena. Equipped as a *retiarius*, instead of fighting he kept running this way and that, failing to use his weapons to any effect. All the while he cast terrified glances at the tribunes, so that "even [his] opponent feels the shame of it more painfully than any wound."[79] It was precisely because the fights put on by Caligula and Commodus, who either themselves killed defenseless men or had handicapped ones fight, did not provide room for a show of courage that our sources condemned them.

How often did the spectators get their wish for a courageous fight, and to what extent was the "ideal," if the use of the word is permitted in so horrible a context, of courage realized? Obviously, considering the above-mentioned criticisms to which Caligula and Commodus were subjected, not always. However, the shows in question were exceptional. In fact it is only for that reason that they appear in the record; Cassius Dio all but apologizes for mentioning them, saying that they are beneath the dignity of history. One very partial answer to the question comes from a graffito from Pompey. Out of twenty men who entered the arena ten were proclaimed winners. Two died – whether they did so during combat itself or after being denied quarter remains unclear. Eight were granted *missio*, meaning that they were allowed to leave the arena alive after asking for quarter by raising a finger of the left hand. Now a display of courage was the reason par excellence why gladiators were sometimes granted quarter in the first place; even so, both the crowd and the presiding magistrate were capricious so that the outcome was by no means certain. It therefore appears that, in at least eight out of ten fights on this list, the spectators got what they had hoped for.

Indeed gladiators themselves, for all their degradation and the ruthless conditions under which they lived and fought, seem to have retained some pride and *esprit de corps*. In one story we are told of a group of gladiators who claimed they lacked for nothing and encouraged travelers whom they happened to meet on the road to follow their example and become gladiators themselves.

subject of some scholarly debate. Here I follow Grant, *Gladiators*, p. 64, and R. Auguet, *Cruelty and Civilization: The Roman Games*, London: Routledge, 1972, p. 43.

[77] Tacitus, *Annales*, 12.65.

[78] Petronius, *Satyricon*, LCL, 1975, ch. 45; Suetonius, *Caligula*, in *Lives of the Emperors*, p. 30.

[79] Juvenal, *Satires*, 8.208–10.

Some took on pseudonyms intended to emphasize their valor and intimidate opponents: either they identified themselves with mythological heroes or else they chose names such as *Pugnax* (the Pugnacious), *Ferox* (the Ferocious), *Velox* (the Fast), or *Tigris* (the Tiger). Some had their portraits painted. Some seem to have complained that they were not allowed to fight, whereas others set up funeral monuments for their fallen comrades.

Most of these monuments show the men fighting and/or triumphing in the arena, but a few carry peaceful, even idyllic, domestic scenes. Many express their owners' pride in their profession. In one or two cases a gladiator, or those who erected his monument for him, took care to note that his death was the result of generosity since the man who killed him was one whom he had previously spared.[80] Some cemeteries dating to Imperial times apparently had special plots set aside for the disposal of gladiators' bodies.[81] Late in the second century AD some of Commodus' gladiators even established a sort of professional association complete with its own patron gods. Unsurprisingly, the main ones were Mars, Diana, Hercules, Victoria, and Fortuna. The first four served as models of prowess whereas the last one directed the fortune to which gladiators entrusted their lives. However, the principal patroness of the shows was Nemesis, the "dark-faced" goddess of justice and retribution. Closely connected to Fortuna, she was a key link between the human world and the divine one. Many amphitheaters had shrines for her built into them; had it not been for the gladiators, indeed, Nemesis would have found few people who worshipped her and practiced her cult.[82]

In thirty-two fights that took place during the first century AD whose outcome is known, six out of sixty-four participants were killed.[83] If each fight ended with a winner and a loser, losers also numbered thirty-two. Statistically, therefore, losers could expect to obtain quarter and survive almost five out of six combats, a surprisingly high figure. If we count both victors and losers, then the chances of emerging alive out of any single encounter were just short of ten out of eleven. However, we have failed to take draws into account. Judging by the career of one gladiator whose epitaph provides us with the necessary information, about a third of the fights ended without a victor.[84] Using this fact – admittedly, we are talking about a sample of one – to recalculate the results, then the chances rise to about thirteen out of fourteen.

---

[80] G. L. Gregori, *Epigrafia anfiteatrale dell'occidente romano*, Rome: Quasar, 1989, p. 68.

[81] See Carter, "Gladiators and Monomachia," p. 307.

[82] See on this Futrell, *Blood in the Arena*, pp. 110–20; also M. B. Hornum, *Nemesis: The Roman State and the Games*, Leiden: Brill, 1993, pp. 55–6.

[83] Ville, *La gladiature en occident*, pp. 318–25; Junkelmann, "Familia Gladiatoria," pp. 142–3; see for this entire subject also T. Wiedemann, *Emperors and Gladiators*, London: Routledge, 1992, pp. 120–2.

[84] *Inscriptiones Latinae Selectae*, H. Dessau, ed., Nabu, 2010 [1892–], no. 5115.

Certainly the gladiators' life was harsh. For a great many, fighting in the
amphitheater was a horrible experience from which even the victor could very
well emerge with grave injuries (one wonders about post-traumatic stress
disorder, or PTSD, but since none of our sources mention it there is no point
in discussing it here). Most gladiators seem to have died aged between twenty
and thirty with between five and thirty-five fights to their names. Not surprisingly, the sources mention a couple of men who chose to commit suicide rather
than amuse the mob by fighting. Still, if it is true that many died early, it is also
true that some are known to have ended their careers and retired more or less
successfully. A few outstanding champions even returned to the arena of their
own free will in return for fabulous sums of money.[85]

The hope for gain and fame explains why there was always a sprinkling of
men (and women) who were not forced into the arena but volunteered for it.
Their number seems to have increased with time until, early in the Imperial age,
they may have made up a considerable percentage of all the gladiators.[86] The
fact that, doing so, they assumed the status of slaves does not seem to have
disturbed them unduly; already in antiquity questions were raised about their
motives as well as what their existence might mean in terms of the nature of
man.[87] Some were probably debtors who hoped to use this desperate method to
avoid payment. A few may have been possessed by sheer lust for fighting, but it
is improbable that they were at all numerous. As we saw, even some emperors
participated, albeit their lives were too valuable for their appearances to deserve
the name fights. If volunteers were in fact common then it is hardly surprising
that their combats raised few eyebrows. Where our sources *do* grow indignant is
when senators or knights (*equites*) engaged in similar pursuits.

The way the Romans saw it, public performances of every kind – not only
gladiatorial ones, but those that involved hunting in the theater, chariot races,
acting, dancing, and making music – were degrading and on a par with
prostitution. Marcus Aurelius at one point even proclaimed that gladiators
and their trainers were not fit to pay taxes.[88] Such performances conflicted with
dignitas, which the Romans considered one of their principal virtues and which,
as the argument concerning the relationship between athletics and war shows,
supposedly distinguished them from the degenerate Greeks in particular. It
simply would not do for spectators to say that so-and-so fighting in the arena is
the descendant of Scipio, or Aemilius Paulus, or whoever.[89] Yet as was so often
the case during the late Republic and Empire,[90] traditional values proved to be

---

[85] Suetonius, *Tiberius*, in *Lives of the Emperors*, 7.   [86] Ville, *La gladiature*, p. 255.

[87] Cyprian, *Ad Donatum*, in *Opuscoli*, Turin: Internazionale, 1935, p. 7.

[88] See C. Edwards, "Unspeakable Professions: Public Performance and Prostitution in
Ancient Rome," in J. P. Hallett and M. B. Skinner, eds., *Roman Sexualities*, Princeton
University Press, 1997, pp. 66–98; and Tabula Italica, line 7, in *Corpus Inscriptiones
Latinarum*, T. Mommsen, ed., Berlin: Reimer, 1869, vol. II, no. 6278.

[89] See e.g. Cassius Dio, *History of Rome*, 61.3.   [90] According to Tacitus, *Annales*, 14.20–1.

of no avail. So many senators and knights acquired experience in the matter that in 65 BC Caesar could ask some of them to train his own gladiators.[91] Now we know that the gladiators in each category had their own specialized coaches;[92] hence the men in question must have had experience not just in war but in the arena too.

Long before that, in 122 BC, Gaius Gracchus had passed a law that excluded knights who had hired themselves out as gladiators from the courts. In 46 BC Caesar himself passed one that banned senators from entering the arena – to no avail, since it had to be repeated eight years later.[93] This was not the end of the matter. In 29 BC a senator by the name of Quintus Vitellius, a distant relation of the future Emperor Aulus Vitellius who reigned for a few months in AD 69, fought as a gladiator. In 22 BC Augustus repeated the prohibition, and this time he saw fit to ban knights who were the descendants of senators as well as females of the upper classes. He even had the measure formally passed by the Senate,[94] to no avail, as far as anybody can tell. In AD 5 a knight, unnamed but said to be "distinguished for his wealth" fought as a gladiator, proving that penury was not the only motive involved. Telling of the episode, Cassius Dio can hardly hide his astonishment; to emphasize just how unusual it was, he adds that, during the same *ludi*, an elephant vanquished a rhinoceros.[95] Similar cases must have abounded. In AD 11 Augustus, notwithstanding his usual conservative bent, saw himself forced to rescind the prohibition which was being disregarded in any case. Since it was assumed that free men would fight better than slaves, contests in which knights participated quickly became centers of attraction.[96] The emperor himself, accompanied by the praetors who supervised the games, came to watch.

Nevertheless, the situation remained ambiguous. In AD 15 "certain knights" wished to enter fights organized by Tiberius' nephew and adopted son, Nero Claudius Drusus Germanicus. The games were held in honor of the latter's victory over the Germans in which he avenged Varro's defeat of AD 9. Yet not only did the emperor refuse to be present, but after one of the knights had been killed he prohibited the other from ever fighting as a gladiator again.[97] On one occasion Caligula put to death a number of knights, some of whom "had merely practiced gladiatorial combat."[98] Yet this was the same emperor who, whenever he felt like it, made whoever he disliked come down and fight. In all probability, subsequent emperors gave up the struggle as useless. Shortly after his accession

[91] Suetonius, *Caesar*, 26.3.
[92] See, for the evidence, Wiedemann, *Emperors and Gladiators*, p. 117.
[93] Cassius Dio, *History of Rome*, 43.23 and 48.43.
[94] *Ibid.*, 44.2 See, on the various unsuccessful prohibitions, B. Levick, "The Senatus Consultum from Larinum," *Journal of Roman Studies*, 73, 1983, pp. 97–115.
[95] Cassius Dio, *History of Rome*, 55.27.   [96] Tacitus, *Annales*, 12.56.3.
[97] Cassius Dio, *History of Rome*, 57.13.   [98] *Ibid.*, 59.10.

Septimius Severus took the senators to task for fighting in the arena.[99] Yet he, too, does not seem to have done anything to stop the practice.

Seen from a modern point of view, all the games did was to pile atrocity upon atrocity. Along with most other things that took place in the amphitheater, such as executions, animal hunts, and the sexual abuse of women who were mounted by animals, they were manifestations of Roman brutality and bloodthirstiness. To quote the most famous modern historian of all, "in terms of morality, combat-games both represented and fed the worst that the ancient world had to offer."[100] Seneca provides us with a vivid record of the crowds' shouts as they encouraged the fighters to thrash and kill their opponents.[101] Still there was another side to the matter. Though atrocities have always been frequent in war, in principle at any rate atrocity and war are not the same. In a sense they may been seen as opposites that exclude one another. War demands courage above all, whereas atrocities, by being committed on the defenseless, exclude it, and in the long run turn those who commit them into cowards.

The point is that, excepting only the handful ordered to fight by a Caligula, a Nero or a Commodus, trained gladiators were anything but defenseless. To the contrary, they were selected men. No *lanista* would invest in men who were obviously unfit, and no *editor* would buy them or rent them. Volunteers too must have considered themselves fit, or else they would hardly have embarked on so perilous a career. As literary sources and the remains of gladiatorial schools show, everything was done to prepare the men for the ordeal as thoroughly as possible. It has even been claimed that they were trained to inflict stabbing wounds which, though fatal, would not cause unnecessary pain.[102] An indication of the quality of the medical care gladiators received is provided by the fact that remedies first developed for treating them were later applied to society at large.[103] Early in his career Galen, who later worked as a private physician to Marcus Aurelius and went on to become one of the most famous doctors in history, was in charge of a gladiatorial training institute. Far from feeling ashamed of the fact, he boasted that, by his care, he reduced the gladiators' mortality.[104]

The ancient Romans were nothing if not class-conscious. Emperors and other members of the higher classes in particular well understood that their privileges depended in large part on the impression they made on their inferiors. They called the fact that men of standing fought as gladiators "perverse"

[99] *Ibid.*, 76.8.
[100] T. Mommsen, *Roemische Geschichte*, Munich: Deutsche Taschenbuch Verlag, 1976 [1888], vol. V, p. 188. I am grateful to Professor Elisabeth Erdmann of Erlangen University for bringing this passage to my attention.
[101] Seneca, Letter to Lucilius, in *Epistles*, LCL, 1925, no. 7.
[102] Wiedemann, *Emperors and Gladiators*, p. 117.   [103] Pliny, *Natural History*, 26.135.
[104] *Medicorum graecorum opera quae extant*, vol. XIII: *Claudii Galeni opera omnia*, C. G. Kuehn, ed., Hildesheim: Oms, 1965 [1827], p. 600.

(the early third-century AD Christian writer Tertullian), but seldom took effective measures to prevent them from doing so.[105] In this they resembled many early modern rulers who, while repeatedly prohibiting duels, were unable or unwilling to end them once and for all. However, few seem to have cared about the lives of low-class people, let alone felt that there was anything basically wrong with the combats. If ordinary people had any objection to others of their own kind killing each other for the spectators' amusement, then we have precious little evidence of the fact. Some Romans even placed mosaics with images of the shows in their dining-rooms, carefully locating them in such a way that guests were able to see and admire them.[106] All the more reason, therefore, to try and find out why they declined and ultimately disappeared.

Decline, demise, and legacy

In all probability, one of the principal reasons behind the games' decline was the enormous and growing costs they entailed as *editores* vied with one another for influence, power, and popularity. They had more than a little in common with the custom, known from many parts of the world, of potlatching in which property is deliberately destroyed to see who is richer and more generous; in Seneca's words, "[the rich] throw into the gladiatorial schools all the best-looking, the most fit for combat." The aforementioned Nicolas Damascus also tells of a rich man who, in his will, designated his best-looking slaves to fight each other to the death at his funeral.[107]

Undoubtedly some persons may keep engaging in potlatching even under adverse economic circumstances in order to disguise the decline in their fortunes. However, in the long run the activity is conceivable only as long as things are going well. Augustus' will did not in fact end the age of expansion – Tiberius added parts of Germany, and Claudius occupied Britain as far as the southern border of Scotland. Early in the second century AD Trajan conquered Dacia as well as, temporarily, Mesopotamia as far as the Persian Gulf. More or less peaceful consolidation in the form of the absorption of client states also continued. After that, the frontiers froze in place. Increasingly the Empire's wars changed their character. Sometimes it was a question of border clashes with Persia which went on for centuries without doing much to change the balance between the two powers. On other occasions barbarian tribes had to be

---

[105] All the following quotes from Tertullian are from *De Spectaculis*, M. Menghi, ed., Milan: Mondadori, 1995, chs. 12 and 22.

[106] See Wiedemann, *Emperors and Gladiators*, p. 24.

[107] Seneca, *Controversiae*, in *Moral Essays*, 1.4.18; Nicolas quoted in Athenaeus, *The Learned Banqueters*, 4.49. On the potlatch aspects of Roman life, see P. Veyne, *Bread and Circuses*, London: Allen Lane, 1990, pp. xvi, xxi, 19.

prevented from crossing into the Empire, or else rival pretenders fought each other for the throne. In AD 275 Dacia itself had to be evacuated, a portent of other withdrawals to come.

The end of expansion dried up the flow of booty and prisoners on which the gladiatorial shows, along with so much else in Roman life, rested. Instead of relying on captives, *lanistae* had to buy convicted criminals from the Imperial treasury which sold them at six gold pieces each. Another factor may have been the growth of the armed forces in comparison with the Empire's resources in terms of both money and manpower. The process, which first becomes visible under Marcus Aurelius, accelerated during the third century AD, straining the treasury. To speak with one modern scholar, it was a clear case of Imperial overstretch.[108] Whereas gladiatorial shows had always been the most expensive by far, now the cost of holding them skyrocketed. As magistrates, instead of being elected, came to be appointed from above, holding games also lost much of its attractiveness in promoting one's career. The growing monopolization of the games by the emperors must have worked in the same direction.

During the fourth decade of the first century AD Caligula already had some difficulty in making consuls and praetors do their duty as *editores* and provide shows of every sort, gladiatorial ones presumably included.[109] By one interpretation, the measures taken by Marcus Aurelius in respect of the games were meant to prevent the price of gladiators from going through the roof, and in this way ruining the magistrates responsible for holding them.[110] Apparently to no avail: during the third century AD the size and frequency of the shows seems to have declined. This happened first in the western provinces, which were more subject to barbarian invasions, and then in the eastern ones as well. Only in Rome itself did the practically unlimited wealth coming in from all directions allow emperors such as Gordianus I and III (reigned AD 238 and 238–44 respectively), Probus (276–82), and above all Philip the Arab (244–49) to proceed as before. The shows of the last-named, held in honor of the first millennium since the foundation of Rome, were especially spectacular. Included among them were the last naval battles on record. All in all, a thousand gladiators were killed. If our calculations are anything near correct, that would indicate that the total number involved may have been ten thousand and more, though one must allow for the possibility that some fought more than once, which would have increased the odds against them emerging alive and reduced the total number.

---

[108] P. Kennedy, *The Rise and Fall of the Great Powers*, New York: Viking, 1987, especially pp. 536–40.

[109] Cassius Dio, *History of Rome*, 59.5.

[110] See M. Carter, "Gladiatorial Ranking and the SC De Pretiis Gladiatorum Minuendis," *Phoenix*, 57, 1/2, Spring–Summer 2003, pp. 83–114.

Enormously popular as the games were, there had always been a few men – we know nothing about women – who did not much like them. In particular, first-century BC Greek Stoic philosophers such as Apollonius and his contemporary Epictetus criticized the shows for the passions they raised among the spectators. Participating in the debate concerning the relative merits of the two civilizations already referred to in the previous chapter, they worried lest Greek cultural superiority would be smothered by Roman vulgarity and brutality.[111] This kind of attitude seems to have been fairly widespread among the urban elites of the Hellenized eastern part of the Empire.

In Rome itself the earliest known reservations were expressed by Cicero. In 55 BC he wrote that there was no pleasure in watching "a variegated display of cavalry and infantry equipment in some battle or other."[112] However, he did admire the courage of individual fighters and has nothing to say about the blood being shed. Seneca, in a letter to a friend, took a different line. His objections centered on the games' effect on the crowd – whose members, he says, were always crying out for more and more violence, proof of their own unruliness.[113] All ran against the Stoic philosophy of which he was the chief representative at the time. It presented passion as the root of all evil – with a man like Nero in power, not an unreasonable attitude to take – and called for self-control and courage in the face of adversity as the greatest virtues of all. Yet Seneca did not take issue with the combats as such. None of his letters or the rest of his *opus* suggest that the shedding of human blood as a form of entertainment made him lose his sleep. Like Cicero, he treated gladiators, always provided they behaved courageously, with considerable respect. The same applies to Pliny the Elder, who tells us that they were taught not to blink even when weapons were brandished in front of their faces. In Tertullian's words, they were taught how to die.

Like Cassius Dio, Tacitus considered the shows to be beneath the dignity of history which, he believed, should concern itself with important public matters rather than with mere gossip. Unlike Dio (and Suetonius) he did not succumb to the temptation of describing particularly nasty episodes that took place in the arena in order to blacken this emperor or that. Instead he is careful to mention only shows that were unusually large or somehow linked to some exceptional event. Several second-century AD Greek writers, including the orator Dio Chrysostom ("Golden Mouth"), and the historian and philosopher Plutarch, did the same. Lucian mentions the protest of a second-century cynic philosopher, Demonax, against the shows; before permitting them, he told his Athenian countrymen, they should pull down the statue of pity.[114] Somewhat later, the Christian apologist Minucius Felix expressed a similar sentiment.[115]

---

[111] Epictetus, *Encheiridon*, LCL, 1925, 33.2.
[112] Cicero to M. Marius, September 55 BC, in *Epistolae ad Familiares*, 7.1.
[113] Seneca, Letter to Lucilius.   [114] Lucian, *Demonax*, LCL, 1913, 28.7.
[115] M. Minucius Felix, *Octavius*, G. W. Clarke, ed., New York: Newman, 1974, 37.11.

His and Demonax's are the only known attacks on the morality of the fights. The rest either followed Seneca in their fear of the passions they roused among the low-born in particular, as Chrysostom did, or else claimed that the shows were a waste of resources better employed in combating Rome's ever-growing list of enemies.

Originating with high-class men, almost certainly these views had no impact on the masses most of whom probably never read a word any of these authors had written; over a period measured in centuries, only once do we hear that a crowd disapproved of an *editor* because of his extraordinary relish for bloodshed.[116] It is, however, true that, during the first centuries AD, some of the harshest aspects of the shows were slowly – very slowly – prohibited or modified. Augustus himself showed the way by trying to ban the form of combat known as *munus sine missione* in which a vanquished gladiator could obtain no reprieve. Under Trajan a law was contemplated, and perhaps passed, allowing a gladiator who survived his fights to retire after three years and regain his freedom after another two.[117] Around AD 130 Hadrian issued a decree which prohibited owners from selling their slaves as gladiators unless they (i.e. the slaves) had either volunteered or been condemned for a crime.

Somewhat to Cassius Dio's consternation, Marcus Aurelius had gladiators fight with blunted weapons, "like athletes, without danger." Inscriptions and images dating to the third and fourth centuries show that this form of mock combat, though it was not universally adopted, did not die with him. All these decrees may well have owed something to humanitarian feeling – Marcus Aurelius, after all, was also the author of the celebrated *Meditationes*. However, other considerations may have been involved. First, the measures can be understood as part of ongoing legislation aimed at increasing Imperial control over every aspects of their subjects' life. Second, *editores* often hired gladiators for specific shows. If they lived, good and well; if not, though, the full price would have to be paid, which could be up to fifty times as high. Hence the last-named reform in particular may have represented a cost-reducing measure.[118]

All these reforms may well act as one indication that, slowly but steadily, the entire cultural-ideological basis on which the combats rested was starting to erode. The way the Romans understood themselves, their greatest quality had always been *virtus*, manly prowess, which in turn was both absolutely necessary for war and best demonstrated by engaging in it. In the *Aeneid*, Virgil, who was

---

[116] Tacitus, *Annales*, 1.76.3.

[117] Ulpian as quoted in T. Mommsen, *Corpus Iuris Civilis*, Nabu, 2010 [1895]; 11.7.4; also T. Mommsen, *Roemische Strafrecht*, Berlin: Akademieverlag, 1899, p. 953.

[118] See on this M. Carter, "Gladiatorial Combat with 'Sharp' Weapons," *Zeitschrift fuer Papyrologie und Epigraphik*, 155, 2006, pp. 161–75.

Augustus' semi-official poet, celebrated this part of their civilization as well as anybody could:[119]

> Strong from the cradle, of a sturdy brood,
> We bear our newborn infants to the flood;
> There bath'd amid the stream, our boys we hold
> With winter harden'd, and inur'd to cold.
> They wake before the day to range the wood
> Kill ere they eat, nor taste unconquer'd food.
> No sports, but what belong to war, they know;
> To break the stubborn colt, to bend the bow.
> Our youth, of labor patient, earn their bread;
> Hardly they work, with frugal diet fed.
> From plows and arrows sent to seek renown,
> They fight in fields, and storm the shaken town.
> No part of life from toils of war is free,
> No change in age, or difference in degree.
> We plow and till in arms; our oxen feel,
> Instead of goads, the spur and pointed steel;
> Th' inverted lance makes furrows in the plain;
> Ev'n time, that changes all, yet changes us in vain;
> The body, not the mind; nor can control
> Th' immortal vigor, or abate the soul.
> Our helms defend the young, disguise the gray
> We live by plunder, and delight in prey.

Virgil's contemporary Horace says that youth was expected to harden its limbs, treat poverty as a friend, learn to fight, and grow accustomed to a harsh life in the open.[120] Once in the army, they were expected to conquer or die with very little leeway in between. Naturally there is always a wide gap between theory and practice, a gap of which many Romans were well aware. The banquets given by Lucullus and Nero's Golden Palace have become proverbial. Still, much in Livius and Polybius confirms what the poets have to say. One does not start as a small city-state and end up by conquering the world for nothing. For centuries hardly a year went by without the gates of the Temple of Mars being thrown open and the citizens assembling at the Campus Martius and going to war; in the words of one modern historian, confronting death was not so much a question of exceptional heroism as of proving oneself a Roman.[121] If only because military service was a prerequisite for entering upon an official career, the *cursus honorum*, until Imperial times few if any aspiring politicians got very far without giving proof of competence as soldiers or commanders. To emphasize the role of military prowess, from Augustus on the first and most important title every emperor carried was Imperator, victorious commander, even if he

---

[119] Virgil, *Aeneid*, LCL, 2001, vol. II, 9.603–13.   [120] Horace, *Odes*, LCL, 2004, 3.2.
[121] Auguet, *Cruelty and Civilization*, p. 198.

had never taken part in a campaign and even if he was, at heart, a coward, as some undoubtedly were.

As Epiphanes may have understood when he adopted the shows and spread them in his realm, what the games really did was to provide a living illustration of this ur-Roman code of values. As each combat opened, everything that normally surrounds fighting – and, often enough, prevents it from taking place, such as distance, friction, and uncertainty – was systematically excluded. So, of course was any possibility of taking shelter or escaping from the field. War was stripped to its most elementary form, i.e. killing and being killed – courageously, relentlessly, without pity or remorse. It was to make sure that this should indeed be the case that weapons were tested for sharpness and the gladiators prohibited from wearing body armor. Yet the gladiators themselves were a special breed: regardless of whether they had volunteered for the arena or been compelled to fight in it, they were condemned men. For them the games represented one last chance to redeem themselves – albeit one that was extremely dangerous and often led to premature death. Conversely, those who tried to flee their opponents might be subject to derisive graffiti, several of which were found at Pompeii; watching such gladiators, the spectators felt cheated and humiliated.[122]

It was at this point that the new and fast-spreading religion coming from Palestine, Christianity, entered the picture. Josephus himself did not explicitly criticize Agrippa for holding the shows at Berytus. However, the context leaves no doubt that they did offend many of his fellow Jews.[123] The Talmud, while it does tell us that some Jews (including one, Reish Lakish, who later became a famous rabbi) sold themselves to a *lanista* to be trained as gladiators, makes no secret of its disapproval of the games.[124] The problem is complicated by the fact that the text uses various terms taken from various languages, with the result that it is often hard to say just what kind of fighter is meant. Jesus' immediate followers probably took the same line. After all, they had started out as a branch of Judaism and one that was more peacefully minded that most. Though the relevant literature does not contain other references to gladiatorial fights, it is explicit in its condemnation of athletics in general.[125]

Later on, references to the games, as well as condemnations of them, multiply. Around AD 200 Clement of Alexandria, the teacher of the great Origen, called the amphitheater *cavea saeviens*, best translated as "a den of savagery."[126] Tertullian, the other outstanding Christian writer of the period, agreed with him. Yet

---

[122] Seneca, *De Ira*, in *Moral Essays*, 1.2.4.   [123] Josephus, *Jewish Antiquities*, 19.7.5.
[124] Gittin, 46b–47a. See on this episode M. Z. Brettler and M. Poliakoff, "Rabi Simeon Ben Lakish and the Gladiatorial Banquet: Observations on the Roman Arena," *Harvard Theological Review*, 83, 1, January 1990, pp. 93–8.
[125] See M. Poliakoff, "Jacob, Job, and Other Wrestlers: Reception of Greek Athletics by Jews and Christians in Antiquity," *Journal of Sport History*, 11, 7, Summer 1984, pp. 53–4.
[126] Clement of Alexandria, *Paedagogus*, Leipzig: Heinrichs, 1905, 3.11.77.

contrary to what a modern reader might perhaps expect, what most disturbed both men was neither the fact that huge numbers of innocent animals were being butchered nor that condemned men and women – including, of course, Christians – were being thrown to the beasts or publicly executed in the most horrible ways. Rather, their main objection was to the gladiatorial combats, the reason being that, to quote Tertullian, "men gave their souls to the gladiators and women, both their souls and their bodies." The way they saw it, for fighters and spectators alike there was only one road to salvation, i.e. the one that led through the Lamb of God and took the believer into the afterlife. The idea that prowess, displayed either in war or in the arena, was the highest virtue of all – higher even than faith, and, since it offered condemned men a chance at redemption of a kind that many might find attractive, a substitute for it – was anathema.

In AD 325, twelve years after he had his famous vision and his army first started operating under Christian symbols, the Emperor Constantine issued an edict in which he "totally prohibit[ed]" the existence of gladiators. At a time when peace reigned everywhere and order had been restored to the known world, he wrote, bloody shows could no longer provide any delight; henceforward condemned criminals would be sent to the mines so they could pay for their crimes without their blood being spilt.[127] This should not be regarded as a sign of humanity on Constantine's part. If anything, being sent to work in the mines represented the more severe sentence. At least gladiators, as long as they remained in training, were well looked after. They also stood a chance, however slight, of leaving the arena alive and even of regaining their liberty. The situation of miners – "wretched manikins ... their entire skin covered with bluish welts, their backs torn into bloody strips" – was entirely different. Invariably they faced a slow, painful, and of course unnoticed and inglorious, death.[128]

In any case the emperor does not seem to have followed up on this decree. First, a mere two years later he passed a law that condemned freeborn kidnappers to fight as gladiators.[129] Since the same decree specified that slaves and freedmen should continue to be thrown to the beasts, obviously it was considered that being made to fight in the arena was not the very worst fate that might overtake a man. Second, there is no record of any attempt on his part to suppress the shows held at Antioch, which at that time was one of the Empire's principal cities, only three years later. Third, towards the end of Constantine's reign a Sicilian senator by the name of Firmicus Maternus prepared a handbook on astrological lore. Not only did he include several horoscopes of gladiators, but he spelled out the exact way in which they were fated to die.[130]

---

[127] *Theodosian Code*, C. Pharr, trans., The Lawbook Exchange, 2001, 15.12.1.
[128] Apuleius, *Metamorphoses*, LCL, 1989, 9.12.   [129] *Theodosian Code*, 9.18.1.
[130] Julius Firmicus Maternus, *Matheseos*, Stuttgart: Teubner, 1968, 3.4.23, 7.8.7, 8.7.5–10.4, 23.4, and 24.7. There is an English translation by Jean Rhys Bram entitled *Ancient Astrology: Theory and Practice*, Park Ridge, NJ: Noyes Press, 1975.

What was true of Constantine also applied to his successors in both parts of
the divided Empire. All but one, Julian the Apostate, were Christians, yet none
is known to have tried to interfere with the fights. It is true that literary evidence
concerning their development is scant. However, though it may be an accident,
some of the largest mosaics that show the combats in all their gory detail date
from precisely this period. Christian propaganda against sports of any kind was
unrelenting: for example, the influential fourth-century theologian Basil of
Cappadocia claimed that "the athlete of Christ" was marked by leanness, pallor,
and weakness of body.[131] We know that Valentian I decreed in 367 that
Christians would no longer be condemned to the arena. Some three decades
later Saint Augustine argued that gladiators, along with prostitutes and pimps,
should be refused baptism, a measure that can only have had any meaning if it
were applied to volunteers whose continued existence is thus confirmed. One
way or another, the opposition made itself heard.

As late as the middle of the fourth century the orator Libanius found
warm words of praise for the gladiators who fought in games held by his
uncle, comparing them with Leonidas' three hundred Spartan heroes at
Thermopylae.[132] In 393 a former consul by the name of Symmachus spent a
vast sum to hold a lavish show in Rome itself, i.e. right under the nose of the
Christian Emperor Theodosius I. His objective was to clear the way for his son,
who at that time was a mere boy under a tutor's care, to mount the first steps in
the Imperial administration; deeply conservative in everything he did, he also
saw it as part of his duty to the Populus Romanus.[133] His letters give a vivid
image of the importance he attributed to the matter and also of the difficulties
any *editor* who was planning to give a large show had to overcome. Animals
destined for the arena died, some Saxons prisoners gave proof of cowardice by
preferring suicide to fighting, and more. Two facts point at the underlying clash
of values between pagans and Christians which had not yet been decided. First,
this was the same Symmachus who, eleven years earlier, had unsuccessfully
tried to convince the equally Christian Emperor Gratian to refrain from
removing the statue of victory, a pagan deity, from the Senate House. Second,
Symmachus was attacked by the contemporary Christian poet Prudentius. The
latter in his *Contra Symmachum*, demanded an end to the shows. But he did not
object to men being thrown to the beasts; instead, he suggested that punishment
as an alternative to the shows he hated so much.

To Augustine the trouble with gladiators was that, as desperate men
who considered themselves beyond fear or hope, they felt free to do as they

---

[131] See on him Poliakoff, "Jacob, Job and Other Wrestlers," p. 55.
[132] Libanius, *Selected Orations*, Cambridge, MA: Harvard University Press, 1977, *Oratio* 1.5.
[133] For everything pertaining to Symmachus, see S. Dill, *Roman Society in the Last Century of
the Western Empire*, London: Macmillan, 1899, pp. 150–1.

pleased.[134] To make things worse, people could not take their eyes off them. In his *Confessions*, written just before AD 400, he described one of his fellow students at Carthage who had long resisted attending the shows. When his fellows dragged him to the amphitheater he kept his eyes shut, determined not to watch. Then a roar from the crowd caused him to open them:[135]

> When he saw the blood, it was as though he had drunk a deep draught of savage passion. Instead of turning away, he fixed his eyes upon the scene and drank in all its frenzy, unaware of what he was doing. He revelled in the wickedness of the fighting and was drunk with the fascination of bloodshed ... He watched and cheered and grew hot with excitement, and when he left the arena he carried away with him a diseased mind which would leave him no peace until he came back again, no longer simply with the friends who had first dragged him there, but at their head, leading new sheep to the slaughter.

Obviously most of the Rome's residents remained just as enthusiastic about the shows as they had been for centuries past. A curious episode of 404 reinforces this impression. According to the church historian Theodoret of Syria, an otherwise unknown monk by the name of Telemachus traveled from his home in Asia Minor to Rome specifically to protest against the combats. In the midst of a performance he rushed into the arena, attempting to stop the fight; the spectators' reaction was to tear him to pieces.[136] The story does not make much sense – the same stringent security precautions (in the case of the Colosseum, a wall twelve feet high) that prevented gladiators and animals from climbing into the tribunes must have prevented the spectators from entering the arena. Theodoret's claim that the incident made such an impression on the Emperor Honorius that he put an end to the shows is contradicted by the fact that they continued to be held both in the city and elsewhere. Incidentally, none of this prevented President Ronald Reagan from repeating the story and embellishing it a bit in a speech he gave at the annual prayer breakfast in February 1984.[137]

In 410 the inconceivable happened: Rome, the city which in its heyday had a million and a half inhabitants and which for centuries had served as the capital of one of the largest, most powerful, and most impressive empires of all times, was besieged, captured, and plundered by Alaric and his horde of Vandals. The conquest did not prove lasting. As the Vandals left for North Africa, Honorius, whose capital was in Ravenna, remained on the throne. In the absence of other evidence, from this point on we have to argue *ex silentio*. In AD 429 the

---

[134] Augustine, *Enarrationes in Psalmos*, Vienna: Akademie der Wissenschaft, 2005, 70.1.
[135] Augustine, *Confessions*, Harmondsworth: Penguin, 1961, 6.8.
[136] The story is told in Theodoret of Syria, *Ecclesiastical History*, Kessinger, 2004, 5.26.
[137] See, for the President's remarks: www.reagan.utexas.edu/archives/speeches/1984/20284a.htm.

Christian writer Salvianus penned a treatise in which he attacked theatrical shows in general and wild animal chases and chariot races in particular. Yet, exceptionally, he did not say a word on the gladiatorial combats; considering that previous Christian authors had uniformly raised stronger objections to the combats than to any other form of entertainment in and outside the theater, one can only conclude that they had already been abolished.[138] Twenty years later, when emperors Anthemius and Armasius issued decrees that prohibited all kinds of shows from taking place on Sundays, gladiators were not mentioned either.

The end of the gladiatorial games did not mean that they were forgotten. Far from that being the case, they proved to be one of the Empire's most enduring legacies, appealing to people's imagination just as much as, if not more than, Roman law, Roman military methods, and Roman roads, baths, and other buildings. During the Middle Ages there was a tendency to associate the games with pagan ritual and to demonize them, which in view of their religious associations is not surprising. Later, during the Renaissance, things changed. For example, a famous statue, dating to Hellenistic times and representing a naked warrior, became known as "the Borghese Gladiator" even though it has nothing to do with the arena. Its existence was recorded for the first time in 1610; later, during the eighteenth century, it became one of the most admired antique statues of all, widely copied and used as a model by countless artists. Such was its fame that Napoleon had it taken to the Louvre where it may still be seen.

A stateroom in the Buen Retiro Palace, built in 1630 for Philip IV of Spain, was decorated with paintings of fighting gladiators. Nineteenth-century "historicist" artists competed as to who could produce the most realist work on the subject. The best-known painting, Jean-Léon Gérôme's *Pollice verso* (thumbs down, 1872) has become all but emblematic. In 1886 John Philip Sousa, who wrote *Semper Fidelis*, composed a *Gladiator March*. In 1899 the Czech Julius Fucik produced *The Entry of the Gladiators* which is still often performed. A 1930s British combat aircraft, a species of sparrow, and a species of frog all had the honor of being called gladiator. The last of these owes its name to the sharp bony spine males have on each hand which they use in mortal combat against others of their kind.[139] The city of Cleveland has a Gladiators football team and the role of football in modern American life has often been compared with that of the gladiators. There are gladiator pickup trucks, gladiator bicycles, gladiator sandals, and gladiator shoes (by Dior, no less). One website offers a gladiator online game in which one can create a gladiator, arm him, and send him into the arena to fight other gladiators; another sells "medieval gladiator

---

[138] That, at any rate, is the view of Meijer, *Gladiators*, pp. 205–6.

[139] *Hypsiboas rosenbergi*, at: www.wildherps.com/species/H.rosenbergi.html.

Corinthian helmets," as if such a thing ever existed.[140] For women there is a "gladiator bra" complete with beaded bronze fringe and gold trim. As the US military was experiencing morale problems when moving from conscription to an all-volunteer force in the 1970s, one sociologist suggested the troops would need a "gladiatorial ethos."

Many of the amphitheaters in which the gladiators fought were left standing. Some continued to be used for various purposes, whereas others were abandoned and gradually disappeared. Either they fell victim to the ravages of time or they were dismantled. The most important one left standing was the Colosseum; not only was it the largest Roman building by far, but its position, near the Palatine Hill where the emperors used to live, meant that it could hardly escape the attention of residents and visitors alike. Perhaps no other piece of ground in the world – the arena, after all, only measured 281 by 177 feet – witnessed so many people fighting and killing each other. For two millennia it has stood as a gigantic memorial to the terrible things that had once taken place there, and one that became the subject of countless legends.[141] Sometimes it was used by architects to provide stones for other buildings, sometimes excavated and carefully preserved. At times its lower arches were occupied by peddlers and prostitutes.

To speak with Henry James, "if nocturnal meditations in the Colosseum [were] recommended by the poets they [were] deprecated by the doctors."[142] Present-day visitors are not as sensitive. To them the structure is a tourist attraction such as few other cities can claim, complete with snacks, souvenirs, and mock gladiators ready to be photographed. It has also become quite common for gladiatorial fights to be reenacted in other cities in and outside Italy; such events are useful both for the excitement (and revenue) that they generate and as instruments in the hands of certain historians. Only by carefully reconstructing various weapons, training volunteers to use them, and trying them out in various combinations can the strengths and weaknesses of each type of gladiator be fully appreciated.[143] The 1990s saw the rise and fall of a TV show called *American Gladiators*. In it muscular young men and women had to make it through a sort of obstacle course. However, the only goal was to earn points (there was no plot of any kind). Since the obstacles were neither dangerous nor at all similar to the kind one is likely to meet in real life the show always remained a little silly. But this did not deter others from setting up something known as Gladiator Challenge, which judging by the relevant website appears to be a traveling martial art show.

[140] See www.gamesolo.com/flash-game/gladiator.html and Chainscheap US, http://chain-armor.chainscheap.us/.
[141] See, for the Colosseum's subsequent history, Meijer, *Gladiators*, pp. 208–19.
[142] H. James, *Daisy Miller*, New York: Harper, 1879, p. 57.
[143] See Junkelmann, *Gladiatoren*, pp. 145–65.

Movies with gladiators as their theme include *The Last Days of Pompeii* (1913), *Gladiator* (1955), *Spartacus* (1960), *Gladiators of Rome* (1962), *Demetrius and the Gladiators* (1964), *See You Gladiator* (1986), *Colosseum, a Gladiator's Story* (2003) and the 13-part TV series *Spartacus; Blood and Sand* (2010). The last-named one, alternately spurting blood and sperm, focuses on the period before the hero escaped and became the rebel leader whose name was immortalized. Furthermore, the term "gladiator movies" has been applied to an entire genre of (often Italian-made) films. They were characterized by (1) stories and characters drawn from ancient history and myth; (2) a muscle-man in the starring role, performing superhuman feats of strength; (3) lurid scenes of bondage and torture; and (4) a host of exotic, often half-naked and very curvaceous, heroines and femmes fatales. Curiously enough, many of the films' protagonists have little or nothing to do with gladiators. Probably most memorable of all was Ridley Scott's *Gladiator* (2000), a vast production that won five Academy Awards, including that for Best Picture. Not only was it hugely successful, but it gave rise to quite a literature ranging from term papers to scholarly discussions.[144] The fact that, like all the rest, it contained many inaccuracies hardly mattered. If anything it added modestly to the film's fame by giving critics something to break their teeth on.

Books about the gladiators that target popular or juvenile readers are legion. More serious works also continue to come off the presses;[145] indeed the library of my own alma mater in Jerusalem seems to have more volumes that deal with the *munera* than with any other kind of games, past or present. In 1582 the famous neo-stoicist philosopher Justus Lipsius estimated the number of men killed in the amphitheater each year at 240–360,000. Yet far from using that vastly exaggerated figure to impress readers with the evils of ancient society, he praised the "beautiful and amusing games" (*pulchri . . . et oblectantes ludi*) so suitable for a people "born to arms." Two centuries later the even more famous Marquis de Sade, while putting the number higher still, made a similar argument.[146] What both men had in common was their admiration for everything Roman. To them it represented the most powerful polity ever seen on earth, whose secret of longevity consisted partly of the games.

At that time opinion had already started to shift. In his admiration for the Roman Empire Edward Gibbon was second to none; yet when writing about the fifth century AD, he rejoiced that "the piety of the Christian princes had

---

[144] See Meijer, *Gladiators*, pp. 220–31; also A. Ward, "The Movie Gladiator in Historical Perspective," University of Connecticut, 2001, available at: http://ablemedia.com/ctcweb/showcase/wardgladiator1.html.

[145] See, for reviews of some works, J. E. Lendon, "Gladiators," *The Classical Journal*, 95, 4, 2000, pp. 399–406.

[146] J. Lipsius, *Saturnalium sermonum libri II, qui de gladiatoribus*, Amsterdam: Brill, 2011 [1582], vol. I, 12, 38, vol. II, 25, 116; A. F. de Sade, *Schriften aus der Revolutionszeit*, G. R. Lind, ed., Frankfurt/Main: Insel, 1969 [1788–95], p. 10.

suppressed the inhuman combats of the gladiators."[147] Gibbon's nineteenth-century successors likewise took a keen interest in the games. They used them as proof of just how sadistic the Romans had been; also, by implication, how enlightened their own modern bourgeois society, which at that time was busily eliminating other bloody spectacles such as public executions, was. Expressions such as "cruel" and "loathsome" abound.[148] One of the last examples of this approach was Michael Grant's *Gladiators*. Grant (1914–2004) was an extra-ordinarily productive British historian whose works tended to be on the popular side. The volume, which first saw the light in print in 1967, was republished several times and now carries the subtitle "The Bloody Truth; The Nastiest Blood Sport Invented." Nasty the games certainly were. Yet what makes the question really important is the way this very quality translated into the vast popularity they enjoyed, and, as the above-listed facts prove, still enjoy.

In 1972 the American anthropologist Clifford Geertz published his enor-mously influential essay, "Deep Play: Notes on the Balinese Cockfight."[149] Based on his fieldwork during the late 1950s, it all but ignored the fights themselves. No attempt was made to describe them, nor was a single word wasted on the fact that they were quite as nasty as those between the gladiators. In fact they may have been worse, given that the victims were not human beings who at least understood what was demanded of them and why, but animals that did not have such knowledge. Instead, with razors tied to their legs, they went after one another by pure instinct. What interested Geertz was the men who organized the fights, trained their cocks to participate in them, watched them, applauded them, and of course placed bets on them. He described them in terms of a sort of poor man's theater in which the values of Balinese society were put on show. Trials, wars, political contests, and disputes of all kinds were compared to cockfights: "cock" (*sabung*) also stood for hero, warrior, cham-pion, man of parts, bachelor, dandy, lady-killer, and general tough guy. The fights served to dramatize, play out, and resolve conflicts between the cocks' owners, thus possibly avoiding more serious violence and helping hold the community together.

Many historians found Geertz grist to their mill; unsurprisingly, his theories have often been applied to gladiatorial fights in particular. Previously they were understood as mere outlets for the sadistic impulses of the ancient Romans, their sometimes mad rulers, and many subject peoples who adopted the games

---

[147] E. Gibbon, *The History of the Decline and Fall of the Roman Empire*, London: Caddell, 1837 [1788], p. 484.

[148] Dill, *Roman Society*, p. 53; W. Warde Fowler, *Social Life at Rome in the Age of Cicero*, London: Macmillan, 1963, p. 303.

[149] Clifford Geertz, "Deep Play: Notes on the Balinese Cockfight," reprinted in *Daedalus*, 134, 4, Fall 2005, pp. 56–86.

and watched them almost as enthusiastically as their masters did. Now they could be interpreted as grand theater rationally used by those in power in order to obtain rational ends. To quote Tertullian again:

> symbolic protection of society reaches its high point in *munera*. The spectators, arranged in good order – important people dressed in signs of their status, soldiers in their parade uniforms, and the emperor in triumphal garb – assist with eliminating and forcing submission of all enemies, real or potential, of order ... How better to associate the masses with rejection of all rebels and troublemakers of every sort? ... What better way to spread among the masses the lessons of fear overcome, of discipline, submission, courage and virile violence?

Some modern historians have used this approach to cast a more favorable light on emperors such as Commodus, whose action in (and out of) the arena had previously been considered models of insane depravity. Others went further still, presenting the games as a metaphor for everything Roman and even for at least some of what it means to be human.

Here no attempt will be made to decide which of these approaches is correct. Probably there is an element of truth in all three or, if we include the sadistic impulses, four. Probably emperors, *editores*, *lanistae*, members of the upper classes, plebeians, and of course the gladiators themselves held very different views of the subject. Some were interested in pleasing the crowd and demonstrating their own power (the emperors), others in both of those things as well as giving proof of piety (the *editores*) or making money (the *lanistae*). Some admired the shows, others treated them with contempt (Tacitus above all). The vast majority must have attended them in the hope of having fun, roaring their heads off, and placing bets. Most gladiators were unfortunates who fought under dire compulsion and were lucky to survive more than a few fights. However, a growing number, apparently including a handful of women, had foresworn life of their own free will. A few may have relished their profession and made as much out of it as they could. In spite of, or more likely because of, the massive bloodshed they involved, no other wargames in history have ever been more popular. Certainly none have engaged the imagination of subsequent generations to such an extent; at a guess, few if any ever will.

3

Trials by combat, tournaments, and duels

A certain kind of justice

As a look at the literature will show, the line between trial by combat on one hand and single combat and combat of champions on the other has always been rather vague. As long ago as the Middle Ages, various authors referred to the same episodes by different terms or used the same terms when referring to very different episodes.[1] In all three cases the fight, rather than being an integral part of ongoing hostilities, is clearly separated from them by means of challenge and response as well as the fact that it took place in a location specially set apart for the purpose. Often it is supposed to act as a substitute for those hostilities or to put an end to them, albeit that in most cases things did not work out as planned, the terms of the preliminary agreement were violated, and hostilities opened or resumed. In all three cases the fight is carefully stage-managed, the objective being to enable as many people as possible to watch it. In all three cases, the fighting serves as an ordeal and is intended to prove a point – either that God is on one's side, or that one's cause is just, or simply that one trusts in one's prowess and stands ready to take on any enemy who dares to present himself. What sets trial by combat apart from the other two is a unique characteristic which justifies treating it separately: namely the fact that, in this case, the fight is neither an exhibition nor a contest but part of a formal judiciary process. As such it takes place at the behest of a judge, or judges, who commands both sides and presides over the proceedings.

Single combat and combat of champions may be found in many different cultures from pre-classical Greece to early modern Japan. Not so trial by combat, which seems to be a uniquely European custom deeply rooted in old

---

[1] A good medieval example is *The Mirror of Justices*, W. J. Whittaker, ed., London: Selden Society, 1895, vol. III, no. 23. A. MacC. Armstrong, "Trial by Combat Among the Greeks," *Greece and Rome*, 19, 56, June 1950, pp. 73–89, uses the term "trial by combat" while referring to episodes which, in the present volume, are included under single combat and combat of champions. So does P. Wilutzky, *Vorgeschichte des Rechts*, Berlin: Trewendt, 1903, pp. 137–40.

Celtic and Germanic law. Quite often it is linked to ordeals by iron, water or fire, and indeed too many modern writers treat the two things as if they were one. Livy, the Roman historian whom we have met many times, describes a dispute between two Iberian chieftains, Corbis and his nephew Orsua, both of whom wanted to rule a city by the name of Ibis. Refusing the offer of the Roman representative on the spot, Scipio (later called Africanus) to mediate, they declared that only the war-god Mars could judge between them. With Scipio presiding, a single combat was arranged from which Corbis, as the older and more experienced of the two, emerged victorious. The year was 206 BC or thereabout.[2] A similar story comes from Livy's slightly younger contemporary, the historian Velleius Paterculus. He tells us that the Germans of his own day practiced the custom and that the Roman commander on the spot, Quintilius Varus, sought to suppress it but failed.[3] This was the same Varus who in AD 9, led three legions into the Teutoburg Forest, not far from modern Wuerzburg, and was defeated and killed.

Our next reference is a decree issued by the Burgundian King Gundobald in 501. In it he reconfirmed the custom, assuming it had ever been abandoned. The relevant passage reads as follows:[4]

> We know that many of our people have become depraved through the failure of litigation and through an instinct of cupidity, to the extent that they do not hesitate to offer oaths in uncertain matters and to perjure themselves over known facts. In order to undermine this criminal habit we decree by the present law that whenever a case arises among our people, and he who is accused denies on oath that the thing in question should be sought from him or that he is responsible for the crime, then ... license to fight will not be denied ... since it is right that if anyone says that he knows the truth of the matter without doubt and offers to take the oath, he should not refuse to fight ... [all in order] that men may delight more in truth than perjury.

Clearly this was not simply a piece of barbaric stupidity on the king's part. Rather, the decree seems to have served two distinct objectives. First, the declared intention was to put an end to, or at any rate reduce, the number of false accusations by making both parties in a dispute back up their claims with their lives.[5] This in turn rested on the idea, characteristic of the Middle Ages, that law was not simply a system arbitrarily made by men but reflected God's will; thus understood, trial by combat was simply a way of discovering what that

---

[2] Livy, *History of Rome*, 28.21.5–10.

[3] Velleius Paterculus, in *Compendium of Roman History*, LCL, 1924, 2.117–18.

[4] Quoted in P. Fouracre, "'Placita' and the Settlement of Disputes in Later Merovingian Francia," in W. Davies and P. Fouracre, eds., *The Settlement of Disputes in Early Medieval Europe*, Cambridge University Press, 1986, p. 16.

[5] See on all this G. Neilson, *Trial by Combat*, New York: Macmillan, 1891, pp. 3–14.

will was. Second, trial by battle, a formal occasion if ever there was one, was meant to replace the feuding that was part of tribal life and, going on almost without interruption, was always threatening to get out of hand. To that extent it served to limit violence and subject it to a well-defined set of rules. It may, indeed, be seen as a step towards a more centralized system of government.

In an age when near-universal illiteracy made written proof of anything hard to get, other peoples, too, practiced the custom. It is found among the Franks, the Saxons, and the Frisians. Like the Burgundians, all these tribes originated in northern Germany and Scandinavia. Some migrated into lands that had previously formed part of the Roman Empire, whereas others remained behind. Among the latter were the Danes: Saxo Grammaticus, the late twelfth-century Danish chronicler, quotes the (legendary) King of Denmark, Frothi III as saying that, in adjudicating a dispute, swords were more trustworthy than words.[6] In sharp contrast to some early modern duels, the fights were neither standardized nor genteel. To the contrary, they were good occasions for berserkers to go into a fury, real or pretend, bellowing, hitting out in all directions, even biting. Perhaps the most deadly of them was the so-called "girth fight" in which the combatants, strapped together, were literally compelled to fight to the death.[7]

From Denmark the custom spread to Norway, home of the Vikings. The latter may have brought it to Muscovite Russia, as well as Iceland, which was known as the Wild West of the Scandinavian world during the Middle Ages.[8] At issue were disputes over land and – how could it be otherwise? – women. It also reached England, though whether this was before or after 1066 is moot.[9] William the Conqueror decreed that persons accused of perjury, murder, homicide, or robbery would be allowed to defend themselves as they preferred, i.e. either by the ordeal of carrying the hot iron or by combat. By the time of Domesday Book (1086) disputes over land could be settled "vel bello vel judicio" – either by combat or by ordeal.[10] Special regulations were made to cover cases when Normans challenged Englishmen, or the other way around. To this day, some circular plots on the Shetlands are known as battle *punds* (pounds), or enclosures.

It was from the Latin word *calumnies*, meaning false accusation, that the term "challenge" was derived. Challenges could arise not merely from civil

[6] Saxo Grammaticus, *The History of the Danes*, p. 143.
[7] Kiernan, *The Duel in European History*, p. 29.
[8] H. W. Dewey, "Trial by Combat in Muscovite Russia," *Oxford Slavonic Papers*, 9, 1960, pp. 21–31; G. Jones, "The Religious Elements of the Icelandic Holmganga," *Modern Language Review*, 27, 3, July 1932, pp. 307–13.
[9] Neilson, *Trial by Combat*, pp. 31–3, 251–4; J. E. R. Stephens, "The Growth of Trial by Jury in England," *Harvard Law Review*, 10, 3, 1896, pp. 153, 155; M. J. Russell, "I. Trial by Battle and the Writ of Right," *Journal of Legal History*, 1, 2, 1980, p. 112.
[10] *Domesday Book*, G. Marin and A. Williams, trans., London: Penguin, 2004, 2.146, 2.176, 2.277b, 2.190.

cases, as one would expect, but from criminal ones too. In the words of a late nineteenth-century English historian whose work appears to be the only full-length study of the subject, the method was

> a remedy for nearly every wrong that flesh is heir to. Nothing was too high for it, nothing too low. It would establish the virtue of a queen, test the veracity of a witness, or re-argue the decision of a judge; it would hand a disputed point of succession, give a widow her dower, or prove a questioned charter. It was also used to settle issues arising out of debts.[11]

As well as serving as a substitute for a trial, combat could take place as a result of it and as a follow-up on it. That was because contemporary convention permitted a defendant to accuse one of his judges, who in a seigniorial court would be his peers, of "false judgment," and demand the right to fight him. Naturally not all judges relished the thought of having to uphold their verdict in this style. To avoid doing so, they might very well deliver it collectively.

In England trial by combat was only allowed in cases when the litigants were of equal rank. Thus a lord could not fight his vassal or a master his servant. The one exception to this rule was treason. In Wales, a country with many peculiarities (in case of a challenge, twins counted as a single person so that two persons fought one), things were reversed: here it was considered that, in case of treason, trial by combat was the *only* mode of prosecution befitting a lord's dignity. In Germany any man could challenge any other who was his equal by birth. But whereas a superior, challenged by an inferior, could refuse the challenge, the opposite did not apply. It was possible to challenge a dead man, but a challenge delivered after the clock had struck twelve was invalid unless the proceedings had started earlier in the day.[12] French noblemen were allowed to challenge villeins, but only on condition that they used the villeins' weapons, i.e. a staff and a shield, and fought on foot. Understandably few chose to do so.

Other restrictions also applied. Making clergymen fight had always been problematic, and in England at any rate they were formally exempted from 1176 on. This put them on a par with women, men under fourteen or over sixty years old, and disabled men. The rules that governed such cases were extremely detailed. They referred to physical defects such as the loss of an eye or an ear, or crooked fingers, or a broken arm. For obvious reasons, castration too was considered a handicap. So was being without teeth, given how useful they were in a fight. Some jurists went further still, distinguishing between different kinds of teeth such as front teeth and molars: the loss of the former constituted "mayhem" whereas loss of the latter did not. The rules in question acted like a

[11] See, for the quote and for what follows, Neilson, *Trial by Combat*, pp. 5–7, 36–53.
[12] *The Saxon Mirror: A "Sachsenspiegel" of the Fourteenth Century*, M. Dobozy, trans., Philadelphia: University of Pennsylvania Press, 1999, pp. 87–8.

one-way street. Though some people did not have to fight if challenged, there was nothing to prevent them if they chose to do so. At least one English case is known when a man of seventy insisted on his right to do combat. He succeeded in obtaining the court's permission to do so, whereupon his opponent promptly withdrew.[13]

In England persons who had gained an exemption from combat were tried by a jury of their neighbors, whereas in other countries holding the trial was the task of the responsible magistrates. In all countries, defendants unable to obtain an exemption but unwilling to fight would have to find a champion who would take their place. In theory, paying a champion was prohibited by law. In practice it went on all the time, giving rise to a class of professional champions ready to answer challengers. Early in the thirteenth century a certain William Copeland is mentioned in connection with no fewer than eight combats that were held in places as far apart as Yorkshire and Somerset over a period of seventeen years. Others had even longer careers.[14] By that time such men had become sufficiently numerous for "Champion" to serve as a well-known surname. The same happened in Germany where they were known as Kempfs. Like gladiators, Kempfs and champions were not highly regarded, socially speaking. Paradoxically in view of their calling, they might even suffer from curtailed legal capacity.[15] Either they would charge on a case-by-case basis or be put on a retainer. Here and there a master might try to use his servants as champions by inciting them to serve separate complaints against his rival whom he did not care to fight in person. Understandably such practices, if they were discovered, were not exactly favored by the courts.

Jews, too, formed a category of their own.[16] Both Charlemagne and his son Louis the Pious issued capitularies that exempted Jews from having to undergo ordeals by fire and by water. Yet neither ruler specifically mentioned trial by combat. One tenth-century case is known when a convert to Christianity accused the Jewish community of Limoges of "destroying" (leshahet, in Hebrew) the local lord and demanded that they send a champion to fight it out with him. He refused to accept the Jewish offer of "lots of money, gold and silver," but since the manuscript that is our sole source is incomplete we do not know how the story ended. The issue must have continued to preoccupy contemporaries, for it is mentioned in two thirteenth-century German sources, the *Schwabenspiegel* and the *Meissner Rechtbuch*. The former denies a Jew the right to challenge a Christian but obliges him to answer a challenge issued by a

[13] M. J. Russell, "II. Trial by Battle and the Appeals of Felony," *Journal of Legal History*, 1, 2, 1980, p. 140.
[14] R. W. Ireland, "First Catch Your Toad: Medieval Attitudes to Ordeal and Battle," *Cambrian Law Review*, 50, 1990, p. 55.
[15] *The Saxon Mirror*, pp. 80, 82.
[16] See S. Eidelberg, "Trial by Combat in Medieval Jewish History," *Proceedings of the American Academy for Jewish Research*, 46–7, 1928–9, pp. 8–19.

Christian. The latter grants Jews the right to judicial combat, but only with the aid of a champion.

In 1244 we find the Duke of Austria not only exempting Jews from having to fight but promising to provide them with a champion in case they suspect somebody of having murdered one of their own number. It is worth adding that the laws in question were not intended to favor the Jews. To the contrary: one thirteenth-century commentator on the *Sachsenspiegel* explains that whereas weapons were forbidden to priests because of their honor, Jews were barred from using them owing to the ignominy in which they lived.[17] Around 1285 in England, a poor Jew who had apparently been accused of something and challenged to battle asked to do it in London because of the bias he expected in Oxford. Nothing seems to have come of it, however, since at the time when Edward I expelled the Jews five years later he was still in prison.[18]

A prominent feature of most modern legal systems is the use of state witnesses. Normally they are lesser criminals who are promised less severe punishment or immunity in return for testifying against their former, presumably more important, bosses and accomplices. During the period under consideration a similar function was sometimes filled by so-called approvers – convicted criminals who agreed to meet a number of malefactors in separate duels. They were needed, one source tells us, because of the vast number of desperate criminals.[19] Apparently there were even some female approvers. To ensure approvers would indeed make an appearance and fight, they were often held in prison and only released just before the fight. Those who won the number of duels specified in their contracts received a pardon; those who were killed died; and those who surrendered often also died. Cynics might say that the system made use of undesirables to take care of other undesirables and that a better method for getting rid of undesirables remains to be devised. In practice it led to numerous cases of false accusation, which is why it was gradually abolished from about 1300 on.

As in ordinary courts of law, a detailed set of rules was developed over time specifying how to proceed. The first step was to issue a challenge. This was done formally by one side throwing down a gauntlet and the other picking it up, all in the presence of judges authorized for the purpose. Next, both parties had to find friends or neighbors who would stand bail in case they failed to present themselves: those who did so lost their cases and were heavily fined as well. Originally it was the challenger who had the choice of weapons, but later that privilege was transferred to the defending party. In Germany it was the judge's duty to provide poor defendants with sword and buckler.[20] The judge or judges would also decide on a time and a place. The latter was known as the *champ clos* or closed field. For example, London had Tothill Field and Smithfield,

---

[17] See G. Kisch, *The Jews in Medieval Germany*, University of Chicago Press, 1949, p. 128.
[18] Russell, "II. Trial by Battle and the Appeals of Felony," p. 140.
[19] Ireland, "First Catch Your Toad," p. 57.   [20] *The Saxon Mirror*, p. 88.

apparently selected for their proximity to the courts at Westminster and the prison at Newgate, respectively. Each of these provided a piece of level ground 60 yards square, double rails to hold back spectators, a dais for seating the judges, bars for the sergeants at arms, and tiered scaffolding for the public. Behind the tiers were located the tents or pavilions where the combatants could make their preparations and, if they won, or at any rate survived, retire after the fight. Most combats took place in similar public installations; however, great lords, secular and ecclesiastical, were sometimes permitted to have their own private fields and fight in them.

In all this, great care was taken to ensure equity and what today might be called transparency. Each protagonist had to swear a solemn oath that his case was just. In case he lost, that meant he would automatically be held guilty of perjury as well. Things were so arranged that neither combatant would have the sun in his eyes. The use of concealed weapons was prohibited. So was wearing magic prayers and charms on one's body; if it is true that the combats were understood as the judgment of God, it is also true that supernatural interference was forbidden and, to the extent possible, prevented. To ensure that no illicit objects were smuggled in, the combatants were strip-searched and had their heads shaved. During the fight itself the ordinary rules of a court of law applied. For any onlooker to do anything to hinder fair play or even to make a noise was an offense; in this respect trial by combat differed sharply from single combat and combat of champions where cheers and groans were not only permitted but expected.

By Scottish law, anybody who interfered with a fight could be punished by imprisonment or else by the loss of life or limb. The thirteenth-century *Sachsenspiegel* prescribed the death penalty for such conduct.[21] In one recorded English case of 1255, a spectator drew a combatant's attention to a pit into which he was about to fall, possibly saving his life. Since the warning was taken up by many others the original caller could not be discovered; however, the magistrate in charge did avail himself of the opportunity to impose a fine on everybody present. As in modern soccer matches, disorder sometimes reached the point where the fight had to be discontinued. Yet the system of sureties and fines also meant that trial by combat could be very profitable for those in charge. As late as the reign of Edward I, i.e. the last quarter of the thirteenth century, it appeared to be an important source of revenue in the royal accounts.

As one might expect from a custom practiced by so many different peoples for so many years, the forms of combat varied considerably. Early Celtic and Germanic warriors probably followed their normal military methods, fighting on foot while using swords and bucklers as their weapons. Later, as cavalry established itself as the arm of the noble and the rich, some of the socially more prominent protagonists entered the field on horseback. At the other end of the

[21] Russell, "I. Trial by Battle and the Writ of Right," p. 115; *The Saxon Mirror*, p. 88.

scale, the poor, unable to afford proper weapons, presented themselves armed with staves, clubs, stones, and knives. A common tactic they used was to throw sand into each other's eyes. Occasionally a woman was allowed to challenge a man, in which case she would have to hire a champion. Very occasionally a woman was allowed to fight a man, in which case the latter was handicapped by being chained to a peg in the ground or else by being buried in a pit up to his waist.[22] In contrast to the gladiatorial games, and as far as I could determine from the literature, it does not appear that women were made to face women.

Unlike "nonsense fights" and some kinds of tournaments, but like single combat, combat of champions, and gladiatorial shows, the fight went on without respite or interruption. It lasted until one side was either killed or called out "craven," meaning that he admitted defeat and "craved" the victor's mercy. God's "verdict" having been pronounced in this way, as in any court of law the judge or judges would pass sentence on the loser. If he was dead already his property might also be confiscated. If he was not yet dead, he might be executed. A coffin stood by to receive the body, which would later be disposed of in the most ignominious way possible. However, it is only fair to add that not all combats were fought to the death and that lighter sentences, mainly consisting of fines, were sometimes imposed. Especially in civil cases, combats that ended by one party being killed appear to have been quite rare.

Most, but not all, trials were fought on a one-against-one basis. In Germany there seem to have been occasions when seven fought against seven, apparently not in a melee but in a series of duels; however, the relevant passage in the *Saxon Mirror* is obscure and we do not know just how it was done and why.[23] Perhaps the largest known group combat took place near Perth in Scotland in 1396. The protagonists were the clans of Chattan and Kay, though the exact cause of their quarrel has been lost. Each side mustered thirty men who were supposed to fight to the death. However, the proceedings had to be halted when it turned out that one man on the Chattan side had absconded. At length a volunteer was found who agreed to fight on condition that, should he survive, his sustenance would be guaranteed to the end of his days.

On the appointed day an immense crowd, headed by King Robert III of Scotland, gathered. With him came countless Scottish, English, and French knights. Each combatant carried a sword, a battleaxe, a dirk, and, most unusually – this, after all, was Scotland, a relatively backward country – a bow with three arrows. Defensive armor was not allowed, perhaps because few would be able to afford it. Stripped to the waist, they waited for the signal. We are told they slew each other "as butchers slay bullocks in the shambles." As evening brought the battle to an end, fifty out of the sixty combatants lay dead and the Clan Chattan's eight survivors had gained a victory. Tongue in cheek, our nineteenth-century historian adds: "It is not for one moment credible that

[22] Wilutzky, *Vorgeschichte des Rechts*, p. 139.   [23] The *Saxon Mirror*, p. 96.

these brave highlanders butchered each other in vain – to make a royal holiday."[24]

Given its nature as an offense committed when no others are present, and also in view of the important role that "women's honor" has played in the lives of all peoples at all times and places, it is hardly surprising that many cases involved rape, real or alleged. The most famous case of this kind unfolded in France in 1385–6 and is known to us from Froissart as well as numerous other sources.[25] The story started when Marguerite, the young and beautiful wife of a Norman nobleman, Jean de Carrouges, told her husband that during his absence from their chateau she had been raped. The perpetrator was one Jacques Le Gris, another nobleman well known to the couple. Though inferior in rank, he was wealthier and better connected. Carrouges' first step was to ask for justice at the hands of the local count. Having failed to get it, he went to Paris, consulted a lawyer, and begged the youthful King Charles VI to allow him to confront his enemy in a trial of battle. The matter was referred to Parliament which launched a formal inquest, and after several months' deliberations granted the request: clearly it was felt that, in the absence of witnesses, combat was the only way to find out the truth. Preparations were made to hold the event at Saint-Martin-des-Champs, a well-known Paris monastery. Its extensive grounds included a large field long used for the purpose and capable of holding as many as 10,000 spectators.

On December 29, 1386 a huge crowd gathered. In attendance were the king, his uncles, members of the high nobility, senior prelates and magistrates, and thousands of others. The most important spectator was Marguerite herself. Dressed in black and seated in a black carriage, she would face immediate execution (by burning) for bringing false accusations if her husband lost his fight. Carrouges approached her and asked her once again whether she had spoken the truth. Upon her answering in the affirmative, the couple kissed. Mounted on horseback and armed in the manner of knights, the protagonists entered the field. They repeated their respective charges and denials for all to see and hear, swore that their cause was just, and, heeded the herald's thrice-repeated call, "Faites vos devoirs." A final command, "Laissez les aller" ("Let them go") was issued and the fight began. The third time they charged, the lances broke and the combatants took out their battleaxes. First the horse Carrouges was riding was killed, then Le Gris' mount. Now they fought on foot, using their swords, and Carrouges was injured in the leg. He was nevertheless able to seize Le Gris by the helmet and hurl him to the ground where his armor prevented him from getting up. He was, however, so well protected that Carrouges could not kill him. The two rolled on the ground, fighting with

---

[24] Neilson, *Trial by Combat*, p. 14.
[25] See, for what follows, E. Jager, *The Last Duel: A True Story of Crime, Scandal and Trial by Combat in Medieval France*, New York: Broadway, 2004, *passim*.

daggers while Carrouges called on his enemy to surrender. Le Gris refused, until in the end he was killed by a stab to the chin.

The fight over, the victory ceremony could begin. First Carrouges turned and asked whether he had done his duty and was told that indeed he had. Next he approached the king and fell on his knees to thank him for graciously allowing justice to be done. Charles raised him, presented him with ten thousand francs, and made him a gentleman of the chamber with a pension of two hundred francs for life. He also ordered his own physicians to look after him. Reunited with Marguerite, Carrouges rode south from Saint-Martin-des-Champs to the church of Notre-Dame where he planned to offer his thanks to God. Meanwhile Le Gris' corpse, stripped of armor, was carried from the field feet first. It was delivered to the public executioner who threw it on a horse-drawn sled and had it dragged to the Porte Saint-Denis and beyond the city walls to Montfaucon, the place where criminals used to be executed. There it was hanged.[26]

Another case was fought out at Valenciennes in 1455 and brought out of obscurity by Huizinga who uses the contemporary Burgundian chronicler Chastellain as his source.[27] This time the adversaries were burghers, the plaintiff Jacotin Plouvier and the defendant Mahuot. Both had their heads shaved and both were sewn up in cordwain dresses of a single piece that did not provide a hold. Both were accompanied into the arena by their fencing masters, and the chronicler notes that both were very pale. Both saluted the old duke, Philip the Good, who had insisted on being present. Servants came up and smeared them with grease. They rubbed their hands with ashes and took sugar in their mouths. Armed with staffs and bucklers, which were painted with the images of saints, they went for each other. Mahuot, the smaller man, used his buckler to throw sand in Plouvier's face. Plouvier seized him, filled his eyes and mouth with sand, and thrust his thumb into Mahuot's eye to make him let go one of his fingers which the latter was biting. Next Plouvier twisted Mahuot's arms, jumped on his back, and tried to break it. Mahuot appealed to the duke for mercy; though some pages are missing from the manuscript at this point, his cries do not seem to have availed him since he ended up half dead and in the hands of the executioner.

By this time, the middle years of the fifteenth century, the custom of trial by combat had already been in existence for over nine hundred years – counting from Gundobald's decree, which formalized it but almost certainly did not mark its beginning. Throughout that period it had met with opposition. As early as 713–35 the Lombard chieftain Liutprand tried to limit it: possibly this reflected the fact that northern Italy was already beginning to draw ahead of the rest of Europe, that literacy was spreading, and that other methods of proof

---

[26] Froissart, *Chronicles*, pp. 113–14.
[27] J. Huizinga, *The Waning of the Middle Ages*, Harmondsworth: Penguin, 1965 [1924], pp. 98–9.

were becoming available.[28] In England attempts to do so started during the twelfth century under Henry I (reigned 1100–35). While leaving criminal justice alone, the king ordained that in civil cases combat would be limited to disputes with a value of ten shillings or more. Later, during the thirteenth century, it became established that parties to a civil dispute who were challenged to a duel might decline and entrust the matter to a jury made up of his neighbors.[29] Throughout the later Middle Ages the kind of crime or dispute for which trial by combat was available kept being restricted. After 1250 or so criminals caught red-handed – "mainour," to use the pidgin French expression that was current at the time – were denied the right to fight. A hundred years later Scottish law still allowed them to do so, but only in case of capital offenses secretly or treacherously committed.

As one would expect, many objections came from the church. Some of the earliest on record were voiced by Agobard, Archbishop of Lyon, probably at some time between AD 800 and 840.[30] Still the church's opposition was not always as strong or consistent as the written protests of some ecclesiastics would suggest. Most clergymen understandably made use of their right to exemption. Some, however, preferred to hire champions, and there were even occasions when they fought in person. To mention a few episodes only, in 1165 Pope Alexander III ruled that a priest who had lost part of a finger in a duel should not be disqualified but could continue to celebrate mass. Though individuals might express their scruples, there was seldom any problem finding a priest who would administer oaths before the fight started and grant a participant absolution after it was over. Cases are even known when trial by combat was used to settle points of Christian doctrine. The Fourth Lateran Council of 1215 denounced the custom, to little effect. In 1251 we find the Abbot of Meaux, east of Paris, hiring no fewer than seven champions, presumably in an effort to prevent them from serving his enemies.[31] As late as 1404 Pope Innocent VII was requested to adjudicate in a duel between two kings, an offer he graciously declined. Throughout the combat between Plouvier and Mahuot the church bells kept ringing.

Another factor working against judicial combat was the revival of Roman law which began during the twelfth century. This particular opposition centered in the universities, which were located in the towns, which were inhabited by burghers who did not like the custom very much. The first English town to gain exemption, presumably after having paid King Henry II a suitable sum, was

[28] C. Wickham, "Land Disputes and their Social Framework in Lombard-Carolingian Italy, 700–900," in Davies and Fouracre, The Settlement of Disputes in Early Medieval Europe, p. 113.
[29] Neilson, Trial by Combat, pp. 33–6.
[30] See Eidelberg, "Trial by Combat in Medieval Jewish History," p. 107.
[31] Ireland, "First Catch Your Toad," p. 55.

Bury St. Edmunds in 1182. It was followed by Norwich (1193), Lincoln (1194), London (1199), Northampton (1200), Rochester (1227), Warenmouth (1247), Canterbury (1256), Melcombe (1280), Devizes (1331) and Bedford (1394). Ireland and Scotland, though more backward than England, followed a similar pattern.[32] As both church and towns gradually turned their faces against it, trial by battle was increasingly confined to the upper classes whose privilege, as well as duty, it long remained. Much later the same was true of the duel, the difference between the two being that duels, instead of being part of a formal process of law, acted as a substitute for it, and to some extent against it.

Across the Channel in France things were moving in the same direction. A significant step was taken in 1256 when Enguerrand IV, Sieur de Coucy and one of the greatest nobles of the realm, was accused of having hanged three squires whom he had caught as they engaged in poaching game. Appearing before King Louis IX, Enguerrand insisted on his right to challenge his accuser to trial by battle, but was rebuffed. After a long and complicated investigation Enguerrand was tried and found guilty. If he was not executed then this was due solely to the intervention of some of his peers who sensed a threat to their own privileges and advised the king against such a step.[33] In the event, the decisive move towards restricting trial by combat was made by Philip the Handsome in 1306. Under his laws, it could only take place provided (1) the crime, whether homicide or treason, was "notorious and certain"; (2) it carried the death sentence; (3) combat was the only means of obtaining conviction and punishment; and (4) the accused was notoriously suspected of having committed the deed. To make sure his wishes were respected Philip reserved the right to authorize it to his own person, which of course meant added bureaucratic difficulties and long delays.

In Germany, criticism of the custom may have surfaced for the first time in Heinrich von dem Tuerlin's *Diu Crône* ("The Crown"), which was written around 1230.[34] The poem deals with the court of King Arthur and may have been intended as a satire on it; if this interpretation is correct, then the author objected to trial by combat precisely because, in his view, it was disrespectful of the noble ideals of chivalry. In any case such a deeply rooted custom could not be eradicated at once. Throughout the fourteenth century, knights continued to receive safe conducts in case they wanted to fight other noblemen with whom their own lords were at war. That was especially true in the borderlands between England and Scotland where judicial combats were more frequent than anywhere else.[35] In 1380 Sir John Annesley, an English knight, accused his squire,

---

[32] See Russell, "I. Trial by Battle and the Writ of Right," pp. 118–19, 131–2.
[33] M. Wade Labargue, *St. Louis*, Boston, MA: Little, Brown, 1968, pp. 175–6.
[34] See on this L. Jillings, "Ordeal by Combat and the Rejection of Chivalry in *Diu Crône*," *Speculum*, 51, 2, April 1976, pp. 262–76.
[35] Neilson, *Trial by Combat*, pp. 161–4 and 218–24.

Thomas Katrington, of having committed treason. When the trial by battle took place at Tothill Field, far more people came to watch it than had turned out to witness the coronation of Richard II three years earlier. Approvers are still occasionally referred to even during the fifteenth century. In 1487, so many persons accused of murder were waiting for their trials that the period during which they were allowed to demand the right to clear themselves by combat had to be extended.[36]

The last judicial duel fought on English soil took place in 1492 in the presence of Henry VII, victor of the Wars of the Roses and founder of the Tudor dynasty.[37] For Scotland, Spain, and France the dates are 1426, 1522, and 1547 respectively. The French case even gave the language a new phrase, the "coup de Journac." It was named after a combatant who delivered the underhand blow that decided the last licensed fight in that country. Just two years earlier, the Council of Trent had still seen fit to rain fire and brimstone on rulers and magistrates who authorized the encounters. In fact, trials that had the epithet "the last" applied to them are as numerous as pieces of the True Cross. In England in 1631 trial by combat was reintroduced in cases involving treason. Seven years later judges confirmed it as a legitimate procedure even in disputes over property.[38] By that time combats that were not only announced but actually fought had become rare indeed. Nevertheless two attempts, made in 1770 and in 1774 respectively, to make Parliament legislate the institution out of existence did not succeed.

This not so benign neglect made possible what may truly have been "the last" challenge of all. It took place in 1818 when the violated body of a young woman named Mary Ashford was found in a pit near Edinburgh where she had been drowned. The putative murderer, Abraham Thornton, was quickly arrested, but a jury believed his alibi and acquitted him. Mary's brother William would not accept the verdict and launched an appeal. Thornton was rearrested, whereupon he demanded trial by battle as his right. Seeing that it had never been formally terminated, the responsible court had no choice but to grant his request. In the event Ashford refused the challenge so that the battle never took place. Well knowing that public opinion was against him, Thornton left the country to start a new life in the United States. The next year Parliament finally took action and abolished the custom once and for all.[39]

The exercise of justice has always been closely bound up with ritual, and this was no less true during the Middle Ages than in any other historical period

---

[36] Russell, "II. Trial by Combat and the Appeals of Felony," p. 137.
[37] Neilson, *Trial by Combat*, pp. 64–5, 203.
[38] J. S. A. Adamson, "The Baronial Context of the English Civil War," *Transactions of the Royal Historical Society*, 5th series, 40, 1990, p. 93.
[39] See for this entire story J. Hall, *The Trial of Abraham Thornton*, London: Hodge, 1926.

before or since.[40] Then as now, litigants and their representatives who did not play by the rules or use the correct formulae were not even allowed to submit their case, let alone argue it. As with any other trial, there was an accuser and a defender. Once the legal problems had been resolved and a trial by combat decided upon, it was scheduled to be fought at the designated time and place. The fight went on in deadly earnest with the best weapons the parties could afford until one side was either killed or called it quits. Yet this seriousness did not prevent the event from being preceded, accompanied, and concluded by elaborate ceremonies that marked it as a special occasion, clearly and carefully separated from "ordinary" life. Precisely because it was a question of life and death, perhaps more than in many other kinds of games everything was done to ensure equity and transparency. Steps were also taken to rule out any possibility of interference on the part of spectators, gods, and devils. But for all these rituals and rules, the trials would have counted as skirmishing at best and as murder at worst. As it was, throngs of spectators regarded them as entertainment pure and simple, discussing the proceedings, carefully studying every move and every gesture, and placing bets.

As the special regulations concerning the Jews show only too clearly, trial by combat was considered both a privilege and a duty. Certainly from the beginning of the twelfth century, and quite possibly earlier too, there were always persons and organizations who expressed their doubts about the system. Either they opposed it as a matter of principle, as the church sometimes did; or else they did what they could to have the powers that be grant them exemption from it. Following its demise, which for practical purposes occurred between about 1450 and 1550, historians seeking to show just how "rude," "superstitious," "weak," and "barbarous" our ancestors were have often referred to the custom as proof par excellence.[41] As one of them wrote, "well it is that those days have gone forever!"[42] Yet human nature has not changed. False claims and counterclaims are no less easily made, no less frequent, and no easier to refute at the present time than in Gundobald's day. Nor do courts find it easier to get at the truth, especially but by no means exclusively when it is a case of the word of one person against that of another. In view of that fact, as well as the lighthearted way in which certain heads of state with no judge above them occasionally send their troops to fight and die for nothing at all, one sometimes wishes it still persisted.

---

[40] See on this E. Cohen, *The Crossroads of Justice: Law and Culture in Late Medieval France*, Leiden: Brill, 1993, pp. 54–73.

[41] These are the terms used by J. P. Gilchrist, *A Brief Display of the Origins of Ordeals . . . and the Decision of Private Quarrels by Single Combat*, London: by the author, 1821, p. 26.

[42] J. B. Hurry, *The Trial by Combat of Henry de Essex and Robert de Monfort at Reading Abbey*, London: Elliot, 1919, p. 26.

The rise and fall of the tournament

Like so much else in the Middle Ages, the origin of the tournament (*hastilude*, "lance game," in Latin) is unknown. Writing some two centuries after the events he describes, Theophanes the Confessor, a Byzantine chronicler, says that the Emperor Herakleios (reigned, 610–43) trained his cavalry by dividing it into two groups which collided with each other and fought without danger. However, the text is cryptic and does not explain how it was done.[43] In the ninth century Nithart, as well as Widukind of Corvey a hundred years after him, tells of cavalry exercises held in the courts of Charlemagne (whose grandson Nithart was) and King Henry I of Germany respectively.[44] Since sharp weapons were not used, the exercises may have resembled maneuvers – known, in the late Middle Ages, as *behourds* – more than they did tournaments proper.[45]

To confuse matters still further, some *behourds* did have victors, entailing competition of some sort. Some authorities believe they were designed to demonstrate equestrian skill, including the kind of skill needed to maintain formation, use weapons, etc. Others assume that they were scripted to replicate historical events. Either method would explain why care was not always taken to have equal numbers on each side, but it is hard to be sure. Nor does it matter much, since many *behourds* seem to have got out of hand to the point where they involved fighting and resembled tournaments in all but name.[46] As if to emphasize the ever-present danger of escalation, the same also applies to the *vesprii* that were sometimes held on the eve of the "real" combat.

In Wolfram von Eschenbach's *Parsifal*, an early thirteenth-century source, so ferociously did the knights go after each other during the *vesprii* that the tournament proper had to be cancelled. The issue is further confused by the fact that many chroniclers, who are our chief source of information, worked for members of the nobility. In this capacity they sometimes antedated "the first" tournaments so as to enable their patrons' ancestors to take part in them and garner the glory of doing so: as a result, the question is unlikely to ever receive a

---

[43] *The Chronicle of Theophanes Confessor*, C. A. Mango, trans., New York: Oxford University Press, 1997, no. 303, p. 435, and no. 304, p. 436. See also E. N. Luttwak, *The Grand Strategy of the Byzantine Army*, Cambridge, MA: Belknap Press, 2009, pp. 10 and 397.

[44] Nithart, *Historiae*, E. Mueller, ed., in *Ausgewaehlte Quellen zur deutschen Geschichte des Mittelalters*, vol. V: *Quellen zur Karolingischen Reichsgeschichte*, Darmstadt: Wissenschaftliche Buchgesellschaft, 1955, p. 442; Widukind of Corvey, *Res gestae Saxonicae*, H. P. Lohman, ed., *ibid.*, p. 78.

[45] See for the *behourd*, or *buhurt* as it is sometimes spelled, J. B. Bumke, *Hoefische Kultur: Literatur und Gesellschaft im hohen Mittelalter*, Munich: Deutsche Taschenbuch Verlag, 1986, pp. 357–60.

[46] See the description in Ulrich von Lichtenstein, *Frauendienst*, Klagenfurt: Wiesler, 2000 [*c.* 1255], pp. 89–92.

definite answer. Different sources do not even agree as to whether the first fatal casualty was one Arnold, brother-in-law to Roger, Count of Sicily (1066), or Count Henry III of Louvain (1095). The latter, we are told, "was hit in the heart by a lance and died instantly" in the course of a *militaris ludus*.[47]

One modern authority has suggested that tournaments grew out of the previously described single combats and combats of champions: in other words that they turned the business of war into the pleasures of peace.[48] However that may be, it is clear that around 1100 the custom had become firmly established. As expressions such as "French combat," "fighting in the French manner," and the word "tournament" itself testify, it first took hold in northern France. From there it spread into the Low Countries and Germany, helping turn French into the language of war and chivalry, a position it retained for some eight hundred years. Tournaments were not entirely unknown in England either; however, kings Henry I and Henry II (1154–89) seem to have been fairly successful in suppressing them so that English knights who wished to participate had to travel across the Channel. Richard I (the Lionheart) (1189–99) permitted them, but only if they were held at certain designated locations and only if the organizers paid a fee to the royal exchequer. We even know the name of the person who was appointed to collect the money in question.[49] By that time they had developed into a real craze so that the career of no knight, real or imaginary, was complete without him having participated in them. By and large, the more active a man's military career the more numerous the tournaments in which he participated.

Early tournaments were spontaneous occasions, organized by individuals who invited their friends to come and play. To some extent this remained the case later too; in particular, sieges, which were often long and boring, were enlivened by tournaments. Both sides would agree to temporarily put their hostility aside and have a little fun instead. Sometimes it was a question of celebrating some special event such as a noble birth, wedding, knighting, or anniversary. For example, in 1284 Edward I held a tournament at Caernarvon in order to celebrate the birth of the first English Prince of Wales, later to reign as Edward II. However, that was by no means always the case. Invitations were sent out three to six weeks ahead of time. Either a circular was published or people were invited by name. One letter dating to 1215, written by a group of English barons addressed to the German knight William von Albine, read as

---

[47] *Chronicon Turoniensis*, quoted in J. R. V. Barker, *The Tournament in England, 1100–1400*, Woodbridge: Boydell, 1986, p. 5; *Passio Karoli comitis*, quoted in Bumke, *Hoefische Kultur*, p. 342.

[48] S. Muhlberger, *Jousts and Tournaments*, Union City, CA: Jousts and Chivalry, 2002, p. 20.

[49] William of Newburgh, "Historia Rerum Anglicarum," in *Chronicles of the Reigns of Stephen, Henry II and Richard I*, R. Howlett, ed., London: Rolls Series, 1885, vol. II, pp. 422–3.

follows: "We greet you and strongly urge that you will present yourself at the tournament in question, complete with horses and weapons, in such a manner that you may leave with your honor intact."[50] Froissart quotes a similar letter that went out in 1390, i.e. in the middle of the Hundred Years War:

> we [three French knights] ... beg all those noble knights and foreign [including English] squires who are willing to come not to imagine for a moment that we are doing this [i.e. issuing the invitation] out of pride, hatred or malice, but in order to have the honor of their company and to get to know them better, a thing which we desire with our whole hearts. And none of our shields shall be covered with iron or steel, nor shall there be any unfair advantage, fraud, trickery, or evil design, nor anything not approved by those appointed by both sides to guard the lists.[51]

One cannot help recalling the alleged motto of modern soldiers of fortune: "meet interesting people – and kill them."

Another area that often saw tournaments held between knights belonging to different nations and involved in campaigning against each other was the border between England and Scotland, a region well known for the intermittent warfare that took place there. The men's motives for taking up the challenge and responding to the invitations varied. Partly it was the simple desire to compete and excel in an approximation of what was, after all, the calling of the class to which they belonged. Especially in England, they sometimes acted under the influence of Arthurian legends, trying to imitate the deeds of a Lancelot, a Galahad, or the Green Knight.[52] The larger and more important tournaments also served as a sort of labor exchange. In them military skills would be demonstrated, compared, and evaluated under the critical eyes of grandees. Most of the latter were themselves knights. They had participated in tournaments during their youth, and some kept doing so even when reaching an advanced age. The male members of some baronial families did so generation in, generation out. With a bit of luck they might notice this or that fighter, take him on as a retainer, launch his career, and, in case he proved his prowess and his usefulness, end up by promoting him and finding him some rich heiress to marry, as Henry II of England did with William the Marshal. Some grandees attended tournaments with the specific intention of recruiting retainers or else sent their representatives to do so for them.[53] Even the church, for all its dislike for the sport, sometimes made its representatives attend in the hope of finding warriors who would take up the cross.

---

[50] The letter is quoted in Matthew Paris, *Chronica Majora*, Edinburgh: Black, 1874, vol. II, pp. 614–15.

[51] Froissart, *Chronicles*, p. 373.

[52] See on this Barker, *The Tournament in England*, pp. 152–3.

[53] Jean le Bel, *Chronique*, J. Viard and E. Deprez, eds., Adamant, 2005 [1904], 2, 35.

Another very important motive was money. Depending on the rules, the victor would obtain either whatever the loser was carrying on his person or everything he could cough up. Either way, the pickings, especially in the form of horses and armor, could be rich. *The History of William the Marshal* tells us that within one ten-month period the protagonist and his partner Roger de Gaugi defeated and captured no fewer than 103 opponents.[54] Der Pleier, the somewhat mysterious thirteenth-century author of a long epic poem called *Tandareis und Flordibel,* mentions three aristocratic brothers who, along with their retainers, were able to capture 40–50 horses in each of the great tournaments in which they participated.[55] In particular, young knights without means – in other words, cadet members of the great families with no prospect of inheritance – spent their time going from one event to the next, even if doing so meant traveling far and wide: a modern analogy would be successful golfers or Grand Prix drivers.

Finally, tournaments, in particular the larger and more important ones, resembled many other kinds of wargames in that they served as politico-social theater. As Geertz, in his role as the cloud column that preceded the Israelites during the Exodus, wrote: "[Tournaments] provided a metasocial commentary upon the whole matter of assorting human beings into fixed hierarchical ranks and then organizing the major parts of collective existence around that assortment. [Their] function, if you want to call it that, [was] interpretive ... a medieval/aristocratic reading of medieval/aristocratic experience, a story they told themselves about themselves."[56] Stripped of social science jargon, this means that they were festive occasions when the values of chivalrous society, built around war and love, were played out for all to see. The fact that many meetings were international and helped spread the values in question all over Europe brings out the importance of this aspect of the matter even more.[57]

Early tournaments often opened with single combat – a wargame within a wargame. They themselves were fought by groups rather than by individuals: accordingly, it was first of all necessary to decide who would be on whose side. Normally good care was taken to ensure that numbers should be exactly equal, though the fact that different barons brought along retinues of very different sizes might make doing so difficult. Either the rule that no knight should fight against his lord had to be violated – there are indeed some indications that the relevant oaths were temporarily suspended[58] – or else some men must have

[54] *The History of William the Marshal,* London: Birkbeck College, 2002, line 3421.
[55] Der Pleier, *Tandareis und Flordibel,* F. Kuhl, ed., Graz: Buchheim, 1885, lines 13199, 13929, 14398.
[56] Geertz, "Deep Play," p. 82.
[57] See W. Strickland, *War and Chivalry: The Conduct and Perception of War in England and Normandy, 1066–1217,* Cambridge University Press, 1996, pp. 149–50.
[58] Muhlberger, *Jousts and Tournaments,* p. 69, following Geoffroi de Charny.

been disqualified. Attempts were also made to keep together men belonging to the same nationalities or originating in the same towns and provinces. The largest meeting of all is said to have taken place at Mainz in 1184 to celebrate the girding of the sons of Emperor Henry VI. No fewer than 20,000 knights are said to have participated.[59] The *History of William the Marshal* describes a tournament in which 1,500 knights fought on each side.[60] If so, then it must have been one of the largest of its kind; most occasions were much smaller. A "huge" tournament held by King Edward III of England in 1350 attracted 250 knights.[61]

Normally the day selected was a Monday. Whereas it was always necessary to arrange a place in which the tournament would be held, early on there were no courts. This allowed the fighting to spread over hill and dale, including both open spaces and wooded ones. The one real restriction was the provision of so-called *recets*. They are perhaps best described "security zones" in which one was free from attack and in which one's prisoners could be kept until the day had ended. Sometimes one party used a town or castle as its base whereas the other set up camp at some distance outside the gates.

Tactically speaking, these tournaments were not free-for-alls but carefully organized affairs. On each side, the highest-ranking knight acted as the commander. Combatants fought in closed units, meaning that discipline was essential. In the words of Ulrich von Lichtenstein (*c.* 1255), "the troop that initiated the tournament rode in close order. They kept together just as one is supposed to do when advancing on the enemy."[62] Commanders repeatedly urged their men to stay in formation so as to charge the opponent, or force him to retreat, or break through his ranks, or take him in the flank. Sources such as *The History of William the Marshal* reserve their highest praise for companies that maintained good order even as the fighting proceeded.[63] A knight who broke ranks was vulnerable. He might even endanger others who would be forced to come to his rescue, possibly putting themselves into an unfavorable position.

This apart, comparatively little is known about the tactics used. The first weapon used in any fight was the lance. It was longer and heavier than the javelins and spears previous cavalrymen had used, meaning that it could not be thrown. Underhand strokes and strokes with the lance pointing downward were also difficult if not impossible to carry out. Instead it was most effectively employed while held under the arm and pointing straight forward; that way the

[59] Giselbert of Mons, *Chronicon Hanoniense*, L. van der Kindere, ed., Brussels: Kiessling, 1904, p. 157.
[60] *William the Marshal*, line 4782.
[61] Adam Murimuth, *Continuatio Chronicarum*, quoted in Muhlberger, *Jousts and Tournaments*, p. 61.
[62] Von Lichtenstein, *Frauendienst*, pp. 94 and 545.
[63] *William the Marshal*, lines 1417–22 and 2497–500.

full weight of knight and horse could be brought to bear against the opponent. Parsifal's brother Feirefitz boasts of having mastered all five different ways of using the lance, and here again the poet's pidgin French provides a clear indication of the tournament's origin.[64] Apparently distinctions were made among frontal attacks, flank attacks, attacks on closed formations, and clashes between individuals. What is clear is that, as the fights became prolonged, the two troops, having exhausted their maneuvers, often became locked in hand-to-hand combat – horse against horse, man against man, and shield against shield. Clearly all this constituted very good training for war; in fact the need to make English knights equal to French ones was one reason why Richard authorized them.

The fighting continued either until one side was pressed back into its "security zone" – though that rarely happened – or else until nightfall. While the horsemen, their lances having been broken or torn away, hacked away at each other with axes and swords, those who had lost their mounts would continue the fight on foot. Sometimes the retainers on both sides, armed with clubs or even with bows and arrows, intervened. They might try to seize the combatants' mounts by the bridle and drag them to the security zones: it hardly requires saying that the lives of low-class men engaged in such activities were not worth very much. The outcome was accusations and counter-accusations as well as cries of foul. Though there were no umpires, a participant who felt that the rules of play had been violated might appeal to his opponent's superior and, with a little luck, win his case. Sometimes an agreement was concluded in advance to prevent such things from happening and make sure the fight would be fair.[65] One late fourteenth-century English ordinance prohibited "they who shall come to see the Tournament" from bringing along sword, dagger, staff, mace, or stone.[66]

Given the importance of order and discipline, the side that succeeded in incapacitating the opponent's commander enjoyed a clear advantage. So did the side that had maintained a reserve and brought it into action at the right moment at the right spot, as happened, for example, at Lewes in 1264 and at Evesham in 1265. In all this there was a strong resemblance between tournaments and real warfare – to the point that, especially in images dating to the period before 1200 or so, it is often hard to say what we really see. One mid-twelfth-century account describes the proceedings as follows:[67]

---

[64] M. Dallapiazza, ed., *Parzifal*, Berlin: Schmidt, 2009, canto 812, lines 9–16.

[65] See Bumke, *Hoefische Kultur*, p. 355.

[66] Quoted in F. H. Cripps-Day, *History of the Tournament in England and France*, London: Quaritch, 1918, p. xxv.

[67] Balderich, *Gesta Alberonis*, G. Weitz, ed., in *Die Wundergeschichten des Caesarius von Heisterbach*, Bonn: Hanstein, 1937 [*c.* 1155], pp. 598–9.

Had you been able to be present [at the tournament held by Alberonis, the Archbishop of Trier in 1148], what a wonderful show you would have seen! The knights, wearing full armor, engaged in mock warfare; the horses, wildly twisting and turning about within the smallest space; the combatants, storming at each other; the lances groaning as they broke; all accompanied by the shouting of the pursuers and the pursued. You would have seen pretend flights followed by sudden turnabouts; sweeping changes of fortune as attackers, drawn into their opponents' formation and breathing closely into their necks, were suddenly enveloped from both sides; and you would have learnt a thousand other maneuvers and ruses as well.

French tournaments in particular were famous, or infamous, for the ferocity with which they fought, to the point that, in Germany, they were sometimes called *Stritt* ("war"). As so often, the difference consisted in that strategy – here understood in Clausewitz's sense of using battles for winning a campaign – intelligence, reconnaissance, and logistics were left out. Also, though some tournaments did involve siege warfare, so important to medieval warfare as a whole, apparently most of the time it was regarded as burlesque rather than as a serious attempt to mimic the serious operations of war. On one occasion a "fortress of love" was built and "manned" by ladies who pelted the knights trying to take it with cakes.[68] Above all, fewer men were killed rather than either being permitted to surrender and withdraw or be dragged off by the main force.

Starting in 1130, when the Council of Clermont prohibited them, the church always put its face firmly against the "despicable" tournaments.[69] Later the prohibition was often repeated. Superficially it was a question of avoiding the bloodshed involved and preventing gatherings that might provide opportunities for all kinds of interesting entertainments. As one cleric explained in some detail, those who attended tournaments were likely to commit all seven deadly sins, from pride through gluttony to fornication.[70] Tournaments also diverted knightly energies away from more useful pursuits such as going on crusades. The thirteenth-century German preacher Berthold of Regensburg compared knights who preferred tourneying to traveling to the Holy Land with the kind of women who wore yellow clothes and makeup.[71] Beneath the surface there always existed a certain tension between God's representatives on earth and the culture of chivalry of which the tournament was the symbol par excellence. Needless to say, the warnings went unheeded. Yet the contradiction between the two traditions should not be exaggerated. Here and there a priest refused burial to a person who had been killed in a tournament, but such cases seem to

---

[68] M. van Creveld, *Men, Women and War*, London: Cassell, 2001, p. 84.
[69] See C. H. Hefele and H. Leclercq, *Histoire des Conciles*, Paris: Letouzey, 1912, vol. V, p. 7.
[70] Jakob von Vitry, *Sermones Vulgares*, in J. B. Pitra, ed., *Analecta novissima spicilegii solesmensias*, Paris: Didot, 1888, vol. II, no. 52.
[71] Berthold of Regensburg, *Predikten*, F. Goebel, ed., Regensburg: Manz, 1882, vol. I, p. 176.

have been rare. Notwithstanding that they engaged in tournaments, most knights probably regarded themselves as good Christians. Many senior ecclesiastics were themselves noblemen and may have sympathized with their tourneying relatives. In 1316 Pope John XXII, a Frenchman who was the first of the Avignon pontiffs, bowed to the pressure of the French King Philip IV and withdrew his opposition. In 1471 a tournament was held in Rome's St. Peter's Square, right under the Pope's nose.[72]

The relationship between tournaments and the various countries' secular authorities was even more complicated, in some respects foreshadowing the eighteenth- and nineteenth-century duel. Medieval counts, princes, dukes, kings, and similar aristocrats all the way to the emperor inclusive were themselves knights. They partook of chivalrous culture, participated in tournaments, and sometimes became casualties. Particularly during the twelfth century, the list of those who died was impressive. In Germany alone in 1185, sixteen knights died within the span of a single year.[73] Yet the danger of escalation was always present; mock warfare, either reflecting existing animosities or stirring up new ones, might escape control and turn into the real thing or something very close to it. The damage to participants and bystanders alike could be considerable. Besides, whereas tournaments could be used in order celebrate chivalry and the government exercised by the more important barons, they also provided good opportunities for malcontents to gather together and perhaps plan their next move. As at all times and places, any ruler who permitted large gatherings of well-trained, heavily armed men to take place without taking precautions was (and is) a fool. One who learnt this lesson to his cost was Edward II, who ended up by being deposed and killed. His son and successor, Edward III, was more successful in this respect.[74] In 1400 a plot to kill another English monarch, Henry IV, on the occasion of a tournament at Oxford was only foiled at the last moment.

These factors – fear of escalation, the human and material damage that tournaments often caused, and the desire to bring them under stricter government control – combined to turn them into less spontaneous, more formal occasions. Possibly, too, we see here the influence of the judicial duel, on which more below. Starting during the second decade of the thirteenth century, the number of participants in each bout went down. Sharp weapons were sometimes replaced by blunt ones.[75] Perhaps more importantly, the open space between two armies was replaced by specially designated courts. The earliest ones are mentioned in "The Good Gerhard" by Rudolf of Ems, a German poet who flourished during the first half of the thirteenth century.[76] Later they

---

[72] See on this entire subject Barker, *The Tournament in England*, pp. 70–83.
[73] Bumke, *Hoefische Kultur*, p. 346.   [74] Barker, *The Tournament in England*, pp. 47, 61.
[75] The earliest reference is in Matthew Paris, *Chronica Majora*, vol. II, p. 650.
[76] *Rudolf von Ems, Der guote Gêrhart*, J. Asher, ed., Tuebingen: Altdeutsche Textbibliothek, 1989, lines 3437ff.

became a standard feature of tournaments until no self-respecting baron could afford to be without one. As so often, the term for single combat, joust, was originally French. Later it entered other languages in more or less corrupt form. As so often, we do not know when the first jousts were held. Some modern authorities believe that originally they may have formed part of the above-mentioned *vesprii*, serving as an introduction for the "serious" business of the next day.[77]

What does seem clear is that jousts were less bloody and less risky than their predecessors. The same appears to be true of so-called round tables, a kind of feast first mentioned at about the same time and in which jousts played a central role. One indication of this fact is the growing presence of women, and indeed the promise that noble ladies would be present was sometimes used to attract participants.[78] With the introduction of jousts, tournaments, and war started drifting apart, causing the value of the former as preparation for the latter to decline. Perhaps this explains why, after 1332, the contracts of English retainers no longer obliged them to tourney with their lords. As foot-soldiers were increasingly armed with pikes and crossbows and thus represented a growing danger to knights, they too were left out. At most, jousters were allowed to bring along two or three unarmed servants. Their primary function was to help the jousters mount their horses before combat, but they were also permitted to pull an opponent from his horse, lead a defeated opponent away, etc. To prevent misunderstandings, servants were made to wear a special cap or badge. In German lands, the higher a combatant's rank the more servants he was allowed to have with him.

By Froissart's day, things had reached the point when only blows against the opponent's helmet or shield were allowed, whereas striking his horse was prohibited. Before the fighting could begin, knights were sometimes made to swear that, on pain of losing their arms and horses, they would obey these rules; two centuries earlier, any attempt to limit the fighting in this way would have been regarded as both preposterous and counter-productive. Yet another indication of the widening gap between mock warfare and the real thing is the growing number of references to horses specifically trained for the former.[79] Though it took time – as late as 1405, a Spanish nobleman visiting France took note of the fact that as many as ten or twenty or thirty knights sometimes jousted on each side – increasingly tournaments became a matter of one combatant against another.[80] Conversely, less is heard about riots and the like.

---

[77] See, for the evidence, Bumke, *Hoefische Kultur*, p. 361.
[78] See on this entire subject below, pp. 302–4.
[79] Barker, *The Tournament in England*, pp. 174–5.
[80] Gutiere Diaz de Gamez, *The Unconquered Knight*, J. Evans, ed., London: Routledge, 1928, pp. 142–3.

The addition, during the first years of the fifteenth century, of a barrier took the process a step further. Originally it consisted simply of a piece of canvas or rope running the length of the court. When that proved insufficient real partitions, about five foot high and often painted red, were constructed. A barrier put an end to all sorts of tactical maneuvers. At the same time it saved the horses from having to go against their nature and collide head on, thus avoiding all kinds of accidents that could result when they swerved or reared and making them easier to control. Jousters were warned to make sure their mounts kept at the right distance from the barrier, neither too close nor too far away. Trying to correct these errors at the last moment, they might miss their opponents altogether.

Given the need to hold a weapon with one hand and the reins with the other, carrying shields on horseback had always been difficult. As the addition of a barrier caused combat with axes and swords to come to an end, shields became smaller and, instead of being carried on the left arm, were bolted onto the breastplate. Meanwhile lances, having been turned from weapons of first resort into the sole ones, grew ever longer and heavier. Handbooks warned jousters against using lances that were too heavy for them, since the outcome could be hernias as well as pain in the back, head, and arms.[81] The longer and heavier a lance, the harder it was to control and aim. This reached the point when, at the beginning of the fourteenth century, armor began to be provided with a special gadget, known as the *restre*, for holding it in place; by preventing the lance from sliding backward, the *restre* also increased the force of the blow it delivered. Tournament armor also developed, becoming more elaborate as time went on.

For all the measures taken to civilize them, tournaments always remained somewhat dangerous – as is clear from the fact that, in one event held by the future Emperor Charles V in 1518, seven cavaliers lost their lives.[82] Forty-one years later no less a person than King Henry II of France was felled by an accidental stroke of the lance. More and more often, though, tournaments were waged not with sharp weapons but with so-called *armes de plaisance*. Rather than capturing the opponent, the objective was to unhorse him, a form of combat also known as tilting. All this meant that encounters, instead of lasting minutes and sometimes even more, were over in a matter of seconds. Tactics were simplified and became less interesting than before: the turning and twisting, the attacks and feint retreats and counterattacks having disappeared, how many different ways were there to couch and aim a lance? Perhaps to compensate for these developments, elaborate point systems, like those used in

---

[81] Dom Duarte, *The Royal Book of Horsemanship, Jousting, and Knightly Combat*, A. Franco Preto and L. Preto, trans., Highland Village, TX: Chivalry Bookshelf, 2005 [*c.* 1438], pp. 75, 76, 79, 100.
[82] R. Coltman Clephan, *The Mediaeval Tournament*, New York: Dover, 1995 [1919], p. 117.

present-day boxing, were introduced.[83] So and so many blows were to be delivered, in such and such a way, with such and such weapons. Mid-fifteenth-century English rules, adapted from Italian ones, lay down that the best jouster of the day was he who knocked his opponent off his mount or sent both rider and horse crashing to the ground. In the absence of such a clear victor, the prize went to the combatant who twice accomplished the difficult feat of striking the coronal on the opponent's lance; or to him who hit the sight of the opponent's helmet three times; or broke the most lances.[84]

Another method often used to enliven the proceedings was to add various fantastic elements – what later generations would call scenarios. Knights swore oaths to undertake dangerous missions, vowed to abstain from this or that activity or food or dress for such and such a time until a fight could be held and honor redeemed, and the like. A popular form of combat was the *pas d'armes*. In it, one or more knights swore to defend a bridge or pass against all comers using either blunt weapons or sharp ones; on one occasion they did so for no fewer than six weeks. Another was the fountain of tears near which was to be found the weeping maiden. She was being held prisoner by a wicked dragon or magician and had to be rescued. Sometimes a lady had to wear a bracelet and could not enter a certain place without a knight coming to her assistance. On other occasions a knight or group of knights went in quest of the Holy Grail. Mythical beasts, unicorns above all, were often used to complete the picture. Sometimes knights defended not positions but propositions (e.g. "noe fare ladie was ever false") much as if they were PhD candidates taking their oral exams.[85] The list of possibilities, many of them taken from twelfth-century romances that described the legendary adventures of even earlier heroes, was practically endless.[86] Detailed handbooks advised people how to organize tournaments, what rules to apply, and so on.

Thanks no doubt in part to the pageantry which accompanied them, tournaments retained their popularity as a spectator sport – as is proved by early prints which often show packed tribunes and people climbing roofs and even trees to watch. At a joust held at Westminster in the presence of Queen Elizabeth in 1581, so great was the throng that many people were injured and some killed. Still, the above changes, as well as the gradual spread of firearms, caused the value of tournaments as training for war to decline. Writing around 1350 Geoffroi de Charny explained that war was the greatest test of martial skills. The tournament came next, whereas the last place was occupied by the joust.

---

[83] J. K. Ruehl, "Wesen und Bedeutung von Kampfsagen und Trefferzhalenskitzzen fuer die Geschichte des spaetmittelalterlichen Tourniers," in G. Spitzer and D. Schmidt, eds., *Sport zwischen Eigenstaendigkeit und Fremdbestimmung*, Bonn: Institut fuer Sportwissenschaft, 1986, pp. 82–112.

[84] See Muhlberger, *Jousts and Tournaments*, p. 30.

[85] Coltman Clephan, *The Mediaeval Tournament*, p. 133.

[86] See Huizinga, *The Waning of the Middle Ages*, p. 81.

The same author described jousts as "attractive to the participants and fair to see," but they might also cause some men to neglect more serious pursuits of arms.[87] Edward III himself, in founding a chivalrous order, made it clear that the way to become a member of it was by martial exploits, *armes de guerre*, and not by tourneying. A century or so after them Jean de Bueil in *Le Jouvencel* gave it as his opinion that those who engaged in "feats of arms" were risking their lives merely to prove their ability to do something that was of no use to anybody better than anybody else.[88]

As war and tournament went their separate ways, the latter tended to become more exclusive, socially speaking. Two processes were involved. First, armor had always been very expensive. With plate taking the place of mail and chain from the middle of the fourteenth century on, it became even more so. The carefully constructed and splendidly decorated late fifteenth-century suits originating in centers such as Milan and Nuremberg, and now on display in many museums around the world, cost a fortune and were far beyond the reach of many ordinary knights. In the end only true grandees could afford these masterpieces. This process peaked around 1530, when a decline set in. Starting with the pieces that protected their legs, slowly but surely cavalrymen discarded their suits. That, however, was too late to save the tournament.

Second, during the fifteenth century organizers increasingly tried to limit participation to true blue-bloods. Previously low-born knights and even mercenaries, provided of course they possessed the necessary equipment, had been able to attend. Even townspeople sometimes organized tournaments in which they competed against one another, which incidentally is one more proof as to just how popular they really were.[89] Later, though, all these different categories of men were increasingly left out.[90] Those directly responsible for this were the heralds, a class of officials who were becoming increasingly professionalized and who, like all professionals, tended to be sticklers for detail. The fenestration of arms, meaning that arms had to be hung outside one's tent or pavilion so that contenders could deliver their challenge by knocking on them, worked in the same direction by leaving out those not entitled to a coat of arms. The two processes reinforced one another: as the cost of tourneying skyrocketed, the number of those granted entry declined. To make things worse still, victors, instead of holding the vanquished to ransom or at least taking away their horses and suits of armor, had to be content with the prizes formally handed out by the organizers. The days when one could make a fortune by going from one event to the next were over. In view of all this, the wonder is not that interest in

---

[87] Muhlberger, *Jousts and Tournaments*, pp. 10, 21.
[88] J. de Bueil, *Le Jouvencel*, Nabu, 2010, vol. II, 100.
[89] J. Larner, "Chivalric Culture in the Age of Dante," *Renaissance Studies*, 2, 2, 1988, pp. 122ff.
[90] See, on mercenaries, Barker, *The Tournament in England*, p. 29.

tournaments declined – far less was written about them after 1500 than before – and eventually disappeared, but that some were still being held even during the early decades of the seventeenth century. In 1645 Sir John Evelyn watched one in Rome, although by that time it was more in the nature of a bloodless reenactment than a bona fide fight.[91]

Compared with the kinds of wargames we have already studied, tournaments show a number of interesting similarities and dissimilarities. Unlike the above-mentioned games of tribal societies, which were open to any adult male, tournaments were normally the exclusive province of the higher classes and tended to become even more so as time went on. Unlike single combats and combats of champions, there was no attempt, however theoretical and however futile, to use them for solving political problems connected with real-life war. It is, however, true that tournaments were often held during lulls in the latter and also that, if care was not taken, they might run out of control and escalate into real warfare; if some organizers tried to arrange things in such a way that friends would not have to fight one another, others deliberately placed well-known enemies on opposite sides. Status-wise, knights were as far removed from gladiators as anybody could be. Neither prisoners, nor slaves, nor degraded because of their choice of occupation, they represented the flower of contemporary society and always entered the lists of their own free will. As countless chronicles, romances, and *chansons* make clear, participating in tournaments was one of the most important and most praiseworthy things a knight, whatever his rank, could do in life. As late as 1515 the *Freydal* of Emperor Maximilian I, a work named after the *nom de guerre* he assumed when tourneying, contained no fewer than 255 carefully executed plates, all of which show the tournaments in which he had taken part. He himself went over the manuscript page by page and corrected some of the details.[92]

Certainly death and injury, present from the beginning, were regarded as unavoidable. Still, the real objective of the fighting was less to inflict them than to incapacitate, capture, and obtain a ransom. On the other hand, there were cases when knights released their captives in order to prove their generosity, or so the sources tell us.[93] Indeed the way prisoners were treated represented one of the major differences between mock warfare and the real thing. Whereas prisoners of war were sometimes held for years, those taken in tournaments were supposed to be released when the event came to an end, usually on the same day. Early tournaments strongly resembled war and were sometimes used to recruit warriors for both licit purposes and illicit ones. However, as time went on and they were

---

[91] J. Evelyn, *Diary*, W. Bray, ed., London: Bickers, 1879 [1818], vol. III, p. 118.

[92] See C. Dodgson, "An Unknown MS of Freydal," *Burlington Magazine for Connoisseurs*, 48, 278, May 1928, pp. 235–42.

[93] E.g. H. von Aue, *Erec*, M. G. Scholtz, ed., Frankfurt/Main: Klassiker Verlag, 2004, [c. 1191], line 2430.

replaced first by jousts and then by tilts – by which I mean the form of combat in which the protagonists were separated by a partition – this became much less so than had initially been the case. By 1420 at the latest, the differences had grown to the point where any military training tournaments could offer had become an illusion, and at times a dangerous one at that. Later still, as the sixteenth century went on, increasingly it was not the fighting itself but the pageantry by which it was surrounded that contemporaries found most interesting.

Intended neither as preliminaries to war nor as judgments, let alone as religious services as the *munera* were, essentially all forms of combat collectively known as tournaments were pure entertainment, joined of course with theater of the kind Geertz has described. Whereas early on tournaments and war went hand in hand, gradually the theater tended to overshadow the fighting. Just as the gladiatorial combats had been an essential element in the process of Romanizing the Roman Empire, so in time tournaments became the focal point of an entire culture. As that culture waned away, to use Huizinga's admirable phrase, so did they.

A question of honor

By the middle years of the sixteenth century single combat, combat of champions, and the judicial duel had clearly turned into anachronisms. While tournaments were still being held, they too were entering the last stages of what was to prove their final decline. However, the idea that men (hardly ever women) should defend their "honor" weapon in hand, fighting and shedding blood if necessary, remained very much alive. As is so often the case, the precise origins of the duel, a highly ritualized form of wargame that now emerged and was to remain in vogue for the next three and a half centuries, are unknown. In 1549, one historian claims, the term itself had not yet been invented.[94]

In essence, two interpretations are possible. The first is that duels were born out of trial by combat, now finally superseded and suppressed, and that they continued that tradition in unofficial form. The other is that they grew out of what contemporaries called *rencontres*, best translated as fights. At times and places when government was weak – as, in the absence of a specialized police force, it often was – the term covered all sorts of ambushes, skirmishes, and small battles waged between private individuals as a method for settling disputes. Originally they could be fought on horseback as well as on foot, by small groups of men as well as by individuals. An excellent case in point is the skirmish between the followers of the house of Capulet and that of Montague in which Tybalt and Mercutio are killed.[95] Later, instead of simply drawing and

---

[94] See, for what follows, S. Carroll, *Blood and Violence in Early Modern France*, Oxford University Press, 2006, pp. 132–49.

[95] W. Shakespeare, *Romeo and Juliet*, Act III, scene I, lines 75–110.

fighting as in Shakespeare's play, they started to formally challenge one another to a duel. In a way, doing so was a method of avoiding the increasingly heavy hand of government. The possibility must also be considered that both explanations are correct, and that duels actually had two parents. One was rooted in now antiquated law; the other originally existed outside it but, having evolved into a different form, came to be more or less tolerated by it. Having entered the world by the fusion of two different traditions, no wonder duels incorporated elements from both.

Formal dueling, rooted in an attempt to limit casualties by having the *rencontres* take place at a designated time and place, as well as defining exactly who would and who would not participate, seems to have been invented in Italy where it was known as the *combattimento della mazza* (*mazza* = staff, club, mace).[96] From there it spread to Spain – at the time, much of Italy was governed from Madrid – and, probably at the hand of mercenary soldiers, to France.[97] There the collapse of royal authority during the last four decades of the sixteenth century enabled it to take root. Subsequently France became the classic country of the swashbuckling swordsman, so much so that in Germany duels were known as French combat.[98] At first there was no attempt to enforce what later became the outstanding characteristic of the duel, i.e. strict symmetry and obedience to the rules. Things, however, gradually changed. By 1642, when two French combatants took off their boots and put on dancing pumps instead, duels had developed from something very close to a free-for-all into what one historian calls "a graceful art defined by its rituals."[99] Some seventeenth-century observers, notably the English political scientist and satirist Bernard Mandeville (1670–1733), even argued that duels grew out of the spirit of politeness that set their own age apart from all its predecessors.[100]

With few exceptions, most previous wargames took place with the consent of the authorities, who organized them, encouraged them, used them for their own purposes, and, in not a few cases, participated in them. Not so duels, which almost from the beginning were a thorn in those authorities' side. England's King James I, who wrote several treatises on the subject,[101] was but one out of many rulers who tried to eradicate them. However, neither in England nor anywhere else could the ban be enforced; it has been claimed that during the

[96] P. de Bourdeille Brantôme, *Memoires contenans les anecdotes de la cour de France . . . touchant les duels*, in *Œuvres complètes*, Paris: Foucault, 1803, vol. VI, pp. 70–1.
[97] Kiernan, *The Duel in European History*, p. 47.
[98] According to K. McAleer, *Dueling: The Cult of Honor in Fin-de-Siècle Germany*, Princeton University Press, 1994, p. 18.
[99] Carroll, *Blood and Violence*, p. 149.
[100] B. Mandeville, *An Inquiry into the Causes of the Frequent Executions at Tyburn*, London: Kraus, 1975 [1725], pp. 31–2.
[101] See M. Peltonnen, *The Duel in Early Modern England*, Cambridge University Press, 2003, pp. 87–8.

reign of Henry IV (1589–1610) over 4,000 French aristocrats were killed in duels. Henry's successor, Louis XIII (1610–43), is said to have issued no fewer than 8,000 pardons for murders associated with duels, and even this figure only covers part of his reign. His, of course, was another period when France was weakly governed. Pictures show duels being fought on a bridge across the Seine not far from the Palais Royale. Voltaire, looking back on the reign from the heights of the Enlightenment a century or so later, considered that this was when the passion for the "gothic barbarism" of dueling had become part of the national character.[102]

The reasons why the prohibitions did not work are not hard to find. On the one hand, monarchs could not but look at duels with a jaundiced eye. This, after all, was the age of growing absolutism. As official ideology, the growth of government, and many forms of art all testify, it was characterized by nothing so much as the royal attempts to impose order on society in general and the aristocracy in particular.[103] On the other hand, rulers themselves were aristocrats. Like other blue-bloods, they owed their status and privileges to their birth. Prohibiting what was usually regarded as an aristocratic custom – in principle, only aristocrats had honor to defend – meant sawing off the branch on which they were sitting. Brantôme, the late sixteenth-century French historian and biographer, claims that King Henry III, who reigned from 1574 to 1589, loved his nobility too much to enforce the prohibitions on dueling he was always issuing.[104]

More specifically, aristocrats were the class from which rulers drew their officers. As long as the *ancien régime* lasted most officers were aristocrats, and in some armies this was even more the case at the end of the period than at the beginning. At a time when Frederick the Great, an acknowledged expert on such matters, declared that "the one thing that can make men march into the muzzles of the cannon that are trained at them is honor," depriving aristocratic officers of their means par excellence of avenging insults to that honor was impossible and counter-productive. In fact Tsar Peter III, who ruled Russia from January 1762 until June of that year and who was an admirer of Frederick, was said to be a failed duelist himself.[105] The same politeness officers were expected to show their opposite numbers obliged them to duel. The outcome was that the duel, like male adultery, was prohibited in theory but allowed in practice. Often punishments were light, or else letters of pardon were issued to those who had fled justice and later begged to return. That such letters could

---

[102] Voltaire, *The Age of Louis XIV*, London: Everyman, 1928 [1751], p. 17.
[103] See, above all, P. King, *The Ideology of Order*, London: Routledge, 1999, especially pp. 255–89.
[104] Brantôme, *Mémoires contenans les anecdotes de la cour de France*, p. 139.
[105] See I. Reyfman, *Ritualized Violence, Russian Style: The Duel in Russian Literature and Culture*, Stanford University Press, 1999, pp. 64–5.

also serve those who issued them as a useful source of income hardly requires saying.

As has been said, a duel was a miniature war, a trial of courage and skill concentrated into a few intense minutes with the lives of the contestants at stake.[106] The duelers themselves understood the system very well. Instead of challenging the authorities head-on, a method that might well lead to dire consequences, they met early in the morning when the chance of discovery was less. Preferably they chose deserted places far from the madding crowd: favorite locations were islands in the middle of rivers where the authority of the state did not apply. For example, the famous duel between Vice President Aaron Burr and former Secretary of the Treasury Alexander Hamilton took place at a spot known as the Heights of Weehawken in New Jersey, the reason being that New York had outlawed the custom. Others too used it, and for the same reason. From 1700 to 1845 eighteen duels are known to have taken place there; the real number may have been considerably higher.[107]

The need for secrecy also explains why duels, unlike many other kinds of wargames, only occasionally developed into popular spectator sports. As if to prove how important they had become, the first half of the seventeenth century witnessed an explosion of manuals that dealt with them. All the most important West European languages of the time – French, Italian, German, and Spanish – were represented.[108] So, though it was not yet considered an important language, was English. All the manuals agreed that duels were, strictly speaking, illegal. However, all also argued that custom permitted them even if secular and ecclesiastical law did not. All the manuals were at great pains to spell out the kinds of offenses for which "satisfaction" might be demanded and that might lead to duels. A protocol was laid down. First there would be an offense directed by one gentleman – depending on time and place, the definition of who was a gentleman varied – against another. Next, perhaps, came a countercharge of lying; next, a challenge to fight; next, it was up to the party that made the challenge to choose the time, location, judge, and weapons. To refuse a duel either as a means to redeem one's honor or when challenged meant losing face in the eyes of society.

These technicalities having been settled, the two men would meet at the appointed place. Each would be accompanied by one or more seconds, called "godfathers" (*padrino, parrain*) in Spanish and French. Their function was to act as witnesses, ensure that the rules were observed, and render what assistance was needed either before the fight or after it was over. The duelists would swear

[106] Kiernan, *The Duel*, p. 145.
[107] See S. Demontreux, "The Changing Face of the Hamilton Monument," Weehawken Historical Commission, 2004, p. 3.
[108] See S. K. Taylor, *Honor and Violence in Golden Age Spain*, New Haven, CT: Yale University Press, 2008, pp. 21–5.

that their cause was just. The signal having been given, the fighting started. If only because the parties would never agree to duel if their chances of emerging as victors were not equal, very great care was taken to balance them in terms of what they could wear, the arms that they could use, the manner in which the engagement was fought, and what their seconds were and were not allowed to do. The selected piece of ground had to be level and free of obstacles, the hour chosen in such a way that neither combatant would have the sun in his eyes, and so on. Even the lamps that the seconds carried had to be held in such a way as to avoid blinding the combatants. The intention behind these precautions was to exclude all kinds of ruses as well as the possibility of surprise. Though there were important differences between one country and the next, on the whole the later the date the more detailed the rules and the more genteel the duels.

Duels rested on a profound paradox. On the one hand they sharply differ-entiated between those who had honor to lose and were able to demand satisfaction and fight and those who did not and could not. On the other, they put everybody who had honor and was eligible on an equal footing. Both issuing a challenge and answering it was as much as saying, "You are my equal and I am yours." Sixteenth-century pictures show duelists wearing armor and using all sorts of weapons, pikes and battleaxes included. Later, things changed. War and wargame were clearly growing apart. Another move towards separa-tion was the introduction of the rapier shortly before 1600. A cut-and-thrust weapon whose use required both strength and skill, it made its first appearance in Italy from where it spread to other countries. Meanwhile, about the only kind of sword still used in real-life warfare was the cavalry saber. Fencing schools – the English term is derived from "defence" – where masters trained their students in the use of swords in case they should be involved in *rencontres* had long done a flourishing business in many European cities. While some were more attuned to the times than others, over time most of them were probably forced either to shift their expertise in such a way that it would serve the more stylized duel now coming into vogue or to close their doors.

Another interesting development was the appearance, around 1750, of the foil. A light thrusting weapon named after the "foil" fixed to the tip to prevent it from doing damage, its introduction marks the moment when fencing, a highly stylized combat sport, and dueling, a deadly serious wargame, finally separated. As if to emphasize that fact, during the last decades of the eighteenth century some duelers started using pistols. Since there could be no doubt that shooting at an opponent without going through the ceremony of giving fair warning first was simply murder, the change made it much easier to distinguish duels from ordinary *rencontres*. This probably contributed to making the former even more ritualized than they already were.

The pistols of the time were single-shooters. Hence the combatants some-times used both weapons, firing first and then, in case no serious damage had been done and no agreement was reached, going after one another sword in hand. The more time passed the more frequent the use of pistols. They were manufactured in pairs and packed and sold in specially made cases that also contained all the necessary ancillary equipment. Often treated as family heirlooms, they were passed from one generation to the next, complete with the stories that surrounded them. Among the English aristocracy in Ireland towards the end of the eighteenth century, family heads who considered giving a daughter in marriage regularly asked whether the suitor had "blazed." Guides to pistol duels began to be published and rules for them were laid down.[109] Schools that taught the art of fighting with pistols also emerged. However, swords never completely disappeared and duelists often had the choice between the two weapons.

Here is a description of a fairly typical eighteenth-century duel, taken from an account by an early nineteenth-century English author.[110] The year was 1772. The protagonists were a Mr. Sheridan, "the avowed suitor of Miss Linley, the celebrated vocal performer," and a Mr. Matthews, "a gentleman" from Bath. The latter had "caused a paragraph to be inserted in a public paper at that place, which tended to prejudice the character of that young lady." A duel was fought, with swords, at a tavern in Henrietta Street, Covent Garden, London. Mr. Sheridan's second was none other than Charles Francis Sheridan, formerly Secretary at War in Ireland. "Great courage and skill were displayed on both sides; but Mr. Sheridan, having succeeded in disarming his adversary, compelled him to sign a formal retraction of the paragraph that had been published."

That was not the end of the matter. Exulting in his triumph, Sheridan published the apology in a Bath paper. Thereupon Mr. Matthews sent him a message challenging him to a second duel. "The victory was desperately contested, and after a discharge of pistols they fought with swords. They were both wounded, and closing with each other, fell on the ground, where the fight was continued until they were separated. They received several cuts and contusions in this arduous struggle for life and honor, and a part of his opponent's weapon was left in Mr. Sheridan's ear." Thus the fight ended inconclusively. Miss Linley on her part "did not suffer a long time to elapse before she rewarded Mr. Sheridan for the dangers he had braved in her defense, by accompanying him on a matrimonial excursion to the continent. The ceremony was again performed on their return to England, with the consent of the lady's parents."

The same author tells us that, "in *one hundred and seventy-two combats* (including *three hundred and forty-four individuals*), *sixty-nine persons were killed;* that in *three* of these *neither* of the combatants survived; that *ninety-six* were *wounded,* forty-eight of them *desperately,* and *forty-eight slightly;* that *one hundred* and *eighty-eight* escaped *unhurt.*"[111] Still these 172 combats only led to

---

[109] E.g. J. Hamilton, *The Dueling Handbook,* Mineola, NY: Dover, 2007 [1829], pp. 1–16.
[110] Gilchrist, *A Brief Display,* pp. 103–7.   [111] *Ibid.,* p. 60. All italics are in the original.

eighteen trials; of those arraigned, six were acquitted, seven found guilty of manslaughter, and three of murder. Two were hanged, eight sentenced to various periods in prison. All this led our author to the conclusion that Parliament should not regard it beneath its dignity "to add to the multiplicity of benevolent plans which their predecessors have already achieved, some remedy which may tend to annihilate that most painful . . . remnant of *gothic* ignorance."[112] No fewer than four British prime ministers engaged in dueling – two of them, William Pitt the Younger and the Duke of Wellington, while in office. One of the four, George Canning (who at the time was no more than an aspiring politician) even received a pistol bullet in the thigh; however, the wound did not prove to be serious. Yet England at the time was already known as the "nation of shopkeepers." In 1841 it became the first to abolish the duel altogether.

While it is probably true that no nineteenth-century nation was without men (and women) who hoped to see duels abolished, in most of them things developed in a different way. A particularly interesting case is presented by the United States. In a country where social classes were less important than anywhere else, it was quite common for men of very different status to face one another. Perhaps that fact, as well as the penchant for self-help arising out of the frontier mentality, helps explain why, very often, the objective was not just to obtain "satisfaction" but to kill. So pronounced and widely known were the differences between the two sides of the Atlantic that each looked down on the other. At least one European expert contrasted the Americans' "irregular and unfair mode of fighting" with the "strictly honorable, spirited, and manly conduct of the Englishman" in particular.[113] An "American duel" referred to an especially unregulated and wild one. Americans in turn proclaimed their disgust at the small number of casualties European dueling produced.

The most prominent American known to have engaged in a duel – more than one, in fact – was president-to-be Andrew Jackson. Apparently even Lincoln was challenged, but used humor to wriggle out of it. Southerners in particular were known as roughnecks, always ready for a fight. Only the South had regular meeting places, the best known of which was "the Dueling Oaks" in New Orleans. Harriet Martineau, the famous writer and traveler, was told that more duels had been fought there in 1834 than there were days in the year, fifteen on one Sunday morning alone.[114] So little did seconds trust the duelists' "honor" – the very quality which had caused the quarrel – that they sometimes presented themselves fully armed, threatening to shoot whomever broke the

---

[112] *Ibid.*, p. 59.
[113] A. Steinmetz, *The Romance of Duelling in All Times and Countries*, London: Chapman and Hall, 1868, vol. II, p. 249.
[114] H. Martineau, *Society in America*, London: Saunders and Otley, 1837, vol. II, p. 60, and vol. III, pp. 55–6.

rules.[115] Officers apart, Americans rarely used swords. Instead they resorted to bowie knives, known after a certain early nineteenth-century Colonel James Bowie, which being much shorter than swords would almost certainly lead to unseemly fights in which practically everything was permitted.[116] Americans were also said to have invented other interesting forms of dueling, such as when the parties, armed with dirks, went after each other in a darkened room or else threw sticks of dynamite at each other. To this day, out of fifty states, thirty still do not have a specific ordinance against dueling in their constitutions. That of course does not mean that it is permitted, but only that lawyers in their wisdom have found other methods for dealing with it.

On the Old Continent, the most important nations that must be considered were Italy, France, Austria-Hungary, Russia, and Germany. Italy, the land where dueling had been invented, was a special case, part European, part African (as adherents of the Lombard League argue to this day). Judging by the number that was mentioned in the press, Italy had far more duels than any other country. However, out of 2,795 fought between 1879 and 1889 just fifty, or 1.8 percent, ended with the death of one or more combatants.[117] As one historian says, perhaps Italians preferred the show to the reality behind it.[118] French dueling, instead of being limited to officers and aristocrats, resembled the American system in that it was comparatively democratic. Especially towards the end of the nineteenth century, many duelists were scandal-mongering journalists. Some papers, notably Le Figaro and Le Gaulois, maintained special facilities where their reporters could practice. Even Jean Jaurès, the socialist leader (1859–1914), fought a pistol duel against a nationalist adversary.[119] After 1789 France never enacted a specific law against dueling. Instead, the matter was dealt with by way of general legislation against murder and assault. Provided no fatalities ensued, the courts were inclined to dismiss the matter. As a result, duels in France were conducted more publicly, even in front of the cameras, than anywhere else. Some were made the centerpieces of elaborate feasts, complete with ladies, waiters, and refreshments.

Most nineteenth-century French duels were fought sword in hand, a method considered a French specialty. The primary objective was to demonstrate one's skill as a beau sabreur. To quote the novelist Guy de Maupassant, himself a redoubtable dueler: "they feinted and recovered with an elastic grace, with a measured vigor, with part sureness of strength, part sobriety of gesture, part

[115] J. K. Williams, Dueling in the Old South, College Station: Texas A&M University Press, 1980, p. 4.
[116] See, for James Bowie, B. Holland, Gentlemen's Blood: A History of Dueling, New York: Bloomsbury, 2003, pp. 154, 190–4.
[117] Figures for Italy, as well as Austria-Hungary, from S. von Bischoffhausen, ed., Mitteilungen der Algemeine Anti-Duell Liga fuer Oesterreich, Vienna, 1903.
[118] Kiernan, The Duel in European History, p. 260.
[119] See, for dueling in France, McAleer, Dueling, pp. 183–95.

impeccable demeanor, part moderation of technique that surprised and charmed the novice crowd."[120] When pistols were used they were often loaded with a reduced charge of gunpowder and quicksilver balls. Thus France resembled Italy in that few duels – between 1880 and 1889, just 16 out of 431, amounting to 3.7 percent – ended in somebody being killed.[121] Another reason for this was that by French law seconds who helped arrange the fights were held co-responsible for any injuries or deaths. They might indeed be punished more harshly than the duelists themselves. To protect themselves the doctors some-times turned around and refused to look; this enabled them to claim that their presence on the spot had been accidental. So low was the fatality rate that foreigners, Germans in particular, sometimes claimed that dueling in the Third Republic was really a joke.

Judging by newspaper reports, which of course only reported the most important cases, the European country with the largest number of deadly duels was Austria-Hungary. Out of 124 fought in 1884–5, nineteen, i.e. no fewer than 15 percent, ended with one of the combatants losing his life. Later, however, Austria became more civilized and the figure went down. In Russia, Peter the Great in his Military Code (*Artikul voinskii*) of 1716 threatened to hang anybody who engaged in a duel, or helped arrange it, regardless of whether there were dead or injured.[122] The next ruler to legislate on the subject was Catherine the Great. More realistic than her predecessor, throughout her reign she opposed dueling without, however, taking firm steps to stop it.

Catherine's own successor, Paul I, took a different line. Like many other European monarchs, he was torn between powerful government and honor. During much of his reign honor came out on top. In 1801 he opened himself up to ridicule by suggesting that a series of duels (in reality, combats of champions) between heads of state, each seconded by their prime minister, could resolve Europe's political conflicts: he himself wanted to fight Napoleon in Hamburg. On the other hand, he often meted out harsh sentences to duelists, including loss of noble status and exile to Siberia, where they were to perform hard labor. Though some sentences were later revoked or reduced, it seems to have worked. The Russian State Military Historical Archive for the years 1797–1801 refers to just three cases of dueling, and of these only one actually took place; it must be remembered, though, that they only referred to officers.

The accession of Alexander I led to more changes. Queen Louise of Prussia, who was infatuated with him, wrote that "such is the heavenly goodness of his character that with each look he makes people happy and contented." Perhaps

---

[120] G. de Maupassant, "Bel Ami," in *Œuvres complètes*, Paris: Dumont, 1979, p. 138.

[121] Figures for France, as well as Austria-Hungary, from "Zweikampf," in K. Birkmeyer, ed., *Vergleichende Darstellung des deutschen und auslaendischen Strafrechts*, Berlin: Liebman, 1906, vol. III, pp. 125–59.

[122] See, for what follows, Reyfman, *Ritualized Violence*, pp. 45–95.

this heavenly goodness helps explain why the prohibitions were relaxed. Under his reign, which lasted from 1801 until 1825, duels proliferated. Another factor was the Napoleonic Wars, particularly the campaigns of 1812–14 which took the Russian Army to Paris. Probably the fact that many Russian officers spoke French helped them perform many heroic deeds both on the dueling ground and in the boudoir. Numerous duels were fought over trifling issues – on one occasion the subject of the quarrel, Avtot'ia Istomina, was described as "a mere dancer" – and ended with the death of one of the combatants. The Decembrists, a group of liberal (by Russian standards) officers who tried to overthrow Alexander's successor Nicholas I in 1825, are said to have been particularly interested in dueling. Possibly this was because they saw themselves as representatives of a new generation seeking equality with older and more senior aristocrats.

Under Nicholas I and his successors dueling continued. As in France, journalists were particularly likely to become involved in "affairs of honor." A Russian peculiarity, and one that begs an explanation, was the enthusiasm with which the literary classes took up dueling. Russia's greatest poet Alexander Pushkin (1799–1837) was all but obsessed with the subject about which he wrote many a story. The same applies to his somewhat younger contemporary, Mikhail Lermontov (1814–41). Both men lost their lives while dueling. Perhaps their fate helped establish the convention whereby many other Russian writers felt obliged to present the duel as proof par excellence of human integrity, independence, and honor. Or else it is hard to see why it became the stock in trade of subsequent nineteenth-century writers such as Ivan Turgenev (1818–83), Fyodor Dostoyevsky (1821–81) and Leo Tolstoy (1828–1910). Dostoyevsky in his private notebooks even blamed the government for the decline of the duel, real or alleged. He need not have worried: in 1894 a law, apparently modeled on German and Austria-Hungarian ones, was passed obliging officers to duel if challenged. Literary men also continued to challenge each other into the twentieth century. One young blood who did so was Boris Pasternak (1890–1960), albeit that the fight in question never took place. Another peculiarity of Russian duels was their emotional character. It was as if duelists felt obliged to laugh, weep, and, as one contemporary noted, go into convulsions "like a hysterical woman."[123] It was left to the Bolsheviks to abolish the "ludicrous, savage, foul and shameful" custom which, the newspaper *Kommunist* claimed, had made two red commissars fight over some Georgian princess.

The final country I want to touch upon in this context is Germany. There are two reasons why German dueling has attracted much attention. One was the student duel or *Mensur*, a unique custom with no real equivalent in any other country. The other was dueling between officers. The latter in particular was often

---

[123] Aleksei Suvorin, quoted *ibid.*, p. 89.

seen both by contemporaries and by subsequent historians as an essential element in the conservative–feudal–imperialist–capitalist–authoritarian–reactionary–patriarchal (add as many derogatory adjectives as you please) complex that supposedly played such an important part in German public life and helped usher in National Socialism and two world wars.

In Germany, as in France, some considered the advent of the duel a step away from barbarism and toward civilization. Eighteenth-century German student duels were little different from ordinary civilian ones. As in other countries the authorities made some feeble attempts to prohibit them. Later, during the nineteenth century, they became an essential part of the culture, if that is the correct word, of the student associations or *Burschenschaften* which arranged them. Arrangement meant that there was no need for either an offender or an offended party. Dueling was considered both a privilege and a duty. It was a privilege because it enabled members of the associations to demonstrate their courage. They did so first by fighting, then by walking around with a bandaged head, and finally, more permanently, by means of the famous scar or scars across the cheek. Socially speaking, so important was that privilege that those who were denied it, as Jews regularly were, keenly resented the fact. It was a duty because anybody who refused to fight was excluded from membership, a fact that could have important repercussions for one's subsequent professional life.

As a traveler commented at the beginning of the twentieth century, in these duels the objective was neither to satisfy offended honor nor to injure or kill one's opponent. Instead, the real victor was the one who emerged with the greatest number of wounds.[124] By that time approximately 6,000 out of 8,000 student duels fought each year were of this kind.[125] Originally students used the so-called *Pariser*, a foil from which the "foil" had been removed. Later it was replaced by the rapier. Every German university town, and there were more of them than in any other country, had a class of fencing masters who made their living by teaching its use. Combatants wore special "dueling dress" consisting of heavily padded leather pants, fencing gloves, silk neckerchiefs, and a felt hat. *Pauken*, to use the original term, was praised as an especially pure and chivalrous form of fighting.[126] Wounds could be quite painful and regularly forced the recipient to be stitched up and spend a few days in bed. However, great precautions were taken to prevent more serious ones, let alone death. This caused outsiders to regard student duels with some contempt. Conversely, students with more serious scores to settle preferred the saber or the pistol and fought without protective clothing. The tendency of some students to go

---

[124] J. K. Jerome, *Three Men on the Bummel*, Bristol: Arrowsmith, 1900, ch. 13.

[125] U. Frevert, *Men of Honor*, Cambridge: Polity, 1995, pp. 102–3, 106.

[126] See H. Ring, "Die Mensur, ein wesentliches Merkmal des Verbandes," in R.-J. Baum, ed., *Wir wollen Männer, wir wollen Taten! Deutsche Corpsstudenten 1848 bis heute*, Berlin: Siedler, 1998, pp. 383–5.

beyond the *Mensur* explains why, out of some fifty cases of dueling between civilians that reached the courts in Germany each year during the 1890s, about thirty were attributable to the student community.

During the eighteenth century the authorities in Prussia, as the most important German state after Austria, did what they could to prevent dueling. Later, with the aristocracy tamed and forming a bulwark around the throne, attitudes changed.[127] As was the case with their opposite numbers in other countries, Prussian officers were especially likely to engage in duels, which often resulted from the most trivial causes. The difference was that those who refused to answer a challenge would be tried in front of a so-called *Ehrengericht*, or court of honor, consisting of their peers. If the verdict went against them, they were almost certain to be dishonorably dismissed from the army. *Ehrengerichte*, incidentally, continued to exist until 1945. Towards the end of World War II they were used to get rid of the conspirators of 20 July 1944, which cleared the way for them to be handed over to the notorious people's courts.

Throughout the nineteenth century the wisdom of these arrangements was the subject of a fierce debate. As in other countries, there were liberals and progressives who regarded dueling as stupid, wasteful, and reactionary. In particular, the representatives meeting at St. Paul's Church in Frankfurt in 1848 wanted to abolish the custom which, perhaps more than any other, marked the special status of the military in Germany.[128] Perhaps more than in other countries, it was defended by those who claimed that honor and courage were the quintessential qualities of officers, and that freeing them from the obligation to respond when challenged would destroy the army's morale. Dueling, indeed, was sometimes seen as a means of strengthening the solidarity of the officer corps.[129] This idea, it is said, was supported by none other than Goethe.[130] Dueling between civilians was defended as a victory of honor over interest and also as proof of the individual's independence over an increasingly omnipresent state. Even Marx, who saw it as a relic of a bygone age, fought a duel during his days as a university student at Bonn and later had some good things to say about the practice.[131] In practice a sort of compromise was

---

[127] See P. Dieners, *Das Duel und die Sonderrole des Militaers: Zur preussisch-deutschen Entwicklung von Militaer- und Zivilgewalt im 19. Jahrhundert*, Berlin: Duncker & Humboldt, 1992, pp. 34–5, 85–7.

[128] *Ibid.*, pp. 128–33.

[129] K. Demeter, *The German Officer Corps in State and Society, 1660–1945*, New York: Praeger, 1965, p. 119.

[130] F. von Mueller, *Unterhaltungen mit Goethe*, R. Grumach, ed., Weimar: Boehlau, 1956, p. 162.

[131] Frevert, *Men of Honor*, pp. 149–50; W. Liebknecht, quoted in F. J. Raddatz, ed., *Reminiscences of Marx and Engels*, Moscow: Foreign Languages Publishing House, 1959, p. 159.

worked out. Compared to that which students engaged in, the number of duels fought by officers and civilians each year was almost vanishingly small.[132]

On the other hand, the combats German officers and civilians did undertake tended to be fought with pistols and were very serious indeed. German ideas concerning what was and was not appropriate differed from the rest. French and British duelers often satisfied their own and their opponents' honor by firing into the air. Not so in Germany, where doing so was considered a mortal insult and might invite a bullet through head or heart. Russian duelers were allowed, even expected, to engage in histrionics. Not so German ones, who were supposed to demonstrate iron self-control. This was taken to the point where they had to face their opponents' fire without so much as twitching a muscle. In duels conducted with the saber, punching with the free hand or the guard, kicking, pushing, touching the ground with hand or knee, transferring a blade from one hand to another, or following up an attack that had disarmed an opponent or caused him to fall were all disallowed. There was to be no talking, screaming, or taunting through word or gesture. Clinches were broken up by the seconds.[133]

In Weimar Germany, student dueling all but disappeared.[134] In April 1933 Hans Kerrl, Reich Commissioner, tried to revive it by sending a circular to public prosecutors throughout the country ordering them not to prosecute students who engaged in saber duels. A month later the law was changed and student duels were expressly declared to be exempt from punishment. In 1934 a challenge for a duel with sabers was actually issued, but nothing came of it. The Nazis also made duels obligatory for members of the SA and SS and for officers of the Wehrmacht. Following the Italian Fascists, they were provided with daggers for the purpose. However, social attitudes had changed. As far as we know, during the twelve-year Reich there took place just one duel. The combatants were the reporter Ronald Strunk and one Horst Krutschinna, adjutant to Reich Youth Leader Baldur von Schirach. The latter had used Strunk's stay in Spain, where he covered the Civil War, to have an affair with his wife. Krutschinna, as the challenged party, wanted to fight with swords. Upon Strunk producing medical proof that he was unable to use one, pistols were substituted. The shoot-out ended with Krutschinna slightly wounded and Strunk dead. Thereupon Hitler, incensed at the loss of Germany's only internationally known journalist, decided that any future duels would have to be approved by him personally.[135]

[132] Frevert, Men of Honor, pp. 133–4.   [133] McAleer, Dueling, p. 161.
[134] See, for what follows, Frevert, Men of Honor, pp. 220–7.
[135] See H. Kater: "Die Ehreauffassung der SS: Nationalsozialismus und das Duell. Himmler als Burschenschafter: Das Duell R. Strunk gegen Horst Krutschinna," Einst und Jetzt, 38, 1993, pp. 265–70.

Probably originating as a cross between the medieval trial by combat and ordinary brawls, the kind of wargames that duels represented could not have existed for as long as they did if the powers that be had really done what they could to stamp them out. If, in spite of countless prohibitions, the games continued to exist, then this fact had everything to do with honor: in other words the realization that the readiness to kill and be killed – the latter perhaps even more than the former – is absolutely essential to war and the fear that, should dueling be abolished altogether, readiness would be hard or impossible to maintain. Going back to the Middle Ages, such ideas were widely held by the aristocracy, including the blue-bloods who sat on thrones and including also the officer corps, most of whose members were themselves aristocrats. As bourgeois officers increasingly began to join the services after 1789, naturally they sought to imitate their betters. Bent on showing that they, too, had honor, civilians of any standing did the same. In England dueling was reserved for gentlemen, an ill-defined class that nevertheless rested on a widely understood code of behavior.

Early on, duels differed little from skirmishes – indeed they *were* skirmishes, often fought by small groups of men with whatever weapons they had in all sorts of deserted places where the authority of the state did not yet reach. However, as the vast number of published handbooks show, later they tended to become more formalized and rule-bound. The variety of weapons duelists were allowed to choose was also reduced. As had also happened with tournaments, time caused duels to become less relevant to the conduct of war at any level. Depending on the country where they were held, some duelers fought to kill, though the percentage of those who did so probably declined as time went on, during the late nineteenth century in particular. Others were happy if honor could be satisfied by means that were less injurious to health. German student duels, being arranged, were especially harmless. This is probably another reason why there were so many of them and why they were tolerated, even encouraged, right into the early years of the twentieth century. Late nineteenth-century French duels also had a reputation of being numerous but relatively bloodless. At the other extreme were American duels – many of which are perhaps better characterized as pre-arranged brawls – Austrian-Hungarian duels, and Russian duels. Duels between German officers, though not numerous, also tended to be more deadly than most.

Though swords never entirely disappeared, starting around 1770 a growing number of duels were fought with pistols instead. Right from the beginning dueling with pistols was considered less honorable than doing so with swords, the reason being that whereas the latter allowed real fighting to take place the former did not. The more advanced the technology in use, the more acute the problem. The introduction of sighted pistols with rifled barrels from around 1870 made it much easier to hit an opponent. It is true that combatants sometimes used old pistols which did not have these technical refinements, but such weapons, as well as the black powder and balls used to load them, were themselves becoming increasingly hard to obtain. Faced by an opponent armed in this manner, it was all duelers could do to prove their courage by sticking to the rules and facing their opponent without flinching.

To put it another way, the point came when technology developed to the point where strategy, in the sense of a two-sided interaction between two parties, became impossible. Either duelers found some way to settle the matter – as far as may be determined, during the last years before 1914 the number of fights with a deadly outcome tended to go down – or else all that was left to them was to look their opponents squarely in the face. Honor, in other words, became almost synonymous with stupidity. Perhaps not surprisingly, that was also the moment when dueling finally came to an end.

4

Battles, campaigns, wars, and politics

From squares to hexes

The wargames discussed in this volume so far were played by real men using real weapons, though admittedly some of them were blunted or otherwise modified to make them less dangerous. Either the games took place out of doors, as most did from the Stone Age on, or else they were held in special structures such as the Colosseum. Without exception, all were somewhat dangerous – danger, in fact, was precisely what set them apart from other two-sided games in which victory was won not by fighting but by other methods. Many, notably single combat, combat of champions, gladiatorial combats, trial by battle, and duels, were very dangerous indeed. In some cases this was carried to the point where the fighting was as real and as deadly as anything in war. The difference consisted in the purpose the games served; also in the ceremonies with which the games started and ended and of which they were a part.

However, between about 1450 and 1525, a vast change came over warfare, and with it wargames. Until then, practically all weapons used by all civilizations around the world had been edged and derived their energy from human muscle. This even applied to those which, like siege engines, used various contrivances in order to combine the energy of numerous individuals. The introduction of firearms, as demonstrated most convincingly at Constantinople in 1453, changed all that. On the one hand it made weapons much more powerful and much more deadly. On the other, this very power and deadliness meant that they were no longer suitable for use in two-sided wargames of the kind discussed so far. In other words, two-sided games and weapon practice were forced apart. Indeed the time was to come when the latter could only be engaged in if and when there was nobody who could possibly get hurt for miles around. The only exception was dueling pistols. However, even they gradually grew so powerful that the games in which they were used ended up by abolishing themselves. Other methods for playing at war, simulating war, and training for war had to be found; building on much older foundations, other methods for doing so were found. In the process, the way war was understood itself underwent a profound transformation.

The wargames in question were played indoors by means of counters, or miniatures, on a board of some sort. As we shall see, these methods enabled all kinds of factors that previous wargames could not and did not simulate to be introduced. On the other hand, as we shall also see, there were certain elements that had to be left out. The oldest known board game, the ancient Egyptian *senet*, was played with dice and pieces on a field of thirty squares. However, what it symbolized was not war but the trial of the deceased in front of thirty judges in the next world.[1] The ancient Greeks had *polis*, sometimes known as *petteia*. It was played by two persons on a large board with the aid of pieces (*pessoi*) known as dogs. The game seems to have resembled chess in that the number of pieces filled two rows at each end of the board. *Polis*, though, differed from chess (but resembled draughts) in that all the pieces were of the same kind. They moved in the manner of chess rooks and captured by the interception method. Apparently the rules made it important to make sure no piece would find itself isolated from the rest. This has caused some modern authorities to argue that it was used to teach players the kind of discipline that hoplites, fighting in a phalanx, required.[2]

The Romans had a different game called *latrunculi* (little robbers). As best it can be reconstructed, it was played on an eight by twelve board by two players using pieces with contrasting colors. Each player had twelve normal pieces plus a king. All thirteen pieces moved as rooks do, except that the king could only move one square in each direction. As best we can reconstruct the game, it resembled *petteia*, in so far as capture was by the interception method. However, kings could not be captured. Apparently the side that immobilized the opponent's king on all sides, or captured all the opponents' normal pieces, or had more pieces left on the board after fifty moves, won.[3] Other peoples, including the ancient Irish, Thai, Japanese, Nubians, Scandinavians, and North and South American Indians all had, or have, their own games.[4]

Most wargames of this kind are played by two persons, but some involve four. Each player commands an "army" on a board that symbolizes a field. Sometimes a lattice pattern is used, as in Go, or else there are squares of contrasting colors. Games are differentiated by the shape of the board (rectangular or oblong) and according to whether the board has other marks on it and, if so, the purpose those marks serve. The number and arrangement of pieces on

---

[1] See Decker, *Sports and Games in Ancient Egypt*, pp. 124–31.
[2] According to L. Kurke, "Ancient Greek Board Games and How to Play Them," *Classical Philology*, 94, 3, July 1999, p. 259, based on Aristotle, *Politics*, 1.2.9–12.
[3] See Ludus Lantruculorum, available at: http://en.wikipedia.org/wiki/Ludus_latrunculorum.
[4] See H. J. R. Murray, *A History of Board Games other than Chess*, Oxford: Clarendon Press, 1952, pp. 53–98.

each side, the types into which they are divided, their various moves, the methods used for capture (interception, leap, or encirclement), and the rules as to what constitutes victory are also different. Most games involve contests between symmetrical armies, but some do not. Since play proceeds by turns, designing a game in which the player who moves first does not enjoy a certain advantage is all but impossible; hence tournaments are often organized in such a way as to neutralize this effect by having players play now one side, now another.

By far the best-known wargame of this kind is chess. It has many variants, including a Chinese one that remains very popular and is often played in the street. Played on a lattice, Chinese chess has two armies drawn up on either side of a "river." The total number of pieces on each side is sixteen, as in Western chess. However, each army also has two counselors (instead of one queen) and two cannon, leaving only five pawns. Not only are the movements of many pieces different, but some of them may cross the river into enemy territory whereas others may not. Those which have done so may move in a different way from those that stay behind. To this extent the game takes into account Sun Tzu's warning concerning the difficulty of waging a campaign far from home, something that Western chess does not do. All this makes it as least as sophisticated and interesting as Western chess, with as many different strategies, openings, endgames, and so on.[5] But whereas Western chess has been widely adopted in China, the opposite had not happened. That is why I shall focus on the development of the former. In doing so, I follow the account of H. J. R. Murray, a great early twentieth-century scholar whose work is unlikely to be improved upon in the future.[6]

This story starts with the *Nitisara*, an Indian work on public policy dating to the first half of the first millennium AD. It says that a *chaturanga*, literally "an organism consisting of four parts," is made up of elephants, horse, chariots, and infantry. A king and his vizier, both of whom represent individuals rather than troops and whose presence on the battlefield is self-explanatory, are added. The text goes on to discuss the best ways these arms should be employed: noting, for example, that a horseman is worth three infantrymen and that the elephants should be stationed in the wings. The parallels with war extend to the way victory is obtained and are both obvious and well understood. To speak with Clausewitz, the objective of war is to overthrow the enemy.[7] This could be accomplished either by the capture or death of the opposing monarch or by the

[5] See H. T. Lau, *Chinese Chess: An Introduction to China's Ancient Game of Strategy*, Tokyo: Tuttle, 1985.
[6] H. J. R. Murray, *A History of Chess*, Oxford University Press, 1962 [1913], pp. 44–50, 123–4, 151.
[7] Clausewitz, *On War*, pp. 75, 77.

annihilation of his army. Both are exactly reproduced by the two methods of winning in early chess – the checkmate and the baring of the opponent's king.

From India the game spread to China and Persia. In the latter it acquired the name of *shach* (king) and went on to conquer the Arab world and Byzantium. Around AD 1000 it began to be played in Western Europe. Over time important changes were made. The original monochrome lattice board was replaced by a checkered one. The elephant, an animal not familiar to Europeans, was replaced by the bishop. Similarly the vizier was replaced by a queen – a change that, though anything but realistic (real-life queens rarely accompanied their husbands to the field, let alone into combat) caused rivers of ink to be spilt as feminist scholars tried to present it as an indication of the higher status of women in Western societies. The most important change took place around 1490. The queen, originally able to move one square diagonally, was allowed to move any number in any direction. This made her much the most powerful one on the board. It also turned a somewhat slow game into a much faster and more aggressive one.[8]

The rules governing the moves of the remaining pieces also underwent long and complex development. Throughout all this, writers of various nationalities never doubted that chess was indeed a wargame, intended and able to capture some aspects of real warfare. This is even truer of Chinese chess with its pieces representing chariots and cannon. Probably the most charming affirmation comes from a Jewish poet in Spain, Abraham ben Ezra (1089–1164):

> I will sing a song of battle
> Planned in days long passed and over.
> Men of skill and science set it
> On a plain of eight divisions,
> And designed in squares all checkered,
> Two camps face each one the other,
> And the kings stand by for battle,
> And 'twixt these two is the fighting.
> Bent on war the face of each is,
> Ever moving or encamping,
> Yet no swords are drawn in warfare,
> For war of thought their war is.

Luigi Guicciardini, an early sixteenth-century Italian author, once wrote an essay entitled, "A Comparison of the Game of Chess with the Notable Treatises on War." Chess, of course, is a two-sided game of strategy aimed at "killing" the enemy in which the enemy's moves are as important as one's own. As in war, strategy consists of attacking, defending, concentrating, dispersing, breaking through, circumventing, and, perhaps most importantly of all, cheating (within

---

[8] See M. Yalom, *Birth of the Chess Queen*, New York: Harper, 2005, especially pp. 15–30 and 213–27.

the rules, of course), misleading, and taking by surprise. Like war, it allows for
very different styles of play: tactical, strategic (meaning, in this context, play
that looks at the board as a whole rather than at the moves of specific pieces),
aggressive, defensive, positional, attritional, and so on.[9]
   Some players show a notable preference for some pieces, such as pawns,
whereas others do not. Some try to occupy the center of the board as fast as they
can, whereas others are more interested in the flanks. Some pay more attention
to controlling "terrain," others less. Quite a few show psychological insight by
varying their style from one opponent to the next. Just as in war every great
commander developed his own methods, so in chess many of these styles are
linked to the names of individual players who invented them. Prominent
among them were François-André Danican Philidor (1762–95), Paul Morphy
(1837–84), and Aron Nymzowitsch (1886–1935). In both chess and war, an
important trick is to combine the various arms so as to bring out the capabilities
of each of them while masking the weaknesses. Another is to orchestrate them
in such a way that each one will carry out not one task but several at once.
   Many of the parallels even extend to detail. In both war and chess, one
excellent method to gain an advantage is to isolate an opposing piece until it can
no longer be defended. Another is to pin the opponent by threatening such an
important target as to force him to defend it and, in doing so, to suffer more
losses than he can afford; another still is to nail the opponent on the horns of a
dilemma or, to speak with Liddell Hart, confront him with a plan with several
branches.[10] As former Israeli prime minister General Ariel Sharon once said, in
real-life battle the worst thing that can happen to troops is to have enemies
appear in their back. The chess (and draughts) equivalent is the queening of
pawns that have reached the last line. To quote Samuel Rosenthal, a Polish-
Jewish player who, living in Paris, became a chess celebrity and adviser to Louis
Napoleon:

> Both soldiers and players, regardless of their talent, must know a certain
> theory and certain principles. Indeed, their theory resembles ours. Isn't it
> true that it teaches them to conduct his troops on a battlefield, according to
> established rules, to reassemble at the opportune moment, to have them
> converge at a determined point in the briefest span of time? Shouldn't they
> try to make the others attack them where they are the strongest, to change
> fronts when the opponent attacks them at their vulnerable point, to
> manage their soldiers' lives for the ultimate moment? ... The two are
> sisters; the path one follows, the method one uses to succeed in chess, are
> absolutely identical to those that the greatest commanders recommend.[11]

---

[9] See, for a simple exposition of the various styles, D. Shenk, *The Immortal Game: A History
of Chess*, New York: Anchor, 2005, pp. 96–7, 100, 103, 142, 166–7, 180.
[10] B. H. Liddell Hart, *Strategy*, London: Cassell, 1967, pp. 343–4.
[11] Quoted in Shenk, *The Immortal Game*, pp. 112–15.

All this shows how strong the strategic paradigm, which is the most important thing chess and war have in common, really is. Unsurprisingly, many famous commanders had more than a passing interest in chess. Among them were William the Conqueror (who once broke a board over an opponent's head), Richard the Lionheart, Edward I of England, Tamerlane (who named a captured city after a chess move), and Napoleon (who tended towards rashness and always remained a mediocre player). Nevertheless, the differences between war and chess are as important as the similarities. The board is much too simple to give a good representation of terrain. The number of pieces is too small. Their moves are stereotyped and have little to do with the real-life tactical possibilities open to the kind of troops they are supposed to represent or, indeed, to any kind of troops at all; this is even more true of Go, which is why it is not discussed here. Not only are logistics ignored, but chess is a game of complete information. Every move by each player is instantly and completely visible to the other: as a result, reconnaissance and intelligence are not required. This in turn means that, though surprise does play an important role, the means for achieving it are completely different. Friction too is left out, including, since all "orders" are instantaneously delivered without any possibility of misunderstanding or disobedience, the kind of friction that operating a mechanism of command and control involves.[12]

Chess has often been praised for the fact that it is a purely intellectual game that involves neither chance nor physical skill of any kind but focuses on strategy alone.[13] In tournament chess, great efforts are made not only to provide a neutral (meaning sterile) atmosphere but also to isolate players from each other and from the public. The intent is to prevent any kind of psychological factor from penetrating and influencing the play. To no avail: in reality, what are being tested are one's entire nervous system, one's fears, one's tenacity, and so forth.[14] Some players were famous for their ability to unbalance their opponents. They deliberately varied the tempo of their moves, rose from their seats, paced around, sat down again, played with their fingers, and so on. One world champion, Mikhail Tal, has been described as "an encyclopedia of kinetic movement."[15] He was also accused of staring at opponents, hypnotizing them, and breaking their will. Some actually tried to protect themselves by wearing dark glasses! Understandably, he himself did nothing to discourage the rumors.[16]

[12] See on this M. van Creveld, *Command in War*, Cambridge, MA: Harvard University Press, 1985, especially pp. 1–16 and 261–77.

[13] Murray, *A History of Chess*, p. 124.

[14] See R. Desjarlais, *Counterplay: An Anthropologist at the Chessboard*, Berkeley: University of California Press, 2011, pp. 63–4.

[15] F. Brady, *Endgame: Bobby Fischer's Remarkable Rise and Fall*, New York: Crown, 2011, p. 112.

[16] See the account of M. M. Botvinnik, *Achieving the Aim*, Oxford: Pergamon, 1981, pp. 36, 56, 158.

One can certainly appreciate what the organizers are trying to do. On the other hand, the purely intellectual character of the game goes a long way to explain why it never became nearly as popular as, say, many kinds of combat and contact sports did. The same applies to all of its successors, however carefully construed and however sophisticated. More pertinent to our subject, the more successful the efforts at making sure that the game should be governed solely by the players' intellect, the less like war it will become. As in any laboratory, perfection can only be achieved at the cost of estrangement from the real world. From this point of view, banishing or trying to banish psychology is the worst thing one can do. Another difficulty is that both in chess itself and in its predecessors and derivatives players take turns in making their moves. Both for this reason and because the moves made on the board are purely symbolic, it excludes fighting – the very factor which, to quote Clausewitz again, is the essence of war.[17] To end the list of problems, strictly speaking what chess simulates is not war but merely a battle. The moves that lead to the battle, or follow it, are excluded.

Some versions of chess could be understood as attempts to correct some of these shortcomings. This applies to Chinese chess, described above, and also to Burmese chess, or *sittuyin*. In it, the initial moves, whose purpose is to arrange the major pieces on the board, form part of the game;[18] to that extent, it simulates not merely a battle but a campaign. In the West attempts to deal with these problems date back to the Renaissance, but little is known about them. The first "chess reformator" whose name has survived was one Christopher Weickmann of Ulm, Germany, who flourished around 1650. As he himself explained, the objective was to present "the most necessary political and military axiomata, rules and ways of playing . . . without great effort and the reading of many books."[19]

Weickmann's work was continued by C. L. Helwig and Georg Venturini. They published their detailed proposals in 1780 and 1798 respectively. All three men claimed that their games had excited the interest of some senior military professionals of their day who regarded them as useful for training purposes. In the case of Helwig and Venturini those claims may have had some base in reality. True, neither of their games ever became very popular. However, both are known to have been close to the Duke of Brunswick, a cousin and close ally of Frederick the Great. He successfully commanded the Hanoverian Army

---

[17] Clausewitz, *On War*, p. 95.

[18] See, for what follows, "Burmese Chess," at: www.chessvariants.org/oriental.dir/burmese.html.

[19] The quote is from P. von Hilger, *War Games: A History of War on Paper*, Cambridge, MA: MIT, 2012, p. 21. See also Perla, *The Art of Wargaming*, pp. 15–60; S. B. Patrick, "The History of Wargaming," in Staff of the Strategy and Tactics Magazine, eds., *Wargame Design*, New York: Hippocrene, 1983, pp. 30–44; N. Palmer, *The Comprehensive Guide to Board Wargaming*, New York: Hippocrene, 1977, pp. 13–7; and many others.

during the Seven Years War; forty years later, while in his seventies, he was decisively defeated by Napoleon at Jena in 1806 and died of his wounds.

As one might expect, all three inventors started by increasing the number of squares on the board. Next, all three gave each side a much larger number of pieces to "command" and modified those pieces' moves in order to provide a better approximation to reality. Different types of cavalry, infantry and artillery were all introduced, as were some other types of contemporary troops. Helwig also added various kinds of terrain – blue stood for water, red for mountains, light and dark green for marshes and forests, and black and white for open fields. Going one step further, Venturini got rid of the squares altogether, replacing them by a grid of no fewer than 3,600 squares which was used to overlay a map of the border area between Germany and France, "the cockpit of Europe" where many campaigns took place. Both Helwig and Venturini allowed units of each arm to advance at different speed over different kinds of terrain. Venturini even factored in logistic elements, including supply convoys, field bakeries – all-important in contemporary warfare, since it was the need to bake bread every five days that dictated armies' moves[20] – magazines, roads, and bridges.

This was a revolution indeed. Logistics had always been part of war: Napoleon may have been the first commander who said that armies march on their stomachs, but he was certainly not the first who knew this to be the fact. So why did they not figure in the wargames people designed, played, and watched either in the field, or in some arena, or on boards? The answer is that, to speak with a modern expert on ancient warfare, war had always been seen as part tourism, part large-scale robbery, punctuated by occasional – seldom more than one or two per campaigning season – large-scale, parade-like, encounters known as battles.[21] On the one hand, so limited was the range of weapons that, raids and skirmishes apart, an enemy force situated more than a mile or so away might as well have been on the moon. On the other, deploying an army of any size into battle array required hours to accomplish. All this meant that such encounters took place by mutual consent, sometimes after armies had been facing one another for days, even weeks, on end.[22] Exactly as in Kishon's story, previous wargames provided a better insight into the way war was understood than war itself did.

Not surprisingly, once Venturini had incorporated logistics into his wargame it was only a matter of time before attempts were made to include other elements of warfare as well. Following in Venturini's footsteps was a Prussian

[20] See M. van Creveld, *Supplying War: Logistics from Wallenstein to Patton*, Cambridge University Press, 1978, pp. 11, 29.

[21] F. E. Adcock, *The Greek and Macedonian Art of War*, Berkeley: University of California Press, 1962, p. 25.

[22] Clausewitz, *On War*, pp. 245–7 and 297.

father-and-son team, Leopold and Georg von Reisswitz. The elder Reisswitz played his wargames with the aid of miniatures, made of porcelain and representing individual soldiers, on a large sandbox. Later the sand was replaced by movable plaster casts of mountains, bodies of water, and so on. Then as today, such devices have the advantage of providing a three-dimensional model of the terrain. Vegetation, roads, rivers, etc. are easily added. What is more, the substitution of a variable "board" for a fixed one for the first time enabled players to be provided with scenarios, thus finally doing away with the rigid symmetry that, in the interest of fairness, had governed almost all previous wargames. It was this aspect of the matter that made it suitable for military training and education. The year was 1811, and Prussia was governed by King Frederick William III of whom Napoleon once said that he could talk of little but "military headgear, buttons, and leather knapsacks."[23] He loved the game, as did his two sons, the future Frederick William IV and Kaiser William I. They introduced it to the future emperor of Russia, their brother-in-law Nicholas I. Incidentally, one of those who looked after the military education of the two princes was none other than Clausewitz.

Toy soldiers have a very long history going back all the way to Greece, Rome, and the Middle Ages. Wargames using miniatures go back at least as far as the Renaissance. It is said that a certain Junellus Turianus got Charles V to play with them on a table top.[24] In 1614 the emperor's great-grandson, Philip IV, then just nine years old, was presented with a complete wooden army. Its creator, Alberto Struzzi, was a political economist whose works were much read at the time. He took care to provide players with stacks of money as well as troops.[25] Later in the century the young Louis XIV owned a set of 5,000 silver soldiers, only to have it melted down to help pay for his "real" wars. Throughout the eighteenth and nineteenth centuries the price of miniature soldiers, now made of tin, kept going down, which enabled growing numbers of people to play with them. Eventually miniatures included not just carefully crafted soldiers but cannon, vehicles of every kind, tents, and much more. Some modern enthusiasts even add field toilets, insisting, no doubt correctly, that without them no army can exist and operate. Apparently the joy of designing figures, painting them and the like predominates over that of making them "fight." As the example of the Prussian "soldier king" Frederick William I (father of Frederick the Great) and some of his successors shows, real-life rulers sometimes showed a similar preference.[26]

[23] Quoted in T. Stamm-Kuhlman, *Koenig in Preussens groesser Zeit*, Berlin: Siedler, p. 255.
[24] According to G. Gush, *A Guide to Wargaming*, London: Croom Helm, 1980, pp. 21–2.
[25] See G. Parker, *The Army of Flanders and the Spanish Road*, Cambridge University Press, 1972, p. 3.
[26] Van Creveld, *The Culture of War*, pp. 353–7.

The rules governing miniature wargames are broadly similar to those of board games. They were very popular in early twentieth-century Europe, especially England where well-known public figures from Winston Churchill down played them.[27] They also became the subject of an amusing little book by the famous writer H. G. Wells. He explained how they should be played, provided some simple rules, and suggested, tongue in cheek, that aggressive leaders everywhere might be locked up in a room and made to play them against each other while thankfully leaving other people in peace.[28] Not such a bad idea, incidentally, and one that has its historical precedents in the combat of champions of which we have spoken. Thanks to the introduction of cheap plastic figures during the 1960s the field still remains a well-developed, if fairly minor, hobby. Miniatures representing troops of almost every imaginable time and place continue to be manufactured in very large numbers. Rules for playing with them also continue to be published.[29] Often it is a question of reenacting historical battles. Indeed it could be argued that by going back centuries and even millennia, miniature wargamers are in a position to make a very substantial contribution to understanding warfare as it was waged during the periods in question. Other miniature wargamers focus on exploring the future rather than the past. Their games incorporate all sorts of fantastic characters endowed with fantastic capabilities. Those include not only the standard military ones of offensive, defensive, and movement but every kind of magic too.

Some miniature wargames use physical devices to enable players to hit the enemy "army." H. G. Wells employed a toy cannon activated by a spring which, he wrote, in trained hands could hit an "enemy" formation nine cases out of ten at a distance of ten yards. His near contemporary, Frederick Jane, a well-known military writer who also devised a naval wargame, invented a "striker."[30] Handheld, it had an asymmetrically mounted pin at its head; players used it to punch holes in ships made of cardboard. The results would then be adjusted according to the part of the ship that was hit. As both writers noted, the method demanded the coordination of mind and body. Thus it brought in some of the "nerve" that fighting requires – precisely the element that most board games, played in a comfortable setting and at a leisurely pace, leave out. Jane even claimed that, in his experience, the closer the game moved to the "combat" phase, the greater the excitement and the harder players found it to aim their strikers. As children we used to roll golf balls against one another's fortresses which were made of wooden blocks. However, so unlike operating real weapons were the actions

---

[27] See K. D. Brown, "Modeling for War: Toy Soldiers in Late Victorian and Edwardian England," *Journal of Social History*, 24, 2, Winter 1991, pp. 237–8.

[28] H. G. Wells, *Little Wars*, Boston, MA: Small & Co., 1913.

[29] See, for all these kinds of games, D. Featherstone and J. Curry, *Donald Featherstone's War Games*, at: Lulu.com, 2008.

[30] See on this D. Featherstone, *Naval War Games: Fighting Sea Battles with Model Ships*, London: Staley & Paul, 1965, p. 148.

required in such games as to be almost ridiculous. As a result, except among children, games based on such means never became very popular.

The great disadvantage of miniature wargames when used for serious training is the difficulty of matching the scale of the figures to that on which the terrain is represented. If the game is played on the floor, as those proposed by H. G. Wells were, then people will find themselves crawling on all fours. They may even be forced to lie down in order to adjust their perspective to that of the "troops" they command. If it is played on a table, then limits are set by the ability of players to reach their figures and move them. The growth of firepower, which was accompanied by a very sharp decline in the number of troops per square yard of territory, has made the problem much more difficult still.[31] Thus such games are best used to reproduce small-scale engagements and skirmishes. Years ago I myself saw them used for this purpose at the Marine Corps officer school in Quantico, Virginia; the officer in charge, incidentally, has since become a very senior general. Even so, the toy soldiers and vehicles used were proportionally much larger than the surrounding terrain features.

A way out was suggested by the younger Reisswitz, whose system of wargaming led to all subsequent ones down to, and in some ways including, the introduction of computers during the 1950s.[32] Reisswitz replaced the model of terrain with a topographic map based on contour lines, a type that first made its appearance at the very end of the eighteenth century.[33] The map was drawn to a scale of 1:8,000. Play proceeded by means of metal counters of different sizes, each representing not an individual but a unit of some kind. As a result, each was able to take up the correct frontage on the map. Not the least important effect of the change was to reduce the size of the necessary apparatus. Instead of requiring a massive six by six foot table it could be fitted in an easily transportable mahogany box. Some are still on show in German museums.

Like all previous games of this kind, Reisswitz's players had to take turns in moving their pieces. The innovation consisted in each turn now representing two minutes of real time. This meant that the distance each type of unit and, even more important, each piece of information directed to or by "commanders" could cover in each period of time, known from actual experience, could be factored in. Commanders, in other words, were required to operate as they would in real war.[34] Instead of pieces capturing one another, as in chess, an elaborate system for determining the outcome of combat was

---

[31] T. N. Dupuy, *Numbers, Predictions and War*, Indianapolis, IN: Bobbs-Merrill, 1979, pp. 28–9.

[32] B. von Reisswitz, *Kriegspiel: Instructions for the Representation of Military Maneuvers with the Kriegspiel Apparatus*, Hemel Hempstead: Bill Leeson, 1983 [1824].

[33] See, for the origin of such maps, the topographic map, at: http://en.wikipedia.org/wiki/Topographic_map.

[34] See, on these critically important aspects of Reisswitz's game, von Hilger, *War Games*, pp. 43–51.

introduced. Based on experiments conducted, among others, by the great military reformer Gerhard von Scharnhorst,[35] it made use of dice and took into account the number of troops on each side as well as the arm to which they belonged. Engagements could end with good or bad effect, with each of the two possibilities being further divided into best, two-thirds of best, and so on.[36] The game, in other words, still left out the actual fighting, which is too complex to be understood by simple causation.[37] To compensate for this fact it relied on statistics – just as quantum mechanics would do in respect to physics a hundred years later.

The new game neither required that the players be precisely balanced nor was content with schematic representations of warfare. Instead it allowed specific scenarios to be produced and played out. The scenarios were devised by an umpire who handed them to the players. They in turn wrote down their general "campaign plans" as well as the specific movements they intended to make. Their notes concerning the latter they handed to the umpire. The umpire made the necessary adjustments to the pieces on the map, which was divided in two by a cloth screen. Sometimes three maps were used, one for each player and one for the umpire. True, intelligence – the systematic gathering of knowledge about the enemy, the use of spies etc. – still did not play a role. However, since the umpire was also responsible for giving each player as much, or as little, enemy information as his patrols would provide him with in reality, each side no longer had complete information about the other. Once again, the game reflected changes in contemporary understanding, as exemplified by Clausewitz,[38] as to what war was all about and what its main constituents were.

In 1824 the entire complex was presented to Frederick William III who was still on the throne. He in turn made the chief of the General Staff, General Karl von Muffling, have a look at it. Much later, the meeting was described by a Lieutenant Dannhauer who had helped Reisswitz develop the game and who was destined to end his career as a general.[39] Apparently the old gentleman was skeptical at first. However, as the presentation continued he grew increasingly excited, finally exclaiming that this was not a game but serious training for war and promising to send a set to every regiment in the army. Not only did he prove as good as his word, but he had the semi-official military weekly, the *Militair-Wochenblatt*, publish an article that gave the game high praise. It had

---

[35] G. von Scharnhorst, *Ueber die Wirkung des Feuergewehrs*, Osnabrueck: Biblio, 1973 [1813].
[36] Von Reisswitz, *Kriegspiel*, p. 9.
[37] See on this point C. Coker, *Barbarous Philosophers: Reflections on the Nature of War from Heraclitus to Heisenberg*, London: Hurst, 2010, pp. 250, 252–3.
[38] Clausewitz, *On War*, pp. 117–18.
[39] E. H. Dannhauer, "Das Reisswitzsche Kriegspiel von seinen Beginn bis zu Tode des Erfinders 1827," *Militair-Wochenblatt*, 56, 1872, pp. 22–4.

succeeded, the author said, in closing the gap between "the serious business of warfare" and "the more frivolous demands of a game."[40]

Von Reisswitz himself did not live to see the outcome. In 1827, having been transferred to a remote garrison town, he shot himself. Later, though, his game spread like wildfire among Prussian soldiers and civilians alike. One indication of this is the fact that the colors he used to mark friendly and hostile troops, i.e. blue and red, were taken over by the military and still remain in use. Numerous *Vereine*, or clubs, were set up to bring enthusiasts together and enable them to play regular matches. The *Militair-Wochenblatt*, as the most prestigious publication of its kind in Germany, provided its readers with at least one new scenario each week. Helmut von Moltke himself is said to have taken up wargaming in 1828, when he was a lieutenant working for the Topographical Bureau of the General Staff.[41] Yet Prussia still remained the least of the great powers. Only after the spectacular victories of 1866 and 1870 did its army acquire an international reputation. The outcome was to turn the kind of *Kriegspiel* practiced by the Prussian General Staff into an export commodity which it still remains. Both in Germany and abroad, a vast number of variations made their appearance. Some applied the principles involved to specific fields such as tactics, strategy, supply, fortress warfare, naval games, and the medical service.[42] Others tried to improve on the original. Here I shall focus on two versions in particular: namely so-called "free" wargames on the one hand and the hexed ones that were popular in the US during the 1970s and 1980s on the other.

"Free" wargames were pioneered by one of Moltke's own officers, Colonel Julius Verdy du Vernois, who in 1876 published a book on the subject.[43] He argued that von Reisswitz's *Kriegspiel* was too complicated. As originally presented by its author, it required a sixty-page booklet of rules and statistical tables. Subsequent modifications, many of which aimed at increasing realism by updating and adding more and more details, made the game more complex still. Play tended to last forever and was often abandoned before it could be brought to a conclusion. In other words, realism – the great advantage of von Reisswitz-type games – and playability – so characteristic of older ones such as chess – had gone their separate ways. The more highly developed the game and the more detailed the rules, the more serious the problem.

The solution, Vernois argued, was to make greater use of the players' professional knowledge. The players he had in mind were not rank amateurs but

[40] Quoted in E. Halter, *From Sun Tzu to XBox: War and Video Games*, New York: Thunder Mouth's Press, 2006, p. 43.
[41] According to Perla, *The Art of Wargaming*, p. 30.
[42] See, for a list of such games, von Altrock, *Das Kriegspiel: Eine Anleitung zu seiner Handhabung*, Berlin: Mittler, 1908, pp. 180–90.
[43] J. von Verdy du Vernois, *Beitrag zum Kriegspiel*, Berlin: Mittler, 1876.

young officers in various stages of training and education. If only one assumed that such players knew how much space a battalion occupied, how fast it could march over certain kinds of terrain, what the range and rate of fire of various weapons were, and so on, many tables and calculations could be done away with. The same would happen if, instead of using dice and then carefully calculating the losses each side would suffer after each kind of engagement, such losses would simply be classified as light, medium, or heavy. After all, the commanders of large formations, such as divisions, army corps, and armies, were not interested in counting every individual casualty either. In maneuvers conducted by real bodies of troops over real terrain, the outcomes were never determined by throwing dice, so why do so in *Kriegspiel?* Playability, in other words, was to be restored by making use of experience and expertise.

To compensate for the "soft" rules Vernois suggested relying on the umpire, whose role in the game was greatly enhanced in this way. Unless the umpire kept things under fairly tight control, deciding when each round had ended and providing new scenarios, the game would either peter out or degenerate into a shouting match. It might even end with participants hitting each other on the head. Yet, paradoxically, of all the numerous factors that separate wargames from the reality they are supposed to simulate, the presence of umpires is perhaps the most important of all: which, of course, is just why many real-life confrontations *do* peter out or *do* end with people hitting each other on the head. As Vernois admitted it would, introducing an umpire also carried the risk of injecting the game with a considerable measure of arbitrariness. Assuming a capable and honest umpire, though, play would become much easier.

Games could be played either with one participant on each side or by opposing teams. The equipment needed for the purpose was fairly minimal – counters representing various kinds of units and troops, and two rooms with the copies of the relevant maps spread out in each. Orders could be delivered in writing, but it was also possible to save time and effort by simply moving counters on the map. Distances were measured with the aid of dividers. The umpire, or exercise leader (*Leiter*) as Vernois, indicating the importance of his role, called him, was supposed to move from one room to another. First he would present a general scenario to each side separately and ask them to formulate their campaign plan as well as their initial moves. Those moves having been made, he would provide the other side with as much information about them as they could expect to receive in reality. In case each side was represented by a team, it was also possible to take account of the time it would take the commander-in-chief to communicate with his subordinates, whose units were stationed at various points on the map, and vice versa. All this, Vernois claimed, would make for a game much more fluid and lively than anything von Reisswitz had been able to provide. To the extent that fluidity and liveliness are characteristic of war, it was also more realistic.

In trying to increase playability by doing away with many kinds of calculations as well as the dice, Vernois was aiming primarily at the military. The
same was true of other Wilhelmine authors, most of whom were officers.[44]
American designers during the 1970s and 1980s, such as Nicholas Palmer, Peter
Perla, and above all James Dunnigan, took exactly the opposite tack. While
aiming their work at civilians, they sought to increase realism by providing
more rules, not fewer. The decisive change was made when squares were
replaced by hexagons, or hexes, as they are commonly called. Dating back to
the 1950s, when the navy experimented with them, superficially they were a
simple invention. Looking back, one is surprised they had not been introduced
much earlier. Hexes had two important advantages. First, they enabled players
to move their pieces in six directions rather than four, vastly increasing
flexibility. Second, when superimposed on a map they enabled frontiers,
roads, rivers, coasts, and the like to be drawn much more realistically.
Depending on the scale on which the map was drawn, anything from minor
topographical features to continents could be represented. As with many
wargames from the time of Helwig on, different types of terrain could be
shown by printing hexes in different colors. Hexed maps, in other words,
represented a cross between the hoary checkered boards and traditional
maps, incorporating some of the advantages of both. Last but not least, each
hex could be provided with a number, as in chess. This allowed the games to be
played by persons or teams geographically far removed from one another, with
the aid of the mail.

In other respects the wargames in question started where the younger von
Reisswitz had stopped. Games were played on maps, albeit highly stylized ones.
Troops, units, and formations were represented by small cardboard counters on
which their most important characteristics such as offensive and defensive
power, ability to move, and so on were printed. Each player started by arranging
his pieces on the map either as he pleased, or, in case a historical campaign was
being simulated, by following a scenario. Movements were governed by terrain,
which either accelerated them or slowed them down. Recognizing the effect of
modern weapons, artillery in particular, many games introduced zones of
control which enemy units could only enter at some cost, such as reduced
speed or offensive power. In some games several counters could be stacked in a
single hex, reinforcing their combat power but also creating logistical problems
which had to be solved by frequent replenishment. Some games simulated the
friction of war by using wild cards, as in Monopoly. Others tried to factor in the
fog of war as well as problems of command and control such as orders that were

---

[44] E.g. von Baerensprung, *Einfuehrung in das Kriegspiel*, Berlin: Mittler, 1913; E. Sonderegger,
Anlage und Leitung von Kriegspiel-Uebungen, Frauenfeld: Huber, 1897; J. Meckel,
Anleitung zum Kriegspiel, Berlin: Vossische Buchhandlung, 1875; and T. von Trotha,
Gebrauch des Kriegspiel-Apparatus, Berlin: Mittler, 1870.

issued but not received, understood, or obeyed. A handful of games, notably one called Atlantic Wall, even required that Allies, Germans, and referees use three different maps; understandably, many amateurs, found them too complex for their tastes.

As in other board games, players took turns. As in other board games, combat could not really be simulated so that its outcome had to be determined with the aid of statistics. Since statistics only works where numbers are fairly large, the smaller the operations being simulated the worse the problem. Normally the method used was to cast dice – some with as many as twenty sides – and weighing the outcome against so-called combat results tables (CRTs). The latter factored in the effect of weather, different forms of combat such as attack and defense (often, in fact, various kinds of both), movement, and even morale. Particularly in the larger games, all this required an immense amount of record-keeping and calculation. Perhaps it is no accident that the years in question also saw the introduction of pocket calculators and adhesive note pads! Notwithstanding these aids, some of the larger games could stretch over weeks, even months. The larger the number of pieces that had to be moved at each turn, the slower the play. This in turn meant that a special table set up in a special room was required.

Games were devised to simulate every kind of engagement, starting with the purely tactical and ending with the grand strategic. Land, sea, air, and space warfare could all be simulated. However, air and space strategy, considered in isolation, tended to be rather simple: hence not many players were interested in spending their money on them. Armored combat, infantry combat, the operations of Special Forces, and an almost infinite number of battles and campaigns were all simulated. Some of the larger games even brought in economic factors, i.e. the ability of the belligerent countries to produce the sinews of war and provide their armed forces with them. For example, a player might be asked to decide whether defeating an enemy army should receive priority over capturing his manufacturing district – a dilemma that has often presented itself in reality as well – or the other way around. Or else it was a question of a blockade imposed by one side causing hunger among the population of the other, leading to a lowering of national morale and perhaps to difficulties in recruiting manpower.

As titles such as Starforce Alpha Centauri and Vengeance Crusaders v. the Monads show, many scenarios were purely imaginary. Others attempted to provide as accurate a simulation of historical campaigns as the available historical data, and the designers' skills, allowed. As with some miniature games, not the least merit of those who produced the games was the immensely detailed historical research in which they often engaged. For example, not only was it necessary to know even the smallest details, such as the caliber of every anti-tank gun used by the Wehrmacht and the range at which they could penetrate the armor of various kinds of allied tanks, but one also had to find mathematical ways of relating their respective values to each other in the same way as a chess queen, for example, is considered to be worth so many pawns. Designers did this by trial and error, repeatedly playing the games and juggling the figures until they felt, on the basis of the outcome, that they got it right.[45] The ability to do that, incidentally, is one very great advantage those concerned with simulating the past enjoy over those who try to peer into the future. All in all, devising a game to simulate warfare as it had been waged at a certain time and place, as one of my students once did, is certainly not the worst way of studying that subject.[46] Indeed it could be argued that, in this kind of game, as well as some others, designers regularly learn more than players do. As in other board games, far too much emphasis was put on intellectual factors as opposed to the players' physical skill, stamina, and morale. In many ways what was being simulated were staff officers at work – the counters wargamers used were modeled on military ones – not troops who fought, suffered, and died.

Starting in 1958, the year when Avalon Hill, the first company that manufactured and distributed them, was founded, demand for this kind of wargame exploded. The main market was in the United States, but other countries such as Canada, Britain and Germany followed. Clubs were founded, magazines with such titles as *The General* and *Strategy and Tactics* published. Reaching a readership numbering in the tens of thousands, they not only turned into a useful publicity tool but enabled manufacturers to conduct public opinion surveys among readers and adjust their products accordingly. Most of those who purchased and played the games were thirty-four or younger. They were also overeducated in the sense that, drawing on published literature, they had learnt a lot about war without being able to apply their knowledge to their professional lives.[47] From my experience most were single which, given that the hobby attracted very few women and was extremely time-consuming, is not surprising. The more thoughtful among them saw the games, provided they were well designed, as a means not only of mastering the details but of familiarizing themselves with the fog of war, the friction of war, and, above all, the two-sided nature of strategy in ways that no narrative accounts, historical or fictional, could match.[48]

Occasionally attempts were made to adapt the games so that real-life armed forces could use them. Generals visited game designers, and game designers were invited to give talks at military colleges. However, perhaps because the equipment required was very cheap, the marriage did not work too well. Civilian designers of wargames tended to be young and self-taught. Some

---

[45] See, on the kind of research involved, D. Isby, "Research," in Staff of the Strategy and Tactics Magazine, *Wargame Design*, pp. 107–16.
[46] Y. Harari, "Wargaming the Battles of the Diadochi Wars," unpublished, Jerusalem, September 1996.
[47] Dunnigan, *Wargames Handbook*, pp. 300–16.
[48] See on all this S. P. Glick and L. Ian Charters, "War Games, and Military History," *Journal of Contemporary History*, 18, 4, October 1983, pp. 567–82.

may even have committed the ultimate crime of those years – wearing their hair long! Their products, instead of being esoteric and costing millions, were available in the shops and could be had by anyone for a few dollars. In 1987, I myself heard James Dunnigan say that he would probably take no more than forty-eight hours to design a wargame that would simulate a war between the US and some country in the Persian Gulf. What if these outsiders proved better than the brass at simulating future warfare and predicting its outcome, as at least some Pentagon officials believed they might? In a culture so committed to the Protestant ethos that physical exercise is known as a "workout," would not the spectacle of officers playing games give rise to negative reactions? In the event, some military colleges *did* use the games in question for teaching purposes. Worried they might be ridiculed, they tried to keep the matter secret – not always successfully, as it turned out.[49]

Even today, with computers all around us, such games still retain some of their advantages.[50] Above all else, hexed games provide players with excellent insight into their own mechanics. To be sure, their rules can be quite complicated. Often they take up dozens of closely printed pages and require a considerable period of time to master. Even so the designers sometimes find it hard to cover all the possibilities and answer all the questions that playing the games may lead to. To that extent, most games have a certain amount of freedom built into them, if not deliberately then accidentally. On the other hand, since the rules are written in plain language and printed, they are easily accessible. The reasoning of those who designed them can readily be understood; without the rules being understood, of course, the games cannot be played at all.[51] Attempting to make the games more realistic or more playable, many players proceeded to experiment with them and to modify them as they saw fit.

All of this cannot be done with the hexed games' computerized successors, most of which are specifically written in such a way as to conceal their programs and make them tamper-proof. Even when that is not the case and attempts are made to use more English-like artificial intelligence languages, doing so only goes so far towards solving the problem.[52] Before we can consider those successors, though, it is first of all necessary to see how defense establishments have used and are using the games in question.

---

[49] R. Smith, "The Long History of Gaming in Military Training," *Simulation Gaming*, 41, 6, 2010, p. 9; L. Bloomfield, "Reflections on Gaming," *Orbis*, 27, 4, Winter 1984, p. 784.
[50] See, for a good discussion, P. Sabin, *Simulating War*, London: Continuum, 2012, pp. 22–8.
[51] Dunnigan, *Wargames Handbook*, p. xii.
[52] P. K. Davis, "RAND's Experience in Applying Artificial Intelligence Techniques to Strategic-Level Military-Political War Gaming," Santa Monica, CA: RAND, 1984, p. 9, available at: www.rand.org/pubs/papers/P6977.html.

By a throw of the dice

From Weickmann to von Reisswitz Jr., those who designed wargames and tried to sell them to the armies of their time hoped to use them for the purpose of military training and education. Accordingly, they made great efforts to reproduce the movements of various troops, the effects of terrain on those moves, and the outcome of combat as accurately as the available technical means allowed. Players were often told that, in playing a game, they should write down their orders exactly as they would on campaign. Late nineteenth-century works on the subject do in fact bristle with such orders, written and delivered according to the relevant regulations; to that extent, what took place was not simulated command and control but command and control, *tout court*. Above all, wargames were, and still remain, not just a very good method of introducing students to the paradoxical – to speak with Edward Luttwak – world of strategy but the only one. The rest, not being two-sided, are simply not in the running.

Training apart, wargames can also be used to prepare for future war in a different, and perhaps even more important, sense. Scenarios can be set up and an officer or team of officers made to represent the enemy. Next, the game can be played in such a way as to examine whether one's plans are sound, what changes may be necessary, and what the outcome of the engagement, or battle, or campaign, or war, is likely to be. Obviously this applies both to offensive wars and to defensive ones. The influence of operational techniques, the impact of new technologies, and so on can also be simulated, if necessary by repeating the games time after time while varying the factors involved.

Preparing to fight France in 1870, Moltke did not game the campaign. Whether this was because he was a bad commander, as one of his critics has claimed, is a little doubtful.[53] However that may be, two decades later wargames had become much more firmly established. Unfortunately little is known concerning the precise methods by which the various general staffs went to work in this respect. Partly this must have been due to the desire to keep their methods secret; partly, perhaps, to the well-founded fear that outsiders might ridicule the proceedings. Scenarios, of course, were always among the best-kept secrets of all. Then as now, armed forces did not like to divulge the kind of campaigns they were planning to fight and the methods they were preparing to apply. However, since we are interested primarily in the changing nature of wargames and the way they were played that fact need not concern us too much.

What little information can be gleaned from the sources suggests that a mixture of "rigid" and "free" games was used, the former to simulate larger operations and the latter, smaller ones. Most were apparently played on maps of different sizes. A few, however, such as the ones held at the US Naval War

---

[53] T. Zuber, *The Moltke Myth*, Lanham, MD: University Press of America, 2008, p. 306.

College, Rhode Island, during the interwar period, used squares (in this case, the tiles on the floor of a large room devoted to the purpose). Much naval combat takes part on the high seas, ship against ship or ships. While it is true that some parts of the sea are more dangerous to navigation than others, the absence of terrain features makes naval wargaming simpler than that which simulates land warfare. For the same reason, seadogs were more likely to resort to miniatures than were landlubbers who continued to prefer counters made of wood or metal. Every game seems to have had an umpire or umpires. Some still used dice to determine the outcome of combat. Occasionally the umpires saw fit to overrule the dice – with interesting results, as we shall see later on.

Whatever the differences among them, all the manuals in use never tired of emphasizing that each game ended, or was supposed to end, with a thorough discussion. The objective was to find out what had been simulated, what had not been simulated, what had worked, what had not worked, why, and what was needed to make what had not worked this time do so next time. Whether that advice was always followed is impossible to say; then as today, as each game ended people were likely to be tired and want to go home. Not surprisingly, the vast majority of scenarios were never translated into reality. Nor can one really blame the game designers for that fact. Scenarios that are possible in theory far outnumber those that actually take place; as a pre-World War I German joke had it, if there were two conceivable ways of solving a problem his Imperial Majesty was certain to find a third. Indeed it could be argued that, since the future is unpredictable, one of the most important – possibly the most impor-tant – objective of holding wargames in the military is precisely to allow participants to try their hand at dealing with the unexpected: to that extent, the question of whether a scenario is ultimately realized or remains imaginary is almost irrelevant.

Contrary to legend, the German chief of the General Staff, Field Marshal Alfred von Schlieffen (served 1893–1905), never gamed the famous plan that has been named after him. What he did do was to make his staff officers, including fairly junior ones, game all sorts of lesser campaigns. When told that the games made players command forces and conduct operations on a scale far beyond their actual rank, he would respond that he could see no reason why the officers in question should not one day be in a position to translate the games into reality.[54] Most scenarios seem to have been con-cerned with the possibility of French or Russian invasions coming from this direction or that and threatening this objective or that. It was up to the players, working either at General Headquarters in Berlin or in some inn during a staff ride, to use the forces at their disposal to contain the invaders and throw them back.

[54] A. von Schlieffen, *Dienstschriften*, Berlin: Mittler, 1939, vol. I, p. 118.

Among the scenarios thus examined, not once but several times, was a *French* invasion of Belgium which had to be turned back.[55] One objective was to simulate what might happen in order that, if it in fact did happen, commanders would not have to reinvent the wheel. Another was to impress subordinates with a number of simple but essential ideas, such as the advantages of operating on interior lines; the importance, in case a smaller army was confronted by a larger one, of taking the opponent in the flank rather than attacking him head-on; and the need, even in the age of the telegraph, for subordinate commanders to take the initiative rather than allow time to be wasted.

As it happened, a scenario that *was* gamed and *did* turn into reality was the invasion of East Prussia by two Russian armies, one coming from the east and the other from the southeast. Given that the Germans intended to use the bulk of their forces in the west, such a campaign, with Berlin as its ultimate objective, would put the Reich in mortal danger. In 1894, twenty years before the battles of Tannenberg and the Masurian Lakes were fought and won, Schlieffen, in a truly prophetic exercise, had his officers game precisely the scenario that was later to ensue.[56] Eleven years later another wargame with the same scenario was held; in his critique, Schlieffen said he could see no reason why the operations it portrayed could not succeed in actual war.[57] Decades afterwards, German officers were still pointing to these episodes as outstanding proof of what wargames, properly and competently handled, could accomplish.[58] Surely their pride is both understandable and justified. However, it is important to realize that Schlieffen used to hold two major wargames each year, and that the vast majority of scenarios worked out in those games were *not* realized.

What makes all this even more interesting is the fact that the Russians also gamed the scenario in question. They too concluded that their invading armies were too far apart to be able to support one another and could there-fore be defeated in detail. However, nothing was done to modify the plan, and the rest followed.[59] Something similar happened to the French during the 1930s. The governing idea behind the Maginot Line was to force the Germans to go through Belgium, which would result in Britain entering the war as it had in 1914 (if the need to invade Belgium could deter the Germans from going to war in the first place, of course, so much the better). That much having been decided upon, a whole series of wargames were held. The

---

[55] T. Zuber, *German War Planning, 1891–1914*, Woodbridge: Boydell Press, 2004, pp. 185–81.

[56] T. Zuber, *Inventing the Schlieffen Plan*, Oxford University Press, 2002, pp. 145–9.

[57] See T. Zuber, *German War Planning*, pp. 173–4.

[58] See the account of the 1894 game in particular, as printed in Generalstab des Heeres, ed., *Die Grossen Generalstabsreisen-Ost – aus den Jahren 1891–1905*, Berlin: Mittler, 1938, pp. 1–50.

[59] According to M. Caffrey, "Toward a History-Based Doctrine for Wargaming," *Aerospace Power*, Fall 2000, p. 40.

objective was to determine what kind of attack the Germans might launch and what the French Army would do to repulse it. The trouble was that, under the French system, a single team played *both* sides. As a result, when the pieces had been put in place in such a way that the Line appeared to be doing its job, there was nobody around to suggest ways in which the Germans might nevertheless try to breach it.[60]

During the 1920s the German Army was laboring under severe restrictions imposed by the Treaty of Versailles. The outcome was to increase interest in wargames. One figure deeply involved with them was General Ludwig Beck, chief of the German Army General Staff from 1935 to 1938. He used them in preparing the famous 1936 manual, *Truppenfuehrung*, with its emphasis on interlocking mobile operations coming from several directions at once. As so often, it would be hard to say whether it was wargames that helped formulate doctrine or doctrine that governed the wargames; however, there is no doubt that the games were used to test the doctrine.[61] That was not the end of the matter. When Hitler started pressing for a German invasion of Czechoslovakia from March 1938 on Beck held a whole series of wargames. They pointed, as indeed they were designed to do, to Germany's ability, or rather inability, to wage war on two fronts.[62] The results were incorporated into memoranda and submitted to Hitler, who called them "childish." Two months later, Beck resigned.

Another German officer who held wargames during the same period was the commander of the submarine fleet, Admiral Karl Doenitz, as part of his attempts to devise new tactics for operating his vessels.[63] Instead of working alone waiting for prey, as they had done in World War I, submarines were to operate in so-called wolf packs. Having discovered a convoy, a submarine would inform General Headquarters, which would direct others to intercept it. Only when enough submarines had been brought together would the attack itself begin. At that point far more torpedoes would be launched at the convoy than a single submarine could carry, confronting the defense with a formidable challenge. Apparently a whole series of games was held, some tactical/operational, others strategic. Two essential conclusions emerged. First, the actual attacks should be commanded not from headquarters but by a senior captain aboard a submarine situated near the scene of action, but sufficiently far away from it to retain an overview. The motto, in other words, was "centralized command, decentralized execution." Second, submarine warfare was capable of defeating Britain, but only if three hundred submarines were available,

[60] P. Bracken, "Unintended Consequences of Strategic Games," *Simulation and Games*, 8, 3, September 1977, pp. 108–9.

[61] R. Hofmann, *German Army War Games*, Carlisle Barracks, PA: Army War College, 1983, p. 7.

[62] *Ibid.*, pp. 29–30.   [63] K. Doenitz, *Memoirs*, London: Cassell, 2000 [1959], pp. 32–3.

one-third of which would be on station at any time. In fact, when World War II broke out, Doenitz disposed of exactly forty-seven.

Preparations for the German offensive against the West involved a whole series of map- and sand-table wargames. They began in December 1939 and lasted until March the following year.[64] In overall charge was the chief of the Army General Staff, General Franz Halder, who observed several of the senior-level games but did not participate in them. Others were the commanders of the two army groups involved, Generals Feodor von Bock and Gerd von Rundstedt, as well as their respective chiefs of staff: General Erich von Manstein, the operational genius who is generally considered the brain behind the plan that eventually emerged; General Heinz Guderian, the creator of the German Panzerwaffe or armored corps; and Colonel Ulrich Liss, head of Foreign Armies West who played the French commander-in-chief. Each time a game was held the scenario took the latest available intelligence into account.

The main question to be resolved was whether the center of gravity (*Schwerpunkt*) should rest with Army Group B opposite Belgium and the Netherlands or with Army Group A opposite Sedan in the Ardennes. The option of building in sufficient flexibility to leave the question unanswered until the last moment, which was Hitler's own favorite solution to the problem, was also considered. However, it proved impractical owing to the sheer size of the forces involved. Possible French and British reactions to each of these moves, as well as the critically important problems of transportation and logistics involved, were repeatedly simulated. Halder personally submitted the results to his Fuehrer who ultimately decided in favor of Army Group A and the Ardennes. Further down, army, corps, division, and regimental commanders held similar games. Particular, attention was paid to the question as to what Guderian's tanks should do once they had reached the river Meuse.[65] In the event the cardinal assumption behind the games, namely that the Allies' first reaction to any German move would be to invade Belgium so as to stop Army Group B as far forward as possible, proved correct. This fact alone justifies the claim of one expert on *Kriegspiel*, writing after the war, that they had made an immense contribution to victory.[66]

Wargames also played a major role in planning Operation Sea Lion for invading Britain. They showed that the landing faced formidable obstacles in the form of insufficient embarkation ports, insufficient shipping space, and the

---

[64] See E. R. May, *Strange Victory: Hitler's Conquest of France*, New York: Wang & Hill, 2001, pp. 215–26, 260–6; also E. von Manstein, *Lost Victories*, London: Methuen, 1958, pp. 119–20; and F. Halder, *Kriegstagebuch*, Stuttgart: Kohlhammer, 1962, vol. I, p. 185, February 7, 1940.

[65] H. Guderian, *Panzer Leader*, London: Cassell, 1951, p. 69.

[66] Hofmann, *German Army War Games*, pp. 15–19.

difficulty of getting men and equipment off the beaches and into the interior.[67] Doing so would take so much time as to enable the British, using their well-developed system of roads, to concentrate against the invader. The conclusion, namely that the operation should be cancelled, was definitely correct. Another series of wargames was held in preparation for the invasion of the Soviet Union.[68] The man in charge was General Friedrich von Paulus of Stalingrad fame. In November 1940 he was serving as deputy chief of the General Staff for operations; unlike many others, the Germans felt that wargaming was too serious a business to be left to junior or even medium-ranking officers. Another round was held in February 1941. This time the games predicted, correctly as it turned out, that in November of that year, six months after the beginning of the invasion, the Wehrmacht would reach the gates of Moscow. They also predicted, incorrectly, that the Red Army would be all but finished. The error can be traced to the fact that German intelligence had vastly underestimated the number of divisions Stalin could command. They believed he had 200, whereas in reality there were 360.[69]

As an episode of November 1944 shows, the Germans maintained their faith in the method to the end. By an extraordinary coincidence, the US Army attacked the front of the German Commander-in-Chief West, Field Marshal Walter Model, in the midst of a wargame designed to simulate just such an offensive. Instead of breaking off the game, Model made it go on. The relevant orders were fed straight to the front, thus saving precious time.[70] Numerous technical details apart, German wargames were governed by three basic principles. First, great emphasis was put on friction – superabundant reports ("information overload"), incorrect reports, out-of-date reports, unintelligible reports, unexpected requests by neighboring units that interfered with one's own operations, and the like. Second, everything had to be done to avoid "schematicism," i.e. school solutions, specifically including those derived from military history. Third, not merely the possible but the impossible was to be gamed, the reason being that, as one expert on the subject pointed out, in war very little is impossible.[71]

Few other countries took wargaming as seriously as the Germans did. For example, in 1872 one Captain Baring, of the Royal Artillery, tried to introduce it to Britain. His game derived from one developed by Captain Werner von Tschischwitz in Germany, who in turn had published rules for a somewhat simplified von Reisswitz-type game, complete with tables and dice.[72] An official

[67] *Ibid.*, pp. 56–7.
[68] *Ibid.*, pp. 37–66; Halder, *Kriegstagebuch*, vol. II, pp. 201, 203, entries for November 29, 1940, December 3, 1941; F. von Paulus, *Ich stehe hier auf Befehl!*, Frankfurt/Main: Bernard & Graefe, 1960, p. 90.
[69] Halder, *Kriegstagebuch*, 2, p. 170, entry for August 11, 1941.
[70] Hofmann, *German Army War Games*, pp. 19–20.   [71] *Ibid.*, pp. 9–11, 22.
[72] W. von Tschischwitz, *Anleitung zum Kriegspiel*, Neisse: Graveur, 1867.

set of British Army war game rules was published in 1895, but regular officers showed little interest it.[73] A game developed by a naval officer and writer, Captain Philip H. Colomb, which represented a duel between two ships, did no better. Royal Navy officers, incidentally, also did what they could to prevent the creation of a naval staff college where they might have to play such games and, which was much worse still, listen to a civilian professor.[74]

Amateurs took a different view. The moving spirit was Spenser Wilkinson (1853–1937), lawyer, art critic, and military writer. He sat on the commission that created the Territorial Army, a sort of reserve, and ended up as Chichele Professor of Military History at Oxford.[75] His best-known work, *The Brain of an Army* (1895) is credited with pushing the British Army to establish its first General Staff. His influence was also brought to bear by way of the volunteer corps, of which he was a member, as well as several gaming clubs. His *Essays on the War Game* were published in the *Manchester Guardian* on which, as if to emphasize the link between games and theater, he also served as the drama critic. His starting point was Verdy du Vernois as "the ablest writer who ever dealt with war games." The actual rules were adapted from another German officer, Captain Nauman, whose *Regimental Wargame*, based on a close study of the Franco-Prussian War of 1870–1, was published in 1877. As Wilkinson wrote, no other form of training was potentially more useful and no other was so easily misused. He was thoroughly aware of the danger, the fatigue, the responsibility and the friction which govern real warfare and which can never be reproduced in games of this kind. However, he believed that this should not prevent them from playing an important role in teaching officers the basics of strategy and tactics.

The most important wargame known to have been played by the British military took place in early 1905, not long after the entente with France had drawn Britain out of its so-called splendid isolation. The scenario was a German–French war. Initially the Germans tried to advance by way of Verdun. Having been repulsed, they sent a 250,000-man army through Belgium instead. In charge of the game was General James Grierson, chief of operations. The role of British commander was played by Colonel C. E. Calwell who nine years later served as deputy director of operations. That of German commander was played by Major General William Robertson, a truly remarkable soldier who had risen from the ranks, was serving as chief of the western section of military intelligence, and later rose to become chief of the Imperial General Staff. Both Grierson and Robertson had visited the theater of operations. Other intelligence

[73] F. Sayre, *Map Maneuvers and Tactical Rides*, Fort Leavenworth, KS: Army Press, 1910, p. 21.

[74] A. Gat, *The Development of Military Thought: The Nineteenth Century*, Oxford University Press, 1992, p. 222.

[75] Wilson, *The Bomb and the Computer*, pp. 7–12.

officers were also involved. The games pointed to three conclusions. First, France on its own would probably go down to defeat. Second, current plans would not enable the British Army to be mobilized and deployed to France fast enough to assist that country. Third, the army was too small to make a difference and might well be annihilated. These pessimistic conclusions did not prevent unofficial, but highly important, Anglo-French staff talks from getting under way the next year. In the event the estimate of what the Germans would do proved right on the mark. Not so, as hindsight shows, of what the British could and would contribute.[76]

Decades later, a British officer claimed that it was the inability of wargames to capture the stress and friction of real-life warfare which prevented them from becoming very popular among the military of his country.[77] Similar considerations do not seem to have disturbed US Army officers who took up German-type wargaming and sought to develop it. Various systems, each named after its originator, were tried. However, all were caught in the now familiar dilemma between realism and playability and none seems to have grown very popular.[78] Instead of being used for planning and rehearsing future operations, as in Germany, they were considered mainly as training devices. When *Military Review*, the official journal of the Staff College at Fort Leavenworth, published a condensed translation of a book of rules by a certain General von Cochenhausen in March 1941 they wrote that the game would provide commanders with the "semblance of actual battle." It demanded "definite decisions and orders for the commitment of troops ... within the realm of time and space, thereby leading to exactitude in troop leading."[79] Not a word was wasted on other possibilities.

Until 1945 the most important wargaming center in the US was the Naval War College. The moving spirit was William McCarty Little, a friend and protégé of the College's founder and first president, Admiral Stephen B. Luce.[80] The first games were held in 1887, just three years after the institution opened its doors. Catching on quickly, during the 1890s they became extremely popular, attracting visits by senior officials from the Secretary of the Navy, Hilary Herbert, and the Assistant Secretary, Theodore Roosevelt, down. As so

---

[76] M. D. Krause, "Anglo-French Military Planning 1905–1914," dissertation submitted to Georgetown University, 1968, Ann Arbor, MI: University Microfilms, 1968, pp. 8–21; G. Aston, "The Entente Cordiale and the 'Military Conversations'," *Quarterly Review*, 258, April 1932, pp. 367–73; W. Robertson, *Soldiers and Statesmen, 1914–1918*, London: Cassell, 1925, vol. I, pp. 24–5.

[77] M. R. J. Hope Thompson, "The Military War Game," *Journal of the Royal United Service Institute*, February 1962, p. 50.

[78] See, on the various American games, Perla, *The Art of Wargaming*, pp. 54–7.

[79] Von Cochenhausen, "Wargames for Battalion, Regiment and Division," *Military Review*, March 1941.

[80] See, for much of what follows, Perla, *The Art of Wargaming*, pp. 63–76.

often, the inspiration was provided by the now famous German *Kriegspiel* which everybody else either imitated or adapted for his – not yet her – own purposes. Games were divided into duels, meaning ship against ship, tactical, meaning force against force, and strategic, meaning navy against navy. The latter two could be played either separately or together, as part of a single exercise.

Ship-to-ship duels were "fought" with the aid of dice, but in tactical and strategic games the outcome of battles was decided with the aid of rather simple rules that reflected the numbers involved on each side. It was a question, in other words, of "getting there fustest with the mostest." The larger the game the more challenging it was, intellectually speaking. Each game was followed, or at any rate was supposed to be followed, by a thorough analysis of what had gone right, what had gone wrong, and why. In Little's own words, wargames were the only form of training which provided "[an] enemy, a live, vigorous enemy in the next room waiting feverishly to take advantages of any of our mistakes, ever ready to puncture any visionary scheme, to haul us down to earth."[81] To prevent players from learning more about their opponents than they should, separate rooms, screens and umpires were employed. All this made the games as valuable as, or more valuable than, any other form of fleet exercise.[82]

Early in the twentieth century wargames were used to investigate, or help investigate, such issues as shifting from coal to oil and from ships with mixed armaments to all big guns vessels.[83] The emphasis on planning did not last. When Admiral William Sims assumed the presidency of the College (for the second time) in 1918, he ruled that games would be held primarily for the purpose of providing players with decision-making experience. The games themselves were made much more sophisticated by adding submarines and aircraft to the order of battle. Also added were extremely detailed tables that reflected the characteristics of each class of vessel separately. Weather, visibility, the distance between ships, the angle at which shells struck their targets, etc. were all taken into account. The crown of creation was the so-called "War College Fire Effect System" by which the outcome of combat was calculated.[84]

As Verdy du Vernois might have predicted, the desire to incorporate one factor after another in the name of "realism" soon caused it to become so complex as to be almost incomprehensible. Following a long tradition, results were presented in terms of the impact of the fourteen-inch shells fired by the

[81] W. McCarty Little, "The Strategic War Game or Chart Maneuver," *US Naval Institute Proceedings*, December 1912, p. 1230.
[82] R. H. Spector, *Professors of War: The Naval War College and the Development of the Naval Profession*, Newport, RI: Naval War College Press, 1977, p. 81.
[83] J. A. Barber, "The School of Naval Warfare," *Naval War College Review*, 22, April 1969, pp. 89–96.
[84] See, for the way it was done, J. McHugh, *Fundamentals of Wargaming*, Newport, RI: Naval War College Press, 1966, pp. 4.14–19.

battleships of the period: hence there was a clear bias in favor of guns and against more recent weapons such as submarine- and air-launched torpedoes. Another problem that afflicted the tactical games in particular were the three-minute turns each player was given to assess the situation, formulate his orders, and make his move or moves. Such a leisurely pace might have sufficed in an earlier age. However, as "fast" carriers – not to mention aircraft with speeds of several hundred miles an hour – entered service during the 1930s, it became hopelessly unrealistic. Perhaps worst of all, the system forced players to immerse themselves in a vast number of technical details. Straining to do so, they tended to lose any ability to see the engagement they were supposed to be leading as a whole.

Of over 300 wargames known to have been played at the College during the interwar period, a little under half were of the operational and tactical level kind. Of those all but nine focused on a possible war with Japan. However, the US Navy during this period does not appear to have used wargaming in the planning process for any specific campaign as the Germans routinely did. What the players did do was work their way through numerous possible scenarios. Admiral Chester Nimitz, who commanded the US Navy in the Pacific during World War II, is credited with saying that, throughout that prolonged and enormously widespread conflict, "absolutely nothing" had come as a surprise except the kamikaze attacks. To that extent the tactical games did indeed prove very useful. This was especially true in working out and testing doctrines of ship movement – the idea that carriers and their supporting vessels should work in groups rather than individually – and the way they should deploy for battle.

The more numerous strategic games were a different matter. Supported by a foreign intelligence department specifically created for the purpose, they were sufficiently sophisticated to take into account factors such as logistics and communications. Based on those, the navy concluded that operating in the western Pacific, where Japan had numerous bases whereas the US had few, would be difficult, time-consuming, and focused on seizing islands by means of amphibious landings. The Marine Corps did in fact start working in that direction from the late 1920s on, holding exercises and developing doctrine.[85] The navy also concluded that modern fleets were so large and fast, and operated in such a dispersed manner, as to make a Tsushima or Jutland-style climactic battle between the main forces of both sides improbable if not impossible. The struggle, if and when it came, would be prolonged and consist mainly of mutual attrition. These conclusions proved broadly correct, except, of course, for the unimportant fact that the attack on Pearl Harbor, which appears to have been completely unforeseen, did take place and changed everything.[86]

---

[85] See J. B. Agnew, "From Where did Our Amphibious Doctrine Come?," *Marine Corps Gazette*, August 1979, p. 53.

[86] E. S. Miller, *War Plan Orange: The US Strategy to Defeat Japan, 1897–1945*, Annapolis, MD: Naval Institute Press, 2007, pp. 3, 81, 168.

BY A THROW OF THE DICE

On the other side of the hill, or rather the ocean, the Japanese also engaged in wargaming. Modern wargaming, as distinct from Go, arrived in Japan almost as soon as the country started modernizing itself. By the end of the nineteenth century they seem to have learnt enough for the games to make a solid contribution to their success in the 1904–5 war against Russia, and in particular their victory in the great naval battle of Tsushima.[87] Like their German mentors, the Japanese did not use the games merely for training purposes, but incorporated them into the planning and decision-making process. One series of table-top games was held at the Imperial Naval War College in 1937. It ended with the "defeat" of the British naval forces in the South China Sea.[88]

As the clouds of war began gathering in the late summer of 1941, another and much more important series of games was held in Tokyo. Apparently the first to go was the army. It gamed the possibility of war with the US, but few details are known.[89] Next, the Imperial Navy entered the picture. Normally the navy held its games in November–December, the season when storms made navigation over much of the Pacific difficult. This time, following the imposition of the US embargo on scrap iron and oil, they were pushed forward into the early days of September. The first round, again held by the General Staff, followed the 1937 pattern by focusing on operations in Southeastern Asia. The next step was to involve the Naval War College which gamed the protection of the sea lanes to that region once "Blue" forces had occupied it.

These were merely preliminary exercises. Much more important was the main round, held at the Naval War College on September 11–17. The participants were the principal commanders of the Combined Fleet. This time the assumption was that a Japanese offensive against Southeast Asia would not only involve the country in war against Britain and the Netherlands (Indo-China was already in Japanese hands) but lead to American intervention as well. Accordingly, in addition to rehearsing that offensive, the exercise dealt with the problem of defending against a US Navy offensive coming from Hawaii. During the first half of October yet another series of wargames took place. The objective was to familiarize the Japanese commanders with their missions, which included the occupation of the Philippines, Guam, Wake Island, Hong Kong, Malaya, Java, and Sumatra. Details such as the size and composition of the forces involved, ports of departure, courses, rendezvous points, and even the individual beaches on which the landings were to take place were studied in detail. Presumably to preserve secrecy, the games were held not at the College but aboard the flagship of the commander of the Combined Fleet, Admiral

---

[87] See McHugh, *Fundamentals of Wargaming*, p. 2.18.
[88] D. C. Evans and M. R. Peattie, *Kaigun: Strategy, Tactics and Technology in the Imperial Japanese Navy, 1887–1941*, Annapolis, MD: Naval Institute Press, 1997, p. 466.
[89] See, for this and what follows, G. W. Prangue, *At Dawn We Slept*, New York: McGraw-Hill, 1981, pp. 181, 193, 223–35, 281–2, as well as Evans and Peattie, *Kaigun*, pp. 463, 439, 473.

Isroroku Yamamoto, the battleship *Nagato*. They worked very well: when Japan joined World War II two months later, many of the operations it mounted followed rather closely in the games' wake.

The strike at Pearl Harbor itself was gamed for the first time in 1927. It was launched by two Japanese carriers, the only ones available, which were accompanied by destroyers, cruisers, and an advance guard of submarines. However, the umpires judged that the damage the Americans had suffered was minimal. Not only was the "Blue" commander, Lieutenant Commander Tagaki Sokichi, criticized for his "rashness," but as the game developed the "Red" side went on to mount a two-carrier attack on Tokyo itself. As if to add offense to injury, the game ended with those carriers making their escape in spite of the Japanese attempts to locate and intercept them. At the time carriers and carrier aviation were still in their infancy and the technology in use was quite primitive. Perhaps this fact helps account for the outcome of the games.

Not surprisingly, the idea of a strike at the main US naval base in the Pacific refused to die. It cropped up repeatedly in accounts of Japanese military planning during the 1930s, and in September 1941 it too was gamed. Two questions in particular had to be resolved: was the operation feasible at all, and could secrecy be maintained? After problems of selecting the correct route – the northern one – and refueling the warships en route had been solved to the satisfaction of the umpires, the time came to ensure that the attackers would not be detected by aircraft flying off Hawaii. The commander of the "Red" forces was a certain Captain Kanji Ogawa. During the 1930s he had witnessed at least one American exercise to defend Pearl Harbor (two were held, one in 1932 and another one in 1938) against just the kind of attack that was now being planned. Both "attacks," incidentally, had been judged successful.[90] As the Japanese concluded *their* games, the outcome was completely different: Ogawa and his team inflicted unacceptable losses on the attackers. Thereupon the plan of attack was changed and it was decided to have the carriers execute the last part of their journey at high speed and at night. This time things went much better.

Admiral Chuichi Nagumo, the officer whose ships were supposed to carry out the attack, remained skeptical. For one thing, attacking Pearl Harbor meant diverting forces away from the coming operations aimed at conquering Southeast Asia, which, he believed, were far more important. Besides, he disliked the choice of the northern route with its stormy waters and considered the plan as a whole too complicated. Others on the staff felt that the games were too theoretical and that too much depended on the umpires. The latter underestimated American strength, put various arbitrary restrictions on the actions of "Red," and slanted their decisions in favor of the "Blue" teams. Some even considered that the games epitomized the Japanese penchant for short-sighted,

[90] C. Reynolds, *Admiral John J. Towers*, Annapolis, MD: Naval Institute Press, 1991, pp. 236–9, 276–9.

self-centered thinking. Others still, while conceding that the plans might be a tactical success, considered them strategically wrong-headed.

Another round of wargames was held in October and resulted in several changes to the plans. On the one hand, the number of participating submarines was increased. On the other, the number of carriers was reduced from four to three; since all of these were long-range vessels, not only was the problem of refueling them made much easier, but more ships were left to participate in the southern operation. Eventually this particular change was cancelled, and the number of carriers attacking Pearl Harbor increased to no fewer than six as new solutions to the refueling problem were sought and found. Yet another round of games, the third in the series, was held. This time they suggested that two out of the six carriers would be lost. This, however, was considered an acceptable risk. Some officers also continued to express their doubts concerning the attack's long-term effect, but they were silenced by Yamamoto.[91]

What actually happened went only so far to confirm the games. First, if secrecy was indeed preserved and surprise achieved, then this was due primarily not to anything the Japanese had done or left undone but to the fact that their approaching aircraft were mistaken for a flight of B-17s due to arrive in Hawaii the same morning. Second, the attackers missed their most important target, i.e. the American carriers, which happened to be at sea on exercises. However, strictly speaking that failure was the result of faulty intelligence, not of a wargame that was improperly set up and played. Third, the attackers did much better than the wargames had led them to expect. Not one of the precious Japanese carriers was lost or even damaged: in other words, American land-based aircraft operating from Hawaii had proved completely ineffective. The only losses were those inflicted by anti-aircraft fire from the guns surrounding the base, and they took a greater toll of the second wave than of the first.[92]

This success, so unexpected in some ways, in turn formed the background to the events that took place before and during the battle of Midway in June 1942. This was not Pearl Harbor. Japan and the US were in the midst of a ferocious war, meaning that achieving strategic surprise of the kind that had largely accounted for the success in the previous year was ruled out. Still the Imperial Naval Command hoped to achieve at least operational surprise concerning the time and place of their next attack. Their main problem was that they did not know the whereabouts of the American carriers; to ensure they would not be present, Yamamoto dispersed part of his forces in the hope of making his enemies follow suit.[93] As in the previous year, the Japanese planners wargamed their offensive not

[91] See R. Wohlstetter, *Pearl Harbor, Warning and Decision*, Stanford, CA: Stanford University Press, 1962, pp. 355–7, 377.
[92] Prangue, *At Dawn We Slept*, pp. 223–30.
[93] J. Parshall and A. Tully, *Shattered Sword: The Untold Story of the Battle of Midway*, Dulles, VA: Potomac Press, 2005, p. 53.

once but twice. The setting was the newly commissioned battleship *Yamato* where the officer in charge, Yamamoto's chief of staff Rear Admiral Matome Ugaki, had set up a large map table on which all moves were shown. The remaining participants had their maps spread out in surrounding cabins, using runners in order to simulate shore-to-ship and ship-to-ship radio communications.

The scenario assumed that the deception had succeeded and that the US carriers would be absent from the scene of action. Accordingly, the main opposition was expected to come from the land-based bombers the US Army Air Force had stationed on Midway itself. Once again, Nagumo had his doubts. He asked what would happen in case the American carriers appeared out of nowhere and took the Japanese in the flank and rear. However, his position was weak – at Pearl Harbor he had erred on the side of caution. Consequently his objections were brushed aside. As it turned out, when the dice were cast to determine the outcome of combat during the second game the Japanese carriers suffered nine hits. Two, the *Akagi* and the *Kaga*, were listed as sunk. At this point Ugaki intervened, arbitrarily reducing the number of hits to three. He also re-floated the *Akagi* and ruled that it had only been slightly damaged. Later in the games the *Kaga* too was restored to the fleet, but that is a different story.[94]

Ugaki and Yamamoto have often been criticized for the rigidity of their plans and their unwillingness to listen to objections. Yet it is necessary to make two points. First, the use of dice inevitably implies the possibility of obtaining statistically very unlikely results. Such results are quite capable of upsetting any kind of human reason and putting it on its head. In fact it is one of the umpire's main tasks to cancel such results if, in his view, they occur;[95] does anyone really think the fate of states and nations should be determined by the accidental throw of a dice? Second, Ugaki's guess that Midway's land-based bombers would be no more effective than those at Pearl Harbor had turned out to be correct. Though the aircraft in question launched several attacks and dropped many bombs, they failed to register a single hit; earlier, the same had happened in the Mediterranean where, until the German dive-bombers came to the rescue, high-level Italian bombing of Royal Navy vessels had been ineffec-tive. What proved decisive was not Ugaki's somewhat high-handed action but the above-mentioned fact that the Japanese deception plan had not worked. It did not work because the Americans had broken the Japanese codes;[96] they were like a man with good eyesight attacking a blind one in the rear while he was otherwise occupied.

[94] *Ibid.*, pp. 61–2, 67, 410; Mitsuo Fochida and Masatake Okumiya, *Midway*, New York: Ballantine, 1955, pp. 87–94.

[95] See on this R. C. Rubel, "The Epistemology of War Gaming," *Naval War College Review*, 59, 2, Spring 2006, p. 119.

[96] See on this S. Budiansky, *Battle of Wits: The Complete Story of Codebreaking in World War II*, New York: Free Press, 2000, pp. 12–13.

Since a fair amount is known about the games in question and also about the way they interacted with reality, this might be a convenient point at which to stop and take stock. Spreading from Germany, where it was invented in the 1820s, military-type wargaming differed from almost all the rest in that it did not try to create conditions where each side would have an equal chance at gaining a victory. Instead players were presented with scenarios supposedly rooted in reality and encouraged to explore what could happen, what would happen, and what they themselves would do in case something similar actually did happen. The wargames were used primarily for two purposes, i.e. planning and preparation on the one hand and training on the other. Often players included not just individual officers but entire teams which thus learnt to work together. Though tending to be complicated and time-consuming, the games could also be used, and were used, for entertainment. But that is a topic we have already discussed.

In McCarty Little's words, when it was a question of training, wargames represented not just the best but practically the *only* method of simulating a conflict against a thinking, acting, and re-acting opponent. When the editors of *Military Review* published von Cochenhausen's game rules in March 1941 they made exactly the same point. Provided the games are carefully handled, arguably this fact compensates for any shortcomings they may have. The games took two basic forms, "rigid" and "free." In practice, as many of the above examples show, there was always a tendency to mix the two in order to rule out unlikely results and/or make the game faster and easier to play.[97] So complex is the reality of war that devising rules to cover all possibilities, as they do in simpler games such as chess, was and remains next to impossible. As Clausewitz rightly points out, too often the results will be pure nonsense.[98]

In all probability, rare was the wargame in which the rules of play were not modified to some extent or another. One could even argue that, since almost all training has to be based on past experience, in games used for that purpose the players' ability to gain insight into the how and why of things by examining the rules and modifying them, if doing so is considered appropriate, represents a bonus and not a problem. Relaxing the rules made an umpire necessary. Often the greatest difficulty consisted precisely in finding one who was both capable and objective. Conversely, it could be argued that, had such an all-knowing, all-understanding person been available in reality, and assuming his authority was unquestioned, then wargames would have become superfluous, and suitable at best for training second-rate operatives. Wargames, in other words, are just as susceptible to human frailties as war itself, and indeed had this *not* been the case most of them would have been completely useless.

---

[97] See, on the various combinations, McHugh, *Fundamentals of War Gaming*, pp. 1.18–20.
[98] Clausewitz, *On War*, pp. 61–2.

Like all other methods used for the purpose, wargames provide only a very partial solution to our basic inability to foresee the future. For every scenario that was wargamed, probably fifty other possible ones never were. (When Nimitz said that every possibility was gamed, it meant that, over a generation or so, every sort of problem was encountered by somebody at some moment in some game. It did not mean that everybody was now prepared for anything, let alone that the navy as such had gamed everything and consequently knew how to cope with any problem that might arise.) Conversely, out of every fifty scenarios that were wargamed probably only one turned out to be correct in the sense that the events it foresaw actually took place in anything like the form that had been foreseen. The random numbers used to determine the outcome of combat, whether produced by dice or by more sophisticated methods, are a very inadequate substitute for extremely complex chains of causality into the dynamics of which we humans only have very limited insight.[99] To be sure some wargames, German ones in particular, played an important role in campaign planning. On some occasions they provided warnings, on others they turned out to predict the future rather accurately, though what percentage of the total they may have formed is impossible to say. But does it matter? When everything is said and done, there appear to be worse ways to try and peer into the future than by doing the best one can to comprehend all of the relevant factors, establish the way they relate to each other as accurately as one can, and play them out, perhaps repeatedly and with variations, against an able and imaginative opponent who has done exactly the same.

Last but not least, recall Wilkinson's warning concerning the things that wargames of the kind discussed in this chapter cannot do. Normally the games are scheduled days, even weeks, in advance. Their location and duration are known: on one occasion, when I suggested to a Norwegian group that, to introduce realism and increase uncertainty, participants in a game should be told neither when it would start nor how long it would last, one could hear the protests all the way from Trondheim to Oslo. While some games last for more than one day, rare is the one that does not allow the players a good night's rest. Evenings are often used for socializing. In one pre-1914 German caricature the location of "headquarters" is marked by a heap of empty bottles; in another, a young officer quartered upon a family during an exercise tells his hosts that whereas wargaming itself is not too exhausting, entertaining a different family every evening is.[100] The games are played in comfortable, well-lit, and if necessary heated or air-conditioned rooms. There are regular breaks for

---

[99] See on this N. N. Talib, *The Black Swan: The Impact of the Highly Improbable*, New York: Random House, 2007, especially pp. 251, 257, 287; also Rubel, "The Epistemology of War Gaming," p. 117.

[100] The caricatures are reproduced in H. Dollinger, *Wenn die Soldaten*, Munich: Bruckman, 1974, pp. 43, 49.

meals – as Napoleon might have said, wargames march on their stomachs. While some of the friction of real war may be simulated, the suffering, the pain, the death, and the bereavement are nowhere in sight.

It is true that in real life everything possible is done to insulate senior commanders from those factors so as to enable them to make the cool, rational decisions they are supposed to make. Even so, the crushing weight of responsibility can only be simulated to a very limited extent, especially, as is normally the case, when the players are relatively junior. It cannot be repeated too often that all this tends to overemphasize the intellectual qualities needed for the conduct of war as opposed to the physical and moral ones. That may be even more true of the next class of games we are now about to consider.

The hilt of the knife

In all pre-1914 wargames, only military factors were simulated. This was as true of tribal mock warfare and of tournaments as of the most sophisticated games conducted by early twentieth-century general staffs. In some of the latter, the forces being simulated numbered hundreds of thousands, if not millions, of men. True, the underlying assumption was that a large part of the male population had been mobilized and was wearing uniform. All the more remarkable was the fact that those forces seemed to glide along like magic, so to speak. Obeying their masters, who drew up the schedules and issued the orders, they made their way on foot, by road, and by railroad. Taking geographical and topographical conditions into account they advanced, retreated, clashed, penetrated, outflanked and encircled one another, and "fired" at one another with such and such results. Naval wargames were similarly organized. To the extent that the underlying economic realities were ignored, once again we see the principle of Kishon's grandson at work: the games gave a better impression of the way commanders *thought* about war than war itself did. At best, what they simulated were campaigns – without exception, brief ones lasting no more than a few weeks – rather than wars.

The experience of 1914–18 changed all that. The idea that economics mattered was hardly new – those in charge of royal and national treasuries had always known it, and it had been raised to the level of theory by Frederick Engels in 1878.[101] Now the rise of "total war" compelled even the most conservative commanders, such as the Frenchman Ferdinand Foch and the German Erich Ludendorff, to admit that military operations were merely the knife that economics, forming the hilt, empowered.[102] Not accidentally,

[101] F. Engels, *Anti-Duehring: Herr Eugen Duehring's Revolution in Science*, Moscow: Foreign Languages Publishing House, 1954 [1878], pp. 188–98.
[102] F. Foch, *Les principes de la guerre*, 5th edn, Paris: Berger-Levrault, 1918, pp. viii–ix; E. Ludendorff, *The Nation at War*, London: Hutchinson, 1936, pp. 11–24.

the interwar period saw the opening in several countries of colleges and research institutes specifically charged with investigating and teaching the links between war and the economic infrastructure on which it rests, the best known of which was the US Industrial College of the Armed Forces. World War II, which in terms of the resources mobilized to wage it probably dwarfed all previous ones combined, provided an even stronger push in the same direction. If the war showed anything, it was that even the best army (the Wehrmacht) with the most brilliant operational commanders could not prevail against a crushing material superiority combined with the kind of political leadership needed to form and maintain a global coalition.[103] Nor did the end of that conflict in August 1945 lead to a change of heart. By the late 1940s the idea that any future wars would be "total" had hardened into dogma – wrongly, as it turned out, for this was just the time when spreading nuclear weapons were making such conflicts between powerful states impossible.[104]

Helwig, Venturini, the two Reisswitzes, and many of their nineteenth- and early twentieth-century successors had all based their work on the belief that the conduct of war is rooted, at least in large part, in the laws of mathematics and physics. Such laws governed rates of advance, fronts, the amount of lead such and such formations might deliver in such and such a time, the number of casualties, and much more. Accordingly, what they really did was to try and find a better way to incorporate those laws into wargames than chess did. Unsurprisingly, that belief was shared by many well-known contemporary experts. They included, besides eccentrics such as Heinrich von Buelow, Antoine-Henri de Jomini. In fact Jomini, who during the first half of the nineteenth century was considered the world's most important military theoretician, often used the chessboard to explain the principles behind the operational movements he recommended.[105] Even Clausewitz, who traced the obsession with mathematics back to eighteenth-century siege warfare and logistics, did not completely reject this approach.[106]

Though it took time, from this it was a relatively small step to including economic factors such as each country's manpower potential, raw material situation, productive capacity, transport network, and the like. In theory, and increasingly in practice too, as the available statistical information improved all of these could be assigned numerical values. All could be related to each other: as in calculating, for example, by how much the mobilization of manpower would affect production or what the economic cost of losing an industrial

[103] On the constituents of national power as they were understood during those years, see H. Morgenthau, *Politics among Nations*, Boston, MA: McGraw-Hill, 1948, pp. 115–64.
[104] See M. van Creveld, *Nuclear Proliferation and the Future of Conflict*, New York: Free Press, 1993, pp. 32–65.
[105] A. H. D. von Buelow, *Geist des neuern Kriegsystem*, Hamburg: Hofman, 1799; A. H. de Jomini, *Précis de l'art de la guerre*, Paris, 1838.
[106] Clausewitz, *On War*, pp. 133–6, 214.

province would be. Military–economic games helped those who played them to determine what resources would be needed, identify bottlenecks, and tackle such problems as the need to create stores, find substitutes for scarce materials, and the like. Compared with this, the operations that earlier wargamers had tried to portray were of secondary importance. What mattered was not so much what military moves each party made but what resources he possessed and the manner in which he used them. To be sure, the resulting models were enormously complex. Often they required that the games be played not by individuals but by entire teams of experts. In principle, though, the need to use mathematics to simulate the factors in question was sufficiently well understood for at least some of them to be incorporated even in some games that amateurs designed and played.

Economics aside, war is a continuation of politics by other means. Historically many wargames were linked to politics in one way or another. In Rome, the repeated attempts to prevent members of the higher classes from fighting as gladiators probably reflected the need to maintain the social and political order on which the Empire rested. The organizers of tournaments tried not to include political enemies in the same team. Many a nineteenth-century politician dueled not because he wanted to but because doing so was essential for maintaining "face" in front of his adversaries. In the military, considerations concerning power and rank often made it impossible for top-level commanders to participate because there was nobody they could fairly play against. A famous story has the German chief of the General Staff, Helmut von Moltke the Younger, gently asking William II to stay away from wargames for that very reason.[107] During the Cold War even chess, the most strictly neutral of all games, was used as a weapon. The Soviets in particular were accused of constructing a "chess machine." It consisted of teams of coaches and advisers who analyzed every move and tried to rig the setting in which championships were held so as to favor their own side.[108] Still, even in this case, once the game got underway politics was put aside. On the board, in the arena, and in the field what counted were the players' skill, strength, and nerve, as well as the quality of the weapons, real or symbolic, they were allowed to use.

Strangely enough, in view of its reputation – asked where the Reichswehr stood, its chief of staff, General Hans von Seeckt, is reported to have said that "the Reichswehr stands behind me"[109] – the first to try and make wargames reflect this fact were the Germans during the Weimar Republic. Seeckt himself, in his critique of the 1923 staff ride, took care to inform the participants that (foreign) policy always impacted on war. Indeed the tools of policy, such as

[107] H. von Moltke, *Erinnerungen, Briefe, Dokumente*, Stuttgart: Der Kommende Tag, 1922, pp. 349–50.
[108] See Shenk, *The Immortal Game*, pp. 171–7; and Brady, *Endgame*, pp. 145–8.
[109] W. Goerlitz, *History of the German General Staff*, New York: Praeger, 1953, p. 237.

diplomatic notes, ultimatums, and economic measures, were themselves a form of war, with the result that the similarities between the two were at least as important as the differences.[110] To modern ears Seeckt's words sound militaristic if not actually warmongering. Yet they represented a radical departure from Moltke and Schlieffen, both of whom had not only insisted on a strict separation between politics and war but had even questioned the right of the former to direct the latter.[111] In so far as adversarial diplomacy too obeys the laws of strategy, moreover, there is no doubt that Seeckt had right on his side.

Six years later the Ministry of War, in a most unusual move for the time, joined the Foreign Ministry to organize what may well be the earliest political–military game of which some trace has survived. Possibly this reflected the often heard charge that, before 1914, the General Staff had failed to coordinate with the Foreign Ministry or anybody else, producing its plans in a vacuum and ignoring the fact that the invasion of Belgium would very probably bring Britain into the war.[112] If only to escape criticism, this was an error they did not want to repeat. Specifically, the objective was to simulate a conflict with Poland in which Polish irregulars operated on German soil, as had in fact happened in 1919–20. For the first time, representatives of the Foreign Ministry were invited. In the event, "the Polish foreign minister" and "the President of the League of Nations" played their respective roles to perfection. The former went on inventing German provocations and the latter kept throwing about empty phrases. Between them they left the German "foreign minister" speechless.[113]

Early in December 1932 the Minister of Defense, General Kurt von Schleicher, personally presented the Chancellor, Franz von Papen, with the results of another game. The objective was to assess the possibility of dispersing the Reichstag, declaring martial law, and using the Reichswehr to rule the country against the wishes of both the parties and the trade unions. The game showed that the chance of success was very slim. It may well have helped convince President Hindenburg that he had no choice but to dismiss von Papen, thus setting in movement the train of events that led directly to Hitler's assumption of power.[114] Finally, in 1938 the newly founded Wehrmachtakademie in Berlin held a large political–military game. Participants included officers from all branches of the Wehrmacht as well as government officials, businessmen, and industrialists, and representatives of Goebbels' Ministry of Propaganda.[115]

---

[110] See F. Von Rabenau, *Seeckt*, Leipzig: Hasse & Koehler, 1940, pp. 228–9.
[111] See on this J. Wallach, *Kriegstheorien: ihre Entwicklung im 19. und 20. Jahrhundert*, Frankfurt/Main: Bernard & Greafe, 1965, pp. 84–6, 95–101.
[112] G. Ritter, *The Sword and the Scepter*, London: Allen Lane, 1972, vol. II, pp. 193–206.
[113] Wilson, *The Bomb and the Computer*, pp. 28–9.
[114] D. Blasius, *Buergerkrieg und Politik: Weimars Ende, 1930–1932*, Goettingen: Vanderhoek, 2006, pp. 126–43.
[115] Hoffmann, *German Army War Games*, p. 27.

Probably other countries held similar exercises, but few details are known. What we do know is that, in the summer of 1941, the Total War Research Institute in Tokyo held a series of political–military games in preparation for the conflict to come. Represented were Japan, the US, the Soviet Union, Britain and other countries. In addition, different players represented divergent views and interests inside the Japanese establishment.[116] The games assumed that Germany would defeat the Soviet Union, a scenario which seemed likely at the time but which turned out to be grossly mistaken. While the conclusion that Japan would defeat Britain in the Far East proved correct, the decision to treat the US almost as a nonentity did not. Having helped lead Japan into a situation where it ultimately had to fight all the above countries plus China simultaneously, the games were not exactly a success. To adapt a phrase, hubris in, hubris out.

In the postwar world, the country that probably engaged in more wargaming, and certainly allowed more details about them to be made public, than any other was the US. The principal pioneer of political–military games during the 1950s was Herbert Goldhammer. Having served as the only civilian member of the US delegation to the Korean War armistice talks, he went on to write several works on the Soviet military, the psychology of deterrence, and gaming.[117] As he saw it, the objective was to bring to light issues that had previously remained hidden and devise novel strategies for dealing with them. By requiring that the players take specific actions and explain them to the umpires, the games also provided an unrivalled educational experience.[118] Later the field was taken over by Andy Marshall, a physicist and a former student of Goldhammer who, as of 2012, continued to head the Department of Net Assessment at the Pentagon. Others, including the political scientists Herman Kahn and Albert Wohlstetter, and the economists Oskar Morgenstern, Paul Kecskemeti, and Thomas Schelling, also owed part of their reputation to their work in the field. Many of them spent at least part of their careers at RAND, the Research and Development institute set up by the Army Air Force in 1946.

A typical political-military game stood somewhere between a Reisswitz-type game and a university seminar. That is why it is sometimes known as BOGSAT, a bunch of guys sitting around a table.[119] It differed from the former in that

---

[116] McHugh, *Fundamentals of Wargaming*, pp. 2–18.

[117] See on him Allen, *War Games*, pp. 148–52, as well as Wilson, *The Bomb and the Computer*, pp. 54–5.

[118] H. Goldhammer and H. Speier, "Some Observations on Political Gaming," *World Politics*, 12, 1, October 1959, p. 77.

[119] See, on the way it was (and is) done, W. M. Jones, *On Free-Form Gaming*, Santa Monica, CA: RAND, 1985, available at: www.rc.rand.org/pubs/notes/2007/N2322.pdf; S. Ghamari-Tabrizi, "Simulating the Unthinkable: Gaming Future War in the 1950s and 1960s," *Social Studies of Science*, 30, 2, April 2000, pp. 172–6; and S. F. Griffin, *The Crisis Game*, Garden City, NY: Doubleday, 1965, pp. 71–86.

there were no detailed rules and no dice to determine results. It differed from the latter in that the objective was to produce a definite outcome, though a good game did not specify what that outcome should be. Each player or team represented a country and occupied as many separate rooms as there were countries and alliances. Two additional rooms housed the game controller and communications center. The widespread availability of modern means of communication such as the telephone enabled the rooms to be located far apart if doing so was considered convenient. Each player or team was provided with a scenario. They then proceeded by turns each of which represented so and so much real time. Often the time represented was not continuous but proceeded in leaps. Players were confronted with successive scenarios separated by days, weeks, or even months.

Players made their moves in writing (in those pre-word-processing days, it was recommended that each team be provided with a typist). The results were submitted to an umpire or team of umpires who passed the information from one "country" to another. Occasionally they withheld part of it or distorted it so as to simulate problems of communication and perception; others added acts of God or else floated rumors in an attempt to simulate the "noise" that, in real life, almost always accompanies "hard" intelligence. Some, notably Schelling, took a more active role still, questioning players concerning their motivations in order to force them to clarify to themselves what they were doing. As the game unfolded the umpires assessed the results of the various moves, developed new scenarios, and fed them to the players to cut their teeth on. A good umpire might also make players operate on partial information, garbled information, and misleading information. Umpires acted as data banks, providing the information players required. The need for data, which had to be collected and stored ahead of time, meant that a month of preparation might be needed for every day of play: a contingency might be over before it could ever be gamed.[120]

Though it is hard to question the role of politics as the factor that governs, or ought to govern, war, no rigorous methodology for doing so has ever been developed. This was not for lack of trying. In fact, building on foundations laid during the 1940s, an entire new discipline, known as game theory, was stamped out of the ground. It probably reached the peak of its popularity during the 1950s when it was touted as "America's secret weapon ... a perfect, fool-proof system for playing all cut-throat games including poker, business – and war." Even as late as the early 1990s some blamed it for having fanned the rivalry between the superpowers.[121] Compared to other methods, the great advantage of game theory consisted precisely in that it focused not on the objectives of this

---

[120] Allen, *War Games*, p. 310; Wilson, *The Bomb and the Computer*, pp. 52–3.
[121] J. McDonald, "Secret Weapons: Theory of Games," *Science Digest*, December 1960, p. 7; M. de Landa, *War in the Age of Intelligent Machines*, New York: Swerve, 1991, pp. 87, 97.

player or that but on the way they interacted and the payoff each one could expect by doing so. By this means the relevant factors in any given game had to be identified, quantified if possible, and related to each other by means of mathematical equations and matrices. The objective was to help policymakers on each side (and, in so-called non-zero-sum games, on both) to "optimize" their decisions so as to obtain the greatest benefit for the least risk and at the smallest cost.

In fact, the impact of game theory on the conduct of international relations and strategy seems to have been negligible.[122] The reason, to quote Nobel Prize-winning game theorist Robert Aumann, is that the vast majority of real-life situations requiring political-military decisions are far too "unstructured" and "amorphous" to be fitted into such a straitjacket.[123] Game theory could not even deal with relatively simple games such as chess and football, let alone the vast number of contingencies, values, attitudes, choices, and alternatives policy-makers face.[124] Ignoring this fact is to risk obtaining outcomes that are non-sensical, dangerous, or both. Conversely, almost all scenarios capable of being handled with game-theoretical tools are far too simple to be of assistance to policymakers responsible for deciding on the conduct of war and the maintenance of peace. That is true even if they understand the relevant tables and equations which, along with the rest of us, 95 percent of them do not. Last but not least, game theory can only tell us what players, exercising pure logic within a rigidly defined framework, should do, not what, based on their hopes and fears, likes and dislikes, they actually will do. All this explains why a figure such as Henry Kissinger, developing from a young analyst into a master diplomat, is said to have lost any interest in it he may ever have had.[125] Certainly it is not mentioned in any of his major publications.

The absence of a proper theoretical framework did not stop wargamers from pushing, or trying to push, ahead. At the time, many universities were setting up departments of international relations and strategic studies. All wanted to demonstrate their sophistication by holding games. Presumably all also learnt that wargames can provide participants, male ones in particular, with shots of adrenalin no other method of study can match. Indeed one of the most surprising things about BOGSATs is precisely the way people tend to forget that they are just exercises in imagination and get caught up in them.[126] Soon

---

[122] B. O'Neill, "A Survey of Game Theory Models on Peace and War," 1990, pp. 1, 3, available at: http://pi.library.yorku.ca/dspace-jspui/bitstream/10315/1425/1/YCI0083.pdf.

[123] Quoted in E. van Damme, "On the State of the Art in Game Theory: An Interview with Robert Aumann," *Games and Economic Behavior*, 24, 1998, p. 184.

[124] L. Freedman, *The Evolution of Nuclear Strategy*, New York: St. Martin's, 1983, pp. 182–9, and M. Nicholson, "Games and Simulation," *Journal of Strategic Studies*, 3, 3, December 1980, p. 82.

[125] Wilson, *The Bomb and the Computer*, p. 151.

[126] Nicholson, "Games and Simulation," p. 85.

the number being held skyrocketed into the dozens, perhaps hundreds, each year. As people moved around from one institution to another, much of the work done by the government, the universities, and the think tanks got mixed up. Goldhammer was heard complaining that he had created Frankenstein's monster.[127] Like so many of their predecessors from the time of Reisswitz on, the games had two basic objectives. One was training, i.e. attracting the participants' attention to all sorts of problems they might not have anticipated and giving them a certain hands-on experience in coping with them. The other was planning, i.e. creating scenarios, allowing them to evolve, and watching where they led in the hope of drawing some lessons for the future. Precision being unobtainable, this was known as heuristic planning or developing options. It was hoped that, when the time came, the options could be submitted to policymakers, who would thus be spared the need to reinvent the wheel.[128]

In the US, the earliest political-military games were held in 1954–5. In 1961 the Joint Chiefs of Staff set up permanent facilities for the purpose. Allegedly the reason for this was President Kennedy's claim, following the Bay of Pigs fiasco, that senior American military did not understand the political implications of their recommendations.[129] Most players were medium-level officials, but senior policymakers sometimes took an interest. As so often in the Pentagon, scenarios tended to be set a few months or years in the future – neither so close as to make preparations impossible nor so far off as to make participants, who were always looking forward to their next election campaign or promotion, lose interest. They dealt with events that the designers thought *might* take place in reality. When a crisis did not exist it had to be invented. Now it was a question of the Soviet Union making aggressive moves in the Middle East, now of a Soviet preemptive attack on China. Now India and Pakistan went to war, now a Castro-type regime was going to be established in Venezuela, and now an uprising was threatening the Shah of Iran.[130] As if to prove how difficult predicting the future was and remains, the last-named scenario did take place, but only after such a long time that few if any of the players remained on the scene. By contrast, neither the building of the Berlin Wall nor the possibility that the Soviets might put missiles in Cuba were gamed – the latter because it was considered too implausible.[131]

All this had more to do with art, especially the art of stage-management, than with science. Absent detailed rules, players had to rely on pretense. Whatever the precise scenario, the principal questions tended to be broadly similar.

[127] Wilson, *The Bomb and the Computer*, p. 55.
[128] Ghamari-Tarbrizi, "Simulating the Unthinkable," p. 172.
[129] Caffrey, "Toward a History-Based Doctrine of Wargaming," p. 48.
[130] See, for this and what follows, Allen, *War Games*, pp. 151–2.
[131] Wilson, *The Bomb and the Computer*, p. 52.

Suppose things developed in such and such a way, how should the US react and what would the consequences of its actions be? What were the possibilities? What were the risks? Was the US prepared for the contingency in question, and if not, what should be done? Some games treated the US and other countries as if they were billiard balls impacting on each other. Others tried to simulate not just interactions among the various countries but the anticipated behavior of various pressure groups within them. Some games factored in the possibility of rushing American troops to the scene of action, a kind of simulation which would generally lead to the conclusion that so and so many men, with such and such equipment, could arrive there within so and so many days. Occasionally it was a question of "horizontal escalation," i.e. the possibility of opening another front. From that point it was a short step to setting up an additional series of lower-level games which would recommend that the process be speeded up by purchasing so and so many additional ships and/or aircraft and setting up such and such additional units and bases.[132] Sometimes the question of how to use the troops once they had arrived was also gamed, but this was by no means always the case.

An important characteristic of political-military games was that, unlike many of their more mathematically oriented predecessors, most of them did not have detailed rules as to what constituted victory. One objective was to make participants think more like their "Red" opponents, which of course might come in handy in case a real conflict developed. Another was to find out what might happen and where things might lead. Since the question as to who "won" did not matter much, individual games tended to end either when the umpire felt enough was enough or when time ran out (most games lasted between a few hours and three days: the more senior any policymakers, the less time they had to devote to gaming).[133] Probably some participants were disappointed by the inconclusive outcomes. Certainly those outcomes were among the factors that enabled critics to question the value of the games. The criticism is understandable but not entirely fair. In "reality," a good many "crises" do in fact melt away of their own accord; others are overshadowed as new ones arise.

Given that future historians are almost certain to point to the Vietnam War as the turning point that first showed the limits of US power, probably the most important political-military games of all were those held in 1964. The intention was to consider the issues surrounding America's commitment to the ongoing

---

[132] See H. Averch and M. Lavin, *Simulation of Decision-Making in Crisis*, Santa Monica, CA: RAND, 1964, pp. 30–1, available at: http://oai.dtic.mil/oai/oai?verb=getRecord& metadataPrefix=html&identifier=AD0605476.

[133] T. C. Schelling, "An Uninhibited Sales Pitch for Crisis Gaming," in R. Levine, T. C. Schelling, and W. Jones, *Crisis Games 27 Years Later*, Santa Monica, CA: RAND, 1991 [1965], p. 23.

conflict in Southeast Asia, which, following the murder of the Vietnamese head
of state Ngo Dinh Diem in November 1963, was entering a critical state. The
first series, called Sigma I, were held in April 1964. Blue players included
Mcgeorge Bundy, White House adviser on national security; John Mccone,
Director of Central Intelligence; General Earl Wheeler, army chief of staff;
General Curtis Lemay, commander of the Strategic Air Command; and John
McNaughton, Assistant Secretary of State. However, apart from CIA Deputy
Director for Intelligence Ray Cline, there seems to have been no senior official
on the Red side. The games concluded that a US bombing offensive against
North Vietnam could not be kept secret, as some rather preposterously suggested it should be. They also indicated that such a campaign, if launched
without appropriate political justification, would lead to massive protests both
outside and inside the US (which did in fact happen), and that it might cause
the Soviet Union "to change the ground rules of the Cold War" by means of
aggressive action in Latin America (which did not).[134] Compared to what had
taken place in Tokyo in the fall of 1941, arguably wargames that got two out of
three important propositions right were a smashing success.

In September of the same year, a month after the Tonkin Gulf Resolution by
which the US officially declared war on North Vietnam, a second round known
as Sigma II was held.[135] By that time Wheeler had been promoted to Chairman
of the Joint Chiefs of Staff. That apart, the list of participants was augmented by
Assistant Secretary of State William Bundy, Deputy Chief of Naval Operations
Admiral Horacio Rivero, and Deputy Secretary of Defense Cyrus Vance.
Though Secretary of Defense Robert McNamara did not participate in person
he did keep a close watch. Except perhaps for a few medieval tournaments,
probably in the whole of history no higher-ranking group of men had ever
played a wargame of any kind, albeit that most of the real work was done by
subordinates and that the senior animals (to translate a German expression)
themselves only dropped in after work. Red was played by some less high-ranking
East Asia experts from the State Department, the intelligence community, and
the universities. Probably this asymmetric setup had two unintended, if almost
certainly inevitable, consequences. First, since the "Reds" were not red at all but
American, culturally induced misunderstandings and friction were much less
pronounced than they would have been in the real world. Second, paradoxically
the fact that the Red players were vastly outranked may have given them a certain
freedom of action which their Blue opponents, carrying heavy responsibilities,
did not enjoy. During the post-game discussion they themselves said as much.
Perhaps an apt analogy would be small mammals running about and eating the
eggs of much larger dinosaurs.

The scenario, which was set in March 1965, was as follows. The number of
North Vietnamese troops in South Vietnam had increased sharply. Chinese

---

[134] Allen, *War Games*, pp. 196–7.   [135] *Ibid.*, pp. 198–208.

advisers were busily helping North Vietnam strengthen its anti-aircraft defenses. The political situation inside South Vietnam was shaky, the Vietcong had shelled Saigon, growing numbers of American troops were being committed to Vietnam, and some of them were getting involved in the fighting and being killed. Over much of the world the war was causing both officials and public opinion to take an anti-American stance. In so far as, by March 1965, much of this had actually taken place, the scenario proved almost uncannily prophetic. But prophecy is not enough: what the games signally failed to do was to suggest a solution to the problem. On one side stood the military men who wanted a powerful bombing campaign and even mentioned the use of nuclear weapons in case they would be needed to stop a Chinese invasion. On the other were the civilians.[136] They worried lest bombing would lead to escalation – not for nothing has Vietnam been called "the War after Korea." They may also have been influenced by some fashionable theories concerning the use of armed force, not for fighting the enemy and defeating him but for signaling, exercising pressure, and threatening.

In the event, the controllers ruled out the use both of nuclear weapons and of large numbers of Chinese troops, judgments that proved to be well founded. Within this framework the Blue civilian players, forming the majority, prevailed. An incremental strategy was adopted, especially in respect to the air campaign over North Vietnam. It quickly turned out that Red, far from being intimidated, would match every Blue move. Even as bombing destroyed much of its industry, transportation network, and central fuel reserve it continued to send troops south. It also intensified its attacks both on South Vietnam and on the US forces operating in that country, inflicted a growing number of casualties, and in general pursued the war. By the time the games ended they pointed to the conclusion that the outcome would not be a North Vietnamese defeat but a growing American involvement attended by serious foreign and domestic political problems. Again the games might be called a smashing success, except that it made no difference. For years and even decades afterwards, the incremental approach adopted both in the games and in reality enabled critics to argue that, had they had their way, the US, and especially its air force, could have "won" the war as early as 1965.[137] The debate is unlikely to be resolved. However, one point stands out. Neither in Afghanistan in 2001 nor in Iraq in 2003 did "shock and awe," delivered from the air with the aid of

---

[136] N. Tannenwald, "Nuclear Weapons and the Vietnam War," *Journal of Strategic Studies*, 29, 4, August 2002, pp. 681–2.

[137] See on this debate R. A. Pape, *Bombing to Win: Air Power and Coercion in War*, Ithaca, NY: Cornell University Press, 1996, pp. 174–211; M. Clodfelter, *The Limits of Airpower: The American Bombing of North Vietnam*, New York: Free Press, 1989; and H. R. McMaster, *Dereliction of Duty: Johnson, McNamara and the Lies that Led to Vietnam*, New York: Harper, 1998.

weapons far superior to those available in the 1960s, prevent a vicious guerrilla war from breaking out and continuing for years on end.

Of the countless political–military games played during this period, the most elaborate as well as the best-known ones were the series of so-called Global War Games held between 1979 and the end of the Cold War. Not accidentally the organization in charge, i.e. the US Navy, was perhaps the one with the broadest responsibilities, geographically speaking, in history. Supported by a dedicated intelligence department to help create a credible Soviet opponent, at first the games had a specifically navy focus.[138] Carrier task forces were always being sent here, there, and everywhere; unlike their Japanese predecessors, Control sometimes allowed some of them to be lost (though critics charged that this did not happen nearly often enough).[139] Soon, however, "[they] evolved, by obvious necessity, into a much broader military and political forum."[140] The overall objective was "to gain insights into how naval campaigns might be conducted on a global scale in the event of conflict between the United States (Blue) and the Soviet Union (Red)." Hoped-for specific insights included the question as to which operations should be given priority, logistic problems, the effectiveness and consequences of various strategic maneuvers, the impact of political and economic forces, the thresholds where nuclear escalation might occur, and problems of command and control. At first sixty people participated. Later, as the focus shifted to bring in additional countries, as many as six hundred did. They included officers from all the services, government officials, and representatives of academia and industry. Organizing all this represented quite a logistic challenge in itself.

As one might expect, in every scenario it was always Red which took the initiative. It attacked now here, now there; in response, the Blue players were expected to see what they could and would do. The 1979 scenario postulated Iraq, supported by the Soviet Union, invading Saudi Arabia in 1985 (in fact Iraq invaded not Saudi Arabia but Iran, not in 1985 but in 1980, and without Soviet military aid). Other scenarios also tended to be positioned a few years in the future. As the 1979 game developed, US forces were sent to the Red Sea and the Indian Ocean to assist the Saudis. The Soviets on their part took the offensive in the Mediterranean, turning it into a Red lake. However, this success was to some extent balanced by the fighting on the "Central Front" where NATO halted the Soviet advance and even mounted some counterattacks. Subsequent scenarios involved fighting, in addition to the all-important "Central Front," in places as far apart as Norway, the Black Sea straits, the Middle East, Iran (both of which came

---

[138] D. A. Rosenberg, "Being 'Red': The Challenge of Taking the Soviet Side in War Games at the Naval War College," *Naval War College Review*, 41, Winter 1988, pp. 86–92.
[139] Dunnigan, *Wargames Handbook*, p. 346; Allen, *War Games*, p. 288.
[140] B. Hay and R. H. Gile, *Global War Game: The First Five Years*, Newport, RI: Naval War College, 1993, "Note for readers" and *passim*.

under Red attack), and the Far East (China against Vietnam, North Korea against South Korea, the US and Japan against the Soviet Union). Fierce "battles" also took place in the Atlantic where Red air and naval forces did their best to prevent Blue from reinforcing NATO forces fighting in Central Europe.

Most of the simulated conflicts were over in a matter of days, which meant that the role played by economic factors was limited. Several involved the threatened and even actual use of nuclear weapons in various outlying areas (outlying, that is, as seen from the White House and the Kremlin, not by the unfortunate people who lived in the areas in question). The point where a large number of strategic warheads were exploded in the territory of the principal belligerents, the US SIOP (Strategic Integrated Operations Plan) and its Soviet equivalent were activated, and the world came to a spectacular end, was never reached. In most games the use, threatened or real, of nuclear weapons was initiated by Blue in the belief that Red's conventional superiority and military successes left it no choice. However, in some cases it was Red, its offensive having been blunted, which introduced them. Most players were extremely reluctant to cross the nuclear threshold. Once they had done so, though, nuclear weapons tended to overshadow everything else. This had the effect of turning the later stages of the games into exercises in escalation control. Either some kind of political settlement was reached, or else they were brought to an end without a clear conclusion.

Early games tended to open with an outright Red offensive aimed at bringing about a fundamental change in the balance of power in Central Europe in particular. In some games the invader got as far as the Channel coast. Subsequent ones were more sophisticated in this respect. They postulated the unintended escalation of what started as some fairly marginal clash and due largely to the fact that neither side wanted to blink first. One reason for the switch was that Red began to be played by intelligence officers on the basis of their estimates of actual Soviet intentions rather than worst-case scenarios. The change had the effect of increasing the role of political negotiations, threat and counter-threat, at the expense of "actual" warfighting. It also caused scenarios to stretch out over periods of two months and more. This caused the role of nuclear weapons to decline but increased that of economic factors: questions such as industrial mobilization, how long it would take, and what its results would be had to be considered. Bringing in economics meant that the database on which players could draw and which they used to determine what they needed and what they could get had to be vastly expanded. This change in turn encouraged, and was encouraged by, the growing use of computers, which might point out, for example, that by day so and so of the simulated conflict Blue or Red was beginning to run out of resources.

As has been said, one should never underestimate the willingness of the state to act out even its most shocking fantasies.[141] Thank goodness, hardly any of

---

[141] D. Delillo, *Underworld*, New York: Scribner, 1997, p. 421.

these scenarios were translated into reality. Afghanistan in 1979 apart, the Soviet Union never invaded any other country, let alone initiated and pursued a war on the "Central Front." In fact, to the extent that the games dealt with finding answers to Soviet "adventurism," by the time they were initiated the peak of that adventurism, as displayed in the Middle East, the Horn of Africa, and Angola during the 1970s, was already in the past. Nevertheless, the basic factors governing the Cold War were simulated quite well. This included (after the first few games) its tendency to flash up in the periphery rather than in the "Central" theater; the need to keep the sea-lanes open; as well as the overriding importance of nuclear weapons and the need to contain them at almost literally any cost. In fact one very important reason why, in most games, wars broke out in the periphery was precisely because most of the countries in question did not have nuclear weapons. A less expected, but equally important, insight was that players on each side rarely if ever understood the political intent of the military moves that the others directed at them.[142] As a result, moves meant to pass a signal or message normally led to totally unexpected consequences. Better proof that man is indeed the animal that invents stories to explain itself to itself (and that each story is different and may have little if anything to do with "reality") is hard to find.

Overall, the games may not have yielded many earth-shaking new insights. Some would argue that they were merely an enormously expensive way to bring out the obvious; if so, however, then the same also applies to many other kinds of research done in many other fields. Others claim that wargames of every kind may actually make the events they simulate more acceptable and thus more likely to take place. On the positive side, they certainly caused players to think about what they were doing. By testing and validating all sorts of concepts, they may even have helped bring about significant shifts in American strategic thought.[143] For example, initially Blue thought it was all it could do to defend so as not to lose, or at any rate make victory expensive for Red. Later it came to believe that it should counterattack and might actually win. This belief was motivated in part by the possibility of revolts in the countries of Eastern Europe which would surprise Red, disrupt his communications, and make him wonder what he should do next. Operationally there was a shift from forward defense, meaning an attempt to stop the Reds as close as possible to the West German border, to much more flexible maneuver warfare, Airland Battle and FOFA (Follow-On Forces Attack). Whereas early on it was thought that the "Central Front" almost totally eclipsed all the rest, later other theaters were rehabilitated.

At first it was thought that, to avoid defeat, Blue would have to start using nuclear weapons at an early stage. Later Blue became more confident; as the introduction of those weapons was delayed, wars tended to become longer. Not

---

[142] R. H. Gile, *Global War Game: Second Series*, Newport, RI: Naval War College, 2004, p. 11.
[143] *Ibid.*, pp. 127–8.

everybody agreed with this. Thus General Bernard Rogers, who served as Supreme Allied Commander, Europe (SACEUR) from 1979 to 1987, explained that the bases in which the weapons were stored were in danger of being overrun within days of the opening of hostilities. Either they would be used, or else they would be lost.[144] As is shown by the fact that the last game in the series, which was played in 1988, focused almost exclusively on war termination, there was a growing emphasis on that problem.[145] Some of the shifts may not have reflected anything in the "real" world but merely the dynamics of the games themselves. How many times can one game a Soviet invasion of West Germany and the precise way it should be countered without trying other scenarios as well? And what is the point of introducing nuclear weapons early on if doing so would almost certainly cause the games to come to an almost immediate end?

As always, it would be hard to say whether the games shaped the strategic outlook of those years, especially the renewed feeling of confidence that resulted from the vast Reagan-inspired increase in the defense budget and the Military Reform Movement, or the other way around. Did the games trigger thought, or did they reflect it and put it to the test? To what extent did they influence policy? After each game teams working for the director stayed behind. They prepared reports which were disseminated among senior decision-makers, who may or may not have studied them. Since such decision-makers seldom discuss their plans in advance (even if they care for wargames, which not all of them do),[146] however, and since a great many scenarios remained secret for years after the games had ended, the answer is left blowing in the wind. Needless to say, the more senior the decision-makers the greater the problem.[147]

As the following example illustrates, the games' value in forecasting the future was mixed. Those held in 1985–7 assumed growing economic and political pressures towards German reunification.[148] East German attempts to counter those pressures by stirring up trouble around Berlin led to escalation and the outbreak of large-scale warfare on the "Central Front" which spread to the Atlantic, the Mediterranean, and the Far East. All this was supposed to happen between October 1989 and January 1991. However, the underlying assumption, which was reflected by the teams responsible for financing the "war," was that it would last for at least two years. It would be paid for by Japan setting aside $2.3 trillion for the purpose. Whether the Japanese had been asked, and what their response was, is not recorded. Like so many scenarios of the

---

[144] See J. Baylis, "NATO's Strategy: The Case for a New Strategic Concept," *International Affairs*, 64, 1, Winter 1987, p. 44. It is only fair to add that Rogers was not specifically referring to the wargames.

[145] Gile, *Global War Game: Second Series*, p. 85.

[146] See D. Ford, *The Button: The Pentagon's Command and Control System*, New York: Simon & Schuster, 1985, pp. 90–3.

[147] Allen, *War Games*, pp. 220, 250. [148] Gile, *Global War Game: Second Series*, pp. 37–67.

period, in some ways it was simply a rerun of World War II with the Soviet Union playing the role of Nazi Germany. With hindsight we know that pressures toward German reunification did in fact peak precisely during the period in question – but also that they did not lead to war either on the "Central Front" or anywhere else.

Designing games in such a way that they will faithfully capture past events is hard enough, but doing the same in respect of the future is harder still. Since validation is impossible, most games will probably get some things right, others wrong. However, it is only in retrospect that the two may be separated. The collapse of the Soviet Union, which some saw as the decisive event that brought the "short" twentieth century to an end,[149] made journalists and scholars engage in a mad scramble to provide explanations as to why it had taken place. On the other hand, there is no evidence that it was gamed in advance.

[149] See E. Hobsbawm, *The Age of Extremes: A History of the World, 1914–1991*, New York: Vintage, 1996.

5

From bloody games to bloodless wars

Toil and sweat (but no blood)

As Clausewitz never tires of telling us, combat is the very essence of war. Paradoxical as it sounds at first sight, the same may be even more true of wargames. Throughout history, the intricacies of higher strategy, intelligence, logistics, command and control, and similar aspects of war have only appealed to a relative handful of people. Indeed it would hardly be an exaggeration to say that, for every person who took an interest in the above-mentioned fields, a hundred roared their heads off as blows were delivered and parried, blood was shed, and some combatants stood triumphant even as others went down to defeat. To be sure, there have always been some wargames, such as chess and its relatives, which did not involve physical combat and focused on the more intellectual aspects of war instead. That was precisely why they never became nearly as popular, or generated nearly as much excitement, as their bigger brothers did.

The spread of firearms put an end to the great fights/nothing fights, *agona*, *ludi, jeux, Ritterspiele*, jousts, or whatever else the more violent wargames were called. For almost five hundred years after that, violent wargames were not two-sided and two-sided wargames were not violent. What weapons could still be used in the latter tended to be rather childish, as when early nineteenth-century Prussian troops facing each other in mock battle used clappers to simulate the sound of musket-fire,[1] and when H. G. Wells enlisted children's toy guns to help him play among fortifications made out of volumes of the *Encyclopedia Britannica* strategically positioned on the floor. It was only the spread of simulators and shooter-type computer games – as we shall see, the two, originally separate, ended by becoming practically the same – from the 1960s on that finally enabled two-sided games to become violent again: albeit only in the form of blips "firing" at other blips on the screen.

---

[1] P. Schrekenbach, *Der zusammenbruch Preussens im Jahre 1806*, Jena: Diederichs, 1906, p. 24.

Furthermore, war has always been the domain of thirst, hunger, heat, cold, discomfort, and fatigue. Whoever cannot cope with these factors need not try his or her hand at it. Surprising as it may appear to some, technological progress has done remarkably little to change this fact. In most wars, for every pilot and other soldier-technician whose weapon system is almost indistinguishable from the machine that simulates it there are perhaps a hundred grunts on the ground. Carrying a heavy pack – given the computers and batteries needed to realize the vision of a "networked army," recently packs have become heavier, not lighter – they gasp for breath as they enter combat.[2] Nor does it look as if things are about to change. If, as some believe, future warfare will be overwhelmingly urban, then it may well become physically more grueling still.[3]

Two-sided wargames that are held in the field, thus providing at least a semblance of the fatigues of war, are known as maneuvers. Originally the term meant the various ways in which a commander could deploy and move his troops prior to, into, and during combat.[4] Later it also came to stand for a two-sided military exercise, and it is in this sense that the term will be used on the following pages. Remarkably little has been written on maneuvers, and their origins remains somewhat of a mystery. Xenophon in his *Cyropaedia*, the work in which he describes the ideal king as he raises and trains the ideal army, may be referring to something of the sort.[5] However, it is impossible to be sure. The same applies to the famous passage in the first-century AD Jewish-Roman historian Josephus where he says that Roman military exercises were bloodless wars and Roman exercises bloody games.[6] *Behourds*, assuming they represented some form of riding exercises in which two sides were made to operate against one another without the use of sharp weapons, may also have fallen into this category. Certainly neither Machiavelli in his *Art of War* nor any of the numerous seventeenth-century drill books refer to maneuvers in our sense of the term.

Equally certainly, eighteenth-century commanders with their standing armies did hold large-scale exercises, often on an annual basis. The favored season for doing so was the autumn, by which time the harvest would have been brought in. September, incidentally, has remained the favorite season for maneuvers right down to the present day. Major exercises might last as long as a couple of weeks. In them thousands and even tens of thousands of troops, carrying full pack and equipped as if for war, took to the field and were put through their paces. One drill-book after another was published, going into

---

[2] D. Lamothe, "[Marine] Corps Researching New, Light, Combat Gear," *Marine Times*, July 31, 2009, available at: www.marinecorpstimes.com/news/2009/08/marines_high_speed_gear_083109w/.

[3] See, for a graphic account of what is involved, G. R. Christmas, "A Company Commander Remembers the Battle for Hue," *Marine Corps Gazette*, 62, 2, February 1977, pp. 1–26.

[4] For example, Guibert as quoted in H. Camon, *Quand et comment Napoléon a conçu son système de bataille*, Paris: no. pub., 1935, p. 173; Clausewitz, *On War*, pp. 541–2.

[5] Xenophon, *Cyropaedia*, LCL, 1914, 1.9–13.   [6] Josephus, *Bellum Judaicum*, LCL, 3.5.1.

minute detail as to the best formations to be adopted and advocating this system or that.[7] Following the outstanding performance of the Prussian Army during the Seven Years War (1756–63) its exercises were held in particularly high regard. It was during that period that the word "maneuver," specifically referring not only to troop movements in general but to those carried out as part of a training schedule, came into vogue. The objective was to allow both the troops and their commanders to practice the complicated evolutions that the tactics of the age demanded.

Yet little in the contemporary literature indicates that the exercises in question were meant to provide a more or less realistic simulation of a two-sided conflict. Instead, what stands out above all is their highly artificial nature. Much of this had more to do with the need to maintain discipline and present the world with a pretty picture of troops acting and marching like robots than with serious preparation for war. As one contemporary story had it, Gustavus Adolphus, while welcoming one particularly exacting eighteenth-century drill-master to wherever commanders go after their death, commented that he had not been aware that, since he himself had been killed at Luetzen in 1632, the world had been made flat.[8] As if to emphasize the total lack of realism, on one occasion Frederick II himself was treated to the spectacle of a battalion turning on its own axis, like a top, in the center of the market-square at Magdeburg.[9] Much later, incidentally, forming a swastika and having it turn in the same way became a much beloved exercise among the Hitler Youth. When Napoleon said that Frederick had been cheating and that the annual Prussian maneuvers at Potsdam were merely meant to mislead the curious foreigners who flocked to watch them, he may well have had a point.[10]

Discussing friction, Clausewitz says that peacetime maneuvers only provide a pale reflection of the reality of war. But whether he was thinking of one- or two-sided exercises is not clear from his work.[11] Large-scale, two-sided maneuvers by divisions and even entire corps appear to have been a nineteenth-century innovation. While their precise origins are hard to trace, probably the factor that really made them possible was the rise of the railroads for war and conquest. Certainly by the last decades of the century every major army was holding them on a more or less regular basis. The major exception was the British one which only acquired the necessary land on Salisbury Plain in 1898.[12]

[7] See on those books and the evolutions they advocated, R. S. Quimby, *The Background of Napoleonic Warfare*, New York: Columbia University Press, 1957.
[8] V. Marcu, *Das Grosse Kommando Scharnhorst*, Berlin: Deutsche Buch Gemeinschaft, 1928, p. 38; G. H. von Berenhorst, *Betrachtungen*, Leipzig: Fleischer, 1796, vol. II, p. 423.
[9] See on this van Creveld, *The Culture of War*, pp. 354–7.
[10] J. Luvaas, ed., *Napoleon on the Art of War*, New York: Touchstone, 1999, p. 40.
[11] Clausewitz, *On War*, p. 122.
[12] E. M. Spiers, *The Late Victorian Army, 1868–1902*, Manchester University Press, 1992, p. 263.

Even so, British maneuvers remained relatively puny. For example, those of 1898 seem to have involved about 33,000 men, corresponding to the wartime strength of one corps and not of two as the scenario demanded. One division, the second, was represented by exactly 767 commissioned and non-commissioned personnel, forming the real-life equivalent of less than two battalions.[13] Only in 1909 did anyone actually see a full British division taking the field at war strength, and even later most maneuvers were held on a considerably smaller scale.[14]

A fairly good idea of the way large-scale maneuvers were planned and executed may be obtained from a German publication entitled *Bestimmungen fuer das Kaisermanoever 1908* ("Instructions for the Imperial Maneuvers, 1908"). The volume was prepared and issued by the headquarters staff (*Generalkommando*) of the XVIth Army Corps. It consists of about a hundred closely printed pages (in Gothic letters), plus several appendices.[15] Subordinated to the XVIth Corps were two infantry divisions, the 33rd and the 34th, as well as "A" cavalry division. However, normally the number of corps participating in the maneuvers each year was four, two on each side. If that applied to those of 1908 too, then the forces assembled for the occasion must have totaled around 180,000 men, fully one-quarter of the entire peace-time army.

Normally the maneuvers were held in a different part of the country each year. Now East Prussia, now Silesia (both of which might become the objects of a Russian invasion from Poland), now the northwestern German plain was selected. The 1908 "theater of war" consisted of northern Lorraine, a hilly region that had seen much fighting during the Franco-Prussian War of 1870–1. Having since been annexed to Germany, most people expected it to become the scene of fighting in the next war, too. However, depots and field hospitals were also set up much further east in Germany proper. The entire gigantic piece of theater was supposed to last for five days. Of these, the first and the last were devoted to approach marches and cleaning up, respectively.

The general outline having been determined, the document went on to deal with the necessary administrative arrangements. They included umpires, who were subject to specially issued regulations and were recognizable by their armbands; the disposition of formations and units, media contacts, uniforms and equipment, command and control, quarters, and supplies; the mail service, sanitary service, veterinary service, and much more. The responsible staffs were told to run all these as they would in real war and even to maintain war diaries as they did so. Specific provisions were made in case a sudden emergency required that the exercise be broken off. Unfortunately for the historian, the

---

[13] US War Department, *Autumn Maneuvers of 1898*, Washington DC: GPO, 1899, p. 73.
[14] William Robertson, *From Private to Field-Marshal*, London: Constable, 1921, p. 160.
[15] Anon., *Bestimmungen fuer das Kaisermanoever 1908*, no place: no pub., 1908.

document does not explain the scenario (known, at the time, as a "general hypothesis," which was divided into "special hypotheses") for the maneuvers, which was kept secret and only distributed to the participants at the last possible moment. All it says is that, the scenario having been issued and "a state of war" declared, the various units, headquarters, and staffs were supposed to operate independently, following their own plans and estimates of the situation.[16]

Formally speaking, overall direction was in the hands of the emperor who was scheduled to take up quarters at Schloss (palace) Urville, not far from Metz. From there he and his suite would move around "exclusively by motor vehicle." A balloon was even used to mark his location at all times. Earlier in his reign William used to command one side in person, always ending the maneuvers with a grand cavalry charge and always emerging victorious against generals who did not, could not, do anything to shatter their master's delusions. However, by this time he had been persuaded to cease doing so, with the result that his role was limited to visiting, inspecting, making speeches, and handing out decorations to those who had done best at various competitions such as riding and shooting. Still he remained very fond of maneuvers, causing a subsequent observer to comment that he much preferred them to war.[17]

To honor William, a special "Kaisermaneuvermarsch" was composed and presumably performed by some of the Imperial Army's 560 bands.[18] In Germany and elsewhere maneuvers tended to be festive occasions. They attracted swarms of observers, both unofficial and official. For example, in 1873, 150,000 people flocked to watch the rather small British maneuvers held at Cannock Chase in Staffordshire. They behaved as if they were attending a fair, complete with stalls that sold food, drink, and souvenirs. Dignitaries of every sort did the same. Churchill twice attended the German maneuvers, once in 1906 and once 1908. In 1910 Emperor William personally invited former US President Teddy Roosevelt to do the same. Later, to commemorate the occasion, he presented his guest with signed pictures of the two of them on horseback, reviewing troops.[19] The guest of honor at the 1937 Wehrmacht maneuvers to be discussed below was none other than Italy's *Duce*, Benito Mussolini. Wherever maneuvers were held, all this publicity entailed the risk that participants, senior ones in particular, instead of focusing on their tasks, would use the exercise to curry favor with their superiors, politicians, and the press.

[16] *Ibid.*, p. 13.

[17] G. A. von Mueller, *Regierte der Kaiser? Kriegstagebucher, Aufzeichnungen und Notizien des Chefs des Marine-Kabinetts Admiral Georg von Mueller*, Goettingen: Musterschmidt, 1959, p. 216, entry for August 25, 1916.

[18] According to B. Matthews, *Military Music and Bandsmen of Adolf Hitler's Third Reich*, Winchester: Tomahawk, 2002, p. 16.

[19] See Theodore Roosevelt Association, *Life of Theodore Roosevelt*, 1998, available at: www.theodoreroosevelt.org/life/biopictures.htm.

On the other side of Germany's western border the French held their annual maneuvers on a similar scale. However, French generals tended to be considerably older than their German opposite numbers. As a result many of the exercises, instead of representing dry runs for war, sometimes degenerated into elaborate retirement ceremonies.[20] At a time when one technological innovation rapidly followed upon another, maneuvers were often used to test new kinds of equipment and weapons. Among them were heavy artillery, the telegraph, wireless communications, as well as motor cars and aircraft. Indeed the exercises provided some of the few occasions when the formidable task of integrating all these into a single smooth-functioning team could be attempted at all. For example, the French maneuvers in 1909 included thirteen aircraft and four dirigibles that flew reconnaissance missions. At the time French heavier-than-air aviation in particular was the most highly developed in the world. Foreign observers were suitably impressed and went on to launch their own efforts.

A year later the Italian Army held a somewhat similar wargame in Monferrato, a hilly region in the northwestern part of the country. Two army corps, a blue one and a red one, maneuvered against one another. Each of them was allocated four aircraft. As was characteristic at the time, and as was also the case in other countries, some of those were privately owned and operated. Since the Italians only had two airships they were put at the disposal of the two commanders, the blue and the red, on alternate days. A detailed description of the moves and countermoves does not appear to be available. Still, the "lessons learnt" from these maneuvers were quite interesting. The airships duly flew reconnaissance missions over a large area. They even helped the "blue" force to take the "red" one in the flank, a maneuver that decided the outcome of the "campaign."

By contrast, the aircraft's ability to do the same was limited by the fact that their pilots were too busy handling the controls. Both airships and aircraft had their performance degraded by the stormy weather, and indeed several of the former were immobilized. Neither, it turned out, could operate without a fairly extensive supporting infrastructure if they were to achieve anything at all.[21] These were important insights, but their value was somewhat diminished by the fact that both aircraft and dirigibles were permitted to fly around without anybody firing at them, notwithstanding the fact that experiments with anti-aircraft defenses had started a few years earlier and quickly brought out the vulnerability of the lumbering dirigibles when flying at low altitude. It was by no

[20] See D. Porch, *The March to the Marne: The French Army 1871–1914*, Cambridge University Press, 1981, pp. 177–8.
[21] See on these maneuvers Anon., "Gli aeroplani et i dirigibili nelle grandi manoevre del Monferrato," in Ufficio storico dell'aeronautica militare, ed., *I prime voli de Guerra nel mondo*, Rome: Ufficio storico, 1961, pp. 10–13.

means the last time that maneuvers were rigged in this way: in fact organizing maneuvers that will *not* be biased, at least in the view of one of the participating sides, appears to be all but impossible.

During the interwar years the armies of several countries used maneuvers in order to test their embryonic armored forces. Particularly important in this respect was Britain's Experimental Mechanized Force. Instigated by the later to be famous Colonel J. F. C. Fuller, the brigade-sized Force began its official existence on Salisbury Plain in August 1927. It consisted of a Flank Reconnaissance Group equipped with armored cars, a Main Reconnaissance Group with tankettes, a Royal Tank Battalion with forty-eight Vickers I medium tanks, a battalion of mechanized infantry, a field artillery battalion with both towed and self-propelled guns, a mechanized light artillery battalion, and a company of mechanized engineers. Communications were provided by 150 wireless sets which supplemented the traditional dispatch riders. Most of the equipment dated back to 1918 and was nothing if not motley. Still the brigade represented the first all-mechanized, all-motorized force in history.[22] Supported by Royal Air Force aircraft, in both 1927 and 1928 it "fought" traditional infantry and cavalry units under the watchful eyes of senior officers (who rode enormous open staff cars), and their parasol-carrying ladies.

A dramatic account of the maneuvers in question comes from the American *Popular Mechanics* magazine, written, as its motto said, "so you can understand it."[23]

> An army of 'robots', mechanical monsters carrying gas-masked men, was mobilized recently [by] the British Army . . . Little two-passenger tanks . . . sped across the fields on endless treads, or switched in a twinkling to rubber-tired wheels and dashed down clear roads. Four-passenger tanks, with guns in conning towers, huge battle tanks, mounting small field artillery, heavy anti-aircraft guns on tractor mounts, and tanks equipped with wireless. Overhead attack and pursuit airplanes soared and dipped while they sprayed the advancing steel armies with bursts of machine gun fire. The maneuvers continued day and night under conditions as nearly as those of actual war as could be produced . . . The engagement was like an evil dream with mythical gray monsters spitting flame and death . . . "Road bombed out of existence," was the message flashed back from the wireless scouts. "Make your own way across country," came the command. Then

[22] See Experimental Mechanized Force, available at: http://en.wikipedia.org/wiki/ Experimental_Mechanized_Force.

[23] Anon., "Radio-Equipped Army Tanks Direct Maneuvers," *Popular Mechanics*, December 1927, pp. 910–11, available at: http://books.google.co.il/books?id=iNgDAAAAMBAJ&pg= PA910&lpg=PA910&dq=salisbury+plain+maneuvers&source=bl&ots=3957js28bk&sig= oSZ58KrQX2wZMmElFRDzVWKe92k&hl=iw&ei=LrJ8TZOqC8ey8QO4xfC6Cw&sa=X& oi=book_result&ct=result&resnum=3&ved=0CCAQ6AEwAg#v=onepage&q=salisbury %20plain%20maneuvers&f=false.

the mechanical army moved ... Suddenly three airplanes, like falcons, dropped out of the bank of leaden clouds ... The unprotected vehicles out in the open field, balancing precariously as their speed increased, hurried for the shelter of the trees. Men in the dragons opened fire with their rifles as the falcons swooped down.

To be sure, not everything functioned perfectly. In particular, coordinating the different units proved to be beyond the commander's powers. The umpires judged the Force to have been, if not a great success then at any rate a good beginning on which the future could be built. The Secretary of War disagreed, however, and it was dismantled.[24]

Meanwhile in Germany, the army of the Weimar Republic, or Reichswehr as it was known, was taking up the tradition of holding maneuvers that World War I had interrupted. During the years immediately after the armistice the scale on which they were held was necessarily small. By 1926, though, it became possible to hold two separate exercises, one in East Prussia and one in south-western Germany.[25] Between them they involved six of the seven available divisions either wholly or in part. Typically for the Germans, who sought to avoid *Schematismus* (roughly, the unthinking adherence to fixed patterns) above all, scenarios were extremely varied. On top of this, commanders were given considerable freedom to act as they saw fit. The American military attaché present, Truman Smith, was particularly impressed by the high caliber of the umpires. They were, he wrote, thorough, sufficient, and efficient, using their sound training to issue their decisions with commendable promptness and judgment. The US Army had nothing similar to this. The exercises did not try to reconstruct the trench warfare of 1914–18. Instead there was an emphasis on mobile warfare and on coordinated teamwork by various arms such as infantry, artillery (carefully camouflaged so as to be invisible from the air), and cavalry. The last-named never rode in mass but always operated in small groups, "fighting" dismounted.

The maneuvers, which made tremendous demands on the troops' physique, also included a river crossing and a night attack. A new tactic, said to have been invented by the future Field Marshal Erwin Rommel at the time he commanded a company on the Italian Front in 1917–18, and consisting of using indirect fire from heavy machine guns instead of artillery to cover an attack, was also practiced. Above all, and again reflecting innovations introduced during the last years of the war, German commanders on maneuver did not try to maintain a continuous front. It took Smith some time to realize that this was not due to any lack of command and control, let alone of tactical and operational expertise,

---

[24] See B. Bond, *British Military Policy between the Two World Wars*, Oxford: Clarendon Press, 1980, pp. 140–7.

[25] See, for what followed, J. S. Corum, *The Roots of Blitzkrieg*, Lawrence: University of Kansas Press, 1992, pp. 183–6.

but to a new doctrine that insisted on units exploiting gaps in the defense and pushing boldly ahead without regard to their flanks.

In one post-maneuver report, the general commanding one side praised the troops for their efforts but wrote that the officers were still not up to par – a most unusual thing to do, as anyone who has served in almost any military knows. By the late 1920s the number of motor vehicles operated by the Reichswehr and involved in the maneuvers was growing. Logistic vehicles, tracked artillery tractors, and even self-propelled artillery on tracks started making their appearance. In 1927, the same year the British maneuvers were held, a complete motorized regiment participated for the first time and attempts were made to coordinate it with a cavalry division in a common operation. Experimentation went on and on: in 1932, for the first time, Krupp-built "tractors" (in reality Mark I light tanks, minus their turrets) figured as the most important component of one of the forces involved, though the problem of coordinating them with the more traditional, slow-moving infantry and artillery remained unsolved.[26] In the same year each division received a permanent reconnaissance battalion. It consisted of a motorized headquarters, a signals platoon, an armored car platoon, an anti-tank platoon, a machine-gun troop, a bicycle company, and a cavalry troop – an organization, as it turned out, that was far too complex to work.

Since the Treaty of Versailles had prohibited the Reichswehr from operating tanks, trucks were dressed up with mockups made of cardboard. Local children who had come to watch would sometimes use pencils to punch holes in them, causing commanders to gnash their teeth in impotent fury.[27] Once rearmament had begun and general conscription been reintroduced in 1935 the picture began to change very rapidly, as armored formations were created and showed themselves on maneuver. At first it was mainly a question of making the various elements work together and demonstrating that capability to skeptical senior commanders. Also, the need to constantly give up stems to help establish new units meant that many formations were rendered dysfunctional for considerable periods of time. By 1937, though, sufficient progress had been made to allow the old tradition of full-scale, two-sided maneuvers to be resumed. In the event the maneuvers in question also proved to be the last, for the looming Czechoslovak crisis caused those scheduled for the next year to be cancelled.

In charge of the 1937 exercise was the then Major General Franz Halder, an training expert who, a year later, was promoted to chief of the Army General Staff.[28] As he wrote at the time, the maneuvers provided a singular opportunity to gain some insight into the approaching reality of war – a war which, for the

---

[26] M. R. Habeck, *Storm of Steel: The Development of Armor Doctrine in Germany and the Soviet Union, 1919–1939*, Ithaca, NY: Cornell University Press, 2000, pp. 163–4.

[27] H. Guderian, *Panzer Leader*, London: Cassell, 1953, pp. 10–11, 18.

[28] See C. Hartmann, *Halder, Generalstabschef Hitlers 1938–1942*, Paderborn: Schoeningh, 2010, pp. 49–50.

first time, would involve large-scale armored formations commanded by wire-less.[29] The location selected was Mecklenburg, a flat, thinly populated region in northern Germany which afforded the necessary space. No fewer than 160,000 troops, 25,000 horses, 21,700 motor vehicles, and 830 tanks – about two divisions – participated. They represented what was probably the largest and certainly the most modern armored force assembled in history until that time. As so often, details concerning the scenario that the two "armies" were presented with and the moves they made are hard to obtain. What we do know is that Hitler, who was present, was excited by the spectacle, almost jumping up and down as he told Guderian, the officer in charge of the armored forces, that those forces were just what he needed to carry out his program.[30]

By Reichswehr standards, wrote the above-mentioned Truman Smith in reference to the 1924 German maneuvers, the exercises at Fort Leavenworth were "archaic." Far from permitting commanders to improvise and avoiding *Schematismus*, they approached war as if it was a question of solving mathematical equations.[31] Not everybody was content with this situation. Among the observers at the 1927 British maneuvers was US Secretary of War Dwight F. Davis (1879–1945), best remembered for the Davis Cup named after him. Impressed by what he had seen, in 1928 he set up an experimental mechanized brigade at Fort Meade, MD. However, so antiquated was the available equipment that it had to be disbanded after three months. The one that replaced it later on was no larger. From 1865 to 1940, nothing characterized US Army maneuvers as much as their small, almost Lilliputian, size. Foreign armies regularly concentrated tens of thousands of men and even more and put them through their paces. Not so the American Army which, owing to its small size, and since its units were scattered in penny packets all over a vast continent, always had great trouble putting together as much as a division. By and large, this meant that any experiments that could be conducted, and lessons learnt, were limited almost exclusively to the tactical sphere.

For example, in October 1929 the largest cavalry exercise since the Civil War was held, with 4,000 men, 3,200 horses, and 1,500 mules taking part. Grouped into two brigades, they engaged in mock combat "over [the] gulches, hillocks, and sagebrush plains" of western Texas. To avoid the attention of the Army Air Corps reconnaissance aircraft flying overhead, white horses were supposed to be painted brown.[32] Other experiments were conducted on an even smaller scale. As late as 1937–9, so limited were the army's resources that, attempting to determine whether the traditional four brigades in each division should be

---

[29] F. Halder, "Warum Maneuver?," *Die Wehrmacht*, special number, September 28, 1937, p. 1.

[30] The story appears in the German version of Guderian's memoirs; H. Guderian, *Erinnerungen einen Soldaten*, Neckargemünd: Vowinckel, 1976 [1951], p. 39.

[31] Corum, *The Roots of Blitzkrieg*, p. 192.   [32] See the account in *Time*, October 10, 1925.

reduced to three, it was only able to field one complete formation of that kind. Its opponent, known as the Provisional Infantry Division (PID) had to be specially formed for the occasion by drawing on troops from all over the United States. Since men and commanders take time to learn to work together, obviously that was no way to rule on such an important issue.[33]

In the winter of 1940, its complacency shaken by the spectacular German victory over Poland, the US Army embarked on the greatest and most rapid expansion in its history. In overall charge was General George Marshall, the steely-eyed chief of staff whom Churchill later called "the organizer of victory." Marshall delegated the task of holding the maneuvers to his de facto deputy, General Stanley Embick.[34] A huge area – ultimately it was to include some 630,000 acres in Louisiana and Texas – was selected. Sparsely populated, sporting thick undergrowth and uncharted swamps, scarred by rural traces that turn to muck at the slightest hint of rain, and crossed by several rivers, it was ideal for the purpose at hand. By May 1940 everything was ready and the maneuvers, involving the participation of approximately 70,000 men, could get under way. First Red Army took the offensive, crossing the Calcasieu in the face of the defenses put up by Blue. The second and the third exercises witnessed various attacks and counterattacks by the two sides. Finally the army's two armored brigades were provisionally joined together, thus forming America's first armored division: they were used by Red to spearhead a mock attack on Blue.

Army Air Corps aircraft flying overhead gathered intelligence and transports delivered troops to newly constructed airfields. Millions of rounds of blank ammunition were issued and used by the troops; to add realism, loudspeakers blared out the recorded sounds of battle, canister smoke shrouded the battlefield, and aircraft dropped white sand bags to simulate the impact of artillery shells and bombs. The entire show – in the US as elsewhere, maneuvers tended to attract spectators like flies – was supervised by hundreds of umpires equipped with armbands and clipboards. They determined the outcome of combat and assessed units and leaders according to a complicated grading system devised by Marshall and his subordinates. Among the participants were Mark Clark, George Patton, and Joe Stilwell. The last-named commanded the "Red" armored division, a task he carried out with commendable efficiency.

At the time these officers carried the ranks of colonel and lieutenant colonel. Neither in 1917–18 nor during the peace that followed did they have the opportunity to exercise command on anything remotely like the scale now

[33] Combat Studies Institute, *Sixty Years of Reorganizing for Combat: A Historical Trend Analysis*, Army Staff College, Fort Leavenworth, KS, 2000, available at: www.cgsc.edu/carl/resources/csi/reportno14/reportno14.asp.
[34] See, for what follows, P. Lauterborn, *Louisiana Maneuvers (1940–1)*, HistoryNet, 2008, available at: www.historynet.com/louisiana-maneuvers-1940-41.htm/print/

being demanded of them. What combat experience they had gathered either dated to the trenches of World War I or to various small-scale campaigns, especially in Latin America and the Pacific Islands. Scant wonder that Embick, who had spent his time crisscrossing the maneuver area observing and questioning commanders, was not very happy with what he had seen. Broken-down vehicles and poorly planned movements that resulted in traffic jams were common. So were failures to coordinate various arms and units as well as the habit, inherited from the past, of trying to exercise command from the rear instead of from the front as modern mobile warfare demanded. He was, however, encouraged by the quality of the troops, raw as they were, of whom he wrote that they did their best and even displayed considerable enthusiasm for their tasks.

In the summer of 1941 the maneuvers were repeated. The man in charge was Embick's successor, General Leslie McNair. His chief concern was to make the exercise as realistic as possible by avoiding elaborate scenarios and giving the commanding generals on each side only enough information to enable them to operate freely against one another. The scale of the maneuvers was gigantic: over 350,000 men and 50,000 vehicles took part. Just one of the two "armies" involved received no fewer than four million 0.30 caliber blanks and 170,000 anti-tank rounds, far more than had originally been allocated for the entire 1940–1 calendar year.[35] Nothing like this had ever been seen on US territory before, and nothing remotely like this was to be staged later.

A conscious attempt was also made to correct the deficiencies that had come to light in the previous year. They included logistics, communications, traffic control, and the tendency of too many aging commanders to exercise their functions from the rear rather than the front. Much attention was paid to air-to-ground cooperation. Hopelessly neglected during the interwar years, that field was ultimately to emerge as one of the US Army's great strengths. The umpires' manual, which in the absence of live fire would have to determine the outcome of "combat" and thus played a critical role in assessing the exercise, was completely rewritten. As the "war" opened on September 15, the Red Army, approaching from the east, and the Blue one, coming from the west, fought for control of the Mississippi River in an entire series of complicated moves and counter-moves. The star of the day turned out to be a little-known colonel named Dwight Eisenhower. Acting as chief of staff to the Red Army, he successfully countered an attempt by Patton, who commanded the spearhead of Blue, to cross the river and decide the "campaign." Later in the maneuvers Patton, who at that time was the more senior of the two, redeemed himself by leading an armored corps in a massive flanking attack against Blue's positions. Following a 200-mile advance he surrounded his opponent. McNair was

[35] C. R. Gabel, *The US GQ Maneuvers of 1941*, Washington DC: Center of Military History, US Army, 1991, pp. 45–6, 49.

impressed and told Marshall as much; from this time on, both officers found the road to high command open to them.

Two-sided maneuvers continued to be held by many armies (and navies, and air forces, these being subjects that cannot be explored here) after World War II. Throughout the Cold War, the technology at the disposal of both sides and their allies kept improving as new weapon systems were introduced. However, except for the fact that some US troops (certainly) and Soviet ones (possibly) were made to drive over terrain made radioactive by the explosion of an atomic bomb, they did not break much new ground.[36] For decades on end, Western commanders looked at the German campaigns of 1940–1 as the acme of the military art, studied them, and, since there were no plans for attacking the Soviet Union, looked for methods to stop them. Red Army commanders for their part tried to find ways to repeat, and improve upon, their own great armored offensives of 1942–5. Meanwhile, the scale on which the maneuvers designed to test the ideas, the methods, and the weapons were conducted declined. For example, the 1964 Exercise Desert Strike held in the deserts of California and Nevada involved 90,000 troops. The 1981 Exercise Certain Encounter involved 70,000 West German, British, and American troops, 17,000 of the latter having to be flown from the US to Europe. There they picked up their pre-deposited equipment and drove to the "battlefield," a hilly region north of Frankfurt, and joined in the fray.[37]

Contributing to the decline was the constant, though highly uneven, process whereby most armed forces around the world, and those of "developed" countries most of all, tended to become smaller and smaller, as well as the enormous and rapidly growing cost of post-1945 weapons and weapons systems. The latter simply could not be mass-produced the way their predecessors were. For example, when the Canadian armed forces held maneuvers, said to be the largest in several decades, in Alberta in May and June 1985, they fielded exactly eighteen tanks – all those they had in the country.[38] In Europe – the "central theater" as NATO planners fondly called it – another factor was the spread of urbanization, sub-urbanization, and conurbation (the process whereby cities spread, grow together, and ultimately merge into one another). In a continent that had long been crowded, finding open spaces sufficiently large for the forces to train in became almost impossible: the more so because the forces themselves tended to operate in an ever more dispersed manner so as

---

[36] See, for the US side of this story, *Operation Upshot-Knothole*, available at: http://en.wikipedia.org/wiki/Operation_Upshot-Knothole; for the Soviet one, M. Simons, "Soviet Atomic Test Used Thousands as Guinea Pigs, Archives Show," *New York Times*, November 7, 1993.

[37] D. Middleton, "In NATO Maneuver US is Hitting its Stride," *New York Times*, September 20, 1981.

[38] C. Wren, "Canadians Debate a Feeble Military," *New York Times*, December 15, 1985.

to avoid the immense firepower, possibly including nuclear warheads, they expected to be directed at them.[39]

The more time passed, the clearer it became that much fighting would take place not *en rase campagne* but in built-up areas; however, the need to maintain daily life meant that training forces of any size in urban warfare was all but impossible. Finally the decades from about 1970 on saw the rise of those who believed that protecting the environment should have priority over war preparation. All this, plus the typical peacetime aversion to incurring casualties of any kind, caused NATO exercises, especially the larger ones, to display a disturbing tendency to degenerate into somewhat childish games. Far from trying to simulate the brutality of war, which is perhaps the latter's most outstanding quality, units and troops had to gingerly make their way among people and their property so as to avoid injury or damage.

Thus World War II seems a good point to stop the discussion and take stock of the kind of wargames in question. Characterized by the fact that bodies of real troops, rather than headquarters or counters, or blips, are made to "fight" each other, such games may go back all the way to ancient Rome, though the record is too spotty to allow clear conclusions about this to be drawn. Eighteenth-century armies may have held them, but again it is impossible to be sure. Really large-scale maneuvers as we know them today first became possible during the second half of the nineteenth century as a direct result of the rise of the railways. These made it possible to concentrate huge masses of troops within a reasonable time and, what was equally important, disperse them once the exercise was over. Soon all armies were holding them, with the German ones generally acting as the model for the rest from about 1870 on. The objective, certainly in theory and often in practice as well, was to exercise and test commanders, troops, equipment, doctrines, and methods under the most realistic conditions that money – maneuvers were enormously expensive – space, and ingenuity could provide. Scenarios considered relevant to future war could also be rehearsed.

As those who direct theatrical performances and movies know only too well, simulating "reality" is always a very difficult task, all the more so when the location is not a stage or a movie set but a huge piece of country dotted with topographical obstacles of every kind and quite often with humans and their habitations as well; and all the more so when the exercise is two-sided and involves strategy. Again as in a theater or movie, to this is added a certain artificial character that is built into the very nature of the exercise – one scheduled in advance and planned to unfold at such and such a place with such and such forces over so and so many days and weeks – and that is almost impossible to get rid of. For these and many other reasons, historically there has

---

[39] Dupuy, *Numbers, Predictions, and War*, p. 28, tables 2–4.

hardly been an exercise that did not attract its share of criticism.[40] Particularly memorable was the claim of Basil Liddell Hart, the British military pundit, that the 1927 maneuvers, the same ones that *Popular Mechanics* had praised so enthusiastically, were "like an attempt to drill a mechanical menagerie into a Noah's Ark procession, and more fitted to fulfill a sergeant-major's dream than a vision of mobile warfare."[41] Now the maneuvers were said to look to the past instead of to the future; now commanders acted in too schematic a manner. Now those in charge had failed to prepare properly, turning the whole thing into a mess with units going off in all directions or simply doing nothing. Now the demands made on the troops were too great, now – perhaps more often – too small. As in many other kinds of wargames, often more intelligence was available to commanders on both sides than there would be in reality.

Whereas warfare is in some ways the least constrained of all human activities, two-sided maneuvers always involve some kind of overall control. The rules of engagement that Control lays down will go a long way to dictate what will happen even before the first move is made. Worse, even: in war, as a free creative activity, scoring a great success often results precisely from a commander violating whatever rules exist; in exercises, to the contrary, he risks being disciplined for doing so. A classic example of this truth was provided by the Israeli maneuvers of 1951. The goal was to simulate an Egyptian invasion – one such had, in fact, taken place just three years earlier – and the response of the Israel Defense Force (IDF) to it. In charge of the "Egyptian" force was the Commander, Southern Front, General Moshe Dayan. Instead of sticking to the roads (and the rules), he had his troops advance cross-country, by-passing the crossroads complete with the umpires stationed at them. Had the chief of staff not cancelled the exercise, he would have captured Tel Aviv. Called to explain himself, Dayan was told that taking the other side by surprise in such a way was "no great feat" (*kuntz*, in the bastardized German that was part of Hebrew slang at the time). "To the contrary," he is said to have retorted, "that is just the greatest *kuntz* of all."[42]

Unless excellent care is taken, in other words, maneuvers by their very nature may well stifle the boldest and most original spirits. The outcome is a "flattened" image of reality that may prove fatal when the real thing comes about. Another element that maneuvers cannot simulate is the one that forms the very essence of war, i.e. fighting. To be sure, modern technology makes it easy to imitate and broadcast the "strange, mournful mutter of the battlefield" (compliments to General Douglas McArthur).[43] Smoke rising from burning vehicles or

[40] See, for an exceptionally thoughtful critique of this kind, Robertson, *From Private to Field-Marshal*, pp. 163–6.
[41] B. H. Liddell Hart, *The Liddell Hart Memoirs*, London: Cassell, 1965, vol. I, pp. 125–6.
[42] Israeli Defence Force Archive, Tel Aviv, file-40/103.53, pp. 5–7.
[43] The speech is available at: www.charmaineyoest.com/2007/06/the_camera_misses_nothing.php.

else forming part of screens can be generated, and so on. Troops can be and often have been issued with blank ammunition, firing away as if their lives depended on it and enjoying every moment doing so. As ballistic weapons are being increasingly replaced by guided ones, though, the astronomic cost of the missiles in question had rendered doing so extremely problematic. Consequently there is always a tendency to cut corners and use simulators instead. These and other measures only go a fairly short way towards recreating the terror of war amidst which commanders and troops have to perform and which forms the background against which, in reality, their performance will have to be evaluated.

Finally, two-sided though they were and are, maneuvers violate Jesus' saying that "by their fruit shall thou recognize them." In the end umpires, however excellent the manuals on which they rely and however godlike their own training, knowledge and objectivity, are no substitute for bullets in deciding what the outcome of combat would be. Conversely, supposing sufficient umpires of a sufficient quality were available (and supposing they would all agree with one another), one would hardly need maneuvers to simulate the future and plan for it. Ever since tournaments had lost their realism at some time after 1300, and certainly since the spread of firearms had made it impossible for units to realistically train against each other, commanders had been looking for something better. In the late 1970s, something better finally made its appearance.

The road to Fort Atari

In sharp contrast to many kinds of previous wargames from antiquity on, after about 1500 the realistic use of weapons and two-sided exercises went their separate ways. Exercises, or call them games, which demanded that players aim and fire their weapons at their "enemies" could not be two-sided: individuals and groups engaged on two-sided maneuvers could not make realistic use of their weapons. Often, indeed, they were reduced to doing no more than lugging them around putting them into position, loading them, and aiming them, only to go through the same routine again as the situation developed and the signal to "move" was given. With the important and very interesting exception of the duel, only children were able to "fight" mock battles. Either they employed slings or else the kind of wooden, cork-firing, pump-action gun Christopher Robin used to bring down the balloon that carried Winnie-the-Pooh aloft. Toy weapons, though, did not have the range for anything like a realistic simulation of real-life combat. From air guns up, weapons that did have the necessary range were too dangerous to use. As time passed and technological progress continued, giving birth to a steady stream of more and more powerful weapons, the problem only became worse.

Attempts to create "firearms" that would be both sufficiently powerful to provide some kind of realistic simulation of fighting *and* sufficiently harmless not to endanger participants in the game have a long history. Apparently the first successful ones were made in the late 1970s when three Americans, Hayes Noel, Bob Gurnsey, and Charles Gaines, came up with the idea of employing pistols similar to the ones farmers and ranchers use to fire balls full of paint at trees and livestock.[44] The fragile balls burst on impact, thus marking their targets. Apparently the public had been waiting for something of the kind: so successful was the idea that National Game Survival, the first company founded to manufacture and distribute paintball guns, balls, goggles, webbing, vests, and the like, began to turn a profit within a mere six months.[45]

As other firms entered the field various technical improvements, including compressed air or gas bottles to increase range and magazines or hoppers that allowed a single gun to fire multiple rounds without having to reload, were introduced. Some are capable of firing balls at 200 miles an hour: that is about 50 percent faster than the strongest tennis player can serve. Some come equipped with a "special operations silencer" which, although it does not actually quiet the shots, will endow a gun with "an awesome tactical look." For those prepared to spend anything between $250 and $1,174 on the hobby, one firm alone sells a variety of guns with such interesting names as GoG G-1 Tactical Paintball Gun, Proto-Reflex Rail Paintball Gun, and Bob Long Victory Intimidator Paintball Gun. A favorite term this particular firm likes to apply to all sorts of gear is "eclipse": whether that fact hints at some underlying sadistic tendencies I leave it for psychologists to decide.[46] Other companies have their own descriptions.

Airsoft guns differ from paintball ones in that they look exactly like "real" weapons. Though the two types work on somewhat different principles and fire somewhat different kinds of ammunition, their use in wargames is sufficiently similar for the two to be treated together. In 1982 the first dedicated paintball field was opened in Rochester, New York. From the US the idea spread to other countries including Canada, Britain, Australia, Germany, and Israel. The world's largest indoor paintball court – covering 28,000 square feet – is said to be located, of all places, in Tehran.[47] For serious players, leagues have been established. By 1987 the game had become sufficiently popular for the first magazine dedicated especially to paintball to hit the newsstands. A monthly

[44] See, for what follows, Paintball, available at: http://en.wikipedia.org/wiki/Paintball.
[45] S. Davidson *et al.*, *The Complete Guide to Paintball*, New York: Hatherleigh Press, 2007, p. 9.
[46] See www.shop4paintball.com/.
[47] See, for Israel, Paintball Israel, at www.paintball.co.il/index_en.asp; "In Tehran, Enjoy a Game of Paintball", Middle East Online, October 28, 2002, available at: www.middle-east-online.com/english/?id=2998.

called *Action Pursuit Games*, it still exists.[48] As in the case of other niche publications, though, much of the activity has been moved to the Internet. There are even teams of professionals who, somewhat like Roman gladiators and medieval knights-errant, will "fight" demonstration games against each other or else take on whoever is prepared to pay for their services. Over two hundred teams participated in the 2006 World Cup tournament alone, and the total number of US players is said to be in excess of ten million.[49] As if to confirm its popularity, a Google.com search conducted in early 2011 resulted in no fewer than 161,000,000 hits.

Paintball/airsoft games are played in one of two kinds of environments: the entirely artificial ones built and maintained by commercial firms who rent them out to interested parties or in the open. The former tend to be relatively small. Many take advantage of parking lots that would otherwise be empty during the weekend. Such courts are usually studded with inflatable, movable obstacles of various sizes and shapes that players can use to take shelter and maneuver about. Natural terrain has the advantage that it is often much larger, allowing more interesting scenarios and tactics to be introduced. Bunkers, streams, and other topographical features can be added or selected at will. Different kinds of terrain may well force players to completely rethink their tactics, a fact that some of them consider one of the great attractions of the game. Provided the area is sufficiently large, thousands of players may become involved in a single game. Even vehicles up to and including armored cars may be accommodated.

The technical limitations of the equipment apart, what most distinguishes the game from real-life warfare are the rules. The most important rules are those that lay down the meaning of victory. Normally it is gained either by deciding in advance how long the game will last and ending it by counting the number of "survivors" on each side or by capturing the opponent's flag. Some large games may have more than one flag with a points system governing the value of each, whereas in others it is a question of finding treasure or shooting the "enemy" general. Other rules may define such things as the minimum distance at which a player may use his weapon on an opponent – being shot at close range may be quite painful – or else the kind of "injury" that will cause participants to leave the game. Some games employ umpires to enforce the rules, particularly those designed to prevent players from wiping off the paint they have received and returning to the game, others do not. Some have detailed scenarios similar to those the military use on maneuver, others do not. New variations keep emerging as players seek to avoid boredom and those who manufacture the equipment and provide the facilities seek to avoid a loss of customers.

---

[48] See www.actionpursuitgames.com/.
[49] Davidson *et al.*, *The Complete Guide to Paintball*, pp. 18, 19.

The games are played not just by individuals and groups on their own initiative but by all kinds of firms, corporations, government organizations, and even universities. The objective appears to be to improve cohesion among employees or simply give them a day of recreation, if hardly rest. To some, the idea of, say, having a stag party or celebrating a birthday in this way may appear childish. Others, though, consider it "an intensified version of what people do everyday. With varying degrees of success, we're all avoiding and confronting obstacles on our way to reaching goals." "Being great at paintball," we are told, "requires you to learn how to take great risks and succeed."[50] As if to prove the point, the military have also latched onto the game. For the first time in centuries, it has enabled them to shoot at each other in a way that, though not quite similar to real-life combat, at any rate is much more realistic than firing blanks or simply yelling "bang-bang." In some cases, the distinction between paintball and the kind of non-lethal weapons police forces sometimes use is being obliterated. So closely related are the tactics of paintball and those used by light infantry in particular that they have started borrowing them from one another.

The title of one booklet, a *Handbook of Infantry Tactics for Paintball*, speaks for itself.[51] The author, one D. Wagner, says he acquired his hands-on experience during the eleven years he spent as an enlisted man in various US Army infantry units. His work, explicitly aimed at enthusiasts, has chapters on basic marksmanship, individual firing positions, close assault, reconnaissance/ stealth, moving through the indoor playing field, contact, ambush, fighting/ defensive positions, and infantry hand and arm signals. Individual sections deal with such problems as crossing danger areas, firing around an obstacle, defending a room/bunker, and so on. The book concludes with a list of military unit map symbols. As the author notes, the ones his readers are likely to find most useful are those indicating smaller infantry units, scouts, and the like. But for those who happen to have "a tank in [their] yard," armor symbols are also included.

Another author, Christopher E. Larsen, "has spent more than twenty years working with warriors from around the world." At the time he published his work, he was "military-analyst-instructional systems designer for the US Army's Command and General Staff College at Fort Leavenworth, Kansas."[52] Helping drive the rapprochement between paintball/airsoft and real-life warfare is the fact that over the last few decades human settlement patterns have been changing. Over much of the developing world, which is where almost all armed conflicts take place, there has been a massive shift towards

---

[50] *Ibid.*, p. 3.
[51] D. Wagner, *Handbook of Infantry Tactics for Paintball, Based Upon US Army and Soviet Doctrine for Light Infantry Combat Operations*, Booksurge, 2009.
[52] C. E. Larsen, *Paintball and Airsoft Battle Tactics*, Minneapolis, MN: Voyeur, 2008.

urbanization.[53] As America's war in Iraq has demonstrated only too well, and as the civil one in Syria was demonstrating through much of 2011 and 2012, most modern combat no longer takes place in the open as it used to do. Its setting is towns and cities with their closely packed, extremely heterogeneous, and often very complex, structures of every kind. In many places around the world the field no longer exists. This is expected to become even more the case in the future.[54]

Urban warfare is often described as hell on earth, and with very good reason. Targets are easily camouflaged and hard to acquire. Tactical movement, usually in small groups, is carried out in extremely exhausting short rushes from one shelter to the next. Obstacles must be negotiated, ricochets and falling debris avoided, hazardous objects such as electricity and gas lines taken care of, and so on. Often it is a question of going house by house, room by room, basement by basement, and even sewer by sewer. High ground retains some of its importance, but other kinds of commanding positions and chokepoints must also be occupied and held. Entries and exits must be covered, communication arteries kept open, squares, streets, and alleys dominated and crossed, doors broken open, stairwells cleared, wounded evacuated, noncombatants evacuated, kept out of harm's way, and/or fed as far as possible, and so on almost ad infinitum. All this must be done under more or less intense fire coming from assault rifles, machine guns, hand grenades – a weapon whose importance in this kind of warfare cannot be overestimated – and short-range anti-tank weapons of which the ubiquitous Soviet-designed RPG is probably the best-known example.

The most important characteristic of urban warfare, though, is that the distance at which engagements are fought is much smaller than in almost any other kind. Postmortem analysis shows that 90 percent take place at a range of under 150 feet. Human targets are generally acquired at considerably less than that.[55] Such figures are not too different from those associated with the most powerful paintball weapons. All this enables paintball to provide an excellent approximation of the reality of combat. Some armies, notably the American, British, German, and Israeli ones, have constructed entire mock villages for the purpose. Others use the facilities private companies provide. The facilities themselves come complete with dummy houses, dummy furniture, dummy noncombatants, and other kinds of dummies. In them soldiers, equipped just as they would be in battle but carrying paintball guns instead of the real

[53] See, for some figures, United Nations, Department for Economic and Social Affairs, *World Urbanization Prospects*, 2005, available at: www.un.org/esa/population/publications/WUP2005/2005wup.htm.
[54] See, for urban warfare in general, R. W. Glenn, *Combat in Hell: A Consideration of Constrained Urban Warfare*, Santa Monica, CA: RAND, 1996.
[55] US Army, *Field Manual 90-10-1, An Infantryman's Guide to Fighting in Built-Up Areas*, Washington DC, 1993, pp. 8-1.

thing, practice their craft against similarly equipped troops who impersonate the enemy.

Since enemy impersonators tend to be more familiar with the setup than the trainees, they are often able give the latter a good run for their money, playing their assigned role with gusto and skill. To be sure, some limitations apply. They include the possibility that firing at close quarters will result in injuries, the difficulty of simulating heavier weapons often used in urban warfare such as anti-tank rockets and recoilless rifles, and the consequent need for umpires or some other system to decide who has been killed, who has merely been wounded, and who has been left unhurt. "Boom," the lieutenant supervising the exercise may say, "you and your squad are dead." Everything considered, though, a more realistic way of training is not easy to think of.[56] Some would add that the (fairly mild) pain caused by a paintball hit is actually a bonus, since it will compel those not inclined to take the game seriously enough to do exactly that. As one player puts it, he will "go ninjas" to avoid the balls.[57]

Thus paintball, a wargame originally invented and played by hobbyists looking for a thrill, has entered the much more serious world of military-inspired wargames. There it will presumably remain until something better is found – armies consisting of bullet-resistant combinations of men and robots, perhaps? The situation in respect to the next game we must consider here, laser tag, was different; hobbyists and the military moved more or less in tandem.[58] Lasers may be briefly described as concentrated beams of light which, instead of scattering as distance increases, remain focused and thus retain their energy. Provided only sufficient power is available, and provided also certain atmospheric conditions are met, in theory there are no limits either on range or on the amount of energy that may be delivered on target in this way.

The first lasers made their appearance around 1960. Unsurprisingly, no sooner had they done so than they gave rise to speculation concerning the eventual generation of "death rays." The idea had been floating about for several decades,[59] but now it seemed much closer to realization. Here and there science fiction heroes started carrying "ray guns" as they visited foreign planets, met various kinds of aliens, defeated them in battle, and departed.[60] One of the earliest military uses of lasers was in range-finding for tanks, a task in which they started replacing the optical instruments and co-axial machine guns from

[56] See, for the kind of training that is available, Bagira Systems, Urban Warfare Training, at www.websplanet.com/var/1059/135467-PAINTBALL%20brochure.pdf.

[57] Yahoo! Answers, at: http://answers.yahoo.com/question/index?qid=20100310053901 AAALH3F.

[58] See, for much of what follows, laser tag, at: http://en.wikipedia.org/wiki/Laser_tag.

[59] "Denies British Invented 'Death Ray': E. R. Scott Asserts He and Other Americans Preceded Grindell-Matthews," New York Times, September 5, 1924.

[60] See, for an all too exhaustive discussion, http://en.wikipedia.org/wiki/List_of_weapons_in_Star_Trek.

the mid 1970s on. From there it was a short step to the idea of using them for training purposes by having soldiers "shoot" each other with them and register hits with the aid of specially designed receivers.

Apparently the first toy to use infrared light for "firing" at an opponent appeared on the market in 1979 under the name, Star Trek Electronic Phaser Guns set. Manufactured by South Bend Electronics, it consisted of two plastic guns (the nine-volt batteries each of them required were not included) and an instruction sheet. There were, however, no receivers yet, meaning that hits, in the form of spots of light, had to be visually identified. By way of a special treat, the wording on the box promised "phaser blast [what is that?] ricochet, and explosion sounds."[61] In fact, however, the only sound produced was a sort of whine. To this day, incidentally, most laser tag weapons emit sounds more like those of movies such as *Star Wars* than the ones originating in a real battlefield. A picture of boy fighting girl (and the reverse, of course), indicated that the South Bend set was meant for children rather than for grownups. That in turn did not take long to change as some of the latter realized lasers' potential for satisfying what one can only call their long-suppressed fighting instincts.

As had happened with paintball, other firms quickly entered the market with their own weapons and equipment. Many of those were designed to increase realism by adding noise, muzzle flashes, and recoil – providing an interesting insight into the things players care about. As had also happened with paintball, commercial arenas for playing laser tag started to be opened. As of 2011 one firm alone, Laser Quest, was running 125 such arenas worldwide. The largest one, located at Mesa, Arizona, covers 13,000 square feet and sports a forest of ramps, towers, and bridges reaching heights of 20 feet.[62] One is reminded of a children's "adventure playground," only much larger. Other enthusiasts, whether because they wanted greater freedom to do their own thing or simply to save money, held their games in the open. However, it was not all smooth sailing: as we saw, wargames have always given rise to opposition. Somewhat like medieval ecclesiastics, politicians in various countries have tried to ban both laser tag and paintball. The most important country in question was Germany. There, on top of being subject to the usual charges of trivializing and encouraging violence, the games were condemned for being popular among "right-wing extremists." In the event, the idea of a ban was dropped within days of it being raised. Childish, dumb perhaps, but not criminal, was the

---

[61] See Star Trek Electronic Phaser Guns, at: www.google.co.il/#hl=iw&source=hp&biw= 1065&bih=664&q=%22Star+Trek+Electronic+Phaser+Guns%22+&btnG=%D7%97%D7% 99%D7%A4%D7%95%D7%A9+%D7%91-Google&rlz=1R2ADSA_enIL420&aq=f&aqi= &aql=&oq=%22Star+Trek+Electronic+Phaser+Guns%22+&fp=91d766f1751cd80f.

[62] International Laser Tag Association, *History of Laser Tag*, at: www.lasertag.org/general/ history.html.

verdict of Konrad Freiberg, chairman of the German Police Union, whose fellow policemen would have had to enforce the ban.[63]

Provided goggles are worn, lasers do not hurt those they hit, meaning that they are perhaps more suitable for young players than paintball is. On the other hand, their range is much greater than that of paint-filled gelatin balls. The best available equipment will register hits 500 feet away in full sun and over 900 in the shade (the difference, of course, is one of the things that separates the game from real war: nothing is perfect). Such ranges mean that, in addition to carrying guns and wearing receivers, players may need to buy or rent sophisticated communications gear so as to be able to operate in teams. Again like paintball, laser tag may be played by amateurs out for a day of fun in an arena or else in the open. It may, however, also be played by highly skilled individuals or groups according to strict rules, thus enabling regular competitions and tournaments to be organized. Especially popular games, or perhaps one should call them scenarios, include capturing the flag, protecting the VIP, and defending the base.

In so far as they pit individuals or groups against each other, all these belong to the realm of strategy. As in real-life war, the list of possibilities is practically endless. New techniques and scenarios keep being introduced. Some of the equipment available on the market not only allows people to shoot each other but uses radio or infrared to hook up guns and receivers with a control computer. By having each gun and each receiver give out a different signal, scores can be kept, cheating prevented, and, in case players are so inclined, lessons drawn for future engagements.[64] As with paintball, players are taught to use tactics very similar to those employed at war. Among them are staying low, mobility – the need to keep moving – making use of terrain (where relevant), putting on camouflage, taking shelter, setting up ambushes and springing them, maneuvering to surprise the opponent, working in teams (but not so closely as to risk being hit by a single shot), sending out reconnaissance and if necessary "sacrificing" a teammate so as to make the opponent reveal his position, and the like.[65]

The qualities that players need most are speed and accuracy, and newcomers to the game are warned that acquiring them takes a lot of practice.[66] Combining the two is sometimes known as taking snapshots, which is said to be the most important skill any player should master. Players are encouraged to experiment and see what their strengths and weaknesses are. Some are slow to pull the

[63] J. Diehl et al., "Germany May Seek Ban on Paintball," SpiegelOnLine, July 5, 2009, at: www.spiegel.de/international/germany/0,1518,623518,00.html.

[64] See, for a description of one such system, Laser Tag System, at: www.lazerrunner.com/mod.php?mod=userpage&menu=13&page_id=30.

[65] Whyteville Lasertag Home Page, Tactics and Strategy, at: www.erikritch.com/wythelasertag/Club/tactics.shtml.

[66] "aashanta," August 16, 2003, at http://everything2.com/title/laser+tag.

trigger but have deadly aim, meaning that, if they are members of a team, they should try to fire from behind cover. They should, in other words, act as snipers. Others are fast actors and should engage in close combat if they can, taking on opponents and out-zapping them while at the same time staying on guard against the kind of bastard who may be lurking in some corner.

While most "combatants" never develop a high level of skill, some do. Videos show them crouching, ducking, leaping, sliding, rolling on the ground, hitting opponents at what look like impossible distances and at incredible range: in short, doing all the things well-trained commando troops are taught to do. At least one website tells visitors to "fight the unfair fight," meaning to operate things in such a way as to enable the many to attack the few.[67] That, of course, has been the essence of strategy in every kind of wargame (and war) from the time chess was invented to the present day. Yet not all the tactics are relevant to real combat: for example, some argue that guns should be kept out of sight as far as possible because the sensors on them are disproportionally likely to be hit. Some of the numerous lists of instructions available on the Net appear to have been written by military professionals. Others were posted by retired ones who now act as laser tag instructors, others still by amateurs with long experience at the game. All this, as at least one site unashamedly tells us, for keeping people amused by seeing which of them can kill the most opponents within the time allowed.

It was at this point that the military entered the picture. As we saw, for several centuries the many kinds of games many armies devised for training, simulation, and planning all suffered from the fact that troops could not do what they do in war, i.e. shoot to kill. This not only detracted from realism but required the use of umpires to determine the outcome of combat. This could yield highly unsatisfactory results – if the umpires were insufficiently knowledgeable, biased, or simply not present at the right place and time – and was clumsy to use even if it did not. While post-action critiques were almost always employed, reconstructing what took place so as to draw the correct lessons from it was always difficult, sometimes impossible. In the words of General Paul F. Gorman, deputy chief of staff for Training at TRADOC (Trade and Doctrine) from 1973 to 1977, neither the US Army nor any other at the time had an effective method for collecting training data, displaying it, and using it.[68]

Attempts to use modern technology for dealing with the problem got under way in the late 1970s. After considerable debate as to whether there should be multiple training centers or just one, the decision was made to select Fort Irwin, a desert area located between Las Vegas and Los Angeles. The prevailing

[67] J. Munro, "Advanced Tactics to Win at the Game of Laser Tag," March 2, 2010, at: www.associatedcontent.com/article/2745151/advanced_tactics_to_win_at_the_game.html.
[68] Quoted in A. W. Chapman, *The Origins and Development of the National Training Center, 1967–1984*, Washington DC: Center of Military History, US Army, 1997, p. 16.

climatic conditions – important if the air force was to participate in the exercises – its size, varied terrain, remoteness, sparse population, and general worthlessness all made it suitable for holding large-scale military wargames. It had, in fact, been intermittently used for that purpose from 1940 until 1972. At that time the end of the Vietnam War and the subsequent reduction in the size of the army caused it to be permanently closed; rebuilding it and equipping it with the most advanced available technology, much of it experimental, proved to be the most costly peacetime training project in the whole of history.

In 1981, after nine years of work, the site was reactivated, complete with quarters, a PX, medical services, and everything else a military base needs for its day-to-day operations. Officially known as the National Training Center, it soon came to be nicknamed Fort Atari, after the company that used to dominate the videogame industry from the mid 1970s to the early 1980s. At the heart of training at Fort Atari, and later at other bases as well, was the use of multiple integrated laser engagement system or MILES. Compared to commercial systems then coming on the market, the main difference was that the lasers were mounted on the barrels of real weapons. When the soldier fired a (blank) round, the laser was automatically activated. Receptors, mounted on helmets, body vests, and vehicles, produced a "beep" when the laser hit them.

To prevent "casualties" from cheating, later versions of MILES replaced the beep with a loud noise which only stopped when the soldier removed a yellow key from his weapon, preventing it from firing again and effectively removing him from the exercise or game. Special devices were also incorporated to make sure that a hit by a "bullet" from, say, an M-16 assault rifle would not result in the "incapacitation" of a tank or an armored personnel carrier. Subsequently similar systems designed to simulate the fire of tanks, armored personnel carriers, anti-tank missiles, several types of attack helicopters, and short-range (point) air defenses were added. Each of these was given a code and linked to a central computer. The objective was to enable the movements and score of each man, each vehicle, and each unit to be recorded and displayed either in real time, for the benefit of the control team, or at some later one.[69] Mobile video units, their movements similarly tracked by computer, also recorded what was going on. Their orders were to blend into the environment as much as possible so as to avoid disturbing the "players" and allow them plenty of room to flex their muscles.

To quote an Israeli saying – what modern country has fought more wars than Israel? – warfare consist of running over the hills, crawling among thistles, and eating sand. All the while carrying heavy loads, and all under what are often extreme climatic conditions. As well as incorporating all the electronic wizardry, Fort Irwin and similar installations allow soldiers to do all these things. It

[69] Multiple Integrated Laser Engagement System, at: http://en.wikipedia.org/wiki/Multiple_Integrated_Laser_Engagement_System.

thus combines the advantages of the shooting gallery with those of two-sided maneuvers. Unit commanders, too, can practice what they are supposed to do with real-life troops in real-life war. During the 1990s the system spread from the US to many other countries all over the world. Among the better-known ones is Hohenfels, in Germany, which, however, only allows two battalions to maneuver against each other.[70] Not just infantrymen but vehicles, including armored personnel carriers and tanks, could be provided with lasers and made to fight much more realistically than before. Not only did a global positioning system enable the vehicles to be tracked, but video cameras could be installed both aboard each one and in the vicinity where they operated, recording every move and permitting subsequent analysis. The entire thing thus assumed the character of a sort of gigantic electronic laboratory. In it human mice, those moved on their own legs as well as those that rode vehicles of every sort, moved about and "fought," with their performance closely watched by god-like commanders and analysts.

What set Fort Irwin apart from the rest was the fact that it spread over no fewer than 642,000 acres (1,000 square miles), enough for two complete armored brigades with several hundred vehicles each to deploy and practice against one another. Normally a brigade assigned to the Fort will spend one week preparing, two weeks "fighting," and one cleaning up and preparing to depart. As with paintball, smaller exercises can include counterinsurgency operations, urban operations, peacekeeping operations, and rescue operations. Gathering steam during the 1990s, those have since come to form the majority of all exercises. Trainees, it is claimed, arrive at the Fort with wide open eyes. Two weeks' worth of intensive training puts them through any number of scenarios, from breaking into a house suspected of harboring terrorists and being confronted with whimpering women and children all the way to coping with an IED (improvised explosive device) discovered by the roadside.[71] The National Training Center, we are told, "prides itself on providing brutally honest and irrefutable feedback on unit performance while providing a forum that encourages candid discussion and self-analysis by the unit."[72] However that may be, certainly such elaborate facilities would have turned past commanders green with envy.

Even so, some problems remain. Direct-fire weapons firing bullets or other kinetic rounds can easily be simulated with the aid of lasers, since in that case only fairly minor adjustments to the fire control apparatus are needed. Not so indirect artillery fire – the most important of its kind by far – and air-launched

---

[70] See, for the details, Hohenfels Training Area, at: www.globalsecurity.org/military/facility/ hohenfels.htm.
[71] See B. Reece, "Training Today's Soldiers at NTC," *Soldiers Magazine*, September 2005.
[72] R. W. Cone, "The Changing National Training Center," *Military Review*, May–June 2006.

missiles and bombs. All of these, instead of moving along a straight trajectory as laser beams do, follow very different ones.[73] It is of course possible to use strategically located pyrotechnics like those moviemakers have long employed and those the army itself often employed in earlier exercises and maneuvers. Activated at the right moment, they can give the troops some feel for the impact that incoming fire of this kind will have and teach them how to deal with it. Tables and computers can then be used to calculate the percentage of rounds that will hit their targets and the damage they will do. Such tables and calculations can even be made to differentiate between attack, defense, daytime operations, night-time operations, and so on. Yet however sophisticated the algorithms, ultimately they are subject to all the limitations that have affected wargames using similar methods from at least the beginning of the nineteenth century on.

Previous methods of assessing military-type maneuvers and wargames often suffered from a lack of detailed information. By contrast, the sophisticated equipment used at Fort Irwin often produces it in such abundance as to make its use impossible. Some take-home packages containing scores as well as visual and auditory material relevant to individual commanders, units and individuals are available. However, it is hard to say what use, if any, is being made of them. Last but not least, Fort Irwin, like many similar if smaller installations around the world, has special units to play the role of Red. Their task is to take on other units seriatim as the latter arrive and present themselves for their scheduled training periods.[74] Since moving units from one base to another is always expensive, the advantage of this arrangement is clear. However, there is another side to the coin. Regardless of whether they represent a Soviet armored brigade or a group of Afghan irregulars, inevitably the locals (OPFOR, for Opposing Force) will get to know the terrain, as well as the general setup, the strengths and weaknesses of the equipment, and so on much better than the visiting units do.

Almost as inevitably, instead of simply simulating the way the baddies are supposed to operate, OPFOR will devise their own tactics best designed to defeat all comers. Doing so, their intimate understanding of the larger organization to which both they and their opponents belong, in this case the US Army, will be of great help. All these advantages mean that they are hard to beat – adjectives often applied to them by visiting units are "awesome," "sneaky," and "redoubtable."[75] In the 1980s, so often did OPFOR defeat its "enemies" that a computer error was suspected.[76] This fact represents both a

[73] See M. Goldsmith et al., Applying the National Training Center Experience: Artillery Targeting Accuracy, Santa Monica, CA: RAND, 1990, available at: www.randproject.com/pubs/notes/2009/N2984.pdf, pp. 4–7.
[74] See, on the way it is done, OPFOR, at: http://en.wikipedia.org/wiki/Opposing_force.
[75] Chapman, The Origins and Development of the National Training Center, p. 88.
[76] Allen, War Games, p. 319.

challenge and a problem. It is a challenge in so far as units sent into the installation to train and practice will normally do their utmost to obtain a good score by defeating the redoubtable OPFOR. It is a problem because, unless care is taken, trying to do so they may learn the wrong lessons and teach themselves the wrong methods. Mirror imaging, in other words, is difficult, perhaps impossible, to avoid.

As so often, one could argue that wargames which provide no prospect for real injury are hardly likely to be taken as seriously as the real thing. As so often, one could turn this argument around on the ground that, early on, the absence of danger allows trainers to focus on their tasks and encourages better learning. Danger is best introduced in carefully measured doses, but even so there are obvious limits. Certainly the line between play, seriousness, and stress is a fine one. That is all the more the case because it varies not just from one individual and unit to another but also in the case of the same individual and the same unit from one time to another. Whether in the form of paintball or in that of laser tag, whether played by amateurs for entertainment or by professionals for serious training, the games discussed in the present section enable a degree of realism to be achieved not seen for centuries past. In so far as some versions of paintball are, or at any rate could be, used in handling "real" situations such as demonstrations and the like, play and the real thing may actually be fusing. In a different way, that also applies to the next, and last, kind of wargames we must now consider.

Reenacting war

Wars being among the most important historical events as well as the most spectacular ones, they have always produced their share of souvenirs of every kind. As the story about Alexander the Great acquiring a suit of armor that had supposedly belonged to the Homeric hero Achilles shows, weapons, equipment, and insignia truly or falsely associated with past conflicts have long attracted buyers and continue to do so today.[77] From there it was a relatively small step to attempts at reconstructing the wars themselves. In Imperial Rome, reenactments of past battles were not rare. Some were held on a spectacular scale and caused the deaths of many who participated in them, though whether things were arranged in such a way as to duplicate the historical outcome, and if so just how it was done, remains unknown; it is hard to imagine how men could have been made to fight for their very lives – which is what the Roman public expected to see – and follow a prepared script. Late medieval knights on tournament sometimes did not fight under their own names but impersonated historical figures or used names taken from the Arthurian legends. During the Renaissance mock battles that pitted Christian warriors against Ottoman ones

---

[77] Arrian, *The Campaigns of Alexander*, LCL, 1929, 1.2.8.

were much in vogue. One such was staged by Cardinal Pietro Riario, a nephew of Pope Sixtus IV, in 1473.[78] Similar displays continued to be held into the early years of the seventeenth century.

That was not the end of the matter. Though tournaments ceased to be held after 1600 or so, reenactments of them – meaning wargames that sought to simulate other wargames – remained quite popular. They continued to be organized throughout the eighteenth and nineteenth centuries. An outstanding example of the genre was the 1839 Eglinton Tournament, funded and organized by Lord Eglinton at his castle in Scotland.[79] The background was formed by the so-called Gothic Revival which, to counter the spreading Industrial Revolution, looked back to everything medieval as simple, healthy, original, and worth preserving. Particularly important in this respect was the novelist Walter Scott (1771–1832) who single-handed brought the Middle Ages, or the image of them that people wanted to see, back to life and whose voluminous opus is full of tournaments as well as knights and their beautiful ladies. Preparations, including the gathering or manufacture of the necessary equipment as well as training, took up almost a year. Some of Britain's best-known aristocrats were enlisted and spent months learning how to joust. Doing so, they took on fancy names such as "the Black Knight," "Knight of the Red Rose," "the Dragon Knight," and so on.

Entry to the show was free, it being assumed that a profit could be made by selling food, drink, souvenirs, and so on. Whereas the organizers had expected 4,000 spectators to attend, on the appointed day, 31 August, no fewer than 150,000 turned up. Among them was the future Napoleon III who was living in England at the time. Unfortunately a thunderstorm broke out in the midst of the opening parade. It turned the field into a swamp, caused the crowds to flee (the ladies, we are told, were helped to their carriages first of all; what happened to the vast majority of female spectators who were not ladies is not on record), and forced the organizers to suspend the event. Even without the centerpiece, i.e. the joust, however, the show was considered a great success in historical consciousness-raising. As one contemporary writer put it, "we heard only one feeling of admiration expressed at the gorgeousness of the whole scene, considered only as a pageant. Even on Wednesday, when the procession was seen to the greatest possible disadvantage, the dullest eye glistened with delight as the lengthy and stately train swept into the marshaled lists."[80] Canceled but not forgotten, in 1989, the tournament was reenacted in what had since become

---

[78] J. Gassner and E. Quinn, *The Reader's Encyclopedia of World Drama*, Toronto: General, 1969, p. 551.

[79] See, for what follows, Eglinton Tournament of 1839, at: http://en.wikipedia.org/wiki/Eglinton_Tournament_of_1839.

[80] J. Aikman and W. Gordon, *An Account of the Tournament at Eglinton*, Edinburgh: Paton, 1839, p. 15.

Eglinton County Park: a remarkable, and perhaps unique, case of a reenactment reenacting another reenactment.

Just as the use of firearms makes it difficult to simulate real war, so it creates complications when it is a question of reenacting the latter. Another period when reenactments were popular was the early years of the twentieth century. In 1903 Pieter Cronjé, a famous Boer general and the victor in several battles against the British in both Boer Wars (1880–1 and 1899–1902), teamed up with an American entrepreneur to form a sort of traveling circus. Allegedly it was made up of 400 real Boer and British war veterans plus 300 horses (which were certainly real). With them he toured the United States, giving exhibitions. In 1904 he was in the city of St. Louis which was hosting that year's World Fair. Twice a day he commanded the Boers in "battle" against the British, the background being formed by a mock village populated by "Swazis, Zulus, and other African peoples."[81] The enterprise must have been profitable, for a year later we find him doing the same on New York's Coney Island, at that time the scene of major amusement parks. As the *New York Times* informed its readers, 1,000 men, "including 200 Kafirs, Zulus, Matabeles, and representatives of other African tribes" and 600 horses were engaged. Though Cronjé was still the outstanding figure, several former Boer and British officers – one of them with a missing arm, "in silent testimony to his service at Spion Kop Hill" – also participated.[82]

The terrain on which the show was held comprised fourteen acres. "Huge basins, zinc lined and installed at enormous cost, with running water, and made to produce the Tugeln and Modder Rivers" were installed. Surrounding the field were hundreds of canvases painted by no fewer than fifty-eight artists to represent the scenery, the towns of Colenso and Paardeburg included. The first scene was laid out near Colenso where the Boers had defeated the British in December 1899. As "the rattle of the deadly Maxim guns" was heard and "the storm of battle [was] waged in this furious fight for supremacy," men and horses went down right and left. The Boers, rough but heroic, captured the British guns, fought their opponents hand to hand, and emerged victorious. Particularly interesting was the performance of one black horse that, having been "killed" early on, rose from the dead upon a signal being made, giving spectators "a sly look." Are wargames the country where even horses have wings?

If anything, the next two scenes, representing the battles of Paardeburg and a Highlander's charge across the Modder River respectively, were considered "a great deal more exciting and even more realistic" than the first one had been.

---

[81] "Reliving the Boer War," at: http://exhibits.slpl.org/lpe/data/LPE240023571.asp?thread=240029422.
[82] *New York Times*, May 21, 1905, available at: http://query.nytimes.com/mem/archive-free/pdf?res=F1071EFB3F5E12738DDDA80A94DD405B858CF1D3.

REENACTING WAR

219

Judging by the fact that the British were always being defeated, perhaps one purpose behind these shows was to help members of the growing Irish-American community to express their sympathy for the Boers. Or perhaps it was because crowds like underdogs – those who, though they deserve to win, go under fighting. In fact games celebrating the Boers' exploits were popular in many countries at the time. That apart, there does not seem to have been any particular political message, and indeed former enemies cooperated in mounting the shows: the objective was simply to offer entertainment and make some money.

In other cases the situation was entirely different. Particularly memorable in this respect were the Russian reenactments of the 1854–5 siege of Sebastopol (1906), the 1812 battle of Borodino (1912), and the 1696 capture of Azov (1918). All three battles were considered important landmarks of Russian history and had been glorified by generations of Russian historians and artists. All three reenactments of them were organized by the authorities or on their behalf. The first two were held more or less *in situ*, and all three were meant to remind spectators of their ancestors' heroism as they resisted invaders or expanded the empire to its natural limit. Not to be left behind, in 1920 the Bolsheviks reenacted the storming of the Winter Palace in October 1917 on the third anniversary of the event.[83] As well as attracting the usual crowd, this reenactment served as the centerpiece of Sergey Eisenstein's film, *October: Ten Days that Shook the World*. Before computer-generated images started taking over during the 1990s countless other directors followed his example. Some used thousands of extras as Cecil B. DeMille (1881–1959) in particular was famous for doing.

In 1913 a Civil War reenactment was held at Gettysburg, said to have attracted no fewer than 50,000 participants, veterans and spectators. As one would expect, the highlight of the event was a reenactment of Pickett's charge.[84] A collection of photographs at the Tropenmuseum (Tropical Museum) in Amsterdam shows what looks like some kind of battle or skirmish being reenacted in Indonesia (of all places) around the time of World War I. Dutchmen and natives, armed and some of them mounted, appear to be charging up a hill, though it is not clear who is impersonating whom.[85]

The reenactments popular in many present-day countries may be divided into two principal types with numerous intermediary ones in between. At one extreme are large public shows. As in the case of the Russian/Soviet ones just

[83] See for these events Historical Reenactment at: http://en.wikipedia.org/wiki/Historical_reenactment.
[84] See 1913 Gettysburg Reenactment at: http://kiki.mx.am/nose.html.
[85] Collectie Tropenmuseum, at: http://commons.wikimedia.org/wiki/File:COLLECTIE_TRO PENMUSEUM_Het_naspelen_van_een_oorlog_door_een_groep_mannen_Karolanden_ TMnr_10004848.jpg.

discussed, often they are staged by, or with the assistance of, the authorities in order to celebrate some occasion and/or remind people of this or that historical event. Some are run on a regular basis. The number of participants can run into the hundreds if not thousands. While such performances often attract huge crowds and give rise to monumental traffic jams, most of the spectators in question know little about the real events being reenacted. That even applies to many performers, who are drawn by the prospect of having a day of fun or perhaps making a few dollars. Hence no very great effort is made to faithfully reproduce contemporary uniforms, weapons, and tactics; often all the organizers seem to care about is numbers of men marching about, "bodies" left lying on the field, and an opportunity sell as many baseball caps, hot dogs, and toy guns as possible.

Outside the US, which has always provided a good market for militaria of every kind, shows of this kind are held in other countries as well. In Italy, the reenactment of the naval battle of Custozza (1866) has now been turned into an annual event. An island as peaceful and as far out of the way as Tasmania has a society dedicated to reenacting historical military events.[86] Even in Germany, where the memory of the Second World War has turned "militarism" into the dirtiest of all dirty words, things are changing: in October 2006 a reenactment was held to mark the two-hundredth anniversary of Napoleon's triumph over Prussia at Jena and was shown on TV. In the words of one spectator, "watching thousands of silly buggers in funny hats line up in full Napoleonic kit before the battle is something I won't forget in a hurry."[87] Most spectators, incidentally, were not youngsters but adults in their fifties. Four years later in the same country another reenactment marked the six-hundredth anniversary of the battle of Tannenberg. It attracted 200,000 spectators who watched 2,200 participants playing the role of knights in a reenactment of the battle. An additional 3,800 participants played peasants and camp-followers. The pageant's organizers claim that the event has become the largest reenactment of medieval combat in Europe. They have been busily trying to repeat their success by turning it into an annual event.[88]

In shows of this kind the maneuvering and "fighting" are scripted and the outcomes predetermined. Consequently there is no real give and take between the sides, no real attempt to overpower or outwit the opponent and achieve victory however defined. Not representing wargames proper, this kind of reenactment will not be further discussed in the present volume. Very different

---

[86] Historical Military Reenactments, at: www.mmmr.com.au/hmr/events.html.
[87] Battle of Jena at: http://forums.starcraft.org/threads/22025-Battle-Of-Jena-200th-Anniversary-Re-enactment.
[88] J. Fowler, "Tabards On, Visors Down: Fans Relive the 1410 Battle of Grunwald," Agence France-Presse, June 17, 2010, at: www.google.com/hostednews/afp/article/ALeqM5h5i MAZg5DRs8GN-80COPjCbuQqbw.

are the sort of small-scale reenactments held by hobbyists for their own satisfaction.[89] Groups of reenactors may number from a handful to several thousands, though for all the members of the larger organizations to come together for a single event is rare. Some players have personal experience of military service and war. Most do not: indeed it has been said of reenactors that they are prepared to do anything normally (and not so normally) done in war except, which God forbid, enlisting and serving in it. In terms of education, profession, and income they come from all walks of life. Incomes range from low to quite high, though perhaps with a disproportionate number of lower-middle-class types: young office workers and salesmen, skilled blue-collar men, and the like. As one website puts it, "mostly, we're average folks who have a hobby that is a bit unusual."[90]

Practically all reenactors are men under the age of thirty-five or so. Probably the percentage of those who are married and have children is somewhat lower than among the general population in the same age range: after all, granting dear hubby leave to spend money on a hobby as well as long weekends away from home practicing it is not something every wife will automatically do. Starting from nothing, just acquiring the basic kit may cost about $1,500, plus membership dues, plus transportation and perhaps lodging, plus all kinds of incidentals. Family men are sometimes called "gappers," after the large gaps between their appearances in the field. They tend to drop out of the game, perhaps to reappear a few years later following a divorce.

Many reenactors will readily admit that their hobby, i.e. dressing up as soldiers from the past and pretending to shoot each other, is somewhat strange. But that does not prevent them from practicing it and enjoying it. Asked about their motivation, they will often answer that they want to understand war and that one cannot really do so without having been in it – as far as possible – complete with all the heart-beat and heightened blood pressure that are the outcome of intensive physical activity.[91] Others explain that they want to honor the men whose deeds they are bringing to life.[92] This is especially true of those interested in World War II, Korea, Vietnam, and so on, many of whom have relatives who served in those conflicts. Thus the Scottish Military Re-enactment Society sets out "to ensure that the memory of those men and women who fought for the allied cause during World War II, shall never be forgotten."[93] A person's ethnic origin may also do much to determine his decision as to whom or what to impersonate: many will only join certain units and not others.

---

[89] The following is based on J. Thompson, *War Games: Inside the World of 20th-Century War Reenactors*, Washington DC: Smithsonian, 2004, especially pp. 76–94, 201–36.
[90] 9th Reenactment Society, at: www.9thsspanzer.com/FAQ.htm#type.
[91] Thompson, *War Games*, pp. 147, 149.
[92] C. Grenand, *So You Want to be a Soldier: How to Get Started in Civil-War Reenactment*, Lynchburg, VA: Schroeder, 2003, p. ix.
[93] The Scottish Military Reenactment Society, at: www.combinedops.com/SMRS2.htm.

If only because of the cost, reenactors who will simply play any kind of soldier at any time and place are hard to find. Many reenactors are interested in socializing above all. As also happens in some real-life militaries, notably those that make extensive use of reservists or consist of civilians who serve an occasional day as in many national guards around the world, reenactments often cause people who would otherwise have led entirely separate existences to come together and feel much closer than would otherwise have been the case. Doing so is considered an important part of the fun.

Some choose to "be" American Revolutionary soldiers serving with Washington and crossing the Delaware. Each year as Christmas comes there is likely to take place a reenactment of that campaign:[94] depending mostly on the weather, sometimes they succeed in crossing the river, sometimes not. Others pretend they are serving in the army of Frederick the Great or in Napoleon's *Grande Armée*. They may represent Crimean War vintage soldiers, or Federals and Confederates, or World War I French *poilus*, or World War II Soviet Guards. The US alone has twenty-three different Roman legions (not counting spare ones) as well as three Praetorian cohorts (I, III and V, based in Florida, Arkansas and New Mexico, respectively). All this, on top of two gladiatorial schools and one "combat simulation organization" calling itself "The Senate and People of Rome."[95] Some reenactors give evidence of being on the peculiar side by choosing to reenact the Waffen SS. One claimed that they were "neat, bad, scary, and . . . top notch soldiers"; another that "reenacting SS is . . . the expression of some fascination for the impressive combat record/ organization/uniforms of those units."[96] Both in the US and elsewhere interest in, and the popularity of, everything pertaining to the German armed forces in World War II is striking. It has created an entire industry dealing in militaria, real real, real fake, and fake.

For example, the New Zealand Military Reenactment Society is prepared to impersonate eight different units.[97] Out of those three are World War II-vintage German. Of those again, one was the "3rd Company, 1st SS Division Leibstandarte SS Adolf Hitler," whose one-time commander, Obergruppenfuehrer (General) Joseph Dietrich, ended up by being tried for war crimes and sentenced to life in prison. Other groups impersonate the SS Viking, Hohenstaufen, Das Reich and 9th Panzer divisions as well as the regiment called after "der Fuehrer" with the objective, as one of them puts it on its website, of preserving their way of life and

---

[94] See, for the details: www.pacpubserver.com/new/enter/12-16-98/crossing.html.
[95] Rome   around   the   World,   at: www.romanempire.net/romepage/Links/roman_ reenactment_groups.htm.
[96] Thompson, *War Games*, p. 68; Axis History Forum at: http://forum.axishistory.com/ viewtopic.php?f=40&t=102045&start=15.
[97] New Zealand Military Reenactment Society at: http://en.wikipedia.org/wiki/Military_ Reenactment_Society.

combat behavior.[98] In 2009, incidentally, the Viking Division alone held no fewer than nine reenactments. One group explains that its members are not forced to reenact SS units exclusively and that they never use the "German raised arm 'Heil Hitler' salute." Another says that it "does not support or hold any political beliefs in any banned political parties or subscribe to any neo-Nazi Movement whatsoever."[99] This particular group boasts of having "eight motorcycle outfits, three Kuebelwagen [a kind of jeep-like vehicle much used by the Wehrmacht in World War II], one Borgward B2000 troop truck, one Zundapp solo KS600 [motorcycle], one 222 armored car, a 2 centimeter flak gun, [and] a pak-37 [antitank] gun." A fine collection indeed: and one that not only cost a lot of money to acquire but requires careful and loving attention if it is to keep running.

All this betrays a certain uneasiness, as it well may: at least one group has gone so far as to reenact the execution by Waffen SS troops of "partisans," probably in France at some time in 1944.[100] Paradoxically, post-1945 German law prohibits public display of symbols dating to the days of the Third Reich. Hence German nationals desirous of doing so are obliged to hold their games in foreign countries where the authorities do not mind people dressed up as Nazis running about; even more paradoxically, many such shows are held in Ukraine, a country specifically selected by those Nazis for permanent enslavement and exploitation.[101] Overall, there probably has not been an important army in history that did not spawn its enthusiasts bent on reenacting its battles. Even an army that had little to show for its efforts except defeats, such as the World War II Italian one, has some enthusiasts who dress up and act like one of Mussolini's units in Russia.[102] Women, one reenactor claims, love the Italians.

Different groups of hobbyists vary greatly according to the degree of authenticity they require. Some will be content if members dress up more or less as the occasion demands and take up some tolerably appropriate weapon. They do not even mind, say, having the soldiers of Frederick the Great, or the Civil War, or World War II, use cellphones. Others are much stricter, not to say fanatical, in this respect. They want to make sure, as far as possible, that history is reenacted exactly as it was and that participants feel exactly as their predecessors did. They insist that every detail should be carefully checked and that the encounters as a whole should be as authentic as close research and money can make them. A rifle, a pocket knife, a watch even, that do not fit the time and the place about to be reenacted are considered enough to spoil the fun. The same applies to a

[98] WWII Historical Reenactment Society at: www.wiking.org/.
[99] The 9th Reenactment Society at: www.9thsspanzer.com/FAQ.htm; Battle Group South at: www.battlegroupsouth.com/recruit.html.
[100] WWII Battle Reenactment at: www.youtube.com/watch?v=0epNR8XKMT8.
[101] See on this "Die Farm der boesen Deutschen," Der Spiegel, 30, July 26, 2010, p. 98; Living – or Falsified? – History at: www.wimag.kiev.ua/index2.php?=pgs20093/92.
[102] See, for some pictures of an event held in May 2006: www.militaryphotos.net/forums/showthread.php?t=80549.

piece of clothing that looks either too new or too old. In the former case this is because the item in question is probably a fake; in the latter, because it does not appear as it did at the time it was actually issued and worn.

These and similar problems often lead to heated arguments. Groups of reenactors, almost always loosely organized because of the voluntary and unpaid nature of the activity, have been known to break up because of disagreements over what is and is not acceptable. May a Napoleonic reenactor drink a bottle of Coca Cola, or should he stick to eau de vie? One website tells enthusiasts how to bake hardtack, a form of dry bread which, though much disliked by those who had to eat it, was a dietary staple for soldiers and sailors for centuries on end. Another advertises everything Civil War reenactors need, starting with a model 1851 US Navy pistol and ending with officers' spurs.[103] There appears to be no limit to what some people may do: for example, in making sure that the gun they carry while reenacting some episode in the 1940 German campaign against France should be a Maschinegewehr 34 and not the slightly different Maschinegewehr 34/41 which only made its debut a year later.[104]

As with most collective activities, "real" military ones specifically included, much, perhaps most, of the time devoted to the hobby is spent making technical preparations on the one hand and socializing on the other. The logistic foundations must be put in place and travel arrangements made. Once the participants have arrived at the appointed location greetings and reminiscences are exchanged, equipment is cleaned and made ready for action, and so on, often with the aid of liberal doses of beer. Post-action hours too may provide plenty of opportunities for a pleasant community life. However, some of the time is spent digging trenches in the soil, dragging heavy equipment into position, running up and down hills under the hot sun, wading through the slush and snow that cover some fields, lying on the ground pretending to be dead, carrying or being carried on litters, eating K-rations, and in general doing almost anything to experience or reexperience what war at the time and place selected was like. Here it should be said that, like the maneuvers of which they are the smaller and less elaborate brothers, reenactments come closest to capturing at least some of the friction, deprivation, and physical effort real-life war involves even in the absence of battle. To that extent they also provide the most realistic training for it: as one reenactor says, being cold, wet, dirty, and miserable is what reenactment is all about.[105]

[103] How to Make Hardtack for War Reenactments at: www.ehow.com/how_2082699_make-hardtack-war-reenactments.html; Civil War Store at: www.aurorahistoryboutique.com/ahb_civilWarStore.cfm.

[104] See, for this weapon, MG-34 at: http://en.wikipedia.org/wiki/MG_34.

[105] Thompson, *War Games*, p, 187.

Above all, reenactors of this kind cannot hope to compete with the public shows in the number of participants they enlist. On the one hand, this has the effect of preventing them from playing out the larger and more important battles that are the stuff of which military history is made. On the other, it provides them with a certain freedom their larger brothers do not enjoy. They do not have the organization and resources required, say, to stage the battle of Gettysburg (although some of the less fastidious among them will participate in such large shows as extras). But they can and do stage what, based on the carefully researched weapons and equipment and modus operandi of the time, must have happened to a "typical" platoon or company at some point and place during that battle. Provided only the terrain is suitable and sufficiently large, many kinds of tactical moves may be and are simulated. Thus, even though there is no shooting and no fighting – this, of course, is something reenactments share with military maneuvers – at least a modicum of strategy is involved.

Forming a genre within a genre, reenactments of this kind are sometimes known as "tacticals." Participants are assigned objectives – say, reaching an objective or capturing a defended position – and engage in reconnaissance missions. They consult maps, prepare plans, move about on the terrain, stalk each other, ambush each other, take each other by surprise, outflank each other, surround each other, and the like. Often the fog of war plays as important a role as it does in real operations. "Soldiers" on mission lose their way, run about in rain or sleet that cover the terrain and bump into the "enemy" who seems to have come out of nowhere and rakes them with withering fire from the flank or pops up at such close quarters that they have no option but to "surrender" – all without having the slightest idea of where the remaining members of the group are, what they may be doing, and what the "big picture" is like. To make up for the absence of "real" fighting, often there are rules to decide who has been killed, injured, or captured, although making people observe them is not easy. Sitting or lying down is boring; nobody wants to set a weekend apart and travel perhaps hundreds of miles to an event simply in order to pretend that, no sooner has the fun got under way, they are dead. As with many computer games, normally even dedicated reenactors are given, or give themselves, several consecutive lives.

Take the following list of instructions, intended for rookie Civil War reenactors:[106]

> When the line moves, you may get pushed or pulled in a certain direction by a line-mate. This is just to make sure that everyone goes in the right direction and stays in their proper place. Make sure you stay with your unit. Remember the faces around you, so that if you do get separated, you'll be able to find your place back in line. If you do get totally lost from your

---

[106] Grenand, *So You Want to be a Soldier*, pp. 258–9.

unit, fall in with the nearest friendly force and follow them until the
conclusion of the action, or until you see a few familiar faces and can
regroup with your unit. If you do end up with another organization, follow
their roles and orders, and respect their officers as your own ... Do not
question the officers' orders to send you straight to a grisly "death". . . Stay
elbow-to-elbow (not shoulder to shoulder), and make sure to fill any holes
made in the front rank with men from the rear rank . . . Stay in line, and do
not charge ahead unless ordered.

The quotation marks before and after "death" apart, did the orders issued by
Confederate company and battalion commanders before Pickett's charge, for
example, sound so different?

Some reenactors are notorious for the deadly seriousness with which they
exercise their hobby. Others do so more in the spirit of light-hearted burlesque:
they play around, engage in all kinds of antics, allow inexperienced spectators to
have a go at it, and the like. Many try to strike a middle-of-the-road posture,
claiming that:

we are a good group of people that are able to straddle the line between a
serious hobby and a fun time. Some groups seem too rigid in some areas,
and they suck the life and fun out of the hobby. Others are too lax, allowing
all sorts of inappropriate behavior and corner cutting. We're positioned
nicely between these extremes. We strive for high authenticity while having
a good time.[107]

However it is done, unkind souls are certain to say that reenactments, being
based on make-believe, merely represent a trivial form of amusement for boys
who have never grown up. Like other wargames they contribute to that dread
disease militarism; perhaps more than other wargames, they may even cause
damage by reviving or intensifying existing rivalries and enmities, as has been
known to happen during reenactments of US Civil War battles.[108]

Up to a point the criticism rings true. Personally I find a photograph of an
American reenactor proudly displaying a trophy he received for participating in
the maneuvers of some Waffen SS division hard to stomach, perhaps even more
so than one that shows the original. It seems to me that the real SS man at any
rate has a kind of innocence. He may have been ordered to do what he did, or he
may have been deceived by a society gone mad. After all most SS men, having
grown up during the 1930s, never heard anything but the most intensive,
comprehensive, most successful propaganda campaign of all times; as the
New Testament puts it, God forgive them because (at least in some cases)
they did not know what they were doing. That is something his latter-day

[107] 9th Reenactment Society at: www.9thsspanzer.com/FAQ.htm#notnazis.
[108] See, above all, T. Horwitz, *Confederates in the Attic: Dispatches from the Unfinished Civil War*, New York: Vintage, 1999, especially pp. 6–9.

reenactor, who is in possession of all the facts, does not share. By choosing to impersonate the SS man, he consciously and deliberately piles evil on evil.

Even putting aside this case as a special one, reenactments, like any kind of historical theater, carry the risk of stirring up memories not all of which may be friendly or pleasant. On occasion a scheduled event has had to be cancelled because the local population did not want to be reminded of a defeat their ancestors had suffered long ago.[109] However, it is also true that organizing reenactments inevitably requires a considerable amount of cooperation between "opposing" groups. War is essentially a zero-sum activity in which each side's gain comes at the other's expense, but reenactors must have quite a lot in common if the event is to take place at all. To that extent reenacting may help to assuage and perhaps overcome the enmities of the past. Indeed northerners have been known to play the part of Confederates, and southerners that of Federals.

The reenactments themselves reflect the close relationship that has always existed between war on the one hand and games on the other. Presumably that relationship will continue to exist until the last testosterone-driven male member of our species gives up the ghost. In a sense, they are part of a wider phenomenon. I am referring to what is sometimes known as the "gamification" of modern life: to wit, the process whereby "serious" activities in such fields as business, administration, and education are being redesigned so as to place a great reliance on point systems and prizes. Such fields as weight-losing, fighting depression, and the like are also being affected. The objective is to encourage performance by making them more game-like, and presumably greater fun.[110] A website dedicated to recreating the history of Yorkshire in northern England puts it as follows: "The days of shuffling around dusty museums or crumbling stately homes to learn about our heritage have long gone. Today, historical re-enactments bring Yorkshire's past to life." Complete with a seaborne attack on the monastic treasures at Whitby Abbey – a ruined building standing on the site of an older one actually demolished by the Vikings – and fully equipped knights on horseback who fight in tournaments almost as real as the real ones.[111]

Experience shows that even some of those who criticize reenacting tend to be caught up by it. Every time an event is held in a settled area people will be flocking to watch. They walk around, examine equipment, take snapshots, and loudly express their approval or disapproval of what they see and hear. Before

[109] L. Steiner, "Historic Battle Reenactment Cancelled [in Canada]," February 17, 2009 at: www.suite101.com/content/historic-battle-reenactment-cancelled-a96929.
[110] See S. McGonigal, *Reality is Broken: Why Games Make Us Better and How They Can Change the World*, London: Penguin, 2011; and B. Reeves and J. Leighton Read, *Games at Work: How Games and Virtual Worlds are Changing the Way People Work and Businesses Compete*, Cambridge, MA: Harvard Business School, 2009.
[111] Enjoy England at: www.enjoyengland.com/ideas/heritage-and-culture/historic-places/re-enactments-in-yorkshire.aspx.

long they start recounting their own military experiences, real or imaginary, and get involved in the reenactors' own debates. Veterans in particular tend to be critical. Probably this is because they fear that the "silliness factor" that is inevitably present even in the best-prepared, most realistic events may cast some doubt on their own deeds and the status they derive from them. Indeed in most reenactments, including those in which weapons are fired, the most serious dangers result not from "combat" but from slipping on ice or else suffering from dehydration or heat stroke. Yet the spirit of reenactment is contagious: onlookers often end up having as much excitement in trying to find out what is and what is not authentic, what can and cannot be reenacted, what should and should not be done, as well as the meaning and purpose of it all, as the reenactors themselves.[112] Some groups will hold special events, known as living history, in order to engage spectators and perhaps attract more of them to join in the hobby.

Compared to other kinds of wargamers, reenactors have the great advantage that they are simultaneously producers, directors, and actors in their own show. Even as they act out history, they watch it unfold. The objective is to experience "what it was really like" (a phrase borrowed, paradoxically, from that most academic of academic historians, Leopold von Ranke), not to watch comfortably or to engage in abstract reasoning. But that is not to say that preparing reenactments, especially those designed to be as authentic as possible, is always easy. At its best it may involve vast amounts of study of a kind not at all inferior to, though very different from, that which "serious" scholarship demands. While many reenactors scoff at the idea that academia should be in charge of the past, some scholars have turned things upside down. They have organized reenactments in an attempt to resolve historical debates concerning, say, the way that ancient Greek hoplites conducted their battles: whether they fought only as part of the phalanx, pushing and shoving, or whether there was sufficient room for individual combat. Given how unusual some of the gladiators' weapons were, reenactments have proved even more useful in reconstructing the way they fought.[113]

Reenactors may disagree among themselves as to what is worth studying and what requires studying – whether, say, it is more important to get the color of a 1916 trench coat exactly right or to make sure the tactics employed are just the ones the British used at the Somme. Some have been known to wonder whether it was OK to use a straw for sipping some water from a cup when wearing a visored medieval helmet (perhaps they should get themselves a real straw rather than one made of plastic). However, almost everybody agrees that study is absolutely essential. Participants who fail to apply themselves and consequently show up with the wrong kind of equipment or put on the wrong kind of behavior are known as "farby" or "farbs," those being the worst derogatory

---

[112] Thompson, *War Games*, pp. 284–5.   [113] Junkelmann, *Gladiatoren*, pp. 148–65.

terms in a reenactor's toolbox. Since it focuses on the trees rather than the forest, largely ignoring both the higher conduct of war and its non-military aspects (although recently there has been a tendency to add medical services, sutlers, camp followers, and the like), the reenacting approach may also be a somewhat narrow-minded one: pedantry may, in fact, be carried to ludicrous extremes.

It is one of the outstanding characteristics of our postmodernist age that most educated people take history less seriously, and know less about it, than at any time since 1850 or so.[114] The best reenactors have the very great merit that they study their own particular piece of history as deeply as anyone can. By acting it out in their own way, they keep it alive for their own edification and that of others. And not without success: whereas all modern armies are shrinking, the number of reenactors and spectators is growing. Of course it is true, as most reenactors are well aware, that their hobby, by taking away the fighting, trivializes the most horrendous activity on earth.[115] Yet the same could be said of most of the wargames discussed throughout this book: in fact this has long been among the most frequent charges leveled against them.

Last but not least, suppose a person who hopes to evade military service by pretending to be mad. That person may well get the discharge he wants – the reason being that, if a person is that good at pretending to be mad, most probably he *is* mad. By granting it, the examining psychiatrist as good as admits that the distance between madness and sanity is small, possibly nonexistent. Could it be that the reason why so many academics and service personnel profess to despise reenactments, reenacting, and reenactors is precisely because the latter, either by sloppiness or by the meticulous way in which they try to duplicate the reality of war, present them with a mirror into which they do not care to look?

---

[114] See, for example, T. Christou, "Gone but Not Forgotten: The Decline of History as an Educational Foundation," *Journal of Curriculum Studies*, 41, 5, 2009, pp. 569–83.

[115] Thompson, *War Games*, p. 59.

6

Enter the computer

Present at creation

Starting in 1945 and lasting for about a decade and a half, a vast wave of change swept over armed conflict as well as the wargames used to simulate it, prepare for it, and, of course, play at it. Largely responsible for the change were two technologies in particular: digital computers and nuclear weapons. Separately and together, so revolutionary were they that those who designed them, developed them, considered ways to employ them, and put them to use (or non-use) could truly claim to have created a new world: one in which humanity, like it or not, will have to live until the end of time.

To speak of computers first, considered from one point of view they have a very long history going back all the way to the ancient Egyptian abacus that Herodotus describes.[1] Considered from another, they only date to the years immediately following World War II when the first multifunction, programmable machines were introduced. Even if visions of such machines that never made it into reality are included, one need go no further back than the "analytical engine" that Charles Babbage and Ada Lovelace built during the first half of the nineteenth century.[2]

Once computers had become available they very quickly proved their worth in designing and playing wargames. One of the first things they did was to take the place of dice in generating random numbers to simulate processes too complex to be gamed in other ways as well as the impact of chance (the so-called Monte Carlo simulation). Not only was such simulation much faster and cheaper than working with multiple dice, but by making possible a much larger number of repetitions it provided a much better statistical basis on which

---

[1] Herodotus, *The Persian Wars*, 2.36.
[2] For a short history of computers in wargaming see Wilson, *The Bomb and the Computer*, pp. 77–85. See also E. D. Swedin and D. L. Svero, *Computers: The Life Story of a Technology*, Baltimore, MD: Johns Hopkins University Press, 2007, pp. 1–46.

to base one's conclusions.[3] Soon computers also started to be used for storing, retrieving, and displaying the information players needed. As we have seen, many wargames, both professional and amateur, require large numbers of calculations to relate the various factors to one another and determine outcomes. The more complex the battle, campaign, or war being gamed, and the more detailed the simulation, the more serious the problem. Computers made it possible both to introduce as many additional factors as those who design the games could think of and to "crunch" the necessary numbers at a speed no human can even remotely match. As computer memory was expanded, the task of record-keeping for subsequent analysis and evaluation was also made much easier. By 1960 the Navy Electronic Warfare Simulator at the Naval War College, built at the cost of ten million dollars (approximately seventy-five million in 2011 dollars) to replace the old wargaming hall with its checkered floor, was performing all these functions. Described as a "two sided . . . electromechanical war gaming device which enables players to make command decisions at real-world or more than real-world time," it would provide them with "significant combat experience in a realistic setting." Other organizations had their own machines, though computer simulations of ground warfare tended to lag behind the rest.[4]

The first attempt to make computers "talk" to each other took place in 1969. Once the Net had become widely available, computers rapidly took the place of messengers, telephones, and other devices in facilitating communication among participants. This often caused the premises where the games were held to look like old-fashioned telephone exchanges with cables snaking about in all directions. Nor did the Net stay limited to its inventors, i.e. the US military. Instead it spread to the civilian world, eventually making possible well-known amateur games such as *World of Warcraft* and *Warhammer* in which hundreds of players can play simultaneously. Last but not least, initially computers were few and far between. Down to the mid 1980s this scarcity provided the fields to which they were applied, wargaming specifically included, with an aura of mystery and sophistication. As Northcote Parkinson of Parkinson's Law fame once noted, that was not the least of their merits.[5] To move around little counters or miniatures on a board, or map, or the floor of a room, or in a sandbox, and pretend to kill them as H. G. Wells and countless other boys aged two to a hundred and fifty did was one thing. To enlist a computer costing millions and functioning in a way few understood in order to do exactly the same was a different and much more respectable one.

---

[3] See H. Kahn and A. W. Marshall, "Methods of Reducing Sample Size in Monte Carlo Computations," *Journal of the Operations Research Society of America*, 1, 5, November 1953, pp. 264–5.
[4] McHugh, *Fundamentals of War Gaming*, pp. 5.2–3, 6.20–1.
[5] N. C. Parkinson, *Parkinson's Law*, Harmondsworth: Penguin, 1957, pp. 60–4.

Not only did computers assist human wargamers but they could, up to a point, take their place. One way of doing this was by using artificial intelligence, meaning a program which, in a certain sense, can "understand" moves and respond to them according to a pre-programmed set of rules. As long as the game is sufficiently simple and structured, indeed, an artificial intelligence program may even "learn" to tailor its moves to the kind of opponent it is playing against, adjusting its play according to whether he is aggressive, defensive, and so on. The potential of this approach has been demonstrated by what in some ways is the most important wargame of all, i.e. chess. The pioneers of chess-playing computer programs were mathematicians such as Norbert Wiener, Claude Shannon, and Alan Turing who did their work during the late 1940s and early 1950s. In 1967 a program called Mac Hac for the first time defeated a human in tournament play. Such programs have been brought to the point where, since 2000 or so, they have been regularly defeating even world champions.[6] The magnitude of the achievement may be appreciated by the fact that, in an average game consisting of a few dozen moves, the number of possible positions is in the order of 1×10^{40}.

The second and in some ways even more radical approach is to dispense with the human player altogether. Games, or perhaps it would be better to call them simulations, can then be run by having two (or more) programs "fight" each other inside the computer itself. Simply juggling the numbers that go into the equations which make up the programs they run will produce different outcomes. Suppose a simulation whose purpose is to help select the best combination of weapons for carrying out such and such a task. Initially each side is given so and so many weapons of such and such a kind. They carry so and so much ammunition and are effective at such and such a range. Given such and such conditions they secure such and such a percentage of hits, inflicting such and such damage on such and such targets defended by such and such means. Changing the numbers will change the results. Hopefully multiple repetitions will enable us to discover the best combination: namely, the one that will produce the greatest number of enemy casualties within the shortest time at the least cost.

Most if not all simulations will be far more complex than this example suggests. Still, the underlying principle is the same. The great advantage of this approach is the fact that, once the equations have been written and the program put in place (once the model has been created) the game, or simulation as some prefer to call it, can be repeated as often as one likes, very fast, and at almost no additional cost. That is not true of humans, who, even if they can be induced to play a game for a second time and even if the cost of doing so is

---

[6] See, for a simple overview of computer chess, Shenk, *The Immortal Game*, pp. 199–221. Another excellent overview of the subject is "computer chess" at: http://en.wikipedia.org/wiki/Computer_chess.

acceptable, will inevitably enter the second game with a set of ideas and assumptions different from the ones with which they entered the first. Thus the ancient Greek maxim that one cannot enter the same river twice applies to wargames as it does to "real" life – an interesting observation in itself.

The benefits of computers were not evenly distributed among various kinds of wargames. One end of the spectrum was occupied by games seeking to simulate not merely war but politics, of which the above-mentioned Sigma Series and Global Wargames were prime examples. To be sure, almost everybody nowadays pays at least lip service to the critical role that politics plays, or ought to play, in initiating war, governing its conduct, and terminating it. However, its imprecise and subjective nature makes developing any kind of rule to model its conduct next to impossible. This specifically includes deterrence, both nuclear and conventional, a "squishy" subject if ever there was one and one that has a lot more to do with psychology than with any branch of natural science.[7] Supposedly game theory is available to help cope with the problem, providing optimal solutions to precisely formulated problems. However, so complex is reality that only rarely can the theory be usefully applied to it. Very often even the most elementary terms are the subject of disagreement among designers.

To illustrate the last-mentioned point let us return to Robert Aumann, surely as qualified an expert on game theory as is alive today. An Israeli citizen, politically Aumann is located on the religious far right. He has criticized the decision by former prime minister Ariel Sharon to evacuate Gaza as "idiotic."[8] In one of his articles he refers to a well-known game named "blackmailer's paradox." In it an insane person, let us call him Brian, forces a sane one, let us call him Alex, to adopt an irrational line of behavior.[9] The logic as developed in the game is impeccable. What is anything but impeccable is Aumann's attempt to fit the Arab–Israeli conflict into the game, or perhaps the game onto the Arab–Israeli conflict, by claiming that "the Arabs present rigid and unreasonable opening positions at every negotiation," blackmailing their opponents.[10] He thus makes a value judgment that not even many Israelis, let alone a single Arab, would accept. The difficulty of agreeing what constitutes blackmail, or, turning back to Brian and Alex, which one of the two of them is insane, explains why, in games designed to simulate politics, computers are largely restricted to performing auxiliary tasks.

[7] See J. Jervis et al., eds., *Psychology and Deterrence*, Baltimore, MD: Johns Hopkins University Press, 1985, as well as B. D. Watts, "Diagnostic Observations on Theater-Level Gaming," Washington DC: National Defense University, April 1985 (unpublished).
[8] *The Marker* [Hebrew], January 12, 2000.
[9] See S. White, "The Blackmailer's Paradox," 2010, at: www.scotworkblog.com/index.php/2010/07/the-blackmailer%E2%80%99s-paradox/.
[10] R. Aumann, "The Blackmailer's Paradox," *The Iconoclast*, July 7, 2010, at: www.newenglishreview.org/blog_direct_link.cfm/blog_id/28397.

At the opposite end of the scale from politics, again specifically including deterrence, stands strategic nuclear warfare. By that is meant the kind of nuclear warfare that is directed against the opponent's homeland. Without any doubt, such warfare is by far the most deadly and destructive form of armed conflict ever invented. So destructive, in fact, that whereas previous weapons only helped change the *ways* war is waged, nuclear ones seem to have altered the reasons *why* it is waged as well as the objectives it may be waged for.[11] To use Churchill's phrase, increasing the power of existing warheads would merely make the rubble bounce. Hence not only is this situation likely to prevail in the future too, but there seems to be little incentive for developing such doomsday methods as "earthquake warfare" and "tsunami warfare."

That much taken for granted, there are several reasons why nuclear warfare is relatively easy to game. First, the number of weapons and delivery vehicles is much smaller than in any other form of war – under certain scenarios perhaps no more than one. Second, owing to the enormous power of the weapons and their residual effects, such as radioactive fallout, it can only be waged far away from friendly troops and populations. Conversely, exercises held as early as the mid 1950s showed that, if it was waged anywhere near those troops and those populations, the outcome might well be to end the existence of both.[12] This requirement in turn means that warheads must be delivered at long distance either through the air or through outer space. However, air and space present much simpler mediums than the sea, let alone the land. While some meteorological phenomena do apply, there are no mountains, lakes, rivers, swamps, forests, various kinds of transportation arteries, villages and towns that must be taken into account in planning one's moves and carrying them out. By comparison, calculating the flight paths of aircraft and the trajectories of missiles is easy.

Third, this very simplicity means that the man/machine balance is markedly different. Starting early in the nineteenth century, the Industrial Revolution caused warfare to become much more capital-intensive than it was before. In this respect, as in so many others, the advent of nuclear weapons marked a watershed. The outstanding characteristic of nuclear warfare is precisely that it is waged with the aid of comparatively few humans. Piloting or launching or otherwise controlling enormously expensive machines, this handful produces a vast bang: as has been well said, instead of equipping the man we now man the equipment.[13] Extremely rigid procedures are put into place so as to exercise

---

[11] The first to realize this was Bernard Brodie: see B. Brodie, *War in the Atomic Age*, Princeton University Press, 1946, pp. 21–69.

[12] H. Speier, *German Rearmament and Atomic War*, New York: Row & Co., 1957, p. 182.

[13] D. R. Segal, "Military Organization and Personnel Accession," in A. Fullinwider, ed., *Conscripts and Volunteers*, Totowa, NJ: Rowman, 1983, p. 17.

complete control and prevent unauthorized or accidental war.[14] Coupled with secure, hardened, redundant communications these procedures are designed to minimize friction of any kind. Last but not least, machines are completely artificial creations. Though their performance may not be entirely error-free, it is far better understood and far more predictable than that of variable, capricious humans. Which means that it is also much easier to model and game.

Even the relatively few humans involved in such warfare are of a very special kind. When it comes to launching missiles, or providing warning against them, or defending against them, most of what Clausewitz calls the *Strapazen* – meaning, strain, fatigue, or suffering – so critical in other kinds of war are all but absent. To be sure, guiding a heavy strategic bomber to its target is not the easiest job in the world. On the other hand, whatever problems they may face, pilots are neither hungry nor thirsty, nor driven half crazy by long periods of enforced sexual abstinence. This is even more true of drone and missile operators who are not expected to face danger or physical discomfort of any kind. Though the stress may be enormous, it is of the kind experienced by air traffic controllers rather than by combat soldiers, who not only operate under what are often extremely difficult circumstances but risk their lives as well. The operators are stationed in specially constructed facilities, possibly located thousands of miles from the scene of action. Everything is done to insulate them and make them comfortable so they can focus on their work. They sit in front of screens, watch blips, talk to other operators, and manipulate controls. In some cases all they are required to do is receive orders that tell them to insert a key into a slot and turn it. This, incidentally, explains why the percentage of women among them is especially high.[15]

During the early Cold War years the Soviet Union was, to quote Churchill's famous expression, "a riddle wrapped in a mystery inside an enigma." To some extent this remained true right down to the final collapse of the Soviet Union; thanks to the development of reconnaissance satellites, though, major parts of the mystery began to be lifted from the early 1960s on. The number of bomber aircraft, missiles, and, later, cruise missiles on each side was roughly known. So, in many cases, were the locations of the bases where they were stationed, their technical characteristics (such as the ability to take off or be launched quickly before a strike by the other side would neutralize them), their failure rate, their range, the distance at which they would be discovered by the other side's radar, the time they would take to reach their targets, their size and shape (which

[14] See, for the part of the arrangements that had been made public, P. Bracken, *The Command and Control of Nuclear Forces*, New Haven, CT: Yale University Press, 1985. For a partial update, R. D. Critchlow, *Nuclear Command and Control: Current Programs and Issues*, Washington DC: CSIS, 2003, at: http://csis.org/files/media/csis/pubs/poni/060503_nuclear_command.pdf.
[15] See on this "Women's Work," Strategy Page, at: www.strategypage.com/htmw/htlead/articles/20090104.aspx (referring to Israeli women).

could be correlated roughly with the number of warheads Soviet aircraft and missiles carried), their accuracy, and the size of the warheads they carried. Those factors in turn could be correlated with population densities, the ability of different kinds of structures to resist blast, and the like. Assuming such and such a target, within such and such a distance from ground zero, so and so many people would be killed and such and such a percentage of buildings demolished. Assuming so and so much radioactivity and winds blowing from such and such a direction, so and so many people could expect to die of leukemia when they were reached by radioactive fallout.[16]

To a lesser but still very considerable extent, the same also applied to whatever defenses had been developed to deal with bombers and missiles. Even specific strategies such as first strike, second strike, and the like could be simulated without much difficulty.[17] To be sure, some things, notably the way each side might interpret the other's preparations and moves and react to them, remained unknown. For example, would a doctrine aimed at targeting the other's delivery vehicles while leaving his cities alone induce the opponent to respond in kind, thus sparing the world from utter destruction in case a war broke out? Or would it merely provide him with an incentive to switch to "launch on warning" (rather than wait for the first hostile missiles to hit his soil) and strike first, thus endangering the balance of terror and making war more likely?[18] Still, such games, and the mathematics that made them possible, were extremely useful in answering questions as to which kind of delivery vehicles, aircraft or ballistic missiles, were preferable; which of one's own forces to use first and which ones to keep in reserve; and so on. Applying similar methods to the other side's armed forces, one could turn the game around and obtain an estimate of one's own losses and how to minimize them, as in choosing between providing the population with nuclear shelters and building an anti-ballistic missile defense system, or in deciding just how such a system should be constructed and organized. All in all, probably never before had such a large part of war been reducible to the laws of physics.

If gaming nuclear warfare is relatively easy it is also exceptionally important. Throughout history, commanders at every level have always based their plans for the future on the experience of the past. Especially from the last decades of the nineteenth century on, one of the most important instruments many of them used for the purpose were wargames. In the case of nuclear warfare, though, no such experience was available. Speculation and science fiction aside,

[16] See, for the kind of calculations involved, R. Ehrlich, *Waging Nuclear Peace: The Technology and Politics of Nuclear Weapons*, Albany, NY: State University of New York Press, 1985, pp. 165–212.
[17] See R. Powell, "Nuclear Doctrine and the Strategy of Limited Retaliation," *American Political Science Review*, 83, 2, June 1989, pp. 503–19.
[18] See on this V. Utgof, "In Defense of Counterforce," *International Security*, 6, 4, Spring 1982, pp. 44–60.

this fact left wargames as almost the *only* available tool for understanding it, planning it, and testing it, vastly enhancing the role that they could and should play. Probably for the first time in history BYMs (bright young men) with no military experience, some of them just out of college, could plausibly claim to know as much about future warfare – or at any rate the most powerful and most destructive forms of future warfare – as the most senior military commanders of the time. Some actually boasted of never having heard a shot fired in anger.

The BYMs' self-imposed mission was nothing less than to invent entirely new techniques for dealing with what they saw, not without reason, as entirely new military problems. In doing so, they sought to combine imagination with rigid quantification. It hardly requires saying that this situation led to numerous clashes between different generations and different cultures: after all, few organizations resemble each other less than the military on the one hand and think tanks on the other. For example General Lemay, during his term as commander of the Strategic Air Command (1949–57), was quoted as saying that, at the time when he himself was directing hundreds of heavy bombers against Japan and dropping atomic bombs on Hiroshima and Nagasaki, Harold Brown, then a young analyst and later Secretary of Defense under President Carter, had been in junior high school. On the other side Herman Kahn, answering critics who questioned his methods, used to ask when they had last fought a thermonuclear war.[19] As the saying goes, old views do not die; it is those who hold them who do. Under McNamara during the 1960s the BYMs' victory seemed complete – until, that is, the Vietnam War caused a reaction to set in. But that is another story.

All this explains why, inside the so-called defense community, thousands if not tens of thousands of nuclear wargames have been held over the years. Most of the details are understandably secret, and at any self-respecting war college the building where the games are held is always the most tightly guarded of all. Still, we know that the Joint Chiefs of Staff, preparing the first Strategic Integrated Operations Plans (SIOPs) in 1961–2, used wargames to determine the level of damage that the US and Soviet Union might inflict on one another in an all-out exchange of nuclear strikes. Not long afterwards, the chief of the Joint Chiefs of Staff, General Lyman Lemnitzer, presented the results to President Kennedy.[20] Lemnitzer never mentioned the possibility of an "out of the blue" US offensive. What he did tell the president was that the number of US casualties would depend primarily on the success of the air force in eliminating as many Soviet bombers and missiles as possible before they could be launched. Yet almost certainly not even the best planned attack, perfectly executed, would prevent some of the Kremlin's nuclear forces from "riding out" the attack – as

[19] See Ghamari-Tabrizi, "Simulating the Unthinkable," pp. 165, 166.
[20] S. D. Sagan, "The Nuclear Plan Briefing to President Kennedy," *International Security*, 12, 1, Summer 1987, pp. 27, 28.

the phrase went – and retaliating in kind. The outcome would be horrendous casualties, even though their exact number was not spelt out in the briefing.

As was noted at the time and later, the SIOP in question was extremely rigid. The objective was to deter, and if necessary safeguard against, a Soviet first strike by using the available forces before they could be knocked out. Hence the plan, and presumably the games on which it was partly based, only provided for all-out nuclear warfare and very little else. Technological progress, specifically the growing number of intercontinental ballistic missiles (ICBMs) and the introduction from about 1965 on of Multiple Independent Reentry Vehicles or MIRVs, led to changes in this respect. ICBMs in their silos were much harder to hit and destroy than bombers on their airfields, thus easing the awesome dilemma of "use them or lose them" and providing their owners with some flexibility in deciding what to do. At the same time, arming ballistic missiles with multiple reentry vehicles capable of being independently guided not only increased the number of targets each of them could hit but also enabled them to do so much more accurately. They could now be aimed not merely at cities but at much smaller targets, which in turn led to the development of smaller warheads. The same applied to the cruise missiles that entered the arsenal from the 1970s on.[21] Escalation, in other words, no longer looked automatic, nor the destruction of the world inevitable.

These developments led the above-mentioned Andy Marshall, as the high priest of wargaming at the Pentagon, to call for games of a different kind. They had to be capable of comparing various force structures, allowing a much richer set of operational factors to be included. Not only strategic nuclear warfare but the much more complex type waged by conventional forces, which might result in escalation, had to be simulated. Another important objective was to find ways of incorporating Soviet points of view on these matters, which Marshall, following discussions he had had with the Soviets years before, thought were likely to differ considerably from American ones.[22] For example, the Soviets might not attribute the same importance to warhead accuracy, silo hardness, and the like. Their methodology for assessing effectiveness, and consequently their plans for achieving it, might also differ considerably. Even if the doctrine was clear, it might not necessarily be understood or adhered to at all command levels. In other words, problems of command, control, and communications had to be brought in as well. The ultimate objective, Marshall wrote, was to design computerized games that would meet the needs of three distinct groups of people. They were, first, those interested in assessing military balances;

---

[21] See, on these weapon systems, T. Greenwood, *Making the MIRV: A Study of Defense Decision-Making*, Cambridge, MA: Ballinger, 1975; and R. K. Betts, ed., *Cruise Missiles: Technology, Strategy and Politics*, Washington DC: Brookings Institution, 1982.

[22] A. W. Marshall, "Problems of Estimating Military Power," 1966, at: www.rand.org/pubs. papers.1005.P3417.pdf, pp. 12–13.

second, those involved in attempts to change those balances by evaluating the merits of alternative force programs; and, third, those involved in devising and evaluating operational plans.[23]

As usual, the principal contractor was RAND which had been working on this kind of problem for over a quarter-century and where Marshall himself had worked for a time. The objective was to automate "all features of political-military gaming from the force calculations to the decision making participants in the traditional wargame," no less. Specific problems to be explored included what might happen in case the Soviets attacked Washington on Inauguration Day, what the effect of the pre-delegation of authority might be, what might happen in case early warning satellites were lost, and the like.[24] Speaking of games, one can imagine the fun the RAND personnel had dreaming up these and other scenarios and trying to find ways of making their computers simulate them as closely as possible. A preliminary report came out in 1982 even as Marshall made the project's existence public.[25] The analysts in charge duly noted how demanding the research was, given that it forced them to make every assumption explicit, find a way to assign to it a numerical value, and create an algorithm to link it to the rest so that the computer could "understand" it. All this implied a major effort to locate the necessary information and using one's imagination where, particularly on the Soviet side, it was not available. Next, no fewer than four hundred different situations had to be created in painstaking detail and decision-making trees for each one devised to enable the computer to "crunch" its way through them. Even that was only the beginning, since care had to be taken to make the program expandable so that even more situations could be incorporated later on.

The analysts also noted that, under this method of gaming, the scenario, instead of being presented before the beginning of play as in traditional wargames, emerged from the interaction of the computer programs themselves. Last but not least, even though the "primitive automated agents are not presently programmed to be very sophisticated, we have been impressed with the complexity of play that evolves from the interactions of several simple automatons." In other words, simply by interacting with each other, programs, though they could not of course violate the assumptions (rules) that had been written into them, often produced highly unpredictable results. "Even at this rudimentary stage of development," the analysts added, "some of us have found

[23] A. W. Marshall, "A Program to Improve Analytic Methods Related to Strategic Forces," *Policy Sciences*, 15, 1982, pp. 47–50.
[24] P. K. Davis *et al.*, "Automated War Gaming as a Technique for Exploring Strategic Command and Control Issues," Santa Monica, CA: RAND, 1983, at: www.rand.org/content/dam/rand/pubs/notes/2009/N2044.pdf, pp. 9–11.
[25] M. H. Graubard and C. H. Builder, "New Methods for Strategic Analysis: Automating the Wargame," *Policy Sciences*, 15, 1982, p. 71.

that the horizons of our own strategic thinking are expanding very rapidly." As so often, perhaps the best way to benefit from a wargame is to design one.

Four years later a more detailed report was published.[26] By this time the scope of the project had been widened so that it comprised not just "Sam versus Ivan" games but some third countries known as Greens as well. The report specifically mentions Saudi Arabia, Poland, Belgium, and France, though it is not clear which and how many of these were included in any specific game. As before, for each country the computer had to be fed not just with data concerning its own forces and behavior but also with the image it had formed, or was supposed to have formed, of the rest. In the case of the superpowers, those images played a major role in the decision to escalate or not to escalate. In the case of the Greens, the images might affect – perhaps determine – their decision as to which side to join, if any. As the number of countries involved in any particular game increased, the resulting level of complexity went up exponentially.

The report also referred to a number of sophisticated features that its predecessor, whether because of its summary nature or because it only dealt with preliminary work, did not mention. One was artificial intelligence, meaning the ability, for example, of Ivan to compare his doctrine in respect, say, of rates of advance or the consumption of fuel and ammunition to the "actual" results that his interaction with Blue produced. The doctrine having been duly adjusted, the effect of the changes might make themselves felt as the game continued. To that extent, it is possible to speak of true wargaming between thinking opponents. An attempt was also made to enable the programs to look ahead towards certain predetermined outcomes and adjust their "play" accordingly. Superficially such a capability was needed in order to simulate the way human decision-makers think and act. However, it quickly led to the problem of what mathematicians call infinite recursion. Infinite recursion is what happens when trying to guess the intentions of an opponent in a strategic-type encounter: I think that he thinks that I think that he thinks that I think . . . Since the series has no logical end, in theory it may last forever. As the analysts noted, under such circumstances the ability to distinguish Sam from Ivan, and the other way around, is quickly lost. That, incidentally, is as true in the real world, especially that of intelligence and espionage, as it is in games, computerized or otherwise.[27]

Interestingly enough, looking forward so and so many moves – currently not even the most advanced supercomputers can work through all the moves in a game, and they probably never will – determining the most favorable interim position, and continuing from there is how modern chess-playing programs work.[28] To be sure, even in a game as circumscribed and as structured as chess, short of meeting the victory condition – mate to the opposing king – defining

[26] P. K. Davis et al., A New Methodology for Modeling National Command Level Decision-making in War Games and Simulations, Santa Monica, CA: RAND, 1986.
[27] Ibid., pp. 78–9.   [28] "Computer chess" at: http://en.wikipedia.org/wiki/Computer_chess.

the exact meaning of a desirable outcome is very hard. Indeed it is precisely in this respect that the differences between various programs are most pronounced.[29] As the RAND analysts admitted, they did not know what outcomes decision-makers might be looking for, much less how they might evaluate those outcomes if and when they did in fact take place. Not to mention the very likely possibility that, in the "real" world, the decision-makers might not know either but would feel their way forward step by step as sleepwalkers are supposed to do. Hence it was all the analysts could do to use their imaginations instead.

Summing up what appears to have been some seven years of work by experts from fields as different as artificial intelligence, military science, psychology, and the history and culture of the countries being simulated, they said that "currently the prototype NCL (National Command Level) models do not contain the richness of detail that is possible and essential for applications work." Nevertheless they considered "prototype development to have been very successful." They also made specific recommendations for further research, suggesting, for example, that the laws of war should be brought in and that greater attention should be paid to problems of command and control as well as "asymmetries" between the ways Sam and Ivan understood the world and each other. The last-named problem, of course was exactly the one they had been asked to solve in the first place. Neither the 1982 report nor the 1986 one wasted a single word on the most important question, namely whether the project produced anything of any use to any of the three groups Marshall had mentioned.

To return from these Pentagon-inspired attempts to build a computerized model capable of simulating the way the world works to the more limited issue of gaming strategic nuclear warfare, it would appear that this kind of gaming never became very popular. Almost certainly one reason for this is that such warfare does not make any great intellectual demands on either strategists or gamesters. To be sure, there may be a first nuclear strike and even a second one. However, a third one is almost inconceivable, as is proved by the fact that practically nothing has been written on it. The rarely used term "broken back warfare," meaning warfare that involves whatever forces may survive a first and second strike, merely confirms this point. A good analogy is presented by some high-level tennis games in which one player serves one ace after another, stunning his opponent and leaving him helpless. In such a game the give and take that both represents the essence of strategy and accounts for much of men's fascination with it is almost entirely absent. This was especially true after ballistic missiles largely took the place of manned bombers from about 1965 on. Even today, though a few anti-ballistic missile defense systems have been deployed by various countries and are supposedly operational, the situation remains substantially the same.

[29] See on this "Alpha-beta pruning," at: http://en.wikipedia.org/wiki/Alpha-beta_pruning.

Throughout the ages, war has always been primarily a question of character attributes such as steadfastness, determination, stamina, and, above all, the readiness to kill and be killed if necessary – to commit, and cope with, bloody slaughter. Many wargames reflected this fact: there are even a few cases, such as the late nineteenth-century duels fought with rifled pistols in which the parties are expected to maintain a stony mien while doing nothing to defend themselves, when courage in particular is almost the *only* relevant quality. By contrast, in nuclear warfare these and other human qualities count for little if anything. At the top, everything is done to ensure that decision-makers and operatives at all levels should act on the basis of rational considerations alone. At the bottom, such is the scale of destruction that there is no coping with it.

Both those who made the decision and many of the rest of us are very likely to end up dead, leaving behind neither leaders nor anybody who may obey them and admire their leadership. In the words of French President Charles de Gaulle, "[in the wake of a nuclear war] the two sides will have neither powers, nor laws, nor cities, nor cultures, nor cradles, nor tombs."[30] The heroic narrative, which, beginning at the time when Homer praised *andreia* (manly courage) as the highest virtue, has always provided much of the motivation behind war and, perhaps even more so, many kinds of wargames, is unable to develop. As one well-known Cold War-vintage Soviet joke put the matter, the citizens of Moscow, when coming under nuclear attack are called upon to don shrouds and crawl *slowly* to the cemetery: slowly, in order to avoid a panic.

Above all, even the most conservative estimates, whether produced by wargames or by other methods, put the number of US casualties resulting from just ten 0.5 megaton weapons over ten urban areas at just under 20 million.[31] This calculation ignored the fact that the real number of available warheads ran into the thousands. Furthermore, it included neither the millions who would die later as a result of radiation-induced cancer nor those who would succumb to the political, economic, social, and psychological conditions in an industrial society abruptly sent back into the Stone Age.[32] As if to highlight the madness, one article on the subject carries the title, "Victory is Possible."[33] Taking a saner approach, most people spoke of "the end of civilization as we know it." To quote a character in the 1983 movie *WarGames*, the only way to win the game was not to play it.[34] In the movie's opening scene the

---

[30] Quoted in J. L. Gaddis *et al.*, eds., *Cold War Statesmen Confront the Bomb: Nuclear Diplomacy since 1945*, Oxford University Press, 1999, p. 226.

[31] T. Calvan, *Crisis Relocation Plans: The Realities of Planning for Nuclear Attack in New York State*, Albany, NY: New York Assembly, 1983, p. 2.

[32] See A. M. Katz, *Life after a Nuclear War: The Social and Economic Effects of Nuclear Attacks on the US*, New York: Ballinger, 1982, pp. 377–83.

[33] C. Gray and K. Payne, "Victory is Possible," *Foreign Policy*, 39, Summer 1980, pp. 14–27.

[34] J. Badham, *WarGames* (1983).

Department of Defense holds an exercise involving the simulated launch of ICBMs with their nuclear warheads, only to discover that one-third of the personnel refuse to turn their keys as told. The movie does not say whether this was because they could not believe that the orders were for real or because, knowing them to be so, they shrank from the task. Coming to the rescue, the BYMs replace the operators with computers, automating the system and opening a nest of nuclear troubles that need not concern us here. Among the consultants who helped create the movie was Peter Schwartz, an engineer/scenario writer/futurist who, as it happened, later worked for Marshall too.

The secrecy that surrounds the issue notwithstanding, there is some evidence that the fear that some humans in the loop might refuse to play ball presented a real concern. Several sources suggest that, in 1980s wargames, players willing to cross the nuclear threshold were hard to find. Explanations for this phenomenon differ. The players may have preferred the devil they knew (conventional war) to the one they did not know; or else they simply did not want to blow up the world. Be that as it may, in game after game they explored every alternative, desperately signaling, dodging, and negotiating with their opponents. This might reach the point where Control found it necessary to push them in that direction even at the cost of producing increasingly implausible scenarios. Should they fail to respond, it might even accuse them of "ruining" the exercise.[35] I personally have heard a slightly inebriated British officer explain how, when the alarm in a nuclear storage installation where he used to work was sounded, those present could not at first make themselves believe it was real and that an accident, involving a bomb that had fallen off its trolley, had taken place.

Marshall himself must have shared those concerns, or else it is hard to see why one of the problems that the RAND analysts he commissioned set out to "solve" for him was the frequent reluctance of human players to unleash such a conflict. They even argued, as Kahn (who happened to die in the same year in which the movie came out) might have done, that, "if gaming . . . the initiation of a nuclear conflict holds any analytical value, it might *only* [my emphasis] be possible with a programmed agent."[36] To that extent, the oft-noted tendency to look at nuclear wargamers as a bunch of Dr. Strangeloves, blame them for some of government's more outlandish policies, and accuse them of making the unthinkable a little less so appears to be fully justified.[37]

---

[35] Allen, *War Games*, p. 315; Watts, "Diagnostic Observations of Theater-Level War Gaming," p. 21; M. de Landa, *War in the Age of Intelligent Machines*, New York: Urzone, 1991, p. 2.

[36] Graubard and Builder, "New Methods for Strategic Analysis: Automating the Wargame," p. 74.

[37] E.g. S. Zuckerman, "Judgment and Control in Modern Warfare," *Foreign Affairs*, 40, 2, January 1962, pp. 196–212; D. Lindley, "What I Learnt since I Stopped Worrying and Studied the Movie: A Teaching Guide to Stanley Kubrick's Dr. Strangelove," *Political Science and Politics*, 34, 3, 2002, pp. 663–7.

Finally, this argument may also be turned upside down. The reluctance of wargamers responsible for simulating the behavior of senior decision-makers in various countries to cross the nuclear threshold may be a cause for concern to a handful of experts who want to know, as closely as possible, at what point a nuclear war might break out, how to prepare for it, what it might look like, how best to wage it, and how to end it short of blowing up the world. Outlandish and disturbing though those concerns may seem to many people, it is hard to question their importance. Yet there is some reason to believe that the reluctance to escalate may faithfully represent the games' unexpected success in capturing the way the real world behaves.[38] If so, then the news is encouraging indeed.

Onscreen war

As the Cold War started winding down during the late 1980s the probability of a Soviet "strike out of the blue," never very likely, declined. So, as a result, did gaming "strategic" nuclear exchanges. On the one hand, as the 1991 Gulf War was soon to demonstrate, the US advantage in waging conventional warfare was so overwhelming as to make resort to nuclear weapons unnecessary. On the other, such was the fear of nuclear weapons that it was, and remains, difficult to imagine a war directed against an enemy who possesses, or is strongly suspected of possessing, even a single such weapon. Indeed some countries, notably India and China, seem to have based their entire strategy on that assumption.[39] As far back as 1965, speaking to the French writer André Malraux, Mao Zedong himself said as much.[40] Increasingly, nuclear wargames at the Pentagon tended to deal with conflicts between third parties such as India and Pakistan or else in the Middle East. Nuclear warfare in Korea must also have been gamed countless times. In an ironic reversal of previous fears that when it came to unleashing a nuclear war human operators might not cooperate as they should, some games focused on the problems of unauthorized war and accidental war.[41]

Having grown from modest beginnings in the 1950s, forty years later wargaming, whether carried out in the think tanks or in-house by various headquarters with the Joint Chiefs of Staff at their head, had acquired a large following. It consisted of highly qualified and extremely specialized experts who, as well as trying to reduce everything to numbers, programmed the

---

[38] See, most recently, T. V. Paul, *The Tradition of Non-Use of Nuclear Weapons*, Stanford, CA: Stanford Security Studies, 2009.

[39] R. M. Bashrur, *Minimum Deterrence and India's Nuclear Security*, Singapore: National University of Singapore Press, 2009; and A. L. Johnson, "China's 'New Old Thinking': The Concept of Limited Deterrence," *International Security*, 20, 3, Winter 1995, pp. 5–43.

[40] Quoted in Chong Pin Ling, *China's Nuclear Weapons Strategy*, Lexington, MA: Lexington Books, 1988, p. 78.

[41] Allen, *War Games*, pp. 314–15.

computers, and understood the highly esoteric language in which many reports were written (e.g. "FSS runs on the Synchronous Parallel Environment for Emulation and Discrete Event Simulation (SPEEDES) framework [which] helps exploit available high performance computational resources and provides much needed functionality").[42] The cost must have run into the hundreds of millions of dollars each year. No wonder the community in question sometimes seemed to take on a life of its own, dreaming up new kinds of games each time changing circumstances made the old ones appear less relevant.

If strategic nuclear wargaming lost much of its relevance, in respect to conventional games the situation was entirely different. As the Global Wargames Series and the success of the contemporary Military Reform Movement in pushing towards "maneuver warfare" both indicate, the 1980s saw a revival of interest in conventional warfare.[43] Partly this was based on the above-mentioned expectation, never really documented, that the Kremlin might permit a conventional war taking place in the "Central" theater to proceed merrily for some time while allowing the awesome nuclear arsenal at its disposal to remain idle.[44] In part it was a reaction to the American failure in Vietnam. The latter caused countless members of the defense community – service personnel, government officials, and analysts in academia and the think tanks – to long for a return to "real" warfare. At the time and later, this was called "shedding the Vietnam syndrome."

There were, and are, several reasons why applying computers, with their insatiable demand for algorithms, to conventional wargaming is considerably harder than doing the same to the latter's nuclear sister. First, in such warfare it is the men's lives, rather than some abstraction such as "civilization as we know it," that is in immediate danger, probably making their behavior harder to predict and simulate. The fact that warfare is a collective activity only makes the problem more difficult still. Second, the participants in such warfare are much more diverse. They range from a simple infantryman with his assault rifle and pack through a twenty-ton armored personnel carrier with its rapid-fire cannon all the way to a 120-ton, eight-engine, B-52 bomber launching JDAMs (joint direct attack munitions) at a discrete target 30,000 feet underneath. Third, their number is larger by an order of magnitude, perhaps more. This is illustrated by the fact that, after a month-long campaign in which hundreds of aircraft participated, just two bombers carrying just two bombs managed to bring about Japan's surrender within days of those bombs being dropped.

---

[42] D. A. Gilmour et al., "Real Time Course of Action Analysis," 2006, at: http://scholar.google.co.il/scholar?q=Real+Time+Course+of+Action+Analysis&hl=iw&btnG=%D7%97%D7%99%D7%A4%D7%95%D7%A9, p. 3.

[43] See, on the military reform movement, A. A. Clark et al., eds., *The Military Reform Debate: Issues and Analyses*, Baltimore, MD: Johns Hopkins University Press, 1984.

[44] See pp. 184–6 above.

Fourth, as I said above, nuclear warfare proceeds in the air and in outer space (what happens on the ground following a nuclear explosion is so devastating that it can hardly be called warfare at all). By contrast, much conventional warfare takes place in the far more complex environments that the sea, and above all the land, present. Not just numbers, capabilities and losses on both sides, but transport arteries, bottlenecks, lines of communication (none of which are present in air warfare), tempo, maneuver, and leverage must be simulated. This, after all, is the paradoxical, infinitely complex, ever-changing, often highly unpredictable world of strategy. Depending on circumstances and the quality of one's moves, two plus two can make now five, now three.[45] Conversely the relative simplicity of air warfare limits the intellectual challenge it presents. Among pilots this sometimes leads to "coning," which means an approach that focuses on capabilities and targets to the exclusion of everything else.[46]

Field maneuvers apart, from the 1950s on probably the best available means for simulating conventional warfare were the kind of hexed wargames discussed in Chapter 4. If they did not solve the above problems then at any rate they tried to do so, often at the cost of immense complexity and the need to perform endless calculations. Hundreds of different ones were published: in 1980, the peak year, two million were sold. At that point computers entered the field. Though hexed wargames did not disappear, in terms of popularity they simply could not compete. Some computers continued to be used as they had previously been. Either they were employed to assist human wargamers, as in the case of the Global Wargames and their competitors in the army and air force, or else they ran programs designed to simulate warfare without human intervention. Thanks to immensely increased speed and memory, however, the number of factors capable of being incorporated and manipulated could be vastly expanded to yield a better representation of conventional war.

A game might figure in the number of troops and units, their weapons (mobility, defensive power, lethality, range, accuracy, ammunition supply, need for maintenance), their equipment, their morale, their logistics, the weather, geography, the kind of human settlement in the theater of war, communications (railways, roads, sea or air transport), and so many other factors as to boggle the mind. This expansion appears to have reached a record of sorts in 1997. Overseen by the Jet Propulsion Laboratory of CalTech, a number of Department of Defense supercomputers located in Dayton, Ohio, and Vicksburg, Mississippi, were made to join forces. They ran a program designed to simulate the activities of precisely 66,239 tanks, trucks, and other vehicles. Typically, some would say, the published report does not mention the number of humans, but by multiplying the number of vehicles by five or six we

---

[45] Luttwak, *Strategy*, pp. 3–68.
[46] D. Gates, *Sky Wars: A History of Military Aerospace Power*, London: Reaktion, p. 22.

arrive at a figure of over 300,000. The results were instantaneously viewed on the conference floor of the San Jose Convention Center which was made to look like the terrain of (where else?) northern Saudi Arabia and Kuwait.[47] Presumably technical progress since then has permitted even larger games, simulating some campaign in this remote theater or that, to be held – certainly doing so would be much easier and cheaper than it was at the end of the twentieth century. The time may come, if it has not done so already, when a game the size of the 1997 one, instead of requiring so many supercomputers, can be played by anyone with a PC. Yet conventional warfare has continued to shrink.[48] Hence it is hard to think why anybody would want to do so: instead it became necessary to include new factors such as space war, infowar, and the like.[49]

Very different from these and similar monster exercises paid for and played by the military were videogames, or, as they came to be known after they began to be played not on dedicated machines but on all-purpose ones, computer games.[50] A common way of classifying such games is by dividing them into operational- and strategic-level games on the one hand and "shooting" games on the other. The two differ in that the latter require players to aim a weapon and pull a trigger, whereas the former do not. To be sure, neither in the games nor in the real world is the distinction absolute. Commanding his army, Alexander fought in person and was wounded many times. As Titian's painting of Emperor Charles V as the Christian Soldier shows, down to the middle of the sixteenth century crowned heads often followed his example, with the result that not a few of them were killed, injured, or captured. As late as World War II, for a German regimental commander to personally lead his men in a counter-attack with submachine gun and hand grenades was considered "a self-evident duty" that did not merit a decoration.[51] Returning to the game world, successful designers must know their target population's secret longings. Accordingly some of them provide players with the wherewithal both to perform command and staff functions and to "kill" opponents. Still, the distinction is useful and we shall stick to it.

To start with onscreen operational- and strategic-level games, they had their origins in the hexed ones of the 1970s. In fact those who played the latter, being

---

[47] Jet Propulsion Laboratory, California Institute of Technology, "Researchers Stage Largest Military Simulation Ever," December 4, 1997, at: www.jpl.nasa.gov/releases/97/military. html.

[48] See M. van Creveld, *The Changing Face of War*, New York: Ballantine, pp. 197–205.

[49] R. P. Haffa and J. H. Patton, "Gaming the 'System of Systems'," *Parameters*, 38, 3, Spring 1998, pp. 110–21.

[50] See, for a general account for their development, J. Lundy and B. Sawyer, *Engines of War: Developing Computer Wargames*, Scottsdale, AZ: Paraglyph, 2004.

[51] See van Creveld, *Fighting Power: German and US Army Performance, 1939–1945*, Woodbridge, CT: Greenwood, 1982, p. 107.

much better educated than the average citizen, also tended to be among the very first to buy computers, install them in their home, and try to see what they could do with them. Some firms that had specialized in hexed games sensed the way the winds of change were blowing. They switched directly from one kind to another, taking existing games and calling in programmers to modify them as necessary. Many of those which failed to do so went under.[52] The levels that the games cover range from the national command authority through army, corps, and division commanders down to brigade ones but not much further. This is because, at battalion level and lower, the distinction between leading and fighting tends to become blurred even today. Indeed the moment arrives when commanders, like the above-mentioned German regimental ones who did not get a medal, are expected to lead *by* fighting and even to cover their men.

In principle games of this kind may be played by two or more persons against each other. In practice most of them seem to involve a human playing against the computer. To play against a human, a computer must first be provided with some kind of artificial intelligence so as to register the opponent's moves and make the appropriate responses. Either way, like chess, Reisswitz-type games and BOGSATs, but unlike shooters, they are played by turns. As in tournament chess, setting time limits for each move or for all of them together would be easy. However, and also as in tournament chess, doing so would merely add an element of artificiality because there is no good way to relate game time to real time. Indeed from Bobby Fischer down many players have suggested their own time schedules, arguing that they were not inferior, and were in some ways superior, to those that FIDE, the World Chess Federation, has set. These games are known by names such as rapid chess, Blitzkrieg chess, and the like. Some of these forms are sufficiently popular to have acquired organizations of their own, which in turn hold regular world championships parallel to the better-established ones.[53]

An excellent early example of a human versus computer game was *Eastern Front*. It was produced in 1981 by Chris Crawford, a wargamer who had studied programming, for the Atari 800 personal computer. This being years before hard disks were introduced, incidentally, that particular computer stored data on a 90 kilobyte floppy disk. It had a maximum RAM of only 8 kilobytes. Thus *Eastern Front* proved, as chess in its own way has always done and still does, that good wargames – good in the sense that they are both able to capture some important aspects of war and playable – can sometimes be designed and produced with the aid of very modest means indeed.

The game recreated Operation Barbarossa, i.e. the German Wehrmacht invasion of the Soviet Union. It covered the months from June 1941 to April

---

[52] See, for the very different publishing dynamics of hexed and computer games, Dunnigan, *Wargames Handbook*, pp. 198–204, 234–7.

[53] See Fast Chess at: http://en.wikipedia.org/wiki/Fast_chess.

1942 when the battle of the frontiers for Leningrad, for the Ukraine, and for Moscow had been fought and the Germans were thrown back from the Soviet capital.[54] The player commanded white, consisting of corps-sized German units. Soviet forces were marked in red and were played by the computer. Apparently the underlying assumption was that people would much prefer directing Hitler's murderous but effective legions than Stalin's no less bloody, but clumsy and lumbering, Red Army: this, after all, was precisely the time when, among members of the defense community, admiration for everything German peaked. Armored and cavalry corps on both sides were marked with crosses, whereas infantry formations appeared as boxes. These formations, instead of moving in six different directions as in hexed games, could be moved only in four. However, the size of the squares was small and their number sufficiently large. Hence this fact did not affect realism or hamper play too much.

The belligerents "fought" their war over a vast area stretching from just north of Leningrad at the top of the screen to Sevastopol at the bottom, and from Warsaw on the left to just east of Stalingrad on the right. Since the theater of war is much too large to be displayed and still maintain sufficient resolution, the players used a joystick to scroll the map as required: the first time, it is said, that such a device was incorporated into any computer game. The terrain displayed was extremely varied, including flat land, forests, mountains, rivers, and swamps. Each of these affected the ability of various formations to move over it in a different way. Adjustments were made according to whether a corps, making an operational movement, entered the "influence" zone of a hostile one and also to reflect different seasons. Thus ice, spreading north to south, gradually made rivers crossable in winter. Conversely, the autumn and spring mud seasons dramatically reduced mobility. Reinforcements and lines of communication were also simulated so that losses suffered in combat were gradually made up (Soviet ones much more than those the Germans took). Given that the German side was heavily outnumbered, the human playing it had to rely on operational finesse in order to surround and cut off as many of the Soviet forces as possible.

Each turn consisted of two stages, an entry mode and combat mode. First the joystick was used to select units and enter movement. Up to eight orders could be entered for any unit, the ultimate objective being to move each unit forward as far as possible in any given turn. Once orders had been entered the player pressed the Start button to enter the combat mode. The outcome was determined by the computer on the basis of calculations similar to those Reisswitz and his successors used to carry out with the aid of dice and tables. Flashes indicated the units that had been attacked, which might either be destroyed or

---

[54] See, for what follows, *Eastern Front* (video game) at: http://en.wikipedia.org/wiki/ Eastern_Front_(video_game).

forced to retreat. Each turn represented one week in-game time, the game ending after forty-one turns on March 29, 1942. Historically this was the moment when the Wehrmacht, having survived the winter, resumed its offensive. Since this was a game aimed at hobbyists rather than at professionals doing serious planning, a great deal of effort was spent ensuring that the game would be both easy to play and balanced. This was done by playing the game time and again while modifying the rules in such a way as to give both players a fairly even chance to win. Nevertheless play remained simple – a major reason why the game was a success.

The hardware – meaning computers – on which the games were played was developing at breakneck speed. Especially important were three factors. First, general purpose machines took the place of specialized ones, allowing as many different games as one could afford to be played on each computer and leading to a dramatic drop in prices. Second, microchips, introduced in 1979, made computers much smaller, lighter, and above all much faster and with greater memories. Whereas Crawford had to make do with 8 bytes of RAM, a few years later 128 and 256 bytes of RAM were common and 512 bytes were in the pipeline. Third, initially screens tended to be heavy and bulky. Some games even came in the form of consoles that had to be hooked up to the domestic TV set. Later the screens became smaller and more easily transportable. Resolution, which is governed by the number of pixels as well as several other factors, was also increased, leading to much sharper, more realistic, images.

Better computers also allowed artificial intelligence to be set at various degrees of difficulty and to adopt different personalities, such as playing offensively, defensively, and the like. As one technical improvement followed another, games were brought out, played for a while, and discarded. New games demanded larger computer memories and larger memories made possible new games. So it went in a merry-go-round that emptied players' pockets, as indeed it was designed to do. Initially games could be produced on a shoestring by individuals with computer skills and a lot of imagination. Later on, doing so became the business of teams of experts taken from various fields who might easily spend months to produce a single one. In addition to planning and programming, the work included devising artistic effects – often a difficult task that demands high expertise, but one that is vital if players are to appreciate the game – as well as musical ones. The process ends with a period of validating and testing. The cost of doing all this can easily run into millions of dollars. Some games ended up on the Net from where they may be downloaded and played for free, a testimony either to their own quality or to people's antiquarian interest in the subject.

In an interview he gave many years later, Crawford said that the commercial success of *Eastern Front* had exceeded all expectations.[55] Unsurprisingly it was

---

[55] See an interview with Chris Crawford at: www.dadgum.com/halcyon/BOOK/CRAW FORD.HTM.

followed by many others. Subsequent games covered almost every possible historical war from antiquity on, not to mention any number of futuristic wars and imaginary wars. As the most important single event in the whole of US history, the Civil War in particular has given rise to a large number of games. One list, last updated in December 2010, provides the names of twenty-three different ones alphabetically arranged and ranging from *Aegod's American Civil War* to *Robert E. Lee: Civil War General.*[56] Land warfare, naval warfare, campaigns, battles, secret missions, and the operations of General Robert E. Lee (who else?) have all been studied, broken into countless computer lines, and reissued in game form. Here I shall focus on one of the most recent and most elaborate games, the award-winning *Forge of Freedom.* Players play against the computer and may choose to be in charge of either the Confederacy or the Union. However, foreign intervention is always a possibility and the game requires negotiations with European powers that must be drawn into the conflict or made to stay out.[57]

Like *Eastern Front, Forge of Freedom* is turn-based. However, the speed of action can be adjusted, producing either a leisurely game or a much more rapid and in some ways more stressful one. The first step is to mobilize resources while setting aside some of them for the purpose of research and development. At a later point in the game, that research and development translates into better weapons. Next one forms brigades – it is at the brigade level that the game is played – by equipping them with one of over fifty types of period firearms and artillery. Brigades may be further customized by adding various kinds of personnel and equipment, including sharpshooters, Zouaves, reconnaissance balloons, horse artillery, raiders, scouts, engineers, and signals personnel. It is even possible to choose one's units' standards "from a collection of over 700 authentic flags." Similar methods are used in building up a navy.

The military action proper takes place on a map covering the territory from Minnesota to Texas and from Maine to Florida. Here the opposing forces advance, retreat, clash, outflank, join, separate, protect lines of communication, or set out to cut them: in short, perform a great many of the things that real-life armies do. Naval action in the form of blockade running, hunting blockade runners, blockading ports, launching amphibious assaults, and bombarding forts is also available. A list of a thousand generals is provided so that players can choose which one they want to put in command of this or that operation. Battles can be resolved either quickly, by having the computer make the necessary calculations and instantly display the results to the accompaniment

---

[56] See "American Civil War Video Games," at: http://en.wikipedia.org/wiki/Category: American_Civil_War_video_game.

[57] See "Battleforge News," at: www.battleforgenews.com/Battleforge-News/7/Build-Unique-Armies-and-Team-Up-for-Epic-Battles-in-a-New-Fantasy-RTS-Game.html, and many similar discussions online.

of a suitable-looking symbol, or else by zooming in on the appropriate place on the map. Doing so yields a detailed representation of hex-covered terrain over which the engagement is "fought" move by tactical move. Fatigue, morale, supply, facing, formation, time of day, reinforcements, command and control, weather, and even battlefield smoke are all included and play a role in deciding the outcome. In these and countless other ways, the progress made since *Eastern Front* is dramatic.

In the case of hexed games, incomplete rules do not necessarily spoil or invalidate a game. This is because players can make them up as they go, proceeding on their own steam. Some, in fact, prefer it that way. They match their ingenuity against that of the designers in an attempt to improve the game – their game – and derive more out of it. By contrast, computerized games do not allow such liberties to be taken but require that every problem be perfectly comprehended and solved in advance. Scant wonder perfection is seldom achieved at the outset so that de-bugging can be a difficult and prolonged process. Even so, few are the games incorporating artificial intelligence of this kind that clever humans cannot outwit if they really want to.

As with all games, the greatest advantage that computerized ones have over conventional learning is the interactive nature of the learning process. So is the opportunity to experiment and discover which factors (within the limits of the program) are most important, how they change over time, and so on. Another option often brought up by players who have bought the games is to incorporate hypertext that will allow them to learn more about what they are doing. Returning to *Forge of Freedom*, some players have volunteered to research and write biographies of the 1,000 generals whom players may call out of limbo, so to speak. Thus study reinforces play, and play reinforces study So much for the often-heard claim that wargaming is a waste of time. Looking back on the days when my own son engaged in it, I believe that it is teachers, many of whom are unfamiliar with the field, who do not understand.

In principle the value of this kind of game not merely for amateurs interested in entertainment or in studying history but for the professional military should be obvious. Provided only the necessary programs are written, commanders can practice their jobs, handling such matters as intelligence, planning, operations, manpower, logistics, medical services, and much more. A well-constructed game, with players working in groups instead of as individuals, may also teach the members of those groups to work together and help mold them into a cohesive, smooth-functioning team. It can certainly help identify troublemakers who may then be weeded out. Provided sufficient intelligence is available before each campaign, a model may be constructed and run, allowing different force mixes, strategies, and outcomes to be tested.

In practice doing all this can be very problematic. First, culling the necessary detailed information and then programming a computer with the necessary algorithms is very time-consuming. One can, of course, use peacetime in order to create a large number of games and keep them in reserve. However, doing so is wasteful and in any case it is impossible to foresee every eventuality. Second, a wide gap usually separates the needs of amateurs from those of professional soldiers. As *Eastern Front* illustrates very well, the former normally demand no more than that a game be up to date – in other words, that it incorporate whatever technology is considered reasonably advanced for the time – that it be sufficiently playable, and that the price will be one they can afford. Realism is certainly a factor, but as the availability on the market of any number of fantasy games shows, not necessarily the most important one.

By contrast, military professionals have no use for games that are clearly and unambiguously disconnected from the "real" world. For them wargames are a much more serious business on which their own lives, and those of others, may eventually depend. While price may be less of a factor, they must demand a much higher level of both realism and of detail. Regardless of whether the objective is training or planning, if that realism and that detail are lacking they may well end up with the wrong lessons. To make the problem more serious still, officers in particular are a competitive lot. After all, that is the way they are selected, trained, and promoted. This entails the danger that, in their eagerness to score a victory either over human opponents or the computer, they will learn how to play the game rather than wage or fight a war.

Focusing once again on the US military as the most important of the lot, and also as the one about which most is known, it would seem that they were slow to get off the mark. Conservatism apart, possibly one reason for this was precisely that early games were not sufficiently realistic and did not simulate war in sufficient detail to meet their needs. According to James Dunnigan, who in many ways is to the world of commercial wargaming what Andy Marshall is to the military one, and who, besides having written a book on it, has worked for the military, they only got in on the act during the mid 1980s. Even then they did so only because the growing numbers of commercial games being produced and sold all around them could no longer be ignored. What information is available points to the conclusion that the field remains split among the services, each with its own training organizations, schools, academies, colleges, and planning agencies. Though the subject is obviously of enormous importance, a coherent picture of what goes on is all but impossible to obtain.

A list of games, drawn up by Dunnigan and dating to the end of the 1990s, does at least provide some idea of the stuff that the military have been interested in.[58] Many seem to have had something to do with Andy Marshall, who for several decades has funded efforts to create them and sponsored conferences dedicated to them. Apparently some were never completed, having fallen victim to interservice friction, or to budget cuts, or to technical difficulties. At the top

---

[58] Dunnigan, *Wargames Handbook*, pp. 239–55.

of the pyramid were the so-called Title Ten (or Title X) games. With a genealogy going back to 1961, they were operated by the Joint Chiefs of Staff and the service chiefs who used them to determine future military needs, as well as testing scenarios, equipment, and methods: examples are the Global Engagement games.[59] Next in importance came the strategic-level games that the theater commanders-in-chief, or CINCs, used to plan, and sometimes fight, campaigns. Further down still were operational- and tactical-level war-games. A good example was Warfighter's *Simulation 2000* (*WarSim*), aimed at training army commanders from theater level all the way to that of battalion headquarters.

Naturally, the lower the level in the hierarchy that any game represented, the smaller the impact it had on the forces as a whole. The lower the level, too, the more it tended to overlap or merge with the kind of simulators, or shooters, which will preoccupy us in the next section. Many games were designed to be played by widely dispersed personnel, a proposition that, though cheap in relation to bringing them together at a single spot, can still be very expensive indeed. The cost ran into many hundreds of millions of dollars and is said to have reached $8.6 billion in 2007.[60] If the figure is correct then it amounts to over 1 percent of the defense budget, trend rising.

Still following Dunnigan, who has extensive experience in working both in the commercial world and with the military, wargames used by the military tend to suffer from several problems. One is the need to satisfy the requirements of many different user organizations each of which does not wish to buy the game off the shelf but actively attempts to pull it in its own direction. Often the outcome is great complexity and compromises that end up, like the famous camel that was created by a committee, by satisfying nobody. Adding more and more features in the name of "realism" also causes the cost to go up, ultimately leading to diminishing returns. Much of the data that goes into the programs is classified: as a result, checking on whether it is correct is difficult, and errors, once they have crept in, tend to stay.[61] Secrecy also makes it hard to update the games as needed. Finally, those who design, manufacture, and market games in the commercial world are obliged to pay attention to users' demands, such as ease of play and creating a good interface between player and game. Their counterparts working in, or for, the military, are not nearly as affected by these concerns. On occasion this can lead to bad games that people simply do not want to play.

---

[59] D. O. Ross, "Investigating the Fundamentals of the Third Generation Wargaming," Rome, NY: AFRL/Rish, 2–8, p. 3, at: http://scholar.google.co.il/scholar?q=Investigating+the+Fundamentals+of+the+Third+Generation&hl=iw&as_sdt=0&as_vis=1&oi=scholart.

[60] Devry University newsletter, at www.devry.edu/assets/pdf/degree-programs/simulation-game-programming-careers-guide.pdf.

[61] Watts, "Diagnostic Observations on Theater-Level War Gaming," pp. 15–16.

Since much of the work is oriented towards the future rather than the past, validation, i.e. making sure that the game represents something "real" and is not simply a figment of somebody's imagination, presents a serious challenge. Too often, too, the adage that the military always plans for the last war it fought comes true. Last but not least, the games played at the Pentagon and similar buildings around the world are anything but independent of the "real" world. To the contrary, they are funded by, and held on behalf of, enormously powerful organizations. The outcomes are often used to advance very concrete goals. The national interest, not to mention billions of dollars as well as many lives, may be at stake. Under such circumstances, inevitably there is a motive for pushing the results in this direction or that or ignoring them if they do not fit one's interests.

As with all other military-type games from Reisswitz on, there is no way to ensure that the games will reflect future reality or that future reality will be reflected in the games. Regardless of how sophisticated and how detailed they are, in the end whether this does or does not happen is almost entirely a question of luck. One way to narrow the gap, as well as motivating participants in the game, is to use real data provided by real intelligence assets. The following story, told by General Norman Schwarzkopf of Gulf War fame in his autobiography, gives some impression of what wargaming at its best can do.[62] In July 1990 Central Command in Florida, of which Schwarzkopf was the commander, was busy preparing its annual wargame, code-named Internal Look. The computerized game, which Schwarzkopf describes as the headquarters equivalent of a flight simulator, was scheduled to stretch over eight sessions lasting twenty hours each. The objective was to enable the participants to practice many of the things they would be doing in war, including sorting out battlefield reports, issuing orders, directing logistic flows, and coordinating the movements of land, air, and sea forces. The scenario, which was first devised in the early 1980s, and was in fact hopelessly outdated, was a Soviet invasion of Iran heading towards the Persian Gulf that had to be stopped.

As the first rumblings of upcoming problems started to be heard, it was decided to change the scenario so as to represent a war with Iraq instead. While some of the data in the computer had to be changed, the fact that the theater of war was roughly the same one must have come in handy. A stream of intelligence coming from the Gulf countries had to be simulated. Where things became really interesting was when real reports coming out of the Middle East started being incorporated, to the point where game and reality became hard to keep apart. So great was the potential for confusion that messages forming part of the game had to be clearly stamped with the word, "exercise." When the decision to send US troops to the Gulf was made, at least the

---

[62] H. N. Schwarzkopf, *It Doesn't Take a Hero*, New York: Bantam, 1992, pp. 336, 337, 348.

preliminary work, involving the mechanics of assembling a huge force, sending it to the Gulf, and deploying and sustaining it there, had already been done.

Lost in virtual reality

The computerized strategy games described in the previous section go back to hexed games, Reisswitz-type games, and ultimately to chess and its equivalents. Nowhere is this more evident than in the fact that, in them as well as BOGSAT-type political-military games, players, instead of directly interacting with each other in real time (which itself may be either "real" time or game time), have to take turns. The turns are both cause and consequence of the fact that the actual fighting, or perhaps I should say violence, is left out. Either the figures capture one another, as in chess, or else they surround each other, as in Go. In other games the outcome of combat is determined with the aid of special tables and random numbers which are generated either by dice or a computer. However it is done, since the nitty-gritty of fighting is absent games of this kind are usually better at simulating the higher levels of war than the lower ones.

The shooting games discussed in the present section have a very different genealogy. Just as the Mississippi and the Missouri meet to form a single river, so the shooters owe their generation to two separate devices, i.e. flight simulators on the one hand and certain amusement machines on the other. To start with flight simulators: the earliest pilots were self-trained. They and their immediate successors used real machines even for the initial stages of training, leading to heavy casualties. During World War I training pilots was turned into a mass enterprise. Many air corps (there were no air forces yet), or branches, or services, or whatever they were called, started using simulators to familiarize trainees with the basic skills that flying an airplane requires. For example, the French, who produced more pilots than anybody else, had a clipped-wing contraption known as the *Bleriot roulant*. Mounted atop a swivel, it gave trainees a rudimentary feel of how the controls worked.[63]

Starting in the late 1920s the firm most associated with simulators was Link, of Binghamton, New York. At first, demand was slow, but it picked up in 1934 following a training disaster during which a dozen army pilots lost their lives in a single week. Later, so much did it dominate the field that for several decades the machines were known simply as Links.[64] With their twelve-foot wingspan, they stood to real aircraft as hobbyhorses stand to real horses and were designed to simulate an aircraft's interior and controls. The latter were attached to hydraulic or pneumatic devices that went some way toward simulating the

---

[63] See, for the technical details, "Bleriot XI," at: http://en.wikipedia.org/wiki/Bl%C3%A9riot_XI.

[64] See, for the history of flight simulators, Flight Simulator, at http://en.wikipedia.org/wiki/Flight_simulator; also Halter, *From Sun Tzu to XBox*, pp. 147–9.

aircraft's movements, i.e. yawing, rolling, and pitching. Later additional controls such as a throttle were also added. Other companies followed. During the salad days of World War II the firm of Link alone produced and installed about 10,000 simulators in the US, Canada, and Britain. They served to teach the basics of flight as well as some specialized skills such as navigation, night flying, and instrument flying. After 1945 both the military and the airlines continued to use them while adding a steady stream of refinements. Chief among them were movies, later replaced by TV images, which simulated the outside environment and were coordinated with the controls. This enabled pilots to practice maneuvers, especially landing at unfamiliar airports, prior to executing them in reality. Emphasizing the connection between training and entertainment, occasionally the machines were stationed in exhibitions and amusement parks where the public could try them out.

As early as World War I some air services also began experimenting with specialized devices to teach pilots how to fire their machine guns while taking into account the relative speed and angle at which their aircraft, and the ones at which they were aiming, were flying. The technique, which takes time and effort to master, is known as deflection shooting.[65] However, firing at real aircraft was much too expensive and much too dangerous. Consequently flight simulators could not shoot, neither could the devices with which firing was taught fly. A way had to be found to build devices capable of simulated shooting at fast-flying, rapidly maneuvering targets. One widely used method was to attach movie cameras to the aircraft's sights and firing button. Provided enough money was available, the moves of each aircraft, shell, or rocket could also be monitored by telemetry devices on the ground. The results could be fed into the all-knowing computer and used for training and post-action analysis.[66] Even so, having pilots and aircraft spend so and so many hours in the air each year preparing for combat that would be over in seconds remained an expensive proposition.

In the event, the initial stimulus toward a solution came from an altogether unexpected direction. From the 1930s on, visitors to arcades had been familiar with games such as pinball which enabled them to interact with machines. Originally these machines had been mechanically operated, but late in the 1950s electromagnetic versions of them started to be marketed. These were the years when television was spreading like wildfire. In principle, if not in

[65] See W. E. C. Crossman, "Dry Shooting for Airplane Gunners," *Popular Science*, 94, 1, January 1919, p. 13, at http://books.google.co.il/books?id=HykDAAAAMBAJ&pg= PA13&lpg=PA13&dq=%22dry+shooting+for+airplane+gunners%22&source=bl&ots=IN soMTg9sL&sig=r9thuUNu6 mg6DH17C8Ikg4-clk&hl=iw&ei=SA9uTZrnNYKj8QPahvj 4Dg&sa=X&oi=book_result&ct=result&resnum=1&ved=0CBYQ6AEwAA#v=onepage&q= %22dry%20shooting%20for%20airplane%20gunners%22&f=false.

[66] See, on AFWET (Air Force Weapons Effectiveness Testing) program, Wilson, *The Bomb and the Computer*, p. 89.

practice, it was a comparatively minor step to get rid of the mechanical elements altogether, replacing them with blips on a screen.[67]

The blips themselves could be made to represent practically anything from primeval monsters to futuristic flying saucers and from individual soldiers trying to bayonet their opponents to tanks firing at anything under the sun (or moon and stars). Depending on the game, the nature of the task that the onscreen images had to perform could vary widely. He, she, or it might be trying to avoid a crash while racing a motorcycle amidst traffic along a winding course. Alternatively the task might be to find a way towards a given goal while overcoming various obstacles, or else – of course – to shoot up virtual opponents. As the game progressed, along with the player's skill, the obstacles with which the computer confronted him or her, or else the speed at which the action proceeded, or both, increased. The outcome was to make play more and more difficult. The game lasted until either time ran out, as in arcade-mounted, quarter-operated machines, or else when the limits of human performance were reached. To make up for the growing difficulty players, or rather the blips that represented them, were often granted multiple lives – an extremely unrealistic feature, or course, but one which, if a game was to be playable, was hard to avoid.

Given that it literally consists of nothing, the environment that was easiest to model in the extremely limited memory of contemporary computers was outer space. Another reason why designers preferred it was because it was unfamiliar, thus appealing to players' imagination and making it harder for them to criticize the game.[68] Both lines of reasoning probably explain why the very first interactive "shooter"-type computer wargame was *Spacewar* (1961).[69] Like many of its successors, *Spacewar* could be played either by one person against the computer or by two persons against one another. Either way, it was a question of maneuvering spaceships, each with a limited supply of missiles and fuel, against one another. Hits produced most satisfying explosions followed by a void. Subsequent versions of the game included a scrolling map of the stars as well as a sun that made its impact felt through the pull of gravity, swallowing up spaceships that came too close to it. These and other additions made the players' task somewhat more complicated and more interesting.

The factor that truly made *Spacewar* revolutionary, though, was that players, instead of taking turns, interacted in "real" time. To that extent it represented nothing less than a return to the kind of wargames, from single combat through gladiatorial fights and tournaments to the duel in some of its forms, described in

[67] See, for the history of the game, "Pinball" at: http://en.wikipedia.org/wiki/Pinball.
[68] C. Crawford, *The Art of Computer Game Design*, 1982, Chapter 3, at: http://arcarc.xmission.com/Magazines%20and%20Books/Art%20of%20Game%20Design.pdf.
[69] See, for what follows, S. L. Kent, *The Ultimate History of Video Games*, New York: Three Rivers, 2001, pp. 18, 64, 67, 116–17.

Chapters 1 to 3 of the present volume. To restate the idea in an even more extreme form: whatever shortcomings *Spacewar* and its successors may have had, it reintroduced time – the very factor Napoleon once said was more precious than space, because having been lost it could never be regained[70] – into wargaming. A greater step towards realism, though it was of a special and in some ways very limited kind, can hardly be imagined. The computer on which the game was designed and played, a Digital Equipment Corporation PDP-1, had the advantage that it was one of the first to sport a screen, or cathode ray tube, as it was known at the time. Small by contemporary standards, it only took seventeen square feet of floor space and cost a mere 120,000 1961 dollars. Scant wonder players were just a few students in first-class academic institutions, as the creator of *Spacewar*, Steve Russell, himself was. Indeed the entire thing was the outcome, not of some deadly serious, goal-oriented effort, but of playful interaction among the members of the MIT Student Tech Model Railway Club.[71]

From Cambridge the game spread to other campuses. By 1963, so popular had it become that Stanford University's Computer Studies Department for one was obliged to announce a "no *Spacewar*" policy during business hours and enforce it rather strictly. As the price of computers started declining in the 1970s, they became more affordable, if not yet by individuals at home, then by commercial operators in arcades. Not all video games designed for the purpose sought to represent some kind of violent struggle, but many if not most did. As one of the early programmers noted, it seemed as if players could not have enough of them.[72] Three notable early games were *Tank* (1974), *Sea Wolf*, and *Space Invaders* (both 1978). The players in *Tank* maneuvered their vehicles, avoided mines, and fired, victory going to the side with the highest number of points at the time the game ended. In *Sea Wolf* they sat behind the sights of a submarine and launched torpedoes at various kinds of "enemy" ships. *Space Invaders* showed the aliens advancing in a massive, relentless, rectangular formation of eight by five. Players had to shoot them down before they could reach the ground while avoiding descending enemy missiles. Additional points could be earned by blowing up flying saucers that flew across the screen from time to time. Since the friendly "turrets" only offered limited shelter, and since the aliens kept on increasing the pace, there was no way a player could stop them in their tracks and win the game. The best one could hope for was to obtain the highest score for the day.

As one of Russell's original comrades in arms later wrote, "these [games] are pretty much all of a piece. After some preliminary foofaraw to get everyone's

---

[70] *La Correspondance de Napoléon 1er*, Paris: Plon, 1863, vol. XVIII, p. 218, no. 14707.
[71] See T. Donovan, *Replay: The History of Video Games*, Lewes: Yellow Ant, 2010, pp. 9–11.
[72] Chris Crawford, quoted in Halter, *From Sun Tzu to XBox*, p. 87.

name right, a bunch of overdeveloped Hardy Boys go trekking off through the universe to punch up the latest gang of galactic goons, blow up a few planets, kill all sorts of nasty life forms, and just have a heck of a good time."[73] Usually that was all there was to it: some subsequent games presenting the player with multiple opponents also demanded that, before responding, he or she evaluate those opponents by the speed with which they made their advance, the amount of "damage" they could inflict, and so on. In a real war of any size, of course, these functions would be performed by numerous individuals working as a team, or else, as with anti-aircraft and anti-missile defenses, by teams made up of both humans and computers or even of computers alone. Unsurprisingly, on occasion so great were the demands that a game made on players that it had to be withdrawn.[74] All the player's actions were carried out not in writing but by manipulating levers, moving joysticks, and pressing buttons. Compared with chess as well as Reisswitz- and BOGSAT-type games, the greatest advantage of shooting games was that players did not have to take turns. To that extent they were much more realistic than any kind of board or map games could ever be. The absence of turns also enabled play to develop much faster than before. Gone was the need for day-long sessions and adjournments. These were major reasons for the shooters' popularity.

    Early on, the fact that the games were associated with pinball, which in turn was supposed to be associated with the Mafia, who were said to be blackmailing arcade owners, worked against them. Some attempts were even made to ban them altogether.[75] Later the reasons for opposing them shifted. Not everybody liked the emphasis the games placed on manual skills as opposed to intellectual ones. Some critics claimed, as they always do when youth is interested in things they themselves are too old to learn, that the games were devoid of "educa-tional" content. As such they were a waste of time, led to that worst of all bad things, addiction, and sometimes involved extreme brutality that might turn players into raging psychopaths (if, perhaps, those who played them were not psychopaths already). Since many players moved their hips in a suggestive way while hitting the firing buttons in particular, the games also threatened their sexual morality. In November 1982 no less a figure than the US Surgeon General, Dr. Everett Koop, publicly stated that the games were causing exten-sive mental and physical harm. Everything in them was "zap the enemy," he claimed, and nothing "constructive" was being done.[76] Apparently learning to "fly," say, a World War II Mustang aircraft, as well as mastering the kind of sophisticated background knowledge required to select various missions and "fight" Messerschmitts in a sensible way, do not count as "constructive."

[73] J. M. Graetz, quoted ibid., p. 76.
[74] Kent, The Ultimate History of Video Games, p. 139.   [75] Donovan, Replay, p. 25.
[76] Ibid., p. 95.

Koop himself was sufficiently fair-minded to concede that he did not have evidence to back up his claims. But this did not prevent the media, parents, and of course scholars from such disciplines as psychology and sociology from taking up the issue. Some of the criticism stuck, leading to "voluntary self-restraint" on the part of the industry and/or the introduction of various rating systems. On other occasions media reports that a game was indeed extremely violent merely led to attempts to get around the systems in question and may actually have increased sales, as controversy, attempts at censorship, and the publicity that attends them so often do.[77] The ability to tolerate the occasionally unearthly noises the machines generated apart, the chief qualities players required and still require are good eyesight, excellent motor coordination, and extreme concentration. All three are highly relevant to waging real war, especially modern war, and especially at the technical and tactical levels where individuals or small numbers of troops fight each other at close quarters. From President Reagan down, this fact caused some pundits, tongue in cheek, to suggest that America's youth might be provided with an unlimited supply of quarters so as to train for it.[78]

Since then, the poor misguided teenagers who played the games during the 1980s have grown up and raised teenagers of their own. *Pace* Koop and countless others, most of them seem to have developed into normal function-ing human beings. Nevertheless, concerns about the games remain as lively as ever. Just one article, entitled "Video Games, Aggressive Thoughts, Feelings, and Behavior in the Laboratory and in Life," was quoted no fewer than 783 times in the scholarly literature alone.[79] Needless to say, it argued that "real-life violent video game play was positively related to aggressive behavior and delinquency ... [whereas] academic achievement was negatively related to overall amount of time spent playing video games." Some games, notably one called *Medal of Honor* and set in Afghanistan, gave rise to objections not because they were time-consuming or addictive or brutal, but because they permitted players to "fire" at troops belonging to their own countries. Both the Canadian and British ministers of defense have denounced the game as unpatriotic, and in the US it was banned from being sold on base.[80] One can only conclude that the rules that govern real-life war also apply to that which is waged onscreen. For us to inflict violence on others is OK, but for them to do the same on us is not.

---

[77] See *ibid.*, pp. 43, 234.
[78] Talk at Epcot, March 1983, at: www.reagan.utexas.edu/archives/speeches/1983/30883a.htm.
[79] C. A. Anderson and K. E. Dill, "Video Games, Aggressive Thoughts, Feelings, and Behavior in the Laboratory and in Life," *Journal of Personality and Social Psychology*, 78, 4, 2000, pp. 772–90.
[80] *Medal of Honor* (2010 video game), at: http://en.wikipedia.org/wiki/Medal_of_Honor_(2010_video_game)

None of this has prevented the game designers from creating more and more sophisticated games. The number of shooter-type games, including those that involved not soldiers but gangsters or aliens, which have been brought to the market must run into the thousands. They sport not only soldiers and guerrillas but cowboys and gangsters and aliens and every kind of imaginary monster. Many only sold a few copies and rapidly disappeared, attracting little notice. A few became bestsellers that enriched those who designed them, produced them, and sold them. *Space Invaders* apart, computerized shooter-type games that have sold millions of copies include *Missile Command, Space Armada, Space Battle, Halo, Call of Duty*, and *Gears of War*.[81] The last-mentioned focuses on the troops of Delta Squad, an elite force made up of somewhat wild-looking types who seem much more like GI Joe characters and "profes-sional" wrestlers than the kind of soldiers one meets in the field, let alone on the street. They fight to save the human inhabitants of a fictional planet from a subterranean enemy known as the Locust Horde.[82] Some games, in particular one called *Doom* (1993), are notable for allowing players a wide choice of weapons. They include a pistol, brass-knuckled fists, a chainsaw, a shotgun, a chaingun, a rocket launcher, a plasma rifle, and the immensely powerful BFG (Bio Force Gun) 9,000 firing green plasma shells.[83] *Doom*, incidentally, made it to the list of the top fifty video game weapons of all time. Some players even claimed it made them "swoon."[84]

In the manner of Hollywood follow-up movies, many games have been updated and expanded at least once. Indeed some are based on movies and TV series, and the opposite is also true. As the number of computers used in every field of life grew, the borders separating entertainment from "serious" gaming and "serious" gaming from war became increasingly fuzzy.[85] Perhaps the best-known movie that was turned into a game was Steven Spielberg's *Band of Brothers*, but others are not far behind. As with a great many other commer-cial products, predicting which game would be a flop and which one would succeed was, and remains, almost impossible. Apparently a number of factors are involved: ease of use (the harder a game is to learn, the fewer, presumably, the people prepared to make the effort needed to master it), imagination (an elusive quality, but one that is absolutely essential), characters that players are able to identify with, and much more. Realism and artistic quality (including the quality of the graphics), special effects (such as sound) can also be very important. Extreme brutality may be attractive to some. Some players would

[81] List of best-selling video games at: http://en.wikipedia.org/wiki/List_of_best-selling_video_games.
[82] See *Gears of War* at: http://en.wikipedia.org/wiki/Gears_of_War.
[83] *Doom* (video game) at: http://en.wikipedia.org/wiki/Doom_(video_game).
[84] BGF 9000 at: http://en.wikipedia.org/wiki/BFG_9000.
[85] See on this T. Lenoir, "All War is Simulation: The Military-Entertainment Complex," *Configurations*, 8, 2000, pp. 289–335.

like nothing so much as to drop a nuclear weapon on Mecca; here and there a designer was shocked to receive letters from players who, contrary to his own intentions, seemed to enjoy killing off entire "populations."[86] However, as with all other features, there seems to be no simple link between the amount of onscreen gore and the number of copies sold.

As with movies, timing may be critically important. Quite often external events that have nothing to do with a game's contents, its characteristics, and its quality will have a determining impact on whether or not it succeeds in the shops; realizing this, producers have been accelerating the speed with which a "real" war is transformed into a game from weeks to days. Finally, customers' demands do not remain stationary but develop over time. As new games are published, older ones, again like so many other products, are pushed aside. Which is not to say that, as also happens with so many other products from vintage cars down, there are no aficionados who will continue to look for them, buy them, and play them for precisely that reason. Indeed some producers, notably id Software, have generously allowed not only some of their games but the code in which they were written to be published online. They thus enable those aficionados to tinker with them and come up with their own versions.

Looking back over the decades since their inception, three inter-related factors in particular seem to be driving computer wargames along. First, individual games often provide far more options than their predecessors did. Many if not most games may be played at various speeds, increasing levels of difficulty, and so on. Instead of only being able, say, to "fly" one kind of aircraft, players may choose among several different ones. "Action" may take place during daylight or, if one prefers, by night. Missions can also be varied. Instead of using one kind of ammunition against the "enemy," many recent games allow players to select among several different ones, thus exercising their knowledge and skill in matching means to ends. All this bears some resemblance to various kinds of gladiators being matched with each other for added interest, and greatly increases what is sometimes referred to as a game's replay value.

Second, contrary to the popular image of them as empty-headed teenagers who get a kick by zapping whomever and whatever they meet onscreen, many players are highly educated and curious. To suit them, many games have special boxes that the player can open by the click of a mouse, allowing him or her to obtain more information, either in order to make an informed choice concerning their play or simply by way of background knowledge. Of course there is the danger that the introduction of too many different features will confuse players. As long as that does not happen, though, it probably makes play more interesting and extends the life of any given game.

---

[86] Richard Garriott as quoted in Donovan, *Replay*, p. 147; Halter, *From Sun Tzu to Xbox*, pp. 302–3.

Third, and in the view of some most important of all, the quality of the graphics has improved dramatically. In first-person games this applies to the window through which the player watches whatever is being displayed. It may, say, be made to look like the cockpit of a real aircraft, complete with functioning instrumentation that will display such things as the aircraft's angle to the horizon, airspeed, a gain or loss of altitude, remaining fuel reserves, and the like. In third-person games it also applies to the figure, say a muscleman or a soldier or a tank or a ship, which represents the player on the screen and whose movements and actions he or she controls. In both kinds of games it applies to the opponent or opponents that must be shot at or otherwise overcome, as well as the environment in which the action unfolds. Gone are the days when games were necessarily played in empty, featureless space. Greater computing power also permitted shading to be introduced, causing games to lose most of their original, rather garish character. Overall, the effect of improved graphics has been to close the gap between reality and what was now known as "virtual reality." As an ad for *Call of Duty 2* (2005) put it, "this is as close to war as you ever want to get."

This was particularly the case because the games' big brothers, i.e. flight simulators, also started making use of computers from the late 1960s. As before, one objective was to help pilots acquire better flying skills, practice various emergencies that were too dangerous to be rehearsed live, and the like. From the point of view of wargames, of greater importance was the attempt to represent the outside world more accurately while also achieving a better match between the moves of the simulator and what the pilot could see of that world. From there it was a short step to adding more blips that represented enemy aircraft as well as other kinds of targets, such as anti-aircraft defenses or oil refineries or power stations, that had to be attacked.

At first it was necessary to build dedicated machines for each type of aircraft and environment, an enormously expensive proposition. Later general-purpose computers with sufficient power changed this situation. To replace an American F-16 fighting an Iraqi Mirage F-1 by a Soviet MIG-29 fighting an American F-15 all a player had to do was to change a cassette or disk. At some time during the 1970s simulators and shooter-type games met, just as the Mississippi and the Missouri do. Later they became almost identical. A simulator was little more than a complex game, whereas a game was but a simplified simulator. An important step in this direction was a game by the name of *Battlezone* (1980), which actually had a sort of periscope players had to press their faces to, creating the illusion of viewing the world through the vision slit of a tank.[87] Indeed a cynic might argue that the most obvious difference between them was that games (and movies) had music whereas simulators (and

[87] *Battlezone* (1980 movie game) at: http://en.wikipedia.org/wiki/Battlezone_(1980_video_game)

everyday reality) did not. A teenager with a personal computer and a few dollars to spend could now play at being, say, an F-18 pilot setting out on a mission to enforce the "no-fly zone" in Iraq. Conversely, the F-18 pilot could do more of his training at home.

As episodes such as the Japanese preparations for the attacks on Pearl Harbor and Midway illustrate only too clearly, high-level wargamers have often come under political pressure to modify either the games themselves or their outcomes. The switch from manual to computerized ones did little to change this fact: the higher the stakes, the less likely it is that commanders and other senior decision-makers will change their views merely because a young computer programmer, exercising what to many people is an arcane art, has made things turn out in such and such a way. By contrast, shooting-type games are used mainly at fairly low levels – hardly ever above that of the battalion. Most represent companies, platoons, squads, or even individual soldiers. Hence there is some reason to think that they are less affected by this problem.

Other things being equal, the best education and training have always been of the kind that soldiers found challenging and that they engaged in not just because they had to but freely. As computer-driven technology enabled simulations that were closer and closer to reality to be created, the distinction between education and training on the one hand and entertainment on the other began to be lost. Nor was it long before the services started thinking of ways to take advantage of this fact. Recruiters prowled arcades, looking for youths who might like to switch from, say, an onscreen tank to the real thing. Generals called on commercial wargaming companies, examined what was available, and signed contracts to modify existing games or design new ones. Among the earliest products was *Army Battlezone*, a variation on the previously mentioned *Battlezone* reprogrammed in such a way as to take into account many different kinds of tanks and other vehicles as well as more realistic ballistics. As in many other fields since 1990 or so, military and civilian technology began to converge.[88]

Particularly successful in this respect, and an example for all the rest, was *America's Army*. Paid for by the government, it may be downloaded for free. To quote the designers, the objective was to offer potential recruits "the most true-to-life Army experience, allowing players to create a soldier and lead him through the excitement of an Army career." Some follow-up versions can even be played on a mobile phone. Needless to say, there were complaints about the game serving as one more tool in the ongoing militarization of American society. Such claims, incidentally, date back at least as far as the last years of the nineteenth century when similar ones were made in reference to toy soldiers.[89] They did not, however, affect the game's popularity.[90] As one

---

[88] "War Games," *The Economist*, October 12, 2009.
[89] Halter, *From Sun Tzu to XBox*, p. 50.
[90] See *America's Army* at: http://en.wikipedia.org/wiki/America's_Army.

insightful critic wrote in the *New York Times*: "Nothing beats going in and seeing what the Army really does . . . without actually having to do it."[91]

Passing from recruitment to training, compared with other training methods that carried on with the aid of computer games/simulators has several important advantages. First, it is cheap: once the equipment is available and the initial program has been written, tested, and debugged, it can be infinitely reproduced, easily distributed, and played over and over again at practically no added cost. The wear and tear that other training methods produce is all but eliminated. Second, it is realistic since opponents can "really" fire at each other. By so doing, they incorporate, at least to some extent, some of the nervous strain of war in ways that many other kinds of wargames, particularly Reisswitz-type ones and BOGSATs, do not capture nearly as well. Third, it is safe since errors do not have fatal consequences. Fourth, training can be interrupted and resumed at any desirable point or location. This increases flexibility and makes it much easier to arrange schedules and timetables of every kind.[92]

Modern simulators are capable of reproducing the aircraft themselves, complete with controls, movements, noise, and much else. To this are added friendly as well as hostile aircraft as well as the external world as perceived by the pilot with the aid of his eyesight, or radar, or FLIR (Forward Looking Infra Red), or whatever.[93] All these different elements, moreover, must be carefully coordinated with each other, a feat that only powerful computers enable the designers to achieve. The outcome is some of the most complex machines ever built. The time was to come when almost any kind of engagement could be simulated as aircraft, ships, and vehicles, either friendly or hostile, received information, maneuvered this way and that, were fired at, and fired back.

For many years play was a matter of one trainee/player per computer, or, perhaps one should say, one computer per trainee/player. More recently the Internet, linking together numerous computers, has enabled entire squadrons or units to "fight" one another onscreen just as those who play *World of Warcraft* do. This is true even when the players remain widely dispersed in geographical space, although in that case some time-lags may become noticeable even when working with machines that exchange information at the speed of light. One example is the Close Combat Tactical Simulation system for training army mechanized infantry and armor units that replicates combat vehicles, tactical vehicles, and weapons systems interacting in real time with

[91] B. Kennedy, "Uncle Sam Wants You (to Play this Game)," *New York Times*, July 11, 2002.

[92] M. Macedonia, "Games Soldiers Play," *Spectrum*, March 2002, p. 35.

[93] See, on the last-named, Forward Looking Infra Red at: http://en.wikipedia.org/wiki/Forward_looking_infrared.

each other and semiautonomous opposing forces.[94] Another is the Joint
Tactical Combat Training System (JTCTS). It is described, somewhat ponder-
ously, as a joint effort by the navy and air force to create a virtual simulation at
the battle group level in which combat participants will interact with live and
simulated targets detected and displayed by platform sensors. A third is the
Synthetic Theater of War (STOW) program. This particular system was meant
"to integrate virtual simulation (troops in simulators fighting on a synthetic
battlefield), constructive simulation (war games), and live maneuvers to provide a training environment for various levels of exercise."

The number of shooter-type simulators used by all three services during the
first decade of the twenty-first century must have run into the hundreds, if not
more. Some were new, some old, some extremely sophisticated, some crude and
out of date. As with many if not most other types of military equipment, what
explains the mix is the cost of the systems which can easily run into the
hundreds of millions of dollars each. Both for technical reasons and because
of the constant need for updates, making all of them work together under the
aegis of the Joint Simulation System or JSIMS is an ongoing task too daunting
for the imagination to grasp. As in the case of the "real" military world which it
is supposed to simulate, most probably it will never be completed.

At a lower level, though, simulators, by drawing on fields as different as
ergonomics, cognitive psychology, painting, acoustics, and a host of others have
been making such good progress that the line between the "real" world and the
simulated (or virtual) one is becoming more and more blurred. One indication
of this fact is the growth of a new phenomenon – known as simulator sickness.
Simulator sickness is much like motion sickness, only in reverse. Apparently the
cause is a mismatch between what a simulator makes a pilot see in virtual reality
and what his or her vestibular system registers. For example, he may be sitting
upright while the image of the outside world being fed to his display board or
helmet tells him that he is "actually" hanging upside down. Symptoms can
include eyestrain, blurred vision and difficulty in focusing, mental disorienta-
tion, apathy, drowsiness, fatigue, headache, and nausea, up to and including
vomiting. Even though fighter pilots are specially selected for their ability to
resist motion sickness, and even though they are used to the machines, between
20 and 40 percent of them are said to suffer from it.[95]

At least one fighting game, *Trekken Torture*, provides players with electrified
armbands that convert each hit taken into a jolt of acute pain. Regardless of who
plays them and why, wargames are developing to the point that they can all but

---

[94] See, for these simulators, Halter, *From Sun Tzu to Xbox*, pp. 152–4, and Dunnigan,
Wargames Handbook, pp. 340–3. Dunnigan's list is also available online at: www.
strategypage.com/prowg/default.asp?target=pwpdefenseprojects.htm.

[95] Simulator Sickness at: www.siggraph.org/education/materials/HyperVis/virtual.env/
percept.iss/simulate.htm.

substitute for certain kinds of war. Conversely, certain kinds of war are being
reduced to wargames. Suppose one is the pilot of a fighter-bomber on a night
mission. Outside the cockpit the world is pitch black. Wireless communications
with headquarters and perhaps other aircraft apart, all the data concerning the
outside world, i.e. the atmosphere as well as friendly aircraft and those belonging to the enemy, will be gathered by some kind of sensors. Much of what takes
place inside the aircraft itself, such as fuel consumption, engine temperature,
and the like, will also be recorded by sensors. Whatever its nature and source,
the data will be translated into electronic signals. Thus transformed, it will end
up either in the form of voice or warning noises or else as blips on a battery of
screens in front of the pilot. Some of it may even be fed directly into his helmet.
To perform his work, the pilot will manipulate the aircraft's controls. Whatever
effect his actions may have will also be displayed in the form of blips.

Now suppose some gnome has taken over the aircraft without anybody
noticing the fact. He continues sending out voice messages indistinguishable
from the "real" ones as well as a stream of electronic blips to be displayed to the
pilot. However, instead of allowing the sensors to generate the signals, he
produces them himself in an arbitrary way. In that case he will have the pilot
acting without any reference not only to the real world, enemies and targets
included, but to his own aircraft. Signals that are impossible or self-
contradictory will either cause the pilot to conclude that something has gone
very wrong with his machine or make him go mad. Supposing the gnome
knows his job, though, he may very well be able to prevent the pilot from noting
that anything has changed and make him carry on as usual, making him
respond to dangers that do not exist while engaging him on a wild goose chase.

To repeat, the most important qualities those who play shooter-type wargames require are good eyesight, excellent motor coordination, and extreme
concentration. While it would be an exaggeration to say that those qualities are
all pilots need, need them they certainly do. No great amount of psychological
study is required to tell us that the performance of a pilot who has to do his
work while his life is in serious danger is likely to drop very sharply[96] – as
Clausewitz puts it succinctly but accurately, under such circumstances even the
bravest are likely to behave somewhat strangely. Training and habituation may
certainly improve things, but only up to a point. Yet we have seen that, from the
pilot's point of view, as long as the signals are consistent it makes no difference
where they come from or even whether they do or do not correspond to
anything in reality. In theory, and perhaps one day in practice as well, it
might therefore be possible to take the opposite approach: namely, to improve
the pilot's performance, and that of other warriors as well, by having them act

[96] See, on this entire subject, P. A. Hancock and J. L. Szalma, eds., *Performance under Stress*,
London: Ashgate, 2008.

under the illusion that what they are engaged on is not real war but merely a game or exercise.[97]

Just such an arrangement is explored in *Ender's Game*, a science-fiction novel by Orson Scott Card first published in 1977.[98] Ender, the eponymous hero, is a boy aged six. Following an exhaustive battery of physical and mental tests, he has been selected to attend Battle School. There, using simulators all the way, he spends several years being trained to wage interstellar war against an alien race known as the Buggers. One day, which to him is just another day at the school, he finds himself engaged in a more difficult struggle than ever before. As absolute concentration is achieved, cause and consequence are abolished. Like some berserker of old he enters a sort of trance, taking leave of his senses even as, paradoxically, he controls them better than at any other point in his life. Days and nights turn into a nightmarish blur. He fights much harder than he ever knew he could fight or that it was possible to fight.

After months of ferocious battles during which several of his highly trained co-fighters are driven to the point of collapse and beyond, Ender manages to win, but only just. The planet that forms the center of the Buggers' universe is blown up onscreen, leaving nothing behind. As he staggers out of the game room for what he does not yet realize is the last time, so drained that he hardly knows where he is or what he is doing, he is greeted by tears and applause. He learns that the struggle that has just ended was not a game or simulation but a real life-and-death war in which the Buggers were defeated and the human race saved from annihilation. Forget about the question, which Ender himself raises, as to whether putting any individual into such a situation is fair. Real reality and virtual reality have become one and the same.

---

[97] See on this J. Der Derian, "The Simulation Syndrome: From War Games to Game Wars," *Social Text*, 24, 1990, pp. 187–92.
[98] Orson Scott Card, *Ender's Game*, New York: Tor, 1991 [1977].

7

The females of the species

To play or not to play

Ever since God created Adam and Eve women have always formed about half of humanity, as they still do. Yet an extraterrestrial being watching participants at almost any kind of wargame, past, present, and presumably future, would never guess that this is the case. Female reenactors form perhaps 2–3 percent of the total. As it happens, the number who served in the Red Army during the Russian Civil War and in the US armed forces during World War II was similar.[1] Many groups, seeking authenticity, do not allow women to join at all. Some appear to regard them as an evil that may or may not have to be tolerated.[2] Others, to the contrary, are constantly on the lookout for female recruits who could fill the ranks of their *cantinières* (canteen women, dating to Napoleonic times), medical corps, signal service, or secretaries. One British group of reenactors has even established an ATS (Army Territorial Service) unit specifically so that women are able to join and play along in a "historically accurate role."[3]

According to the best available book on the subject, most women get involved in the hobby in the wake of their male relatives or boyfriends.[4] Most are found at the larger, more public, and less authentic events; reenactments that try to capture the fatigues of real war, such as operating under difficult weather conditions or camping outdoors, tend to attract fewer women than the rest. But it is not just a question of avoiding physical effort and what are sometimes somewhat Spartan living conditions; as far as the available figures

---

[1] E. A. Wood, *The Baba and the Comrade: Gender and Politics in Revolutionary Russia*, Bloomington: Indiana University Press, 1997, p. 56; B. Mitchell, *Women in the Military: Flirting with Disaster*, Washington DC: Regnery, 1997, p. 4.

[2] J. Hendershott, "Annoying Reenacting Types ," at: http://wesclark.com/jw/annoying_2.html.

[3] See Clash of Steel Reenactment Groups, at www.clash-of-steel.org/pages/links_groups.php?cat=ww2.

[4] Thompson, *War Games*, p. xxi.

go, women playing computerized wargames also form a small minority.[5] Based on the surveys, Dunnigan says that, at the time when he was selling his hexed wargames by the hundreds of thousands, the number of women who showed any interest in them only amounted to perhaps 1 percent of the total.[6] Women who participate in the more physical wargames are rare, but they do exist. It is said that in Taiwan 10–20 percent of airsoft players are female.[7] That seems rather high: one American player put the figure at 2–10 percent.[8] Several websites I have found either seek to bring in more women or complain that the game needs more of them.[9]

Going further back in time, in 1890 a French female journalist by the name of Séverine d'Estoc (meaning, "of the rapier") was challenged to a duel by a man about whom she had written a scurrilous article. She, however, preferred to have a man fight in her stead, a fact that brought the wrath of the Paris League for the Emancipation of Women down on her head. The outcome of the affair is not on record.[10] One American woman, Ella Hattan (1859– after 1909), was an accomplished expert at fencing, including the very specialized art of horseback fencing. Advertised as "The World-Renowned Jaguarine, the Ideal Amazon of the Age" she gave many demonstrations of her skill against male opponents. However, in an age when duels fought with edged weapons were common she does not appear to have participated in a real one.

In 1817 one newspaper in Georgia carried the following story:

> Last week a point of honor was decided between two ladies near the South Carolina Line, the cause of the quarrel being the usual one – love. The object of the rival affections of these fair champions was present on the field as the mutual arbiter in the dreadful combat, and he had the grief of beholding one of the suitors for his favor fall dangerously wounded before his eyes. The whole business was managed with all the decorum and inflexibility usually practiced on such occasions, and the conqueror was immediately married to the innocent second, comformably to the previous conditions of the duel.[11]

Fighting females seem to have been more numerous in the eighteenth century. The weapons they used included not just pistols and stilettos but quarterstaffs

---

[5] J. Cassell and H. Jenkins, eds., *From Barbie to Mortal Kombat: Gender and Computer Games*, Cambridge, MA: MIT Press, 2000, pp. 7–11.

[6] Dunnigan, *Wargames Handbook*, p. 301.

[7] R. Brownlow, "Airsoft Hits the Mark," *Taipei Times*, April 19, 2007.

[8] See: http://groups.google.com/group/rec.sport.paintball/browse_thread/thread/5972d15a03499c1b/f2b745c919930a30?pli=1.

[9] Wichita Area Airsoft at: http://airsoftwichita.informe.com/20id-airsoft-dt6435.html; Airsoft Reload at: www.taipeitimes.com/News/feat/archives/2007/08/19/2003374955.

[10] R. Baldick, *The Duel*, London: Chapman & Hall, 1965, p. 177.

[11] Quoted in Holland, *Gentlemen's Blood*, p. 81.

as well.[12] In 1792 two Englishwomen, Mrs. Elphinstone and Lady Almeira Braddock, held a pistol duel at London's Hyde Park. After Elphinstone's ball had pierced Braddock's hat they switched to swords and went on fighting until Mrs. Elphinstone in turn was nicked in the arm. With that the affair came to an end. In 1715 the Countess de Polignac faced a certain Marquise de Nesle over the affections of the Duke de Richelieu, a younger relative of the famous cardinal, said to be the most charming nobleman at Versailles. The encounter was watched by an enthusiastic crowd of men and women. Depending on whom one believes, it ended with the marquise wounded either in the breast or in the ear. However, the injuries were not serious and nobody was killed. Yet fights between high-class women were rare; contemporary wisdom had it that actresses and prostitutes were especially likely to duel. Thus the opera singer Julie d'Aubigny (1670–1707), known as La Maupin after her husband, was said to have fought several duels against young aristocrats. She and her paramour, a fencing master named Seranes, also gave dueling demonstrations for payment. In them she put on male garb without, however, concealing her sex. In 1898 a novel about her was published, complete with a drawing of her dressed in such clothes.[13]

In 1552 two young women from Naples, Isabella de Carazzi and Diambra de Petinella, dueled one another for the love of a gentleman, one Fabio de Zeresola. Much later, an imaginary rendition of the fight was created by the Spanish artist José de Ribera. His *Duelo de Mujeres* hangs in Madrid's Museo del Prado.[14] Earlier still, most women involved in judicial duels had champions fight on their behalf (as did many men). However, here and there it is possible to find women fighting men. A 1467 German-language manual sheds a somewhat lurid light on the question. The author, one Hans Talhoffer, was a well-known fencing master. The *Fechtbuch*, or fighting book, in question was one in a series of six he wrote and published and the only one of them that contains a section on women. Apparently aimed both at those who organized the fights and at the combatants themselves, the volume contains detailed instructions concerning the tactics each party should employ. The wood-cut illustrations that accompany the text show the man being handicapped by being buried up to his waist in a pit. This had the effect of leaving the woman free to decide on the beginning of combat and, in case she succeeded in evading his grasp, bringing it to an end.[15]

[12] See for this entire subject Kiernan, *The Duel*, pp. 133–4.
[13] See Julie d'Aubigny, at: http://en.wikipedia.org/wiki/Julie_d'Aubigny.
[14] A reproduction may be found at: www.kunst-fuer-alle.de/english/art/artist/image/jusepe-de-ribera/7891/49/144263/duelo-de-mujeres/index.htm.
[15] See on Talhoffer and his *Fechtbuch* Hans Talhoffer, at: http://en.wikipedia.org/wiki/Hans_Talhoffer.

There is no record of ladies fighting in tournaments. Indeed tournaments, as far as is known, are among the very few wargames in which no women took part at all. By contrast, Rome did have some female gladiators. We know that they volunteered for the arena, trained for it, and perhaps fought in it. Judging by what Petronius says in the *Satyricon*, having them on the program was considered a special treat. Of them, a modern female scholar says that they were "one element in a picture of . . . imperial luxury and decadence."[16] Possibly they were placed in between the main acts as a sort of lighthearted relief, much as modern cheerleaders are. A shard of red pottery, discovered in Leicester, England, and reading "VERECUNDA LUDIA LUCIUS GLADIATOR" (Verecunda the dancer, Lucius the gladiator) supports this interpretation.[17] The shard has a hole in it and may have been worn on a necklace. Perhaps it records a love affair between a male and a female member of the same troupe.

Augustus, who socially speaking tended to be on the conservative side, issued a ban on women gladiators. The prohibition, which paralleled the one on high-class men, was probably aimed at high-class women, the only ones considered worth taking notice of. The emperor's intention must have been to prevent them from degrading themselves, and by extension their male relatives on whose shoulders the burden of running the empire and keeping the population in its place ultimately rested. Several subsequent emperors repeated the prohibition, apparently to no avail. Others, including Nero and Domitian, took a special delight in arranging gladiatorial shows in which women as well as men participated, sometimes having them fight against dwarfs.[18] Looking back, it is hard to decide which of the two practices – barring women from the arena or permitting them to make a show of themselves and fight in it – was more degrading to them. Perhaps this conflict explains why the tug of war between the two views went on for about two hundred years. Not even Septimius Severus, who issued a decree on the subject in AD 200, was able to make it stick.[19]

Fighting apart, women were often seen in the arena. They were mutilated, executed, thrown to the beasts, or made the centerpieces of sexual demonstrations in which they were forced to copulate with beasts.[20] One statuette shows a naked woman tied to the back of a bull being mauled by a tiger which is biting – what else? – her breast. When it came to punishments the Romans were exceptional in that they rarely hesitated to treat women as badly as they did

[16] McCullough, "Female Gladiators in Ancient Rome: Literary Context and Historical Fact," *Classical World*, 101, 2, 2008, p. 208.
[17] See Jackson, "Gladiators in Roman Britain," *British Museum Magazine*, 38, 2000, p. 18.
[18] Cassius Dio, *The History of Rome*, 62.3.1; Suetonius, *Domitian*, 4.1.
[19] Cassius Dio, *History of Rome*, 76.16.1. For this entire question see McCullough, "Female Gladiators in Ancient Rome."
[20] See, for a particularly nasty case of this kind, Martial, *Spectacles*, in *Epigrams*, LCL, 1993, 21.

men. However, the fact that among thousands upon thousands of known gladiators' tombstones, mosaics, reliefs, and objects of every kind and source, only one shows two women (distinguishable by their names as well as their hairdo) engaged in actual fighting probably indicates that they were not very common. Even the grave discovered in London in 1996, which some consider contains the remains of a female gladiator, is open to other interpretations.[21] The fact that Latin never developed a term for a female gladiator points in the same direction.

Going further back in time, Herodotus in his ethnographic survey of the Mediterranean world mentions two tribes, the Machlyes and the Auseis. They lived in the area around Lake Tritonis in what today is southern Tunisia.[22] Once a year, he says, a festival was held in honor of the goddess Athene. As part of the festivities, two groups of maidens were made to fight with sticks and stones. Some were injured or even killed. There must have been something to the story because Augustine, a native of the area, was still inveighing against the custom 850 years later.[23] That reference apart, however, anthropologists know of few if any tribal women who engage in mock combat in front of spectators.[24] Finally, I have not been able to find any cases when female champions and single combatants fought it out in front of their assembled armies. And no wonder: such encounters would negate their very purpose, which was either to serve as a substitute for war – at any rate, in theory – or to obtain a psychological advantage over the enemy.

I shall skip the question as to whether more boys than girls participate in mudball fights, snowball fights, and the like. Considering the above facts, two separate questions seem to present themselves. First, how do we explain this vast gender gap? And, second, can its existence teach us anything concerning the nature of both men and women, and if so, what? What makes the first question even more interesting is precisely the fact, which Huizinga and others before and after him have noted, that games are the domain of free-dom. It is one of the outstanding characteristics of human life that many, perhaps most, activities we engage in are more or less obligatory. We go to school, we work, we pay taxes, we enlist for war (in countries that have conscription), we do a thousand other things, not necessarily because we like to do them but because we have to or are made to either by economic need or by the organized power of society. Indeed our ability to distinguish between obligatory activities and voluntary ones is one of the key constituents of what makes us human.

[21] See H. Pringle, "Gladiatrix ," *Discover*, 22, 12, December 2001, pp. 48–55.
[22] Herodotus, *The Histories*, 4.180.2.
[23] Augustine, *De Doctrina Christiana*, R. P. H. Greene, ed., Oxford: Clarendon Press, 1995, 4.53.
[24] Kelly, *Warless Societies*, pp. 32, 35–6.

However, among all the many kinds of players mentioned so far, perhaps only gladiators and soldiers on active service were compelled to participate in wargames. All the rest, including in some cases the highest and the mightiest in the land, did so out of their own free will. Even some of those who did not, as in various kinds of duels, almost always had an escape route open to them. It was only if they were unwilling to forfeit their "honor" that they were obliged to fight. Indeed the ability and the right to refuse a challenge is precisely the feature that distinguishes a duel from a brawl or a skirmish and justifies its inclusion in the present volume. To this extent, games in general and wargames in particular provide us with a sort of laboratory of human behavior. Thus the question remains: what accounts for women's near-complete absence from an activity which was, and remains, almost entirely voluntary?

Prohibitions like the ones Augustus tried to put in place may explain some of the gap, but by no means all. Perhaps one answer is that to engage in fighting can provide men with an erotic kick that women do not seem to share in the same way, if at all. To be sure, ever since "shell shock" made its appearance in 1914–18, war has often been blamed for producing various psychological symptoms in soldiers, impotence and loss of sexual appetite specifically included.[25] On the other hand, one need hardly go far beneath the surface of things to come across the close connection that has always existed between weapons of every sort and phalli, between penetrating an enemy's flesh in war and doing the same to a woman (and, for some of us, a man, but this is not a subject that has to preoccupy us here) in bed.[26] Both English and many other languages, Latin and my native Hebrew included, provide strong evidence for this. In this respect there is little difference between the more physical kind of wargames and war itself: as one reenactor, losing control of himself, was heard to shout, "Man! I get a hard-on firing this gun!" (apparently a World War II German machine gun).[27] The strong, and to some people objectionable, link between shooter-type wargames and sex has already been noted. Some designers had huge success creating so-called "sperm games" in which fear, thrill, and skill were combined with the need to defend the innocent and punish the guilty.[28] To clinch the argument, there is some experimental evidence that such games, especially the more violent ones, do more to arouse aggressive feelings in men than in women.[29]

[25] See on this e.g. M. Kotler *et al.*, "Sexual Dysfunction in Male Posttraumatic Disorder Patients," *Psychotherapy and Psychosomatics*, 69, 6, 2000, 309–15.

[26] See on this, most famously, S. Freud, *The Interpretation of Dreams*, New York: Macmillan, 1913, especially pp. 131–62, as well as C. Cohn, "'Clean Bombs' and Clean Language," in J. B. Ehlstain and S. Tobias, eds., *Women, Militarism, and War*, Boston, MA: Rowman & Littlefield, 1990, pp. 33–42.

[27] Thompson, *War Games*, p. xxiii.   [28] Donovan, *Replay*, p. 88.

[29] B. D. Bartholow and C. A. Anderson, "Effects of Violent Games on Aggressive Behavior: Potential Sex Differences," *Journal of Experimental Social Psychology*, 38, 2001, pp. 288–9.

Even that is probably but one element in a much more complex puzzle. Following Freud, many psychologists, specifically including some of the most prominent female ones, have argued that the decisive moment in any boy's life arrives when he has to switch from dependence on his mother, under whose care all children spend their infancy, to identifying with his father.[30] War being the male activity par excellence, playing at it could be interpreted as one way to act out the transition and fix it in the psyche, so to speak. All over the world, many rites of initiation seem to be designed specifically with this objective in mind. The rites require that boys engage in all kinds of wargames until they are considered ready to be enrolled as mature men and/or permitted to marry. Conversely, had any number of girls been allowed to play along with the boys, then of course the games would have been unable to serve that function.

Last but not least, earlier in this study we saw that play appears to be limited to vertebrates, and more specifically mammals. Our relatives the primates are particularly likely to engage in play-fighting. Whether or not females participate in play-fighting appears to depend primarily on how sexually dimorphic the sexes are: in other words on the relative size of males and females. In primate species where males and females have approximately equal size, weight, and strength, as is the case with gibbons, animals of both sexes participate equally. However, theirs is an exceptional case because most primates are strongly dimorphic. Among most of them young females are less involved with play-fighting, and stop engaging in it at an earlier age than young males. Chimpanzees have been specifically mentioned in this context.[31] This does not necessarily mean that females have less "fun"; rather, they seem to get it in a different manner, spending more time grooming as well as handling infants.[32] Close observation seems to show that vervet monkey mothers do not interfere in the play of their female offspring more often than they do in that of their male siblings. Females, in other words, are permitted to play-fight as much as males are, but choose not to.[33] The fact that female primates do not engage in play-fighting as much and for as long as males do, points to some real biological differences between the sexes. At least

---

[30] E. A. Rotundo, *American Manhood: Transformations of Masculinity from the Revolution to the Modern Era*, New York: Basic Books, 1994, p. 37; N. Chodorow, *The Reproduction of Mothering: Psychoanalysis and the Sociology of Gender*, Berkeley, CA: University of California Press, 1978, pp. 169–76; W. Ong, *Fighting for Life: Contest, Sexuality and Consciousness*, Amherst: University of Massachusetts Press, 1989, p. 89; A. Dundes, *From Game to War*, Lexington: University Press of Kentucky, 1997, pp. 25–46.

[31] C. Loilzos, "An Ethological Study of Chimpanzee Play," in J. S. Bruner *et al.*, eds., *Play: Its Development and Evolution*, Harmondsworth: Penguin, 1976, p. 360.

[32] See Aldis, *Play Fighting*, pp. 101–4.

[33] P. Govindarajulu *et al.*, "The Ontogeny of Social Play in a Feral Troop of Vervet Monkeys," *International Journal of Primatology*, 14, 5, 1993, p. 716; J. B. Lancaster, "Play-Mothering: The Relation between Juvenile Females and Young Infants among Free-Running Vervet Monkeys," in Bruner *et al.*, *Play: Its Development and Evolution*, p. 378.

one expert has argued that nowhere are such differences as evident as precisely in play.[34]

Humans, too, are dimorphic, though not nearly as much as some closely related species such as gorillas and orangutans. Right from their first appearance on this planet human males have always been considerably larger and stronger than females.[35] Indeed some biologists believe that natural selection has made them stronger precisely "in order" that they may fight.[36] Thanks in part to the decision to open the military to women, we now have a large number of studies which document the differences rather precisely. They show that the average US female army recruit is 4.7 inches shorter, 31 pounds lighter, has 37 fewer pounds of muscle, and 5.7 more pounds of fat than the average male recruit.[37] All this leads to her having only 55 percent of the upper-body strength and 72 percent of the lower-body strength of the average male. Since fat mass is inversely related to aerobic capacity and heat tolerance, women are also at a disadvantage when performing the kind of aerobic activities of which warfare is full. Even when the experiments were controlled for height, women only turned out to have 80 percent of the strength of men. Overall, only the upper 20 percent of women can do as well physically as the lower 20 percent of men.

Intensive training, far from diminishing the physical differences between the sexes, tends to increase them still further. This has been linked to some differences in the chemistry of their muscles.[38] After eight weeks of such training male plebes at West Point demonstrated 32 percent more power in the lower body and performed 48 percent more work at the leg press than female ones. At the bench press, the men demonstrated 270 percent more power and performed 473 percent more work than the women. One biologist claims that, if the hundred strongest individuals were to be selected out of a random group consisting of one hundred men and one hundred women, then ninety-three would be male and only seven female.[39] Another has calculated that only the upper 5 percent of women are as strong as the median male.[40]

---

[34] S. S. Suomi and H. F. Harlow, "Monkeys without Play," in Bruner *et al.*, *Play: Its Development and Evolution*, p. 490.

[35] M. F. Small, *Female Choices: Sexual Behavior of Female Primates*, Syracuse, NY: Cornell University Press, 1993, pp. 189–99.

[36] R. Wrangham and D. Peterson, *Demonic Males: Apes and the Origins of Human Violence*, New York: Houghton Mifflin, 1996, p. 181.

[37] Data summarized in Mitchell, *Women in the Military*, pp. 141–2.

[38] G. Zorpette, "The Mystery of Muscle," *Scientific American*, 10, 2, Summer 1999, p. 48; J. F. Tuten, "The Argument against Female Combatants," in N. Loring Goldman, ed., *Female Soldiers*, Beverly Hills, CA: SAGE, 1976, pp. 247–8.

[39] D. Morris, *Manwatching: A Field Guide to Human Behavior*, New York: Abrams, 1977, pp. 239–40.

[40] Presidential Commission on the Assignment of Women in the Armed Forces, *Report to the President*, Washington DC: Government Printing Office, p. C-74.

278 THE FEMALES OF THE SPECIES

Morphologically, too, women are less well adapted to war. Thinner skulls, lighter bone ridges, and weaker jawbones make them more vulnerable to blows.[41] Many women develop large pendulous breasts that impede movement and require special protection. Shorter arms makes it harder for women to draw weapons from their scabbards, stab with them, and throw them; possibly a different brain structure renders them less adept at guiding or intercepting projectiles.[42] Women's legs are shorter and are set at a different angle, making them less suitable both for sprinting and for running long distances; tests among Reserve Officers' Training Corps cadets showed 78 percent of men, but only 6 percent of women, could run two miles in under fourteen minutes.[43] Once a woman has given birth the difference in pelvic structure becomes even more noticeable. All these qualities have always been relevant to war and many kinds of wargames too. While perhaps no longer quite as dominant as they used to be, they remain so to the present day.

These biological facts go a long way to explain why, historically speaking, few women have participated in war – and in wargames. Given the considerable difference in physical strength, having women fight men would inevitably result in severe injuries if not in a massacre. That is why, in the few cases when women did confront men either of their own free will (as in judicial combat) or because they were forced to do so (as seems to have occasionally happened in the Roman arena),[44] they were matched either with dwarfs or with handicapped men; to differentiate a fight from an execution, equality of some sort is absolutely necessary! The difference in physical strength between men and women goes a long way to explain why the latter have always been reluctant to face the former. But it also explains why the former have usually been rather reluctant to face the latter in combat, whether real or simulated. A man who loses to a woman loses; a man who defeats a woman also loses.

But why are women so hard to find even in the many kinds of wargames in which physical strength is not required? In part, women's non-participation in wargames that do not require physical force may have resulted from the fact that they did not participate in war either – after all, throughout the nineteenth and much of the twentieth centuries many of the former were seen mainly as education in, and preparation for, the latter. It is also possible that men deliberately "steered" women away from what they saw as their own domain. Yet this does not end the mystery which was giving people food for thought throughout the nineteenth century. Take the case of chess as one of the best-known,

---

[41] Morris, *Manwatching*, pp. 230–2.
[42] D. Kimura, "Sex Differences in the Brain," *Scientific American*, 10, 2, Summer 1999, p. 27.
[43] Presidential Commission on the Assignment of Women in the Armed Forces, *Report to the President*, p. C-64.
[44] Cassius Dio, *History of Rome*, 61.17.3 and 7516.1.

longest-lived, and most intellectually challenging wargames of all. Some have tried to enlist psychoanalysis to explain women's voluntary absence from the field; others have blamed that absence on motherhood and menstruation which, they claim, do not leave women the necessary peace of mind.[45] In view of the game's history, though, these attempts do not appear to carry conviction.

During the Middle Ages quite a number of ladies played chess. Some considered it especially suited for women, given that they tended to stay indoors and did not spend as much time in the open, either hunting or tourneying or fighting, as their male relatives did.[46] Both in Christendom and, what may be more surprising, in Islam, skill at the game was counted among the accomplishments that made the fillies of the upper classes presentable as well as nubile. Noblemen and perhaps other well-to-do persons appointed chess masters to instruct their daughters in it so as to enable them to entertain guests.[47] Anne of France (1461–1522), the eldest daughter of King Louis XI who after his death acted as regent throughout the reign of her son Charles VII, recommended the game to her daughter Susanne as a way of escaping from "our fragility and wicked way of life."[48] Numerous charming tales tell of challenges delivered and accepted and matches being won and lost. Legend has it that the game was sometimes used as a test to decide whether a suitor was good enough to receive a lady in marriage.

More than one Renaissance male painter produced works showing women as they played chess. So did at least one female painter, Sofonisba Anguissola, an aristocratic Italian lady. In 1555 she painted *The Chess Game*, a truly beautiful canvas. It shows her playing a match with one of her sisters with two others looking on.[49] Female rulers who played included Louise of Savoy (1476–1531), mother and regent of the French King Francis I; Margaret of Angoulême (1492–1549), the king's sister, and the even better-known Queen Elizabeth I of England and Mary Queen of Scots. The beautifully carved sets made for some of these ladies still survive. Yet another female chess player, albeit a fictitious one, was Miranda, Prospero's daughter in *The Tempest*. Interestingly, Shakespeare makes her use the game to express the intensity of her love for Ferdinand, thus suggesting that she cared much less about it than

---

[45] R. Fine, *The Psychology of the Chess Player*, New York: Ishi, 1967, p. 25; J. Shahade, *Chess Bitch: Women in the Ultimate Intellectual Sport*, Los Angeles, CA: Siles Press, 2005, p. 17.

[46] M. Yalom, *Birth of the Chess Queen: A History*, New York: HarperCollins, 2004, p. 57.

[47] *Mai und Beaflor*, W. Vollmer, ed., Leipzig: Cotta'sche Buchhandlung, 1848, lines 230–6.

[48] Anne de France, *Les enseignements d'Anne de France ... à sa fille Susanne de Bourbon*, Nabu Press, 2010 [1878], part 1, p. 9.

[49] See on these paintings M. D. Garrard, "Here's Looking at Me: Sofonisba Anguissola and the Problem of the Woman Artist," *Renaissance Quarterly*, 47, 3 Autumn, 1994, pp. 556–622.

about him.[50] Supposing her attitude is in any way true to life, it would explain why, even during this period, the real experts on the game, those who made their living teaching it and writing books about it, were, as far as we know, without exception male.

By this time the queen, originally one of the weakest pieces on the board, had been turned into by far the most powerful one. Some authors have claimed that the change reflected a wider social process in which "women off the board also witnessed a period of increased leverage in exchanges of power."[51] Perhaps so, perhaps not; in both Europe and India, it is worth noting, chess was equally popular among top-of-the-line courtesans eager to attract clients by providing them with more than sex alone.[52] In any case the period in question only lasted a short time. As the seventeenth century progressed conditions changed and male dominance of the game became more pronounced than ever. Except in the Netherlands, the bourgeois country par excellence and the first in which middle-class women ceased to work outside the home, paintings of women playing chess either with men or with other women, which earlier on used to be common, all but disappeared. Possibly this had to do with the fact that the game began to move out of the home into the coffee houses; such places were seen as promoting license, which sometimes led to decent women being prohibited from entering them.[53] Another cause might be the increasingly competitive atmosphere which surrounded the game. The two processes reinforced each other. Publicity led to increased competitiveness, and increased competitiveness to greater publicity.

Once world championships had been established during the late nineteenth century, competition, as opposed to mere social play, became even more important. By that time chess had long ceased to be a skill that ladies were expected to master. That paragon of femininity, Jane Austen, does not mention it either in her works or in her correspondence. Some (male) contemporaries regretted that fact. They tried to inquire into its cause, suggesting that "every young lady will do wisely in acquiring the power of adding its fascination to the attractions of Home." Women, it was claimed, had both the opportunity to play – more so than men, since their responsibilities were lighter and they did not have to work for a living – and the ability to do so.[54] William Steinitz, the

---

[50] W. Shakespeare, *The Tempest*, V.i.174–6.

[51] R. L. Oshea, *Queening: Chess and Women in Medieval and Renaissance France*, MA thesis submitted to Brigham Young University, 2010, pp. 43, 53–4, at: http://contentdm.lib.byu.edu/ETD/image/etd4018.pdf.

[52] See, for Europe, A. L. Prescott, "Translatio Lupae: Du Bellay's Roman Whore Goes North," *Renaissance Quarterly*, 42, 3, Autumn 1989, p. 403; for India, see Maharishi Vatsyayan as quoted at: www.shvoong.com/humanities/2082545-arts-womans-02/.

[53] Anon., "Coffee History," at: http://web.archive.org/web/20070915014128/http://www.humboldtcoffee.com/History.htm.

[54] Anon., "Chess and the Fair Sex," *Chess Player's Chronicle*, March 15, 1881, pp. 121–2.

American who was world champion from 1886 to 1894, is said to have been "enthusiastic" about female players. He thought that "undoubtedly there is a great field for women in this science."[55] Yet none of these appeals did much to attract women to the game.

Early in the twentieth century special women's chess clubs and leagues began to be established. However, so small was their number that when Arpad Elo, a professor of physics and a chess master, first started devising his Rating System in the 1960s he encountered a problem with the separate women's list. There simply were not enough women players around who had played tournament chess, making it impossible either to rate them against each other or to relate the female list to the male one.[56] Several years ago I was lucky enough to host Professor Alla Kushnir-Stein. Before moving to Israel in 1976, she had been the Soviet Union's joint women's chess champion. I asked her why there were so few women grandmasters around. She answered that when boys and girls started playing as young children they showed equal aptitude. Later, though, most girls left the game behind. The few girls who continued to play after puberty formed a much smaller pool of candidates from which champions could be selected and trained: where quantity was absent quality could not develop.

Professor Kushnir's hypothesis, which she kindly communicated to me over dinner, has since become part of the common wisdom. It has been used, for example, to explain why the world's highest-ranking player, Judit Polgar, was the only woman among the top hundred. In 2009 she came in at no. 27 on the ladder, though earlier in her career she had twice been ranked among the top ten; incidentally, no other woman has ever done remotely as well. In the same year this common wisdom received support from a piece of serious academic research. A team of British scholars focused on Germany, the reason being that records in that country are more complete than most. It turned out that just 6 percent of rated players were female. From these facts they went on to calculate that exactly 96 percent of the gender gap in the quality of play was due not to differences in innate ability but to the fact that few females invested enough in chess to become grandmasters.[57] One doubts whether any figures pertaining to social life can ever be that accurate. Assuming that this one is reasonably so, however, the question becomes even more pointed: if the natural abilities of men and women at the many kinds of wargames that do not require physical force are in fact quite equal, then why do male players outnumber female ones by as much as they do?

---

[55] Quoted in Anon., "These Women Can Play Chess," *Washington Times*, July 15, 1895.
[56] According to Anon., "Famous Woman Chess Players," at www.chess-sets-and-more.com/women-chess-players.html.
[57] See M. Bilalic *et al.*, "Why Are (the Best) Women so Good at Chess? Gender Differences in Intellectual Domains," 2009, at: www.ncbi.nlm.nih.gov/pmc/articles/PMC2679077/.

One student feels that girls stop playing because they find more interesting things to do – they discover that dating is more fun than checkmating.[58] Showing their skill at chess might actually cost them in terms of the number of boys who are attracted to them; conversely, they are not very interested in boys whom they could beat at the game. Even if they go on playing, most of them appear to be less obsessed by the game, and less inclined to put as great an effort into it, than their male colleagues. This in turn might have something to do with the fact that, in chess as in all other fields, a woman can improve her social status by associating with a man who is good at what he does. That is not nearly as true for a man: for him, indeed, things might just as well work the other way around. Whatever the answer, only in Hungary, the Ukraine, and China does the number of woman chess players even come within an order of magnitude of that of male ones.[59] Worldwide no more than 5 to 7 percent of rated chess players are female. In the United States the number is just 3 percent.

Only in 1978 did the first woman, Nona Gaprindashvili of Georgia, which at that time was still part of the USSR, become a grandmaster. Even then she did not win her title in quite the same kind of competition men had to engage in; the first woman to travel the entire road was the Hungarian Judit Polgar in 1991.[60] Since then a handful of top-ranking female chess players have suggested that the FIDE-mandated method whereby women need 200 points less than men to earn the title of grandmaster is insulting. Women, they say, should voluntarily renounce titles they did not really deserve; however, the idea has found no takers. As is also the case with other fields in which "affirmative action" is practiced, the argument goes round and round. Some women, notably Judit's sister Susan, insist both on their own right to play in men's tournaments *and* on the continued existence of all-female tournaments. Participating in the former enables Susan to claim that she is the equal of men; doing the same in the latter, to win her matches without too much difficulty. The bottom line is that, as of 2011, women made up just one 1.6 percent of all grandmasters, living or deceased.

Female participation in Reisswitz-type wargames is even lower. As always happens to minority groups, the outcome was, and still is, a certain tendency to look at women who did play as somehow deviant. Women have stubbornly stayed away from wargames (and many other kinds of games, but these are not under consideration here) even when every effort was made to engage them. I am referring to the kind of game that started coming on the market during the 1970s and that is played onscreen. They were promoted by two groups: feminists, and game-making companies. The former were trying to prove that

---

[58] Shahade, *Chess Bitch*, pp. 154–5.
[59] *Ibid.*, p. 3; R. Kruk, *Dame aan Zet/Queen's Move*, The Hague: Koninklijke Bibliotheek, 2000, p. 46.
[60] See for all of this Shahade, *Chess Bitch*, pp. 49, 97, 109.

women could do anything as well as, or better than, men. The latter hoped to double their sales by attracting women, the more so because, by baby-sitting and the like, girls often get their own independent money at an earlier age than boys.[61] Success was slow in coming. I personally know one American lady who started a firm to produce this kind of game and sell them to women, only to go bankrupt.

By way of solving the riddle, it has been suggested that girls are repelled by violence.[62] Gadgets to zap their friends with simply do not interest them. A different and perhaps better answer is provided by the above-mentioned game designer Chris Crawford. In an entertaining aside, he tells us how his wife, who like most women did not think much of the "silly" games he was working on during the 1980s, took an instant liking to *Excalibur*.[63] What set it apart was the emphasis it put on social interaction between King Arthur and his band of forty knights. Not only do they fight, but they set tithes for their vassals, send plagues and pestilences (with the help of the magician Merlin), rebel against the king, and are either rewarded for their loyalty or banished. Other designers have also noted, albeit often only after years of failed attempts, what one of them calls "the tremendous attraction for girls of complex characters and narratives . . . [as well as] the overwhelming importance of relationships."[64] These words are confirmed by the fact that some 20 percent of those involved in 1980s-vintage fantasy games such as *Dungeons and Dragons* were female.[65]

More recently, the advent since 2000 or so of the kind of networked games in which hundreds if not thousands of players can participate simultaneously has made a difference. Popular games such as *World of Warcraft* and *Warhammer* do not try to capture anything that exists or could exist in reality. Instead they focus on goblins, dwarves, elves, dragons, and similar imaginary beings. Creating relationships among these creatures is what they are all about. In these games onscreen fights, and there are quite a few of them, are waged as much by means of magic – which, not being dependent on physical strength, women know they can wield just as well as men – as with the aid of conventional weapons and martial skills so characteristic of men's games.

Furthermore, *World of Warcraft* and *Warhammer* differ from other onscreen games – those that focus on both strategy and simulators of every kind – in that, like *Excalibur*, they put a heavy emphasis on socializing. One estimate is that as many as 40 percent of *World of Warcraft* players are female.

[61] See Cassell and Jenkins, *From Barbie to Mortal Kombat*, pp. ii, 48, 50, 53.
[62] Lee McEnnay Caraher in Cassell and Jenkins, *From Barbie to Mortal Kombat*, p. 204; P. M. Greenfield, "Video Games as Cultural Artifacts," *Journal of Applied Developmental Psychology*, 15, 1, January–March 1994, pp. 3–12.
[63] Crawford, *The Art of Computer Game Design*, ch. 8.
[64] Brenda Laurel in Cassell and Jenkins, *From Barbie to Mortal Kombat*, pp. 122–3.
[65] J. Kim, "Gender Disparity in RPGs," 2005, at: www.darkshire.net/jhkim/rpg/theory/gender/disparity.html.

However, others put it at less than half of that. The difference is explained by the fact that, online, anybody can adopt any identity he or she chooses. Apparently many of the female avatars floating about are actually created by males who use this method in order to "realize" their fantasies. It has been claimed that big-breasted avatars are particularly likely to be created by males.[66] On the other hand, female players are unlikely to take on male avatars.

One survey suggests that female players in these games tend to be rather older than male ones. They are also much more likely to enter play along with a real-life romantic partner.[67] Some, indeed, consider wargame romance better than the real thing, particularly in the early stages.[68] One female expert tells us that "while most female gamers say they love the competitive element of the game, the social aspect is equally important. Women say they can catch up with friends, flirt, and even find love in this virtual world. It's like Facebook. But with dragons. And swords."[69] Another wrote that a woman who enters online games of this kind had better be prepared to fight off the guys, who probably out-number her by between three to two to six to one, with a stick. Her best strategy is to join one of the larger guilds and pair with others to go on mission.[70] One New Mexico woman became so caught up in *World of Warcraft* that she allowed her three-and-a-half-year-old daughter to starve and dehydrate to death.[71]

In sharp contrast to the above stands a game called *Whyville*. While involving no combat, it enables players to design their own avatars – modding, as it is sometimes called. Using the avatars, people gather, meet others both real and virtual, visit all sorts of secret places, share impressions, and expand their knowledge about themselves and others. In the process they can even earn a regular "salary." An estimated 68 percent of those who play it are women. Another series of non-combat videogames is *The Sims*. Reputed to be the most popular in history, it is also played predominantly by women. In general, one female games designer says, female players tend to avoid head-to-head con-frontations. Instead they look for other ways to resolve conflicts.[72]

---

[66] C. Pearce and Artemisia, *Communities of Play: Emergent Cultures in Multiplayer Games and Virtual Worlds*, Cambridge, MA: MIT, 2009, p. 22.

[67] N. Yee, "Maps of Digital Desires: Explaining the Topography of Gender and Play in Online Games," in Y. B. Kafai et al., eds., *Beyond Barbie and Mortal Kombat*, Cambridge, MA: MIT, 2008, pp. 84, 85.

[68] S. Rosenbloom, "It's Love at First Kill," *New York Times*, April 22, 2011.

[69] P. Frangoul, "The Women Finding Love in the World of Warcraft," *The Times*, February 25, 2010.

[70] B. Childs, "Felicia Day Explains How to Meet Girls in *World of Warcraft*," November 24, 2008, at: www.asylum.com/2008/11/24/felicia-day-explains-how-to-meet-girls-in-world-of-warcraft/.

[71] Associated Press, "New Mexico Mom Gets 25 Years for Starving Daughter," June 3, 2011, at http://beta.news.yahoo.com/mexico-mom-gets-25-years-starving-daughter-145411042.html.

[72] Sheri Graner Ray, quoted in Kafai et al., *Beyond Barbie and Mortal Kombat*, p. 322.

Yet another reason for women's disinterest may be the link that has always existed between the games and real-life war, a field from which women have traditionally been all but excluded. What is the point of spending time and effort preparing for an activity in which one is not supposed to participate? Another is men's frequent reluctance to allow women to share their activities even when the latter are meant for entertainment only. Such participation, they believe, is very likely to cause the value of their own accomplishments to be questioned by both men *and* women.[73] However, as the history of chess in particular shows, these two aspects only form part of the story and possibly not even the most important part. Even if they did apply, in many cases there would be little to prevent women from designing their own games and forming their own organizations for playing them against each other to their hearts' contents. Rarely, though, have they done so; instead, some of them complain about men who play "commando-type games" in which they themselves cannot, or will not, participate.[74]

Whereas men seem to be more interested in playing games that involve fighting, women like those that provide them with the opportunity to socialize, interact with one another, and reach some kind of desirable outcome. One might, perhaps, go further still: whereas for many men fighting *is* socializing – albeit a highly destructive form of it in which deaths replace gifts – with women that is much less the case. Judging by observations of our closest animal relatives, i.e. primates, probably there is a link between this fact and the biological differences between the sexes, their dimorphism in particular. When one is relatively weak, physically speaking, trying to use force against greater force is simply stupid. Turning this argument around, ultimately the real reason why so many women take leave of gaming in general, and wargaming in particular, at the onset of puberty may be because, to speak with Crawford's wife and others,[75] they see these activities as somewhat silly – which, in comparison with leading a full social life and especially the great task of obtaining a partner, conceiving children, carrying them, delivering them, and looking after them, they undoubtedly are. Could it be, in other words, that most women are just too sensible to play with war?

Play and display

Though women may have been reluctant to play with war, to the extent that they did play they often did so at the behest of men. What attracted men was

[73] See, most trenchantly, M. Mead, *Male and Female*, London: Gollancz, 1949, pp. 159–60.
[74] J. Webster, *Shaping Women's Work: Gender, Employment and Information Technology*, London: Longman, 1996, p. 63.
[75] Gisela Gresser, nine-time American women's champion, as quoted in Shahade, *Chess Bitch*, p. 156.

less the women's prowess at fighting than their sex appeal. For reasons that Freud might explain, from the day the first Greek artist took up his brush to paint the first Amazon, the combination of cleavage and weapons of every kind has always been a fascinating one. Talking of the Amazons, indeed, the later the date of the image the more they displayed their charms and the less they fought.[76] The link retains its potency to the present day.

Legend apart, there seem to have been few if any cases when ancient women encountered each other in single combat as men sometimes did. However, on occasion they were made to don arms – light ones, we are told, made especially for them – and put on a performance, albeit one that had to more to do with a dance than with a real fight. Xenophon in the *Anabasis* describes one such spectacle. It was organized by an Arcadian officer in a Greek army in Asia Minor. He had a slave girl in his possession take up a shield and perform in front of some Paphlagonian chieftains. The latter, having watched the show, applauded. Being in a jocular mood, they asked their guests whether they also had women fight alongside them in real-life war.[77]

In ancient Rome the most desirable single quality men were expected to possess was *virtus*. The corresponding quality of women was *pudicitia*, best translated as a combination of modesty, chastity, and sexual virtue in general. Finding expression in modes of dress and behavior, it was exemplified by Lucretia. Legend had her killing herself after having been subjected, through no fault of her own, to *stuprum*, a shameful act; in its personified form, *pudicitia* was worshipped as a goddess and two different temples were erected to honor her.[78] A man, even a criminal or a slave, who fought in the arena thereby obtained a last desperate chance to display his *virtus* and redeem himself. Not so a woman, who, whatever else she may have stood to gain, instantly lost any *pudicitia* she may ever have had. Instead of upholding an ideal, she discarded it. Publius Sempronius Sophus, who was consul in 268 BC, divorced his wife merely for *watching* some games without obtaining his permission first.[79]

A relief discovered at Halicarnassus, the present day Bodrum in southwestern Anatolia, shows women gladiators in action.[80] Originally presented to the British Museum in 1846, to date it remains the only one of its kind. Who set it up and why is unknown. However, it may well have formed part of a series commemorating events in the arena. At the top, a Greek inscription tells us that the two women received an honorable discharge that was often the result of a

---

[76] See W. B. Tyrell, *Amazons: A Study in Athenian Mythmaking*, Baltimore, MD: Johns Hopkins University Press, 1984, pp. 44–5.

[77] Xenophon, *Anabasis*, LCL, 1961, 6.1.5–13.

[78] See, on the nature of *pudicitia*, R. Langlands, *Sexual Morality in Ancient Rome*, Cambridge University Press, 2006, pp. 37–77, 186, 346.

[79] Valerius Maximus, *Memorable Deeds and Sayings*, 6.3.12.

[80] See, for the details, K. Coleman, "Missio at Halicarnassus," *Harvard Studies in Classical Philology*, 100, 2000, pp. 487–500.

draw. They are presented armed in the normal manner of *provocatores* complete with loincloths, greaves, arm guards, and shields. Conspicuously absent is the breastplate (*pectorale*), causing the women to fight bare-breasted; most unusually, helmets are not worn either. Modern archaeologists have spun theories to explain the latter fact in particular. Yet to anyone familiar with subsequent and present-day representations of fighting women it hardly comes as a surprise: it is primarily their long hair which distinguishes such women from men.

The really interesting thing about the tablet, seldom noted, is that, as their names indicate, what we see is not a straightforward fight but a reenactment of the mythological combat between an Amazon – a legendary creature that never existed in reality – and Achilles. On this occasion, it seems, the "normal" world has been put upside down not once but twice: first, by having women fight at all, a fairly rare event that spelt the loss of their chief female quality, that even the Romans, who concerning everything else that took place in the arena were anything but prudish, considered somehow perverted; and second, by having one of them represent not herself but the male hero whose name was a household word throughout the ancient world.

Modern movies such as *Gladiator Eroticus: The Warrior Lesbians* and websites such as *Gladiator Girls* are essentially pornographic by nature. So are some present-day illustrations of their fights.[81] In fact the term "gladiators" has often been applied to all sorts of half-nude performing women regardless of whether they did or did not engage in actual fighting. One company's website offers customers a "gladiator girls" swimsuit competition. A second tries to sell them "gladiator girl fancy dress" to wear on "wild nights" ahead of them, and a third tells them how to prepare a gladiator girl costume for Halloween. Briefly, in many, if not most, cases the combination of "female" with "gladiator" has to do as much with sex as with combat, real or simulated. At a guess, the same was probably true in the ancient world.

The Halicarnassus tablet apart, classical antiquity has not left us with any images of females engaged in combat sports (though we do have representations of Atalante, the virgin runner who did not want to marry, grappling the male hero Peleus). This fact did not prevent subsequent artists, nineteenth-century ones in particular, from using their imaginations to paint "Spartan" girls doing so. In China, female wrestling seems to have been popular during the Three Kingdoms era (AD 220–80) and again during the reign of Emperor Song Shenzong (AD 968–1022). In both periods it was a question of exhibition matches that involved sex as much as violence.[82] Several sixteenth- and seventeenth-century Italian, French, and German artists produced beautiful

---

[81] See Single Female Combat Club, "The Bravest Women the World Has Ever Known," 2011, at: www.fscclub.com/history/gladiatrix-e.shtml.
[82] Thanks to my friend, Major Dr. Li Ting Ting, for pointing this out to me.

sculptures of naked women, or nymphs as they are sometimes called, wrestling.[83] Apparently such matches, combining naturalism, drama, and eroticism, were a popular form of entertainment in some contemporary courts.

The artists in question appear to have struggled with a dilemma. They wanted to make the female figures appear big and strong – close inspection reveals that some are of truly Amazonian proportions. The problem was to do so without stripping them of their sex appeal. In some of these and subsequent works, it is hard to say whether the women are engaged in wrestling, bathing, dancing, or a not so thinly disguised lesbian love act.[84] Eighteenth-century Japan had female sumo wrestlers. Osaka in particular was known for the brothels where many matches were held. From there they spread to Edo (Tokyo) and other towns where they were sometimes associated with Shinto rites. To make the fights more equal, some women had to fight blind men. As in ancient Rome, the authorities regarded the shows as immoral and repeatedly imposed bans on them. Finally prohibited in 1926, they have recently experienced a revival.[85]

In England, too, women sometimes engaged each other in wrestling matches or gave non-lethal public dueling demonstrations for payment. For example, the London Journal of June 1722 provides an account of "boxing in public at the Bear-garden . . . When two of the feminine gender appeared for the first time on the Theatre of War at Hockley in the Hole, and maintained the battle with great valor for a long time, to the no small satisfaction of the spectators."[86] Hockley was a polygonal structure, probably located in Southwark on the south bank of the Thames, where low-class forms of entertainment such as bull- and bear-baiting had traditionally been held. From other sources we know that the fights, some of which involved black African women, took place on a raised platform like the ones used in modern boxing and "professional" wrestling.[87]

Similar shows continued to be held throughout the century. An advertisement for one of them read: "I, Ann Field of Stoke-Newington, ass-driver, well known for my abilities in boxing in my own defence wherever it happened in my way, having been affronted by Mrs Stokes, styled the European Championess, do fairly invite her to a trial of the best skill in boxing, for ten pounds, fair rise and fall." Rising to the challenge, Mrs Stokes promised to hit

[83] See, for pictures, Old Time Female Combat Club, "Old Time Female Combatants," at: www.fscclub.com/history/zhened-old2-e.shtml.
[84] See Female Single Combat Club, "Motion and Fighting in Fine Arts," 2011, at: www.fscclub.com/muse/dynamics3-e.shtml.
[85] Chie Ikkai, "Women Sumo Wrestlers in Japan," International Journal of Sport and Health Science, 1, 1, March 2003, pp. 178–81.
[86] Quoted in D. Dugaw, Warrior Women and Popular Balladry, 1650–1850, London: University of Chicago Press, 1989, pp. 125–6.
[87] Herr Zacharias Conrad von Uffenbachs Merkwuerdige Reisen durch Niedersachsen, Holland und Engelland, J. G. Schelhorn, ed., Frankfurt/Main: Gaum, 1753, 2, p. 532.

her rival harder than the latter had ever beaten her asses. In 1792, two women fought each other at Chelmsford while their husbands acted as seconds and egged them on. "Being stripped, without caps, and their hair closely tied up, they set to, and for forty-five minutes supported a most desperate conflict" until the spectators separated them. In other fights, too, at least some of the women were stripped to the waist. By that time spreading middle-class respectability was causing a growing number of people to take a jaundiced view of female boxers. Among the first to condemn them was Mary Wollstonecraft (1759–97) whose book, *A Vindication of the Rights of Women*, is sometimes described as the most important feminist tract in history.[88] To her they were one of the innumerable methods men use in order "to degrade the sex from which they pretend to receive the chief pleasure in life."

Such strictures notwithstanding, female fencing, boxing, and wrestling matches retained some popularity. One painting of such a match, entitled *An Affair of Honor* and showing two topless courtesans going after one another rapier in hand, was produced by Émile Bayard (1837–91). Exhibited at the 1884 Salon, so popular did it and its counterpart, *Reconciliation*, which showed one of the women (still topless) dying and the other (equally so) tenderly bending over her, become that they were not only shown in France but sent to travel abroad as well.[89] Many well-known artists, including Eugène Delacroix, Camille Pissarro, Aristide Maillol, Max Bruning, Egon Schiele, and Jean Veber, also produced images of wrestling women. To the extent that the episodes they showed were real rather than imaginary, most of these encounters took place in brothels, saloons, and the vaudeville circuit. Usually they involved low-class women who fought for payment in front of crowds consisting primarily of men: a single match might earn such a woman as much as a laborer could make in several weeks. However, there were always exceptions. Like the men, the boxing women fought bare-knuckled. Judging by drawings, this often resulted in nasty bruises all over their bodies.

In France, Germany, and England before 1914 teams of female wrestlers and boxers were fairly commonplace. Shown on the postcards they or their managers commissioned in order to advertise them, they were often hired to exhibit their prowess at fairs or else at private parties.[90] Real or simulated – the latter is sometimes known as "foxy boxing" – women's boxing still retains some popularity, especially among what one female writer has called "leering males" who, seeking "candy for the eyes," fill the stands.[91] They walk into the arena in high

[88] Mary Wollstonecraft, *A Vindication of the Rights of Women*, London: Unwin, 1811, p. 33.
[89] The paintings are available at "Master Paintings of the World": www.iment.com/maida/family/mother/vicars/p177.htm#color.
[90] See W. Sonntag, *Kampfes Lust*, Ostfildern: Laufen und Leben, 2002, pp. 592–610.
[91] D. Montoya, *Women Boxers: The New Warriors*, Houston, TX: Arte Publico, 2006, p. 12.

heels, wave, blow kisses – imagine a male boxer doing that – and do whatever they can to put their charms on display before the fighting begins. One female boxer is said to have fought one thousand exhibition matches against men but only eighteen real ones against women.[92] Another favorite twentieth-century form of female combat appears to be mud wrestling. Some matches are known to have been held at least as far back as the 1930s. Apparently they owe their popularity to a 1966 movie, *Mondo Freudo*. Classified as a "shockumentary," the film took viewers on a "hidden camera" tour to expose all kinds of "bizarre" sexual practices of which the "combat sport" in question was considered one.

Spreading from the United States to the rest of the world, contests of this kind have become more popular still. Nowadays most are held in specially designed rings made of bales of straw. Others take place in a sort of rubber bath with thick inflatable walls. Normally the material used to make mud is sodium bentonite clay, a sticky, gray-yellow material that will swell to twice its size when water is added to it. Here and there other slippery materials such as gelatin, pudding, creamed corn, and mashed potatoes have been substituted. However it is done, all contestants enter the ring (occasionally fountains) barefoot and scantily clothed – this applies to both women, the majority, and the men against whom they are sometimes made to "fight." On other occasions it is a question of several women taking on a single man. In theory the objective is to win the match. In reality it is to entertain the crowd by combining a display of mostly female flesh with humiliation. Why so many men want to humiliate women or else see them humiliate each other is a question that a Darwin, a Nietzsche, or a Freud might try to answer. Here all one can say is that the desire to do so undoubtedly exists and that female combat sports represent one important proof of that fact.[93]

Some of the larger shows draw tens of thousands of spectators, all screaming their heads off. In the words of one, presumably male, advertiser, "sexy angry half naked girls kicking each other's ass in the mud for your entertainment . . . can it get any better than that?" Like male combatants in boxing and wrestling matches, female participants in mud wrestling will boast, dance, and prance in an attempt to entertain the crowd and gain a psychological advantage before the match itself gets under way. Unlike the men they will try to make their shows as sexy as possible, thrusting out their breasts, fondling them – one team of mud wrestlers calls itself the Chicago Knockers – and engaging in something very similar to lesbian sex. Some promoters make the link explicit, seeking to attract customers by promising mud wrestling by lesbian women. If, as sometimes happens, the upper parts of their bikinis are torn off in the tussle, they do not

---

[92] Missa Merz, *The Sweetest Thing: Inside the World of Women's Boxing*, New York: Seven Stories, 2011, p. 108.
[93] Sonntag, *Kampfes Lust*, pp. 298–324.

seem to mind too much. Here and there, nude mud wrestling shows have been put on offer. Dirty talk and name-calling abound. So do breast slapping and grabbing, nipple twisting, pulling at hair (including pubic hair), and even aggressive sexual acts in the form of violent kissing, sitting across each other's faces, and more. Some matches end in a shuddering orgasm, real or simulated. Had similar techniques been employed in a male homosexual or heterosexual context, no doubt they would have caused the police to be called in and the performers carted off to jail. Whatever the precise way things are done, rarely do participants suffer injuries of any kind. Nor does it look as if anybody cares who "won" a match and who "lost" it.

To conclude this list of not so respectable combat sports in which women participate, male "professional" wrestlers sometimes enter the ring with their female partners in tow. The women carry imaginative *noms de guerre* such as Midnight, Mad Maxine, Lady Vendetta, and Black Venus. Several countries even have leagues of female professional wrestlers. Most women's wrestling moves are the same as those of men. However, they are not viewed in a similar way. To avoid any hint of homoeroticism, in men's performances overt sexuality is rigidly suppressed in favor of mock athletic prowess in mock dangerous combat. By contrast, women's performances are deliberately sexualized.[94] Scantily clad, made up in as provocative and as vulgar a way as possible, the women walk around displaying their charms. They engage other women in scripted fights, egg on their masters, and from time to time mount sneak attacks on opposing males. Some "professional" female wrestlers are even allowed to grab men by the genitals, something their male colleagues will never do.

Had the fight been real any of these ladies would have been beaten half dead before they could have even come close to the men. In fact male wrestlers are prohibited from hitting the women. That is why the women always work in pairs so they can hit each other. Often they do so using implements that only women carry, such as handbags. Seen from the organizers' point of view the added value the women bring to the shows is enormous. In the words of one of the best known among them, Missy Hyatt (real name Melissa Ann Hiatt):

> two guys beat each other to pulp for half an hour, slugging each other in the face, kicking each other in the groin, banging metal chairs over each other's heads, body-slamming each other through wooden tables, and the crowd just sits on their hands. Like, *Snore!* But then, suddenly, a couple of chicks – I mean, 'valets' – jump into the ring, grab one another in headlocks, and start rolling around, and now the crowd's on their feet, jumping up and down, climbing onto their chairs, shoving and elbowing for a better view, yelling 'catfight! catfight! catfight!'[95]

---

[94] Mazer, *The Doggie Doggie World of Professional Wrestling*, pp. 106, 116.
[95] Missy Hyatt, *First Lady of Wrestling*, ECW Press, 2001, p. v.

One advertiser, publishing online in March 2011, says he is looking for "sexy female wrestlers."[96] Their own ads often show them posing topless or near beds. There even exists, or used to exist, something known as the Naked Women's Wrestling League (NWWL). Individual wrestlers have had their photographs published in magazines such as *Playboy* and *Penthouse*. Events are said to have been broadcast around the world to thirty-eight countries in Europe, South America, and Scandinavia. In the videos, no attempt whatsoever is made to conceal the real objective, which is titillation through humiliation. Women photographed in a website named Airsoft Reloaded are also characterized mainly by their provocative dress.[97] To this extent the strictures of Wollstonecraft and many later feminists appear fully justified. Still, since participation is voluntary, there is little anyone can or should do.

Even in a wargame as staid and as neutral as official tournament chess is supposed to be, the participation of women has given rise to new questions concerning the kind of dress they should wear while playing. It all started around the year 2000 when the advent of computers capable of beating even the best human players sent the game into a crisis. They threatened to reduce its ability to attract spectators, sponsors, and prize money; some have compared observing a match to watching paint dry. As so often when entertainment goes awry, one way out was to bring in attractive female players. For example, a "blondes versus brunettes" competition was held in Moscow on April 1, 2011.[98] The stated aims of the tournament were the popularization of chess and raising the sporting mastery of female chess players. Incidentally, "blonde" versus "brunette" has long been a favorite method of pairing female participants in "professional" wrestling matches and similar events.

Following these developments, one website started rating female players not by the quality of their play but by their looks. Predictably, some of the women consider it degrading. However, many others have sent their photographs in the hope of obtaining a high rating. Without their cooperation the site could not have operated at all. In the words of Maria Manakova, a grandmaster (mistress?) who at one time used to be Russia's fourth-highest ranked woman player: "We are not as strong as the male players; so why shouldn't we cash in on our beauty?"[99] On another occasion she explained that "when two people

---

[96] Actors and Extras Job Finder, at: http://actors.pillowtalkjapan.com/acting-jobs/sexy-female-wrestlers-nynnj/.
[97] See: www.taipeitimes.com/News/feat/archives/2007/08/19/2003374955.
[98] Mishap, "Blondes versus Brunette," *Chess in Translation*, April 1, 2011, at: www.chessintranslation.com/2011/04/blondes-versus-brunettes/.
[99] T. Allen-Mills, "'Soft Pawn' Row as Chess Discovers Sex," *Sunday Times*, December 4, 2005.

make moves, like in sex, like in love, they do some moves to win. Yes, not only he, but she, the woman. There are very close parallels between these two things: chess and sex. No, I don't mean sex. I mean the game of love." British international master Jovanka Houska agrees that chess, "the clash of wills, the intellectual battle, the power struggle between a man and a woman [is] quite romantic."[100]

A case in point is Alexandra Kosteniuk, said to be one of the world's best female players (though I was unable to find her among the 100 top-rated ones of both sexes). Russian-born, young and beautiful, she now lives in Florida and has a website operated by her husband who is a high-level chess player as well as a marketing expert. It is said that, in terms of the number of hits, no other grandmaster's website comes close. Photographs often show her wearing décolleté dresses and even swimsuits while playing.[101] She herself explains that she considers her career as a model ancillary to the one she has built up by playing chess, and that she will only engage in it if some aspect of "the wonderful game" can be seen somewhere in the background.

Kosteniuk's double nature as both a successful chess player and a model has led to quite some debate. Some think that by putting her charms on display she denigrates both chess and women; others, to the contrary, would like her to dress more sexily during tournaments. Most women players are jealous of her and many will not talk to her. Some other female players also flaunt their beauty in and out of competition. Others still complain about their looks, claiming that the attention they receive from their male colleagues prevents them from concentrating and quashes their motivation.[102] So great is the attention the media pay to young good-looking female players during tournaments that their accomplishments at the gameboard are sometimes all but overlooked. ChessBase.com, the most popular chess news source on earth, has plenty of photographs of young and beautiful chess-playing women but says little about their games. Male players too have complaints. Many resent the fact that their accomplishments at the game are overshadowed by young fresh-looking women. Others say that their women opponents' feminine attributes interfere with their ability to concentrate, causing them to lose games.[103] These problems have become sufficiently serious for the possibility of introducing a dress code to be considered.

Those who like to combine chess with sex will be intrigued by Henri Matisse's 1928 series of paintings *Odalisques*. Set within what looks like a

[100] A. Lusher, "She Looked into his Eyes, He Made his Move," *Daily Telegraph*, March 18, 2007.
[101] Alexandra Kosteniuk's website, at: www.chessblog.com/2009_06_01_archive.html.
[102] Shahade, *Chess Bitch*, p. 67.
[103] D. L. McClain, "Sex and Chess: Is She a Queen or a Pawn?," *New York Times*, November 27, 2005; "Chess Player Cites Foul over Revealing Rival," *Melbourne Herald Sun*, April 1, 1998.

harem, the paintings are said to have been inspired by his travels in Morocco in 1912–13. They show a number of women, some dressed in oriental clothes, others nude, either in the vicinity of a black-and-white chessboard or playing in a lackadaisical sort of way. The artist's fascination with checkered patterns apart, just what the message is supposed to be is not clear. In 1963 another famous French artist, Marcel Duchamp, had himself photographed playing chess with a naked woman.[104] She was Eve Babitz, a self-styled American "antisociologist" who repeated the exercise with several other male players. One particularly nasty product is Lovechess, a series of chess sets whose pieces, molded in epoxy resin, are all shaped like nude or semi-nude men and women. In one onscreen variant, "Egyptian" figures stand about stark naked. They wear helmets, carry spears and shields, and, as play unfolds, engage in all kinds of sexual acts. Still the manufacturers insist that theirs "is not a game with hardcore pornographic scenes."[105]

The place where the largest number of sexy female fighters can readily be found is in videogames. Readers will recall that most of the games in question are bought and played by men, young men in particular. Presumably this explains why, though warlike female characters form a minority in such games, when they do appear they tend to have much more bosom than muscle. Take a game named, significantly enough, SiN (1998). It sports a long-legged, big-busted female heroine. She goes by the name of Elexis – not, for some reason, the more common Alexis. She wears a sort of shiny plastic swimsuit and high boots with heels so high they must make walking all but impossible. Dressed in this somewhat improbable costume, she leads the biotech firm she has inherited from her late disappeared father, Thrall Sinclair. Occasionally she also brandishes a submachine gun while fighting off bad characters who try to destroy the world with the aid of mind-altering drugs. In doing so, her partner is Colonel John R. Blade, the head of the largest private security firm in the city of Freeport.[106]

Or take Elena (Erena) the Street Fighter. Like many others of her kind she was created by a man, the Japanese designer Yoshinori Ono who launched her in 1997. A member of a small tribe from the African savannah, she has white hair and blue eyes. Armed with these attributes she is sent by her father to study first in Japan and then in France. Her attire, consisting of a white bikini and red, sky blue, gold, and purple bands that she wears around her neck, arms, wrists, shins, and ankles, is carefully designed to stand out against her dark-brown skin. It is also light-years removed from what one would expect a ferocious fighter to wear. Snake-like in her movements, she is an expert at the art of

---

[104] The photograph is available at: Google.image under "Eve Babitz."
[105] Lovechess, at: http://centralsdownload.blogspot.com/2011/02/lovechess-greek-era-15.html.
[106] See SiN (video game), at: http://en.wikipedia.org/wiki/Sin_(video_game).

capoeira; using nothing but her long and flexible legs, she turns even the biggest, burliest, most wicked males into helpless heaps of bloody flesh.[107]

Other sexy heroines include Nariko (*Heavenly Sword*), Rayne (*Blood Rayne*), Joanna Dark (*Perfect Dark Zero*), and Cate Archer (*The Operative*). Some, such as *Tabula Rasa*'s Sarah Morison, will readily strip to their underwear or show glimpses of it as they lie on the ground, helpless and apparently beaten. Some wear metal bras obviously designed to attract the players' eyes to what is inside: had they been real, they would have directed the points of swords and spears to the wearer's most vital organs.[108] Of all such female characters the best known one by far is, or was, Lara Croft.[109] First onscreen in 1996, she was inspired by various characters that had graced comic books for years if not decades previously. Her British designer, Toby Gard, is said to have set out to counter "stereotypical female characters." If so, he does not seem to have succeeded very well. To be sure, Lara is presented as intelligent, athletic, and good-looking. The last-named quality is perhaps the most important of all: had she not been beautiful and quite sexy, then presumably neither men nor women would have wanted to play games with her or even taken the trouble to look at her. Her own mistress, unencumbered by either a husband to limit her movements or children to look after, she is an archaeologist–adventurer bearing some resemblance to Steven Spielberg's Indiana Jones.[110] In videogames and else-where, too often a "liberated" woman is simply one who has been caught up in the dreams of men.

Lara has brown eyes, brown hair, and a long ponytail – the last style any combatant, real or virtual, male or female, would want to wear while fighting. She is a traveler, venturing into ancient, hazardous tombs and ruins at various places around the world in order to discover their secrets. She does so while dressed – again most improbably – in a shiny, tight-fitting turquoise sleeveless tank top, light brown shorts, heavy calf-high military-style boots, long white socks, and exposed thighs. Originally her accessories included fingerless gloves, a backpack, a utility belt with holsters on either side, and two pistols. So large and heavy were the latter that, had they and she both been real, probably she could only have fired them by using both hands. At times she also resorted to other weapons, such as submachine guns and harpoons, to kill her opponents.

As additional games built around her were published, Lara Croft developed into the kind of female character that blows men away in both senses of the word. The tank top was replaced by a kind of one piece swimsuit. She also

---

[107] See Elena (Street Fighter), at: http://en.wikipedia.org/wiki/Elena_(Street_Fighter).

[108] See on this interesting point "Ryan," "Fantasy Armor and Lady Bits," December 2011, at: http://madartlab.com/2011/12/14/fantasy-armor-and-lady-bits/. The author introduces himself as an armorer who makes armor for certain kinds of wargames.

[109] See on her Lara Croft, at: http://en.wikipedia.org/wiki/Lara_Croft.

[110] D. Breger, "Digital Digs, or Lara Croft: Replaying Indiana Jones," *Aether*, 2, April 2008, pp. 41–60.

received a variety of accessories such as black leather belts with large metal buckles as well as thongs wrapped around her arms, legs, and torso. Again the resemblance to some types of pornographic attire is obvious and deliberate. More remarkably still, even when she was made to wear clothing suitable for a cold climate or underwater exploration she still retained her sexual allure. Not only did she appear in at least thirteen different videogames, but so successful was the character that she won a considerable following.

That in turn led to a movie being made around her exploits. The first actress to play Lara was Angelina Jolie (rumor has it that Pamela Anderson had also been considered). To increase her bust size to the 36D the producer, Lawrence Gordon, and the director, Simon West, thought would be appropriate for her, she had to wear padding. Indeed most female videogame characters have large busts – notwithstanding the fact that in reality such busts, being soft and vulnerable, make it hard for their owners to engage in combat of any kind. Other regularly occurring features are wasp-like waists, long legs, and relatively delicate, slender, arms. None of these look as if their owners have ever use them to accomplish difficult physical tasks.

Though she only exists in virtual reality, Lara Croft's exceptional popularity has caused her to be surrounded by quite some literature that seeks to understand her qualities and the place she occupies in the world.[111] Some reviewers see her and her sisters as liberated women who act as men supposedly do in doing their own thing and beating up anybody who dares to stand in their way. With their "stunting bodies," it is claimed, they "explosively take up space within a particularly masculinized landscape – the desert, dark urban landscapes, caves and tombs – and in doing so offer a powerful image of the absolute otherness of femininity within this space." Lara's "occupation of a traditionally masculine world, her rejection of particular patriarchal values and the norms of femininity and the physical spaces that she traverses are all in direct contradiction of the typical location of femininity within the private domestic space." The fact that, like many other characters, she has multiple lives and will return to the action almost as soon as she is killed helps. However, not everybody would agree with this analysis. Some see Lara as a sex symbol created by young men for the delectation of other young men (which of course she was); others see her as a "cyberbimbo" who might represent a dangerous role model for impressionable young girls to follow. Pretending to forget that she is only a host of shifting electronic dots, there are even those who speculate on what she might and might not do with and to them in bed.

Thirty or so years since they made their first appearance on the computer screen, so numerous and so varied have female videogame combatants become that no single attempt at categorization and description will fit them all. What is

---

[111] See, above all, H. W. Kennedy, "Lara Croft: Feminist Icon or Cyberbimbo?," *International Journal of Computer Games Research*, 2, 2, 2002.

clear is that the contrast between them and the male characters could not be more sharply drawn. With the exception of some small agile characters using speed and wit to beat the bigger guys, among the males size, musculature, and fighting strength tend to go hand in hand. While some are handsome, many – the wicked ones in particular – are exceedingly brutish and ugly. For example, *Starcraft*'s Jim Raynor looks as if he has swallowed a snake and is ready to swallow another. *Halo*'s Master Chief carries such heavy armor that he seems to be encrusted in it. Virtual though these characters are, one can almost smell their bad breath. Not so the females, who somehow contrive to combine it all – lots of exposed flesh, grace, beauty, the kind of sex appeal only women seem to have, *and* superhuman strength and resilience that enable them to fight and defeat opponents of both sexes who seem much stronger than themselves.

When men engage in wargames of every kind, what they put on show is the kind of strength that most other men would like to have. By contrast, so strongly sexualized are the female characters in some onscreen wargames that they can actually deter women, not all of whom relish having their avatars being drooled over by male players, from enjoying the games in question. Even those – and there are some – who are incurably wicked rarely lack sex appeal, albeit tending to be of the shrewish kind, perhaps asking to be "tamed." They tend to come with a weird combination of long hair, snarling faces, big nude or semi-nude mammaries that never get in their way even when they perform the most amazing athletic feats, impossibly narrow waists, equally impossibly long legs, shiny one- or preferably two-piece swimsuits, thongs made of black, white, or red leather, and sometimes flashy jewelry as well.

Needless to say, none of this has anything to do with reality. Even in our enlightened age, very few women see combat – in Iraq in 2003–10 just 2 percent of US military dead were female. The same applies to the smaller, but even longer war in Afghanistan. As these figures show, normally where there are bullets there are no women and where there are women there are no bullets. To top it all, in real life some weapons have had to be modified so that women can use them. Not so onscreen, where many female characters are armed with various kinds of edged weapons and firearms clearly much too big and heavy for them to handle. Often the link between weapon size and sex is too obvious to overlook. One can only wonder how on earth they manage to do it. Until, that is, one remembers that nearly all of them were conceived, designed, created, brought to virtual "life," tested, and marketed specifically in order to satisfy the fantasies of the men who play with them.

Men, women, and wargames

If it is true that many men like to watch a catfight, it is equally true that many women are by no means averse to watching men shed each other's blood. In this as in many other things, women appear to have their feet more firmly planted on the ground than men. Men may be content with counters on a checkered board or else with virtual combatants shooting one another on the screen; but women prefer the real thing.

To begin at the beginning, there may or may not have been any women present when David slew Goliath in front of the Israelite and Philistine armies assembled in the Valley of Ellah. Later, though, they celebrated his feat by chanting "Saul hath slain in his thousands, and David in his tens of thousands." This, the Old Testament tells us, understandably made Saul "very wroth."[112] With great fights/nonsense fights the situation was very different: on such occasions women, while enjoying immunity, often *were* present. They were even expected to encourage their menfolk and assist them by holding the ring, serving refreshments, dressing the wounded, and the like. One suspects that, had they been absent, the fights would not have been nearly as popular as they appear to have been. Unfortunately it is too late to find out.

In the single combat between Menelaus and Hector, Helen herself served as the prize. As the story about Sempronius' wife going to the circus without his permission proves, Roman women loved gladiatorial shows as much as men did. The man about town and amatory expert Ovidius, who was a contemporary of Augustus, noted that the amphitheater was a good place for picking up girls. "As bees, having gained their dells and fragrant pastures, flit over the blossoms and hover over the thyme; so hasten the smartest women to the crowded games ... They come to see, they come that they may be seen, to chastity that place is fatal." So numerous were they that they made one's head spin; one could approach them by helping them arrange a cushion, or else by setting a stool under a dainty foot.[113] No less a person than Claudius' fourth wife Agrippina is described as watching the bloody spectacle. To do so she was dressed in a beautiful gold-woven chlamys, a kind of military cloak. It was closed with the aid of a brooch or pin and was normally worn by active men; numerous sculptures show that it was often draped around the body in such a way as to conceal nothing. Whether, on this occasion, that was how Agrippina wore it is of course a little hard to say.[114] The empress's box was located right opposite that of the emperor. Other elite women had the very best seats, known as the *summum maenianum in ligneis* (Maennius' top-ranking wooden balcony, called after the man who invented it) reserved for them. It was situated in such a way as to prevent the sunshine from spoiling their complexions.

Another group of privileged female spectators were the Vestal Virgins, the priestesses of the hearth-goddess Vesta who had sworn to spend thirty years of their lives practicing sexual abstinence. In the theater they were assigned ringside seats. Of them, the fourth-century AD poet Prudentius has the following to say:[115]

---

[112] 1 Samuel 19.7–8.   [113] Ovidius, *The Art of Love*, LCL, 1929, 1.96–100.
[114] Cassius Dio, *History of Rome*, 60.33.
[115] Quoted in Symmachus, *Relatio*, Oxford University Press, 1973, 2.1095–1101.

What a sweet and gentle spirit she has! She leaps up at each stroke, and every time that the victorious gladiator plunges his sword into his opponent's neck, she calls him her sweetheart, and turning her thumb downward this modest maiden orders the breast of the prone gladiator to be torn open so that no part of his soul should be hidden, while the *secutor* looms above him, panting as he presses in with his weapon.

Tertullian, in a famous passage already quoted in a different context, says that men committed their souls to the gladiators, and women both their souls and their bodies.[116] There is plenty of evidence to back him up. Almost to a man, gladiators were social outcasts. This did not prevent them from receiving the kind of female attention nowadays reserved for actors, football players, and boxers.[117] Graffiti found among the ruins of Pompeii have an eloquent tale to tell. "Cresces, lord of the girls" reads one of them; "Celadus, the Thracian who makes the girls' hearts beat faster," runs another. Aware of their attractiveness, some gladiators took on erotically charged names.

According to Festus, a second-century AD grammarian, it was customary for newly wed brides to have their hair parted with the point of spear, preferably one which had been dipped in the blood of "a defeated and killed gladiator." The link between the arena and sexuality is also brought out by a relief from Beneventum in southern Italy showing a heavily armored gladiator fighting an enormous penis. A somewhat mysterious metal object now housed at the archeological museum in Naples depicts a small male figure, a gladiator. He has a huge sexual organ: however, the glans is formed like the head of a ferocious dog with powerful jaws. The dog's head points back towards the gladiator, threatening to bite him, while the gladiator is about to castrate himself by cutting off the head with the aid of a dagger. The exact significance of the contraption, from which four small bells are suspended, is unknown. However, the link between gladiators and the god Priapus is impossible to overlook.[118]

One modern authority believes that the reason why high-class women were placed as high up in the amphitheater as they were – in the Colosseum, they had to climb at least 220 steps to reach their seats – was to prevent them from getting too close to the fighters.[119] The jewelry of one such woman has been found in a school for gladiators at Pompeii where she was caught by the eruption of Mount Vesuvius, prompting speculation as to what she might have been doing there – a secret tryst, perhaps? At least two empresses were involved with gladiators. One was Messalina, Claudius' third wife. Famous for

---

[116] Tertullian, *De Spectaculis*, 22.

[117] See, for what follows, Meijer, *Gladiators*, pp. 68–76.

[118] See, for these objects, K. Hopkins, *Death and Renewal: Sociological Studies in Roman History*, Cambridge University Press, 1983, p. 22.

[119] D. L. Bomgardner, *The Story of the Roman Amphitheater*, London: Routledge, 2000, p. 17.

her promiscuity, she was said to have maintained a room in a brothel where she entertained men. Among them was a gladiator by the name of Sabinus. Cassius Dio says that he was defeated in the arena and that Claudius and the spectators wanted him killed. However, Messalina intervened, gave an eloquent speech on his behalf, saved his life, and went on to enjoy the fruits.[120] The other was Faustina, daughter of the Emperor Antoninus Pius and wife of his successor Marcus Aurelius. She was said to have fallen in love with a gladiator whom she saw marching by in a procession. Unable to get near him, yet obsessed by him, in the end she confessed to her husband. He consulted the soothsayers who advised him to have the gladiator killed and make Faustina bathe in his blood before she slept with her husband. It worked, and the spell was broken. However, evil tongues claimed that the affair resulted in the birth of Commodus who himself acted, or pretended to act, as a gladiator.[121]

For as long as the world has existed, one way in which members of the lower classes could revenge themselves on powerful men was by spreading scurrilous rumors about their wives. A millennium and a half after Rome's fall, whether or not they were true is impossible to establish. What is clear is that the phenomenon was sufficiently widespread to attract the attention, not to say envy, of contemporary writers. They wondered, or pretended to wonder, just what the heroes of the arena possessed that caused women, even high-class women, to fall for them like flies on sticky paper. Juvenal has the following to say about this:[122]

> Whose youth and charm have loosed such passion
> In Eppia? For whom does she put up with mockery
> And bear the name of 'gladiatrix'?
> Look, look: it's Sergius. Hardly any beard left
> and declared unfit for combat,
> after one of his arms was severed in a fight.
> And there's a lot else wrong with him besides.
> His skull has been dented by his helmet
> there's a wart on top of his nose
> between two permanently wet, red and swollen eyes.
> But he was once a gladiator, and that confers such radiance
> That she does not care at all about fatherland, family,
> hearth and home,
> these are matters of indifference to her; she is in love
> with the iron of his sword, for if this idiot had
> not held a sword, she would never have pleasured him!

---

[120] Cassius Dio, *Roman History*, 60.28.2; Pliny *Natural History*, LCL, 1938–, 10.172; Juvenal, *Satires*, 6.114–32.
[121] *Scriptores Historiae Augustae, Marcus Aurelius*, 19.7.   [122] Juvenal, *Satires*, 6.103–13.

We do not know who Eppia was. Yet she must have been a lady of some standing, or else the poet would hardly have bothered to write about her. Readers should also be aware that the last line carried a punch because, in Latin, a sword (*gladius*) is slang for penis.

As we have seen, many trials by combat also revolved around women, especially those who claimed to have been sexually attacked without adducing any evidence to back them up. Seeing that the whole of chivalric culture was built around war and women, the role the latter played in tournaments was equally great.[123] Early hastiludes did not take place inside specially designated courts or arenas but in an open field, even spilling over into villages. Such arrangements were hardly suitable for spectators of any sex, male or female. Perhaps the first reference to the presence of women at a tournament may be found in Geoffrey of Monmouth. Writing in the first half of the twelfth century, he says that King Arthur once held a celebration at Caerleon in Wales. First there was a banquet. Next, a tournament took place "while the dames and damsels looked on from the castle walls."[124] The anonymous German *Kaiserchronik* (Imperial Chronicle), which was written around 1150, has a somewhat similar tale to tell. "One day the King [Tarquinius] wanted to celebrate. The Romans organized a large tournament. The news reached the town of Viterbo. Thereupon all the ladies mounted the battlements to watch. When the Romans saw the ladies they did their best to ride as well as possible, in order that the ladies would say what excellent knights they were."[125]

Both of these instances are clearly legendary. Equally clearly, they could not have been presented as historical if the presence of ladies at tournaments had not been commonplace. More evidence comes from *Moriz von Craon*, an anonymous German-language poem the earliest extant copy of which dates to around 1500. Apparently it is based on a much older story that was written down some two and a half centuries earlier. The events described in the poem took place, or were supposed to have taken place, during the 1170s. The beautiful Countess of Beaumont had already received various proofs of her eponymous lover's devotion. Now she asked that he organize a tournament near her residence, justifying her request by claiming that she had never seen one. Moriz, good knight that he was, obliged, spending an immense amount of money in the process.[126] One need not accept every detail as correct to realize

---

[123] See, for what follows, Bumke, *Hoefische Kultur*, pp. 366–9.

[124] Geoffrey of Monmouth, *History of the Kings of Britain*, New York: Dulton, 1958, p. 202.

[125] *Kaiserchronik*, F J. Schmale and I. Schmale-Ott, eds., in *Ausgewaehlte Quellen der deutschen geschichte des Mittelalters*, vol. XV, Darmstadt: Wissenschaftliche Buchgesellschaft, 1972, lines 759–62.

[126] *Moriz von der Craon*, M. Haupt, ed., Berlin: Weidemannsche Buchhandlung, 1871, p. 15.

that, as soon as the sport ceased to endanger their persons, ladies flocked to watch it and even sponsored it.

The History of William the Marshal, written around the time of its hero's death in 1219 but referring to events that took place during his youth forty years or so previously, may be the first historical account to mention women attending a tournament. We are told that, when William arrived at the Castle of Joigny in Burgundy, he found the countess and her ladies waiting for the planned tournament to start. To help keep them amused, he even performed a song. Once the assembled knights perceived the women coming out they could contain themselves no longer. Seizing their weapons, they threw themselves into the fight. Some ten years later this poem was followed by Heinrich von dem Tuerlin's Diu Crône. We learn that the ladies handed over their jewelry to the knights so that they would deliver and receive powerful blows.[127]

Another interesting custom first mentioned by von dem Tuerlin was that of handing over captured knights to the ladies for custody, presumably as a means of making sure that shame would prevent them from trying to escape. One knight, Peter von Stauffenberg, is specifically mentioned as doing so, lance in hand.[128] By this time tournaments were no longer the wild unregulated battles they had originally been, but had long been turned into ordered affairs in which the risk to life and limb was much smaller. Ulrich von Lichtenstein's Frauendienst dates to the middle of the thirteenth century. It purports to be both a first-person narration of the author's deeds in serving women and a handbook for knights who desire to serve them. Among the very first activities mentioned is participating in tournaments: indeed the author claims to have done so no fewer than twelve times in the course of a single summer. He took on the strongest and most powerful in both collective and single combat, all so as to honor his lady, thanks to whose inspiration he won every bout. Only the onset of winter and cold put an end to the games, to the author's great regret. His love, however, reminded him there were other ways in which he could serve her. On a later occasion he broke forty lances in a single tournament, which ended in making him "tired and as weak as a woman."[129]

Some women probably attended because family relationships and their own social status demanded that they do so. For example, in 1279 the English baron Roger Mortimer held a round table at Kenilworth, in Warwickshire, for a hundred knights and their ladies. Many others were present as vendors, seamstresses, and the like. Others still came in the hope of catching a husband, others still with less moral encounters in mind. Standing on the nearby castle wall or sitting on the specially built tribunes, or simply milling around, they watched

[127] Diu Crône, A. Ebenauer, ed., Tuebingen: Niemeyer, 2005, lines 4563–72.
[128] E. von Stauffenberg, "Peter von Stauffenberg," in M. Lemmer, ed., Der Goldene Rosenbogen: Deutsche Erzaehler des Mittelalters, Cologne: Anaconda, 2007 [1977], p. 321.
[129] Von Lichtenstein, Frauendienst, pp. 17–18 and 295.

the proceedings, stimulated their favorites by giving them tokens to wear or carry, and awarded prizes. When in a position to do so, they themselves organized the games. The English barons who sent a letter inviting William of Albine to participate in a tournament in 1250 did not forget to add that the victor would receive a bear contributed by "a certain lady."[130] Herzeloyde, the legendary queen in *Parsifal*, offered herself as the trophy. She ended up in the arms of Gachmuret, the mysterious, powerful, and incredibly rich giant who won the tournament.

This does not seem to have been a unique episode. At a meeting held in Magdeburg ("maidens' town") in 1280, reputed to be the first one in which burghers rather than knights participated, the prize consisted of a prostitute, albeit that the intention seems to have been to reenact some historical episode rather than simply allow him who won her to enjoy her as he pleased. In 1331, so overfilled were the stands that carried Queen Philippa of Hainault during a tournament that they collapsed. She and her ladies-in-waiting fell on top of the knights, who were sitting further down.[131] Philippa's husband, King Edward III, is known to have issued specific orders for ladies to attend tournaments on at least three occasions. In 1342 five hundred of them were summoned to London to attend a series of jousts he was holding in honor of the Countess of Salisbury on whom, so rumor had it, he had developed a crush. Two years later he again called "women and girls *(dames et demoiselles)*, knights and esquires, and everybody else, without excuse," to participate in a great feast held at Windsor. The third occasion took place in 1358. The purpose was to celebrate the conclusion of peace with France. To honor King John II, who had been captured at Poitiers two years earlier and was still being held prisoner in England, he requested the presence of "the most beautiful and best-dressed ladies" of his realm.

If knights were duty-bound to have lady-mistresses and serve them by participating in tournaments, ladies were obliged to watch them, encourage them, and love them. Certainly we may imagine that not all did so with enthusiasm. As Edward's order that they and their menfolk attend "without excuse" shows, some probably resented the expense that was involved in finding the appropriate dress, making the journey, and paying for food and lodging. On the other hand, the opportunity that tournaments and the feasts with which they were associated offered for every kind of licentiousness was one very important reason why the church objected to them. Geoffrey IV de La Tour Landry (*c.* 1320–91), a French noblemen who in 1371–2 wrote a popular *Livre pour l'enseignement des filles* for the benefit of his daughters, has the following

---

[130] See above, p. 112.
[131] The episode is mentioned in J. Stowe, *Survey of London*, Oxford: Clarendon Press, 1908 [1603], vol. I, p. 268. For this and what follows, see also Barker, *The Tournament in England*, pp. 101–10.

story to tell in this connection. A certain lady, well known for her love of pleasure, used to attend jousts on her own without her husband being present. On one occasion, the lights having gone out, she was seen in a corner with a knight. Though nothing had happened between them, her brother-in-law reported the incident to her husband who never trusted her again. The lesson that La Tour's daughters were supposed to learn was clear. The atmosphere at tournaments was very conducive to sex, both licit and illicit. Respectable women in attendance should take the necessary precautions.[132]

At Cambrai in 1385 both the King of France and the Duke of Burgundy attended a tournament held to celebrate the duke's daughter's marriage to the Count d'Ostrevant. The prize, Froissart says, was a clasp of precious stones taken straight from the bosom of the duchess. Ladies also routinely gave tokens to knights to wear during tournaments (and, as various anecdotes reveal, real-life war as well). Particularly popular were pieces of clothing such as hats, mantles, chemises, sleeves, and veils. To encourage their favorite knights, ladies were even prepared to go about disheveled.[133] As time went on, women's role in tournaments tended to grow more important and more formal. They participated in the opening parades and in the *mise en scène* that surrounded the fighting, often taking the role of the tearful damsel in distress who had to be rescued from her wicked captor, human or animal. Calling his noblemen to participate in a tournament in 1395, King Richard II of England promised that:

> At those jousts, the noble ladies and damsels will give a horn garnished with gold to the knight who jousts best of those without; they will give a white greyhound with a collar of gold around its neck to the one who jousts best of those within. And the following Wednesday . . . the noble ladies will give a circlet of gold to the one who jousts best of those without . . . And the lady or damsel who dances best or leads the most joyful life . . . will be given a golden brooch by the knights.[134]

Most of the time women's role as prize-givers was probably symbolic, the real work of judging the outcome being left to learned specialists in the form of the heralds. However, from time to time they must have acted as actual judges, or else it is hard to see why Honoré Bonet in his *Tree of Battles* (1387) should argue against that practice.[135]

Some of these medieval ladies went further still. They pressed their cavaliers to fight not only in tournaments and jousts but in the much more dangerous

---

[132] *The Book of the Knight of La Tour-Landry: Compiled for the Instruction of his Daughters*, Nabu Press, 2010 [*c.* 1450], pp. 29–30.

[133] Huon de Mery, *Le tournoiement de l'Antéchrist par Huon de Mery*, Reims: Regnier, 1851, pp. 16, 38, 47.

[134] Document quoted in Muhlberger, *Jousts and Tournaments*, p. 25.

[135] H. de Bonet, *The Tree of Battles*, Liverpool University Press, 1949, pp. 193–4.

single combats and combats of champions too.[136] Throughout the early
modern period and down to the early years of the twentieth century quarrels
involving women were among the most important ones over which duels were
fought. That also applies to the last recorded duel of all, i.e. the 1937 one
between Strunk and Krutschinna. Allegations of adultery, of course, were one
cause. But so were sexual insults and insinuations: in short, anything that
could cast doubt on a woman's chastity and fidelity. Here and there a woman
may have tried to prevent a man from fighting a duel for her sake, as
Rousseau's heroine Julie did.[137] However, outside the pages of fiction such
cases are hard to document. One early nineteenth-century English male writer
begged "the mothers, sisters, wives, and daughters of the world" to banish "the
habitual duelist" "who kills his man and triumphs over his maid" from their
affections.[138]

On the whole, women's own attitudes in respect of dueling were ambivalent.
A woman who suffered an insult through no fault of her own could feel proud
in having some male volunteer to defend her honor. As Georg Weerth, a well-
known German writer and a close friend of Marx and Engels, put it in 1849: "Is
there any way [but for the duel] that men can give women greater pleasure than
by proving to them that they are men?"[139] On the other hand, a woman who
had brought about the affair through her own loose morals could expect to
carry the blame. If a fatal injury resulted, she might well be ostracized.[140] Men of
the pre-Civil War American South were said to be particularly touchy about
their women's honor. Conversely, Southern women sometimes insisted that
their men challenge or accept a challenge and fight on their behalf. Rather like
the Spartan woman who demanded that her son return from war with his shield
or on it, one belle wrote that being the widow of a brave man was better than
being the wife of a coward. Another threatened to take her husband's place if,
claiming illness, he did not show up. Among the many duels fought by the
future president Andrew Jackson at least one involved a slur cast on his wife,
Rachel. The affair ended with Jackson gravely wounded and his opponent,
Charles Dickinson, dead.[141]

Some duels may have been arranged without the women's knowledge, but
again such cases are hard to document. Perhaps situations in which wives
avenged themselves on their husbands or other male relatives by arranging
things in such a way as to compel them to fight were more common.[142] Even
when female honor was not directly involved, many duels originated in social

---

[136] Barker, *The Tournament in England*, pp. 153–4.
[137] Jean-Jacques Rousseau, *La Nouvelle Héloïse*, Amsterdam: Rey, 1765, part 1, letter 57.
[138] Hamilton, *The Dueling Handbook*, p. 35.
[139] G. Weerth, *Vergessene Texte*, Cologne: Leske, 1976, vol. II, p. 149.
[140] See Frevert, *Men of Honor*, pp. 186–7.
[141] Williams, *Dueling in the Old South*, pp. 18–19.   [142] See McAleer, *Dueling*, p. 161.

events such as theater shows, balls, tea parties, and the like when people of both sexes intermingled. The impact the presence of women could have on men's propensity to quarrel, refuse to compromise, and challenge each other hardly needs explaining and was much commented upon at the time. For example, the English newspaper owner–editor Rachel Beer (1857–1928) wondered why men should consider themselves so much more attractive when they quarreled.

The demise of the duel, as well as the legal changes that led to it and the social ones that surrounded it, marked the end of a chapter. For good or ill, perhaps for the first time in history men found themselves in a situation where society no longer permitted them to engage in *any* kind of wargames in which they might deliberately set out to shed each other's blood. Increasingly, even accidental deaths suffered in the course of the rougher games were likely to result in investigations, lawsuits, and punishments. Numerous attempts were made to abolish those games altogether, a fact that some might attribute to the "civilizing process." All that was left were chess and Reisswitz-type games – subsequently supplemented and largely replaced by free games, BOGSATs, and computer games – on the one hand and combat and contact sports on the other. Probably owing to their overwhelmingly intellectual character, the first four have never roused nearly as much enthusiasm, or attracted nearly as many spectators, male or female, as did the more bloody wargames that have been discussed in the present volume. The necessary drama and shots of adrenalin simply do not appear to be there. Much the same applies to paintball, laser tag, and reenactments of every kind.

The situation in respect of combat and contact sports is entirely different. Women have long formed a minority among the spectators who attend the games in question.[143] Attempting to attract more of them, here and there organizers have often issued them with free tickets, sometimes with success, perhaps more often without. Being a lone woman among a crowd made up of wildly cheering or groaning men is not easy. On the other hand, women who do attend often engage in blatant sexual displays with the objective of drawing attention to themselves. Rarely, it seems, do men enjoy seeing women tearing each other apart in earnest. When such displays do take place they tend to be terminated by the male spectators, which may well account for the very low number of women killed in duels. For whatever deep-seated psychological reason, though, those spectators do like having them humiliate themselves and each other. Doing so is somehow considered erotic, to the point that many videos of the events in question border on pornography if they do not actually contain it.

For their part, many women are not at all averse – to put it mildly – to watching men physically tackling each other and pummeling each other half to

---

[143] See University of Leicester, Department of Sociology, "A Brief History of Female Football Fans," 2004, at: www.le.ac.uk/so/css/resources/factsheets/fs9.html.

death. Proceeding backward through duels, tournaments, and judicial combat all the way to the gladiators of ancient Rome, they were almost always present as spectators. Sometimes they organized the fights in question and instigated them. At other times they were offered, or offered themselves, as the stakes in them. Quite often they went wild over men actually killing one another. If, like male deer fighting over a female, they do so as part of their competition for the women's own bodies, so much the better.

Now, as in ancient times, women applaud the male players during the matches and swamp the victors with their attentions during the intervals between them. For good or ill, perhaps in no respect do wargames, especially the more strenuous and more bloody among them, mirror war more closely than precisely in all that concerns the relationship between men and women.

8

Conclusions: The mirrors and the mirrored

Where did wargames come from? What purposes did they serve? Who partici-pated in them, why, and what for? What forms did they take? What factors drove their development, and to what extent did they reflect changes in the art of war itself? What did they simulate, what didn't they simulate, how, and why? What do they reveal about the conduct of war at the times, and in the places, where they were played? How useful are they in training for war and preparing for it? Why are some so much more popular than others, how do men and women compare in this respect, and what can the way the sexes relate to wargames teach us about their nature and the relationship between them? Finally, what does all this tell us about real war, fake or make-believe war, the interaction between the two, and the human condition in general? These are the sorts of questions the present volume has set out to answer; now that the voyage is almost done and the port is in sight, it is time to try and answer them.

Like all things with a long history behind them, wargames are almost impossible to define. They appear to have their origins in four basic human needs. The first is religion – meaning either the will to appease the gods by shedding blood in their honor or to determine, with the aid of combat of champions and judicial combat, what their wishes might be. The second is the perceived need for some mechanism to enable adversaries to settle certain kinds of disputes while risking all, but without endangering the rest of society, as in the case of single combat, trial by battle, and the duel. The third is the wish to prepare men – rarely women – for wars to come by making them engage in some kind of mock warfare. The fourth is the wish for entertainment pure and simple, as in almost all of them. Needless to say, the four motives have often become inextricably mixed. Did knights tourney because they liked doing so or because, early on at any rate, participation provided training for war? Aren't the movies, the game-manufacturing industry, the military and the hobbyists starting to converge? Nevertheless the distinctions are useful and I shall stick to them here.

Of the various kinds of games, those rooted in the first of these elementary needs may very well be the oldest. Gladiatorial games and judicial combat in particular originated in religion and have always maintained their ties with it. Either they were held in honor of the gods or else they were supposed to show

God's will. Both forms of wargames, however, seem to be more or less defunct: stamped out by the disappearance of many older religions as well as the rise in many places of secularism. Games whose purpose is to settle disputes between individuals, such as the duel, may still be alive in some places. However, in well-ordered modern societies that have found, or claim to have found, better ways to settle conflicts among their members they have all but disappeared. By contrast, wargames grounded in the third and the fourth of the above motives – the need to prepare for war and the desire for entertainment – remain as important, as numerous, as varied, and as popular as they have ever been in history. Tens, perhaps hundreds, of millions of people all over the world either engage in such games or watch them. Not only are billions of dollars being spent on them, but it does not appear that this situation is about to change anytime soon.

As one would expect, the kind of people who engage in wargames not only varies enormously from one society to another but reflects the structure of the societies from which they come or which they represent. As in Kishon's story, indeed, arguably the kind of (war)games a society allows and does not allow, does and does not engage in, can act as a kind of litmus test for its nature. Let us put aside, at least for the moment, games such as hunting, combat sports, and contact sports which have been included here mainly owing to the long-standing debate over their usefulness in military training on the one hand and what they tell us about the differences between men and women on the other. Starting, then, with great fights/nonsense fights, we discover two things. First, the societies in question were quite egalitarian and, to that extent, democratic. Hence every adult male was able to participate on a fairly equal basis. Second, in the absence of strong government that could either force people to play or prohibit them from participating, entry was based on the individual's own free will, although, in the long run, tribesmen who stayed away from the games for no good reason would probably be made to feel the consequences of their behavior.

The open-ended character of the games in question made it imperative that certain rules be applied and/or certain weapons blunted so as to limit casualties and prevent escalation into real warfare from taking place. The case of single combat and combat of champions was entirely different. To be sure, participating in them was equally voluntary – nobody compelled either Goliath or David, Paris or Menelaus, Hector or Ajax, or any of the rest to step out of the line, deliver a challenge or respond to it, and fight it out in front of their assembled armies. If anything, people would try to hold them back, as Agamemnon did when Menelaus wanted to fight Hector. Yet doing so was open only to men who were specially selected for their fighting ability, normally though not exclusively members of the social elite. These encounters also differed from great fights/nonsense fights in that no effort was made to render them relatively harmless. On the contrary, both combatants, armed with the very best weapons available at the time, did their best to kill their opponent(s). Any "positive" outcome – positive in the sense that the fight would fulfill its stated purpose and settle the quarrel – depended on the defeat or death of one fighter. Only an explicit agreement to down arms prevented escalation, and then only for as long as the fight lasted; once it was over "real" hostilities were almost always either opened or resumed.

Very different from these two were the gladiatorial games. Though there was always a trickle of volunteers, the great majority of fighters were either convicted criminals or prisoners of war. Indeed the fact that men of the latter kind became scarce from the time of Marcus Aurelius on may well have contributed to what appears to have been a sharp increase in the price of gladiators and thus to the growing reluctance of urban magistrates all over the Empire to hold the games. For these men participation in the shows was not voluntary but compulsory. If necessary, the most brutal available means were used to make them fight: the more brutal the fights, the more the spectators liked them. Furthermore, gladiators, far from being prominent or even ordinary members of society, were outcasts who had been excluded from it for a variety of reasons. They thus reflected the structure of Roman society with its powerful government, rigid class divisions, and above all sharp distinction between free and slave. The fact that the combatants' lives were forfeit in turn enabled the fights to be waged à outrance, as the medieval phrase was later to go, with the aid of real if often bizarre weapons. Presumably these were introduced to increase variety and maintain interest. Yet escalation was prevented by the status of the combatants, as well as formidable physical obstacles to separate them from the spectators.

Judicial combats and duels resembled gladiatorial games in that the expected outcome was very often death. Considered from this point of view, tournaments were more like modern combat sports. Fatalities did occur and were even expected. But most of the time they grew out of accidents, not design. To prevent accidents special blunt lances were sometimes used and elaborate arrangements to enable combatants to surrender put in place. In so far as few if any men were ever compelled to participate in any of them, all three forms of wargames take us back to the territory of volunteers. Originating in tribal societies, in principle at any rate judicial combat was open to any member of society who had quarreled with a neighbor and wanted to resort to it, though in practice doing so seems to have become more difficult as feudalism established itself and government became more sophisticated. Not so the other two which were only available to members of the elite, either noblemen or the members of the more "respectable" classes who imitated them. To that extent, indeed, duels – some of which were initially fought on horseback – can be seen as a continuation of the tournament. Being voluntary, all three kinds of wargames resembled single combats and combats of champions in that like fought like: commoner was pitted against commoner, nobleman against nobleman. Only in the United States, a relatively classless society with an exceptionally strong egalitarian ideology, did men of very different social standing sometimes confront one another in duels.

Some wargames were rooted in personal enmity, as the one between Paris and Menelaus was. In others the combatants had never had anything to do with one another but represented the hostile groups to which they belonged, and in some – including the gladiatorial ones, which paradoxically were among the most bloody of all – it is probably hard to speak of any enmity at all. A few, notably great fights/nonsense fights and early tournaments, provided more or less valuable military training, but most were designed with entirely different purposes in mind. However that may have been, one must agree with Clifford Geertz when he says that, in all of them, the participants put on an act. That was and is as true of single combat as of gladiatorial games, of trial of battle as of tournaments. It also provided onlookers with a living, and often a very lively demonstration of the structure and values of the societies to which both they and the combatants belonged, thus helping to reaffirm them. If, as often happened, it was also possible to make money out of the show, then so much the better.

It is, however, also necessary to make another point which Geertz seems to have missed. Once they have entered the arena all cocks regardless of who owns them are equal. Victory goes to the stronger bird, not to the one whose owner is rich. Similarly inside the field, or the amphitheater, or the court, or the lists, or the ring, all of the combatants regardless of rank enjoyed equal status. First, equality or a presumption of it was needed in order to enable the games to take place at all – or else a baron would hardly joust with an ordinary knight or a colonel answer a captain's summons to duel with him. Second, where the protagonists were too unequal the fight between them could neither deliver a valid judgment (if that was the objective) nor be exciting to watch. There were even cases, as with the various kinds of gladiators and when men fought women in judicial combat, when the organizers went out of their way to ensure equality by deliberately handicapping one party. As well as reflecting and reinforcing class differences in prestige, wealth, and power, in other words, wargames of all times and places created their own special kind of equality: in that, in fact, lay a large part of their attraction. Not only did some knights enter tournaments in disguise for precisely that reason, but noble prisoners of war were sometimes allowed to participate in their captors' games.[1] The outcome was agonistic competition. Conversely, when equality could not be imposed, as when a Roman emperor "fought" in the arena, the outcome was not competition but a farce: cruel, foolish, or both.

Without exception, what all the games discussed so far in this chapter simulated was not war but battle. This was hardly an accident. As late as the middle of the seventeenth century Thomas Hobbes in *Leviathan*, though

---

[1] Barker, *The Tournament in England*, pp. 36, 132.

admitting that "war consisteth not in battle only," argued that the intervals between battles were merely "tract[s] of time, wherein the will to contend is sufficiently known."[2] War as opposed to battle, in other words, was seen as a situation, not as an event. This in turn caused strategy – here understood not as a two-sided interaction but in the Clausewitzian sense of the higher conduct of war – operational art, logistics, intelligence, and, in most cases, command and control to be left out. On the other hand, many games did resemble real-life warfare in that they were extremely violent. Combatants – one hesitates to call them players – used the most lethal weapons available in life-to-death fights. Many of them differed from real battles only in being pre-arranged, carefully circumscribed as to space and time, and free from external interference. Some games, notably the gladiatorial ones, may actually have been *more* deadly than the reality that they tried to capture. In battle those who ran away often stood a chance of saving their lives and fighting another day; by contrast, the arena did not permit any kind of escape.

To quote a well-known cliché, in war short moments of the greatest excitement alternate with long periods of boredom. In this respect it differs from wargames which, if well planned, can deliberately combine excitement with relaxation. Most of the time wargames tended to make use of the normal weapons of war, more or less. Where the most common weapon was the bow, bowmen engaged bowmen; where it was the sword, swordsmen fought swordsmen; where mounted knights wore armor and wielded lances in war they did the same in tournaments. Provided proper precautions were taken this fact allowed them to be used for training, as several were. As firearms took over from about 1500 on, the situation underwent a fundamental change. Firearms, whether muskets or cannon, were much too powerful and much too dangerous to be used in two-sided wargames of any kind. Those "firing" blanks apart, the only ones ever used for that purpose were pistols: even so it was necessary to install all sorts of precautions to prevent bystanders from being hurt. When rifled barrels took the place of smooth ones during the last decades of the nineteenth century the game was up. Duels fought with such deadly weapons had more to do with Russian roulette than with strategy. Under such circumstances it was all that duelists were able to do to provide a demonstration of raw courage by squarely facing their opponents without flinching. It was an exercise in futility, and it soon ceased.

The fact that most wargames no longer involved any kind of physical fighting with weapons led to a very great reduction in their value as spectator sports. At the same time it caused their value for training purposes, and indeed the very meaning of training, to be reassessed. The outcome was a shift towards more symbolic representations of war, such as chess. Chess, of course, seems to have antedated the period of which we are speaking here by about a millennium.

---

[2] T. Hobbes, *Leviathan*, Oxford: Blackwell, 1946 [1652], p. 82.

There is no evidence that it ever served any purpose except entertainment. What makes it unique is its ability, which it shares with a few other games such as Go, to combine a small number of simple rules with an almost infinite number of extremely sophisticated strategies. Like many other board games similar to it or derived from it, though, chess was much better at portraying battle than at representing war. It is therefore interesting to observe that Weickmann's efforts to develop it in such a way as to make it more like real-life armed conflict date to the very year when Hobbes published his great book.

Whether or not this was a coincidence, from then on efforts in this direction, made either by professional soldiers in order to improve training or by amateurs more interested in entertainment, have been unceasing. Seeing that the best training is also the one that keeps those who engage in it motivated, and that one very good way to motivate people is to entertain them by providing them with a game that is playable, demanding, and varied, quite often the two things went together. The efforts to make commanders take an interest in the games in question, adopt them, and put them to military use also depended, at least in part, on the entertainment value that they offered.

Weickmann's efforts mark the starting point of a fairly straight line of development. It led through the various eighteenth-century men who hoped to provide a more realistic wargame to the Reisswitzes, father and son, early in the nineteenth. It was in keeping with the military thought of the age that these attempts should be based on mathematics, and especially plain geometry of the kind that theorists such as von Buelow and Jomini also tried to use. In particular, the Reisswitzes were professional soldiers who sought to combine serious training for war with entertainment. Their objective was to represent tactics, though not the fighting proper, which board games could not incorporate in any form, as realistically as possible. They and their successors also factored in additional elements such as topography, logistics, intelligence, command and control, and friction. In doing all this they kept pace with the growing scale of war and the emergence of a clear distinction between the various levels of its conduct. Their efforts had much to commend them: particularly important was the introduction of scenarios and of turns based on real time, as well as dice to represent the role of chance. All three continue to play a major role in many kinds of present-day games. As the Reisswitzes and others ought to have known and almost certainly did know, however, was that anything even approaching absolute realism was impossible. The more efforts were made in this direction, the more numerous and complicated the rules and the harder the games became to learn and to play.

After 1870 attempts to escape from this dilemma led to the introduction of so-called "free" games. Compared to the "rigid" ones they were supposed to replace, free games were much easier to learn and to play. Another advantage was that they made it easier to ignore all sorts of ancillary issues and focus on the main points. Dice were still often used to decide the outcome of combat;

however, participants, normally officers, no longer had to constantly consult the rulebook over such questions as the distance a battalion could march in the course of a day or how many bullets a company could fire per minute. Instead they had to use their professional knowledge and make their moves accordingly. Disputes were resolved by an umpire who also made himself useful by providing, or not providing, each side with information about the other.

The absence of detailed rules and the heavy dependence on professional knowledge, that of the umpire in particular, meant that playing wargames of this kind was more of an art than a science. As the games spread from Prussia, where they originated, to other countries, dozens of different variations appeared. Each armed force and service seems to have developed its own methods. Some, especially those used by navies (which tended to operate in relatively simple environments and were heavily depended on technology) were more rigid, others less so. Fun apart, all were used for two main purposes: namely, training on the one hand and planning for the future on the other.

Criticizing the use of such wargames for training military personnel has always been easy and remains so today. Particularly important in this respect is, first, the frequent lack of realism that may lead to the wrong actions being taken and the wrong lessons learnt; second, the danger, which a perceived lack of realism can only enhance, that players will become more interested in winning the game than in using it to gain a better understanding of real war; and, third, the near impossibility of simulating the full stress that participating in real-life war involves. Last but not least, participants in wargames are inevitably confined by the rules. Not so in war, where, as the story about Moshe Dayan illustrates very nicely indeed, it is often the side that surprises the opponent by *breaking* those rules which emerges victorious. Above all, one should keep in mind that two-sided games are not just *a* method to instruct commanders in the practical conduct of strategy: they are the *only* method. Without them, peacetime commanders would be like chess players who, though they may be thoroughly familiar with the rules and have analyzed countless old masters' games, have never actually played a match. That is why they keep being utilized in spite of all the difficulties: as Galileo might have said, "eppure si muove" ("but nevertheless it moves").

Lack of detailed information often hampers attempts to assess the usefulness of wargaming for looking into the future and planning for it. On the whole, though, it appears to be quite uneven. Having pioneered the field, during the early years of the twentieth century the Germans claimed greater expertise in it than anybody else. While there is no evidence that the Schlieffen Plan was ever gamed, they were justifiably proud of the contribution that games made to the great victory at the great battle of Tannenberg. In early 1940 a large number of wargames held at many levels from the top down helped the Wehrmacht prepare for the very successful campaign in the west. They also played an important role in the decision, which was undoubtedly correct, not to risk an invasion of the British Isles. In the next year, however, wargaming Operation "Barbarossa" did not save it from committing what in retrospect was perhaps the greatest blunder in the whole of military history.

On the other side of the hill, more is known about US Navy wargaming than about similar activities by any other military service. Apparently it was useful in helping shape strategy in the form of a gradual advance across the Pacific. It also provided training for a large number of contingencies. However, there is no record of senior officers using it to plan and test any specific campaign. Finally, Japanese wargaming in 1941–2 resembled what was practiced by the Germans. It provides a fascinating tale of how complex the interaction between games and reality can be. Sometimes it worked, sometimes it did not: in both cases, often for the wrong reasons.

The first recorded attempts to game not only war but the politics of which it forms a continuation got under way in Germany between the wars. Perhaps this is another proof that there is nothing like defeat to make people think. At least one game, organized on the initiative of Kurt von Schleicher, may have played an important part in shaping real-life politics. It helped convince the right-wing establishment that it could not forever rule against the will of the parties and the people. Others, set afoot by the Army General Staff to persuade Hitler not to risk another world war, were simply put aside: in dealing with such matters, Hitler preferred to rely on his intuition alone.

During the 1950s political-military games crossed the Atlantic to the US, multiplying until no self-respecting think tank, academic institution, or military college was without them. In crisis games or BOGSATs, as they were sometimes known, participants pretended to be officials in their own countries and others that were allied with them or opposed them. They resembled "free" wargames in that there were few rules. The role of the umpire, now often known as "control," was critical in proportion. As with all wargames, the greatest advantage of BOGSATs was that players were obliged to make choices. Furthermore, each view expressed and each move made was countered by an immediate, and often bruising, critique. Here and there games proved remarkably prescient – but of course they were only a handful out of the huge number played. No one could tell ahead of time which ones would or would not hit the mark. As with many other kinds of games, moreover, BOGSATs were normally considered too time-consuming to allow senior decision-makers to take a serious interest in them. That is probably why, in the US as in Nazi Germany, there is little evidence that even the best-organized ones had a real impact on the course of events.

Nor was wargaming limited to soldiers and defense officials. Playing with miniatures seems to have originated during the Renaissance. Its popularity increased during the eighteenth century when cheap figures made of tin began to be manufactured in large numbers. During the years immediately before World War I even some very well-known public figures engaged in miniature

wargaming. Then as later, play led to charges of "militarism" and warmongering. One very refreshing exception to the rule was the indefatigable H. G. Wells.
His *Little Wars*, he wrote, were "a homeopathic remedy for the imaginative
strategist." "Here is the premeditation, the thrill, the strain of accumulating
victory or disaster – and no smashed nor sanguinary bodies, no shattered fine
buildings, nor devastated country sides, no petty cruelties." If he had had his
way, he would have put "this prancing monarch and that silly scare-monger,
and these excitable 'patriots', and those adventurers, and all the practitioners of
Weltpolitik [the more chauvinist type of German professors, whom he absolutely detested]" into a cork-lined room and let them fight it out to their heart's
content.[3]

Too often, miniatures had the disadvantage that they diverted attention from
strategy to producing the most exact replicas possible. That is a fascinating
activity, no doubt, but since there is no opposition it has hardly anything to do
with war. Another disadvantage was that, if anything like correct proportions
were to be maintained, miniature games took up lots of room. This made them
most suitable for simulating small-scale engagements: since modern tactics
require soldiers to spread out and disperse, the more recent the engagement
being simulated the worse the problem, which cheap plastic models did not
solve. To play out campaigns, let alone wars, the tokens used by professional
soldiers, each of which could be made to represent as large a unit as one desired,
were much superior. The amateurs' motives differed from those of the professionals. Often they cared less about training and planning, more about entertainment. Often entertainment centered less on imparting specific skills than on
acquiring an in-depth understanding and the sense of power it brings in its
wake. As a result, historical games seeking to simulate campaigns of all times
and places abounded. The introduction of hexed maps during the 1950s did
wonders for amateur wargaming and ultimately led to two million sets being
sold in a single year. Considering the games' highly intellectual character, not to
mention the numerous tedious calculations they required, this popularity is
surprising. Perhaps it could serve as proof that some people want more than
bread and circuses alone. There were also some contacts between those who
designed, produced, and sold the wargames and the military. However, the
latter never warmed to the games in question.

Wargames played on floors, tables, and boards of every kind are one thing.
Having two real units take the field and fight one another as part of their
training is a very different one. The idea goes back to ancient Rome, if not
before. It may have been realized in some way by the medieval *behourd*, though
we do not really know. However that may be, the introduction of effective
firearms around 1500 made its realization impossible. Nineteenth-century
armies often held two-sided maneuvers, even very large ones. The method

---

[3] Wells, *Little Wars*, p. 26.

reached its peak during the first decades of the twentieth century when hundreds of thousands of troops, complete with all their equipment, sometimes participated. It continued to be used after 1945, though only on a sharply reduced scale. The great advantage of maneuvers was, and is, that they can go a considerable way to capture not just the intellectual part of war but the physical one, including not least the friction it involves. On the other hand, they were always hampered by the fact that the forces could not fire at one another. This fact in turn necessitated other, often highly arbitrary, methods to decide what worked and what did not.

It took almost five centuries to restore real-life weapons to the wargames from which they had been banished. What made this development possible were two games: paintball and laser tag. On the face of it paintball appears somewhat childish, as two groups of people tumble about a court or in the open in an effort to "kill" each other for no reason except fun – but that is something they share with many other wargames. What made it useful to the military, though, was the latter's growing interest in urban warfare. Reversing an age-old trend, such warfare was mostly fought at very short range for which paintball and its close relative, airsoft, could provide very good training. Laser tag also had the additional advantage that the equipment could be added to many kinds of "real" weapons. Like the other two, provided proper precautions were taken they could be fired at live opponents without any adverse results. To be sure, there were limits. Lasers could not simulate projectiles traveling along curved trajectories or else munitions with an explosive effect such as artillery shells. Still, compared with blanks they represented a very great improvement indeed. Moreover, provided proper instrumentation was available, every move in a "battle" could be observed and recorded for subsequent analysis. In many cases, so abundant was the resulting information that it could hardly be used.

As the billions invested in the National Training Center and similar installations around the world show, training of this kind is anything but cheap. For those unable to play at the taxpayer's expense, a substitute of sorts is available in the form of reenactments. While two-sided in principle, most reenactments have more to do with play-acting, which is sometimes taken to ridiculous lengths, than with strategy. The fact that the outcome of the larger engagements in particular is known in advance works in the same direction. Still, in some of the smaller and less farby reenactments sufficient room is often left for something like real strategy, real intelligence (or at any rate reconnaissance), and real command and control to be practiced. Like maneuvers large or small, they also do much better than most computerized games in simulating the physical experience of many kinds of war. Finally, while aimed at fun rather than at any other purpose, reenactments, if properly prepared, organized, and led, provide participants with an entry into military history that is as good as, if very different from, any other method. Perhaps it is for that very reason that service personnel, who do not like competition, tend to look down on them.

In the 1950s computers started making their mark. Inside and outside the military, computers appealed to those who considered themselves progressive in ways that hexed maps and little cardboard counters with all sorts of numbers printed on them could not. At a time when few understood just how they worked they seemed to provide the illusion, though not always the reality, of accuracy and precision. They were also very expensive: to some people, eager to obtain funding, that may have represented an advantage. The first field to which computerized wargames, or simulations as they were often known, were applied was nuclear warfare as conducted with the aid of bombers or, later, various kinds of missiles. Thousands of games were held in an effort to find out which were the best weapons, how many of them were needed, how they should be deployed and defended, what their first targets should be, how many casualties they would cause, what the consequences of using them might be, and so on. A growing number of attempts were also made to apply similar methods to conventional and even sub-conventional (guerrilla and terrorism) warfare: the more complex the environment in which the latter was waged, however, the more difficult the task.

As the advent of microchips caused the price of computers to come down from the late 1970s on, computerized wargaming developed along two parallel paths. The first was represented by increasingly sophisticated versions of the earlier Reisswitz-type games. Here computers, with their vast capacity for making quick calculations, made it possible not only to produce much larger and more sophisticated games but to speed them up very considerably. Games could be played either by humans against each other or, using artificial intelligence, by humans against the computer itself. They were played both by professionals, who used them for the standard twin purposes of training on the one hand and preparation for the future on the other, and by amateurs primarily interested in entertainment and study. Even chess, as one of the oldest wargames of all, was increasingly being played onscreen with the computer as the opponent.

A much more radical departure was presented by games of the second type, broadly known as simulators or shooters. Simulators replaced the hardware of war – troops, vehicles, and so on – with blips on a screen. Early versions tended to be somewhat primitive. Later the combined efforts of wargame manufacturers, the movie industry, and the military enabled much greater verisimilitude to be achieved. Quite often this was done at a price even individual hobbyists could afford. Above all, the need for taking turns, so characteristic of almost all wargames, many forms of the duel included, from the demise of the tournament on, was finally eliminated. With the computer doing the necessary calculations at lightning speed, so was the need for umpires.

In the military, trainees could "fight" either the computer or each other, in pairs or in groups, even if they were located geographically far apart. Outside the military countless people did the same, enjoying themselves as they "fought" all kinds of opponents from the most "real" to the most "imaginary." The more electronics went into both real-life weapons systems *and* the machines that simulated them *and* their opponents *and* the environments in which they operated, the more they converged, until in some cases they became all but indistinguishable. Generally the further down we go from strategy towards tactics, and the more important the role of machines as opposed to flesh and blood humans, the more true this is. To speak with the French cultural critic Jean Baudrillard, the simulation is taking over from the simulacra. Being completely man-designed and manufactured, the latter is better controlled, less mixed up with other things, and in this sense more "authentic," than the original.[4] Whether this is a good thing, as those who use the games to prepare for wars to come claim, or a bad thing, as those worried about the Dr. Strangeloves of this world fear, is moot.

Like their cousin, war, wargames have always been driven by technological, social, and military forces. Technology helped to govern which factors should be simulated and how, as well as the weapons that were and were not used. Especially after 1800, no sooner was some new technology invented than attempts started being made to introduce it into wargames as well. Social factors dictated the purpose of the games as well as who would and would not engage in them, whereas military ones usually resulted in efforts to make the games as much like war as possible. Quite often these factors pulled in opposite directions. For example, the deadly power of firearms prevented them from being used in maneuvers, which meant that, until the advent of paintball and the National Training Center, the latter always carried a strong element of make-believe. Miniatures may in some respects give a better impression of war than cardboard counters, but only if the scale of the simulated engagements is small.

Some games are too structured by their rules to give a good approximation of war. Others are so unstructured as to appear completely arbitrary and even senseless. A game that successfully navigates between these extremes and incorporates *all* aspects of war has yet to be devised. This gap between the two is precisely why, in military games, postmortem analysis is critically important. But for this, a game may do more harm than good, imparting the wrong lessons and convincing players that they know more than they do. Such analysis can and should make use of the entire toolbox available to military historians. Even so, there are always limits. First, it is important to remember that games and real warfare are not the same and that, for better or for worse, a person may perform very differently in the dangerous environment created by the latter than in the benign one presented by the former. At a more fundamental level still, the quest for realism is limited by the fact that war is essentially a zero-sum activity. That is not true of many wargames. They can

---

[4] J. Baudrillard, *Simulacra and Simulation*, Ann Arbor: University of Michigan Press, 2004, pp. 2, 11, 35.

take place only if the two parties agree to hold them at a certain time and place – and then only if the rules are observed.

In respect to wargames, even more than war itself, men and women seem to come from different planets. That fact sheds a fascinating and occasionally lurid light both on the games' nature and on the character of those who do or do not play, do or do not watch. First, starting with great fights/nonsense fights all the way to the most advanced computer games, far fewer women play at war than men. As the case of chess seems to show, those who do so are on the average less motivated. The great majority seem to prefer socializing to fighting. Indeed it has been suggested that for women Facebook-based games such as *Bejeweled* and *Insaniquarium* are what wargames are for men.[5] Some feminists attribute the difference to society, claiming that it "steers" woman away from the games in question. However, the fact that the situation among primates is similar strongly suggests that different factors are at work. Part of the explanation may be men's greater physical strength. Unless there is some redeeming factor, such as aesthetics, playing games where one is forever doomed to be second-best is foolish. Many men who play wargames, especially the more violent ones or those that involve shooting, find them highly erotic. Few women do so.

Second, when women do participate in wargames of all sorts their perform-ances, real or virtual, regularly have more to do with sexual display than with combat. Perhaps, too, it is their ability to use sex in order to get ahead that accounts for their lack of motivation. Whether in games such as mud wrestling or naked wrestling or lingerie football (said to be broadcast in eighty-five countries, no less), and the like it is men who "exploit" women or the other way around is moot. Most likely people of both sexes use them each for their own purposes. Men, it appears, can never have enough of half-naked female flesh displayed in various exciting positions and movements, whereas women seek money and perhaps a certain kind of fame.

Third, whether acting on the initiative of men or acting on their own, women have often helped to spice up wargames of every sort. They have instigated them, encouraged the male players, rewarded the victors, and served or offered themselves as prizes – again, acting either on the initiative of men or on their own. Nor is the relationship between the sexes on the one hand and wargames on the other one-sided. If men find women's wrestling sexually arousing, many women enjoy watching men as they fight and even kill each other. To speak with Plato, men and women are alike in some ways but differ in others.[6] Precisely because participation is largely voluntary, perhaps nowhere can the truth of this proposition be better observed than in wargames.

---

[5] M. Ingram, "Average Social Gamer Is a 43-Year-Old Woman," Gigaom, February 17, 2010, at: http://gigaom.com/2010/02/17/average-social-gamer-is-a-43-year-old-woman/.
[6] Plato *Republic*, LCL, 1959, 5.454.D.

War is by far the most horrendous of all activities we humans engage in. So why is it, as Josephus noted two millennia ago, that the business of war so often turns into the pleasure of peace?[7] And how come grown men – much less often grown women – so often abandon their families, forget their worldly obligations, and put their all into playing and watching the games? To be sure, the role of the intellect in the conduct of both war and wargames cannot be overestimated. It is also true that this aspect of the matter finds an echo in the minds of those who design the games, play them, watch them, and try to understand them. In particular, the challenge involved in coping with an equal opponent fully capable of countering one's own moves has great appeal. It demands sharp observation, deep understanding, creativity, and a certain kind of craftiness: hence the attraction of countless games of strategy from chess up, or down.

Nevertheless, when Marcel Duchamp, who devoted the second half of his life almost exclusively to chess, said it was a sport whose inherent violence detracted from its appeal he could not have been more wrong.[8] To the contrary: if chess is not exactly the most popular sport in the world, then that is precisely because it is not violent enough. It is the open, extroverted, often unrestrained, display of passion made possible by the creation of an artificial world, the temporary escape from one kind of reality into another, which turns the most violent wargames, independently of any other value they may or not have, into what they are. If violence can be mixed with sex, as it invariably is when women play or display or are involved in any other way, then so much the better. Mirror, mirror on the wall, why were the deadliest games in history also the most popular of all?

---

[7] Josephus, *Jewish Antiquities*, 19.335–7.
[8] Quoted in D. Hooper and K. Whyld, *The Oxford Companion to Chess*, Oxford University Press, 1992, p. 116.

INDEX